GROC's CANDI
CRETE
As well as
Athens City & Piraeus

for package, villa, backpacker &
ferry-boating holiday-maker,
whether travelling by air, car, coach or train.

by
Geoffrey O'Connell

Published by
ASHFORD
1 Church Road
Shedfield
Hampshire
SO3 2HW

British Library Cataloguing in Publication Data

O'Connell, Geoffrey
    Crete, Athens and Piraeus — 2nd ed. — (The Candid
    guides) — (The Greek islands).
    1.   Crete — description and travel — 1981 —
    — guide-books.
    I   Title   II   O'Connell Geoffrey   III   Series
    914.99'80446   DF901.C8

        ISBN 1 85253 090 1

CONTENTS

ILLUSTRATIONS

Please do not forget that prices are given as a guide only especially accommodation and restaurant costs which are subject to fluctuation, almost always upwards. In the last year or so transport costs, especially ferry-boat fees, have also escalated dramatically but the increased value of other currencies to the Greek drachmae has compensated, to some extent, for these seemingly inexorably rising charges.

The series is entering its fifth year of publication and I would appreciate continuing to hear from holidaymakers and travellers who have any additions or corrections to bring to my attention. As in the past, all correspondence (except that addressed 'Dear filth' or similar endearments) will be answered.

I hope readers will excuse the odd errors that creep (well gallop) into the welter of detailed information included in the body text. We manage, in order to keep the volumes as up to date as possible, to cut the period down from inception to publication to some six months which does result in the occasional slip up...

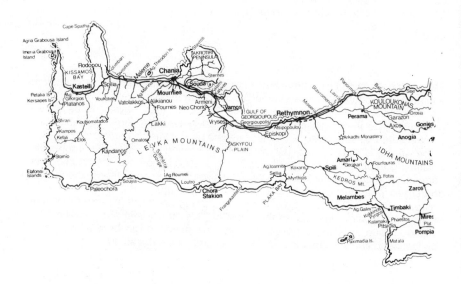

Cape Spatha

Agria Grabousa Island

Imeria Grabousa
Island

Rodopou

KISSAMOS
BAY

Spilia

Kastelli

Kolimbari

Gavrohnis

Maleme

Ag.Marina

Ns.Theodori Is.

Chania

Sternes

AKROTIRI
PENINSULA

Stavros

Souda

Petalia Is
Kersapes Is

Ag
Georgios

Platanos

Voukolies

Vatolakkos

Alikianou

Mournies

Fournes

Neo Chorio

Armeni

Kalives

Vamos

GULF OF
GEORGIOUPOLIS

Rethymnon

Panormo

Bali

KOULOUKONAS
MOUNTAIN

Drosia

Stavromenos

Lavri

Perama

Garazon

Axos

Gonies

Shrari

Koutsomatados

Lakki

Georgioupolis

Alsipopoulou

Episkopi

Masari

Arkadhi Monastery

Anogia

Kampos

Kefali

Elos

Omalos

LEVKA MOUNTAINS

ASKYFOU
PLAIN

IDHA MOUNTAINS

Stomio

Kandanos

Samaria
Gorge

Amari

Gerakari

Fourfouras

Elafonsi
Islands

Ag Roumeli

Loutro

Ag.Ioannis

Sellia

Koxare

Myrthios

Spili

KEDROS Mt.

Ag. Fotini

Zaros

Paleochora

Souyia

Chora
Sfakion

Frangokastelo

PLAKA BAY

Melambes

Ag Galini

Kokkinos
Pyrgos

Timbaki

Mires

Pitsidia

Kalamaki

Phaestos

Plat

Pompia

Paximadia Is.

Matala

vi

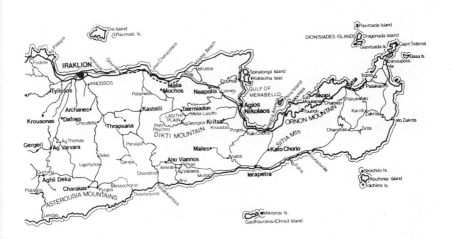

Dia Island
Paximadi Is.
Paximada Island
DIONISIADES ISLANDS
Dragonada Island
Gianitsada Is.
Cape Sideros
Elasa Is.
Fodele
Agia Pelagia
Ermoupolis
Vai
Toplou
IRAKLION
Ammisos
Gournes
Kato Chersonisos
Milatos Beach
Milatos
Palaikastro
Sitia
KNOSSOS
Spinalonga Island
Kolokitha Islet
Elounda
Tylissos
Malia
Mochos
Neapolis
Limnes
GULF OF
MERABELLO
Mochlos
Skopi
Mouliana
Chamezi
Piskokefalo
Potamies
Psira Island
Tourloti
Karidi
Zakros
Archanes
Kastelli
Tzermiadon
Mesa Lasithi
Agios
Nikolaos
Kato Zakros
Krousonas
Dafnes
Choudetsi
LASITHI
PLAIN
Ag.Georgios
Kritsa
Ziros
Thrapsana
Plati
Psychro
Kroustas
Pirgos
ORNON MOUNTAIN
Chandras
DIKTI MOUNTAIN
Kato Chorio
SITIA M'IS
Gergeri
Ag Thomas
Panagia
Males
Anatoli
Kato Chorio
Ag Varvara
Tefeli
Garipa
Ligortynos
Ano Viannos
Pefkas
Ag Fotia
Koutsouras
Strochilo Is.
Gortyna
Chondros
Ag.Vasileos
Amiras
Mirtos
Ierapetra
Koufonisi Island
Trachilos Is.
Aghii Deka
Charakas
Messochorio
Arvi
Platanos
Pyrgos
Tsoutsouras
Kofinas
Kofinas
ASTEROUSIA MOUNTAINS
Lendas
Mikronisi Is.
Gaidhouronisi (Chrisi) Island

INTRODUCTION

This volume is the second edition of Crete, another book in the popular and proven series of GROC's Candid Guides to the Greek Islands. The rationale, the *raison d'etre* behind their production is to treat each island grouping on an individual and comprehensive basis, rather than attempt overall coverage of the 100 or so islands, usually described in one volume. This obviates attempting to do justice to, to, Crete in amongst an aggregation of many other, often disparate islands.

Due to the size of Crete very few, if any, vacationers can possibly visit all of the island, even if as much as four weeks is available.

It is important for package and villa holiday-makers to have an unbiased and relevant description of their planned holiday surroundings, rather than the usual extravagant hyperbole of the glossy sales brochure. It is vital for backpackers and ferry-boat travellers to have detailed and accurate information at their finger tips, on arrival. With these differing requirements in mind factual, 'straight-from-the-shoulder' location reports have been combined with detailed plans of the major ports, towns and/or cities as well as a topographical island map.

Amongst the guides on offer there are a number of earnest tomes dealing with Ancient and Modern Greece, its mythology and history, there are a number of thumbnail travel booklets and there are some worthy, if rather out-of-date books available. Unfortunately they do not necessarily assuage the various travellers' differing requirements which must include speedy and accurate identification of one's position on arrival; the location of accommodation and the whereabouts of banks, post office and tourist offices. Additional requisites are a swift and easy to read resume of the town's main locations, cafes, tavernas and restaurants; detailed local bus and ferry timetables as well as a full island narrative. Once the traveller has settled in, then and only then, can he or she start to feel at ease, making their own finds and discoveries.

I have chosen to omit lengthy accounts of the relevant, fabulous Greek mythology and history. These aspects of Greece are, for the serious student, very ably related by authors far more erudite than myself. Moreover, most islands have a semi-official tourist guide translated into English, and for that matter, French, German and Scandinavian. They are usually well worth the 200 to 300 drachmae (drs) they cost, are extremely informative in 'matters archaeological' and are quite well produced, if rather out of date, with excellent colour photographs. Admittedly the English translation might seem a litte quaint (try to read Greek, let alone translate it), and the maps are often unreliable but cartography is not a strong Hellenic suit!

Each new Candid Guide is finally researched as close to the publication date as is possible and naturally any new ideas are incorporated but in the main they follow the now well tried formula. Part One deals with the preliminaries and describes in detail the different aspects of travelling and enjoying to the full the unforgettable experience of a Greek island holiday. Part Two gives a full and thoroughly redrafted account of Athens, still the hub for Greek island travel, and the relevant mainland port for connections to Crete. Part Three introduces Crete followed by a detailed description of the island, the layout being designed to facilitate quick and easy reference.

The exchange rate has fluctuated quite violently in recent years and up-to-date information must be sought prior to departure. For instance at the time of writing the final draft, the rate to the English pound (£) was hovering about 210 drs but prices are subject to fluctuation, usually upward. Annual price increases vary between some 10-20% but fortunately the drachma tends to devalue by approximately the same amount.

Recommendations and personalities are almost always based on personal observation and experience, occasionally emphasised by the discerning comments of readers or colleagues and may well not only change from year to year but be subject to different interpretation by other observers.

The series now incorporates a number of innovative ideas and unique services including:

The Decal: Since 1985 some of the accommodation and eating places recommended in the guides may display a specially produced decal to help readers identify the particular establishment.

Addendum: An updating information sheet incorporated, where possible, in the second year which includes, for instance, corrections, alterations as well as the relevant price and fare increases that have come to hand.

The publisher (and author) are very interested in considering ways and means of improving the guides and adding to the back up facilities, so are delighted to hear from readers with their suggestions.

Enjoy yourselves and **Ya Sou** (welcome).

Geoffrey O'Connell 1987

ACKNOWLEDGMENTS

Every year the list of those to be formally thanked grows and this edition shows no diminution in their number which has forced the original brief entry from the inside front cover to an inside page.

There are those numerous friends and confidants we meet on passage as well as the many correspondents who are kind enough to contact us with useful information, all of who, in the main, remain unnamed. One constructive critic, who I have never met but deserves a mention for oh so gently cajoling me over this or that, is Iain Morris, *Editor of The Camping and Caravanning Club*.

Rosemary who accompanies me, adding her often unwanted, uninformed comments and asides (and who I occasionally threaten not to take next time), requires especial thanks for unrelieved, unstinting (well almost unstinting) support despite being dragged from this or that sun kissed beach.

This second edition of Crete is the result of close collaboration between myself and Anne Merewood who was herself aided and abetted by her husband Mike Makrigiorgos, when his army duties permitted. Anne, not only carried out the updating research but proof read a draft of this book, thus deserving all my grateful thanks.

Although receiving reward, other than in heaven, some of those who assisted me in the production of this edition require specific acknowledgment for effort far beyond the siren call of vulgar remuneration! These worthies include Linda Fehrenbach, Graham Bishop, Ted Spittles, Viv Hitie and Maureen Burness of *Type Setting*.

Lastly, and as always, I must admonish Richard Joseph for ever encouraging and cajoling me to take up the pen – surely the sword is more fun?

The cover picture of Loutro is reproduced by kind permission of GREEK ISLAND PHOTOS, Willowbridge Enterprises, Bletchley, Milton Keynes, Bucks.

PART ONE

1 Packing, insurance, medical matters, climatic conditions, conversion tables & a starter course in Greek

Leisure nourishes the body and the mind is also fed thereby; on the other hand, immoderate labour exhausts both. Ovid

Vacationing anywhere on an organised tour allows a certain amount of latitude regarding the amount of luggage packed, as this method of holiday does not preclude taking fairly substantial suitcases. On the other hand, ferry-boating and backpacking restricts the amount a traveller is able to carry and the means of conveyance. The usual method is to utilise backpacks and/or roll-bags, both of which are more suitable than suitcases for this mode of travel. The choice between the two does not only depend on which is the more commodious, for at the height of season it can be advantageous to be distinguishable from the hordes of other backpackers. To promote the chances of being offered a room, the selection of roll-bags may help disassociation from the more hippy of 'genus rucksacker'. If roll-bags are selected they should include shoulder straps which help alleviate the discomfort experienced when searching out accommodation on hot afternoons with arms just stretching and stretching and stretching.

In the highly populous, oversubscribed months of July and August, it is advisable to pack a thin, foam bedroll and lightweight sleeping bag, just in case accommodation cannot be located on the occasional night.

Unless camping out, I do not think a sweater is necessary between the months of May and September. A desert jacket or lightweight anorak is a better proposition and a stout pair of sandals or training shoes are obligatory especially if very much walking is contemplated. Leave out the evening suit and cocktail dresses, as the Greeks are very informal. Instead take loose-fitting, casual clothes, and do not forget sunglasses and a floppy hat.

Should there be any doubt about the electric supply (and you shave) include a pack of disposable razors and ladies might consider acquiring one of the small, gas cylinder, portable hair-curlers prior to departure. Take along a supply of toilet rolls. They are useful for tasks other than that with which they are usually associated, including mopping up spilt liquid, wiping off plates, and blowing one's nose. It might be an idea to include a container of washing powder, a few clothes pegs, some string for a washing line and a few wire hangers to hook up washing.

Those visitors contemplating wide ranging travel should consider packing a few plastic, sealed-lid, liquid containers, a plate and a cup, as well as a knife and fork, condiments, an all-purpose cutting/slicing/carving knife and a combination bottle and tin opener. These all facilitate economical dining whilst on the move as food and drink, when available on ferry-boats and trains, can be comparatively expensive. Camping out requires these elementary items to be augmented with simple cooking equipment.

Mosquito coils can be bought in Greece but a preferable device is a small, two prong, electric heater on which a wafer thin tablet is placed. They can be purchased locally for some 1000 drs and come complete with a pack of the capsules. One trade name is *Doker Mat* and almost every room has a suitable electric point. The odourless vapour given off certainly sorts out the mosquitoes and is (hopefully) harmless to humans. Mark you we did hear of a tourist who purchased one and swore by its efficacy, not even aware it was necessary to place a tablet in position!

Consider packing a pair of tweezers, some plasters, calamine lotion, after-sun and insect cream, as well as a bottle of aspirin in addition to any pharmaceuticals usually

3

required. It is worth noting that sun oil and small packets of soap powder are now cheaper in Greece than much of Europe and shampoo and toothpaste cost the same. Including a small phial of disinfectant has merit, but it is best not to leave the liquid in the original glass bottle. Should it break, the disinfectant and glass mingled with clothing can prove not only messy but will leave a distinctive and lingering odour. Kaolin and morphine is a very reliable stomach settler. Greek chemists dispense medicines and prescriptions that only a doctor would be able to mete out in many other Western European countries, so prior to summoning a doctor, try the local pharmacy.

Insurance & medical matters

While touching upon medical matters, a national of an EEC country should extend their states National Health cover. United Kingdom residents can contact the local *Department of Health and Social Security* requesting form number *E111 UK*. When completed, and returned, this results in a *Certificate of Entitlement to Benefits in Kind during a stay in a Member State*. Well, that's super! In short, it entitles a person to medical treatment in other EEC countries. Do not only rely on this prop, but seriously consider taking out a holiday insurance policy covering loss of baggage and money; personal accident and medical expenses; cancellation of the holiday and personal liability. Check the exclusion clauses carefully. It is no good an insured imagining he or she is covered for 'this or that' only to discover the insurance company has craftily excluded claims under a particular section. Should a reader intend to hire a scooter ensure this form of 'activity' is comprehensively insured. Rather than rely on the rather inadequate standard insurance cover offered by many tour companies, it is best to approach a specialist insurance broker. For instance, bearing in mind the rather rudimentary treatment offered by the average Greek island hospital, it is almost obligatory to include Fly-Home Medicare cover in any policy. A couple of homilies might graphically reinforce the argument. Firstly the Greek hospital system expects the patient's family to minister and feed the inmate 'out-of-hours'. This can result in holiday companions having to camp in the ward for the duration of any internment. Perhaps more thought-provoking is the homespun belief that a patient is best left the first night to survive, if it is God's will, and to pass on if not! After a number of years hearing of the unfortunate experiences of friends and readers, who failed to act on the advice given herein, as well as the inordinate difficulties I experienced in arranging cover for myself, I was prompted to offer readers an all embracing travel insurance scheme. Details are to be found on Page ii. **DON'T DELAY, ACT NOW**.

Most rooms do not have rubbish containers so why not include some plastic bin liners which are also very useful for packing food as well as storing dirty washing. A universal sink plug is almost a necessity. Many Greek sinks do not have one but, as the water usually drains away very slowly, this could be considered an academic point.

Take along a pack of cards, and enough paperback reading to while away sunbathing sojourns and long journeys. Playing cards are subject to a government tax, which makes their price exorbitant, and books are expensive but some shops and lodgings operate a book-swap scheme.

Many flight, bus, ferry-boat and train journeys start off early in the morning so a small battery-operated alarm clock may well help save sleepless, fretful nights. A small hand or wrist compass can be an enormous help orientating in towns and if room and weight allow, a torch is a useful addition to the inventory.

Readers must not forget their passport which is absolutely essential to (1) enter Greece, (2) book into most accommodation as well as campsites, (3) change money and (4) hire a scooter or car.

In the larger, more popular, tourist orientated resorts Diners and American Express (Amex) credit cards are accepted. Personal cheques may be changed as long as accompanied by a Eurocheque bank card. Americans can use an Amex credit card at their overseas offices to change personal cheques up to $1000. They may also, by prior arrangement, have cable transfers made to overseas banks, allowing 24 hrs from the moment their home bank receives specific instructions.

It is wise to detail separately from the following items the credit card, traveller's cheques and airline ticket numbers in case they should be mislaid. Incidentally this is a piece of advice I always give but rarely, if ever, carry out myself. Visitors are only allowed to import 3000 drs of Greek currency (in notes) and the balance required must be in traveller's cheques and/or foreign currency. It used to be 1500 drs but the decline in the value of the Greek drachma has resulted in the readjustment. With only 3000 drs in hand it is often necessary to change currency quite quickly after arrival, which becomes a problem if this is over a weekend or the banks are on strike, which sometimes occurs. *See* **Banks**, **Chapter Seven** for further details in respect of money matters.

Imported spirits are comparatively expensive (except on some of the duty free Dodecanese islands) but the duty free allowance, that can be taken into Greece, is up to one and a half litres of alcohol. With this in mind, if a whisky or gin drinker, and partial to an evening sundowner, acquire a bottle or two before arrival. Cigars are difficult to buy on the islands, so it may well be advantageous to take along the 75 that can be imported. Note the above applies to fellow members of the EEC. Allowances for travellers from other countries are only 1 litre of alcohol and 50 cigars. Camera buffs should take as much film as possible as it is more costly in Greece than in most Western European countries.

Officially, the Greek islands enjoy some 3000 hours of sunshine per year, out of an approximate, possible 4250 hours. The prevailing summer wind is the northerly Meltemi which can blow very strongly, day in day out during July and August, added to which these months are usually dry and very hot for 24 hours a day. The sea in April is perhaps a little cool for swimming, but May and June are marvellous months, as are September and October.

For the statistically minded:

Monthly average temperatures on Crete are:

		Jan	Feb	Mar	Apr	May	June	July	Aug	Sept	Oct	Nov	Dec
Average monthly air temperature	C°	12	13	14	17	20	24	26	26	24	20	17	14
	F°	53.6	55.4	57.2	62.6	68	75.2	78.8	78.8	75.2	68	62.6	57.2
Average days of rain		14	12	7	4	3	1	–	–	2	5	8	14

The best time of year to holiday

All the above indicates that probably the best months to vacation are May, June, September and October, the months of July and August being too hot. Additionally, the most crowded months, when accommodation is at a premium, are also July, August and the first two weeks of September. Taking everything into account, it does not need an Einstein to work the matter out.

Conversion tables & equivalents

Units	Approximate Conversion	Equivalent
Miles to kilometres	Divide by 5, multiply by 8	5 miles = 8 km
Kilometres to miles	Divide by 8, multiply by 5	
Feet to metres	Divide by 10, multiply by 3	10 ft = 3 m
Metres to feet	Divide by 3, multiply by 10	
Inches to centimetres	Divide by 2, multiply by 5	1 inch = 2.5 cm

5

Centimetres to inches	Divide by 5, multiply by 2	
Fahrenheit to centigrade	Deduct 32, divide by 9 and multiply by 5	77°F = 25°C
Centigrade to fahrenheit	Divide by 5, multiply by 9 and add 32	
Gallons to litres	Divide by 2, multiply by 9	2 gal = 9 litres
Litres to gallons	Divide by 9, multiply by 2	

Note: 1 pint = 0.6 of a litre and 1 litre = 1.8 pints

Pounds (weight) to kilos	Divide by 11, multiply by 5	5 k = 11 lb
Kilos to pounds	Divide by 5, multiply by 11	

Note: 16 oz = 1 lb; 1000g = 1 kg and 100g = 3.5 oz.

Tyre pressures

Pounds per square inch to kilogrammes per square centimetre.

lb/sq.in.	kg/cm	lb/sq.in.	kg/cm
10	0.7	26	1.8
15	1.1	28	2.0
20	1.4	30	2.1
24	1.7	40	2.8

The Greeks use the metric system but most 'unreasonably' sell liquid (i.e. wine, spirits and beer) by weight. Take my word for it, a 640 g bottle of wine is approximately 0.7 of a litre or 1.1 pints. Proprietory wines such as *Demestika* are sold in bottles holding as much as 950 g, which is 1000 ml or 1¾ pints and represents good value.

Electric points in the larger towns, smarter hotels and holiday resorts are 220 volts AC and will power any American or British appliance. Older buildings in out of the way places might still have 110 DC supply. Remote pensions may not have any electricity, other than that supplied by a generator and even then the rooms might not be wired up. More correctly they may well be wired but not connected!

Greek time is 2 hours ahead of GMT, as it is during British Summer Time, and 7 hours ahead of United States Eastern Time. That is except for a short period when the Greek clocks are corrected for their winter at the end of September, some weeks ahead of the United Kingdom alteration.

Basics & Essentials of the language

These notes and subsequent **Useful Greek** at the relevant chapter endings are not, nor could be, intended to substitute for a formal phrase book, or three. Accent marks have been omitted in the main, that is except where they are left in!

Whilst in the United Kingdom it is worth noting that the *British Broadcasting Co.* (Marylebone High St, London W1M 4AA) has produced an excellent book, *Greek Language and People*, accompanied by a cassette and a record.

For the less committed a very useful pocket sized phrase book that I always have to hand is *The Greek Travelmate* (Richard Drew Publishing, Glasgow) costing £1.50.

The Alphabet

Capitals	Lower case	Sounds like
A	α	Alpha
B	β	Veeta
Γ	γ	Ghama
Δ	δ	Dhelta
E	ε	Epsilon
Z	ζ	Zeeta
H	η	Eeta
Θ	θ	Theeta
I	ι	Yiota
K	κ	Kapa

Λ	λ	Lamtha
M	μ	Mee
N	ν	Nee
Ξ	ξ	Ksee
O	o	Omikron
Π	π	Pee
P	ρ	Roh
Σ	σ	Sighma
T	τ	Taf
Y	υ	Eepsilon
Φ	φ	Fee
X	χ	Chi
Ψ	ψ	Psi
Ω	ω	Omegha

Groupings

αι	'e' as in let
αυ	'av/af' as in have/haff
ει/οι	'ee' as in seen
ευ	'ev/ef' as in ever/effort
ου	'oo' as in toot
γγ	'ng' as in ring
γκ	At the beginning of a word 'g' as in go
γχ	'nks' as in rinks
μπ	'b' as in beer
ντ	At the beginning of a word 'd' as in deer
	In the middle of a word 'nd' as in send
τζ	'ds' as in deeds

Useful Greek

English	Greek	Sounds like
Hello/goodbye	Γειά σου	Yia soo (informal singular said with a smile)
Good morning/day	Καλημέρα	Kalimera
Good afternoon/evening	Καλησπέρα	Kalispera (formal)
Good night	Καληνύχτα	Kalinikta
See you later	Θα σε δω αργοτερα	Tha se tho argotera
See you tomorrow	Θα σε δω αύριο	Tha se tho avrio
Yes	Ναι	Ne (accompanied by a downwards and sideways nod of the head)
No	Οχι	Ochi (accompanied by an upward movement of the head, heavenwards & with a closing of the eyes)
Please	Παρακαλώ	Parakalo
Thank you	(Σαζ) Ευχαριστώ	(sas) Efkaristo
No, thanks	Οχι ζυχαριστώ	Ochi, efkaristo
Thank you very much	Ευχαριστώ πολύ	Efkaristo poli
After which the reply may well be:-		
Thank you (& please)	Παρακαλώ	Parakalo
Do you speak English?	Μιλάτε Αγγλικά	Milahteh anglikah
How do you say....	Πως λενε...	Pos lene...
...in Greek?	...στα Ελληνικά	...sta Ellinika
What is this called?	Πως το λένε	Pos to lene
I do not understand	Δεν καταλαβαίνω	Then katahlavehno
Could you speak more slowly (slower?)	Μπορειτε να μιλάτε πιο αργά	Boreete na meelate peeo seegha (arga)
Could you write it down?	Μπορειτε να μου το γράψετε	Boreete na moo to grapsete

7

Numbers

One	Ενα	enna
Two	Δύο	thio
Three	Τρία	triah
Four	Τέσσερα	tessehra
Five	Πέντε	pendhe
Six	Εξι	exhee
Seven	Επτά	eptah
Eight	Οκτώ	ockto
Nine	Εννέα	ennea
Ten	Δέκα	thecca
Eleven	Εντεκα	endekha
Twelve	Δώδεκα	thodhehka
Thirteen	Δεκατρία	thehka triah
Fourteen	Δεκατέσσερα	thehka tessehra
Fifteen	Δεκαπέντε	thehka pendhe
Sixteen	Δεκαέξι	thekaexhee
Seventeen	Δεκαεπτά	thehkaeptah
Eighteen	Δεκαοκτώ	thehkaockto
Nineteen	Δεκαεννέα	thehkaennea
Twenty	Εικοσι	eeckossee
Twenty-one	Εικοσι ένα	eeckcossee enna
Twenty-two	Εικοσι δύο	eeckcossee thio
Thirty	Τριάντα	treeandah
Forty	Σαράντα	sarandah
Fifty	Πενήντα	penindah
Sixty	Εξήντα	exhindah
Seventy	Εβδομήντα	evthomeendah
Eighty	Ογδόντα	ogthondah
Ninety	Ενενήτα	eneneendah
One hundred	Εκατό	eckato
One hundred and one	Εκατόν ένα	eckaton enna
Two hundred	Διακόσια	theeakossia
One thousand	Χίλια	kheelia
Two thousand	Δύο χιλιάδες	thio kheeliathes

2 Getting to & from Crete, Athens & the mainland ports

If all the year were playing holidays, to sport would be as tedious as work. William Shakespeare

To start this chapter off, a word of introductory warning. Whatever form of travel is used travellers must not pack money or travellers cheques in luggage that will be stowed away, out of sight. Some years ago, almost unbelievably, we met a young lady who had at the last moment, prior to checking-in at the airport, stuffed some drachmae notes in a zipped side pocket of one of her suitcases. On arrival in Greece, surprise, surprise, she was minus the money.

BY AIR
From the United Kingdom

Scheduled flights To get to Crete it is possible to fly direct to Iraklion (via Athens) by courtesy of Olympic Airways. The alternative is to fly to Athens East (international airport), transfer by bus to Athens West (domestic) airport and then fly Olympic Airways to the island. Note both international and domestic Olympic flights use the West airport.

Heathrow to Athens (3¾ hours): daily, non-stop British Airways, Olympic and others.

Scheduled airfare options include: 1st class return, economy, excursion, APEX (Advanced Purchase Excursion Fare), PEX (instant purchase, and the cheapest scheduled fare) and Eurobudget.

Charter flights & package tours Some package tour operators keep a number of seats available on each flight for, what is in effect, a charter flight. A nominal charge is made for accommodation (which need not be taken up), the cost being included in the return airfare. These seats are substantially cheaper than the scheduled APEX fares and are known as 'Charter Cheapies'. Apart from the relatively low price, the normal two week holiday period can be extended by a further week or weeks for a small surcharge. There is a variety of United Kingdom departure airports including Birmingham, Gatwick, Glasgow and Manchester. But, as one correspondent has pointed out, the frequency of charter flights tails off dramatically between October and March, as does the choice of airport departure points. Do not forget this when contemplating an out-of-season holiday.

To ascertain what is on offer, scan the travel section of the Sunday papers, as well as the weekly magazine *Time Out* and, possibly, *Private Eye*. There are many, varied package tours with a number of the large tour operators and the smaller, more personal, companies, offering a bewildering array of multi-centre, fly-drive, budget-bed, self catering and personally tailored holidays, in addition to the more usual hotel accommodation.

Exceptionally reasonable charter flights, with the necessary accommodation vouchers, are available through *Owners Abroad Ltd*, Ilford, who also have offices in Manchester, Birmingham and Glasgow. Example fares and routes for 1987 include:

Two week return fares	Low Season	Mid-season	High season
Athens leaving Gatwick Thursday, Friday	From £ 93.75	£ 99.75	£126.75
Athens leaving Manchester Thursday	From £106.75	£114.75	£136.75
Athens leaving Birmingham Thursday	From £105.75	£113.75	£135.75

CANDID GUIDE TO CRETE

Athens leaving Glasgow Thursday	From £131.75	£149.75	£164.75
Iraklion (Heraklion) leaving Gatwick Tuesday	From £ 99.75	£109.75	£131.75
Iraklion leaving Birmingham Tuesday	From £138.75	£146.75	£170.75
Iraklion leaving Manchester Tuesday	From £113.75	£121.75	£145.75
Iraklion leaving Glasgow Tuesday	From £145.75	£164.75	£178.75

These rates are subject to inexcusable surcharges and airport taxes totalling £14.95 per head. The fares for three weeks are those above plus £30, for four weeks £35 and for five to six weeks, an additional 50 per cent is charged. Note that the total number of weeks allowed in Greece for travellers who arrive and depart by charter flights is six, not twelve, weeks.

Perhaps the least expensive flights available are *Courier Flights*. These scheduled seats start off at about £65 return to Athens for the low season period. BUT passengers can only take a maximum of 10 kg of hand luggage, one holdall measuring no more than 1ft x 2ft – no other baggage. Other restrictions result in only one passenger being able to travel at a time and for a minimum period of ten or fourteen days.

Olympic Airways has joined the charter flight fray with their 'Love-a-Fare' service. (Yes 'love-a-fare' which is an APEX option in summer dress!), the London to Athens return fare costing from £166. The booking must be made at least two weeks in advance and allows a maximum of four weeks stay. There are Olympic offices in London as well as Manchester, Birmingham and Glasgow.

Amongst companies offering interesting and slightly off-beat holidays are the *Aegina Club Ltd,* and *Ramblers Holidays*. *Aegina* offer a wide range of tours, three different locations in up to three weeks and, additionally, will tailor a programme to fit in with the client's requirements. *Ramblers*, as would be imagined, include walking holidays based on a number of locations with half-board accommodation. More conventional inclusions, some in smaller, more personal hotels, pensions and tavernas than those used by the larger tour companies, are available from *Small World* and *Martyn Holidays*. Both brochures have one or two more out of the way locations but equally the two firms allow a fair amount of 'glossing' to creep into individual descriptions which I suppose is to be expected and, if taken into account, can be allowed for in any deliberations.

Students Young people lucky enough to be under 26 years of age (oh to be 26 again) should consider contacting *World-Wide Student Travel* who market a number of inexpensive charter flights. Students of any age or scholars under 22 years of age (whatever mode of travel is planned) should take their *International Student Identity Card* (*ISIC*). This will ensure discounts are available whenever they are applicable, not only is respect of travel but also for entry to museums, archaeological sites and some forms of entertainment.

If under 26 years of age, but not a student, it may be worthwhile applying for membership of *The Federation of International Youth Travel Organization* (*FIYTO*) which guarantees youth discounts from some ferry and tour operators.

From the United States of America
Scheduled flights
Olympic flights include departures from:
Atlanta (via John F Kennedy (JFK) airport, New York (NY): daily
Boston (via JFK or La Guardia, NY): daily
Chicago (via JFK): daily
Dallas (via JFK): daily
Houston (via JFK): daily
Los Angeles (via JFK): daily
Miami (via JFK; 15 hours): daily
Minneapolis (via JFK): daily
New York (JFK approximately 10½ hours); daily direct
Norfolk (via JFK): daily except Saturday
Philadelphia (via JFK; about 11 hours): daily
Rochester (via JFK): daily
San Francisco (via JFK; about 14½ hours): daily
Seattle (via JFK or London): daily
Tampa (via JFK): daily
Washington DC (via JFK or La Guardia): daily

Note that flights via New York's John F Kennedy airport involve a change of plane from, or to, a domestic American airline.

USA domestic airlines, including *TWA*, also run a number of flights to Greece and the choice of air fares is bewildering including economy, first class return, super APEX, APEX, GIT, Excursion, ABC, OTC, ITC, and others, wherein part package costs are incorporated.

Charter/standby flights & secondary airlines As in the United Kingdom, scanning the Sunday national papers' travel section, including the *New York Times,* will disclose various companies offering package tours and charter flights. Another way to make the journey is to take a standby flight to London and then fly, train or bus on to Greece. Alternatively, there are a number of inexpensive, secondary airline companies offering flights to London, and the major Western European capitals.

Useful agencies, especially for students, include *Let's Go Travel Services.*

From Canada
Scheduled Olympic flights include departures from:
Montreal: twice weekly direct
or (via Amsterdam, JFK and/or La Guardia NY): daily except Mondays
Toronto: twice weekly (via Montreal)
or (via Amsterdam, JFK and/or La Guardia NY): daily except Monday and Friday
Winnipeg (via Amsterdam): Thursday and Sunday only.

As for the USA, the above flights involve a change of airline and there is a choice of domestic and package flights and a wide range of differing fares.

Student agencies include *Canadian Universities Travel Service.*

From Australia
There are Australian airline scheduled flights from Adelaide (via Melbourne), Brisbane (via Sydney), Melbourne and Sydney to Athens. Flights via Melbourne and Sydney involve a change of plane from, or to, a domestic airline. Regular as well as excursion fares and affinity groups.

From New Zealand
There are no scheduled flights.
Various connections are available as well as regular and affinity fares.

From South Africa
Scheduled Olympic flights include departures from:
Cape Town (via Johannesburg): Fridays and Sundays only.
Johannesburg: direct, Thursday, Friday and Sunday.

Flights via Johannesburg involve a change of plane from, or to, a domestic airline. South African airline flights from Johannesburg to Athens are available as regular, excursion or affinity fares.

From Ireland
Scheduled Olympic flights from:
Dublin: daily via London which involves a change of airline to Aer Lingus.

Note that when flying from Ireland, Australia, New Zealand, South Africa, Canada and the USA there are sometimes advantages in travelling via London or other European capitals on stopover and taking inexpensive connection flights to Greece.

Scandinavia
including:
Denmark Scheduled Olympic flights from:
Copenhagen (via Frankfurt): daily involving a change of aircraft as well as non-stop flights on Wednesday, Friday, Saturday and Sunday.
Sweden Scheduled Olympic flights from:
Stockholm (via Copenhagen and Frankfurt): Tuesday, Wednesday, Friday, Saturday.
Norway Scheduled Olympic flights from:
Oslo (via Frankfurt or Copenhagen): daily.

All the Scandinavian countries have a large choice of domestic and package flights with a selection of offerings. Contact *SAS Airlines* for Olympic Airways details.

AIRPORTS
United Kingdom Do not forget if intending to stay in Greece longer than two weeks, the long-stay car parking fees tend to mount up – and will the battery last for a 3 or 4 week layover? Incidentally charges at Gatwick are about £31.65 for two weeks, £41.80 for three weeks and £51.15 for four weeks. The difficulty is that most charter flights leave and arrive at rather unsociable hours, so friends and family may not be too keen to act as a taxi service.

Athens Hellinikon airport is split into two parts, West (Olympic domestic and international flights) and East (foreign airlines). There are coaches to make the connection between the two airports, and Olympic buses to Athens centre as well as city buses.
   At the Western or domestic airport, city buses pull up alongside the terminal building. Across the road is a pleasant cafe/restaurant but the service becomes fairly chaotic when packed out. To the left of the cafe (facing) is a newspaper kiosk and further on, across a side road, a Post Office is hidden in the depths of the first building.
   The Eastern airport is outwardly quite smart but can, in reality, become an expensive, very cramped and uncomfortable location if there are long delays. These occur when, for instance, the air traffic controllers strike elsewhere in Europe. Remember when leaving Greece to have enough money and some food left for an enforced stay, as flight departures are consistently overdue and food and drink in the airport are costly. There are simply no facilities for an overnight sleep and the bench seats are very soon taken up. You have been warned.

BY TRAIN
From the United Kingdom & European countries (Illustration 1)
Recommended only for train buffs and masochists but one of the alternative routes

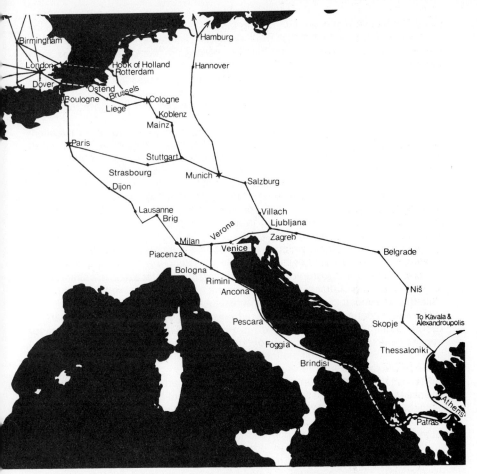

Illustration 1 European Railway Routes

to be considered when a visitor intends to stay in Greece in excess of 6 weeks. The quickest journey of the three, major scheduled overland routes takes about 60 hours, and a second-class return fare costs in the region of £250. One advantage is that travellers may break the journey along the route (a little difficult on an airline flight), and another is that it is possible to travel out on one route and back by an alternative track (if you will excuse the pun). It is important to take along basic provisions, toilet paper and to wear old clothes.

A recent return to the 'day of the train' reinforced my general opinion and introductory remarks in respect of this particular method of travel, bringing sharply back into focus the disadvantages and difficulties. The list of drawbacks should be enough to deter any but the most determined.

Try not to have a query which involves making use of the overseas information desk at Victoria Station as the facility is undermanned and the wait to get to a counter averages ¾ hr. The staff are very willing but it is of interest that they overcome the intricacies of the official British Rail European timetable ("it's all Greek to me guvnor") by overtly referring to the (infinitely) more managable *Thomas Cook* publication.

The channel crossing is often on craft that would not be pressed into service if we declared war on the Isle of Wight; the sea journey is too short for any cabins to be available; the duty free goods on offer are very limited and there are inordinate delays between train, boat and train.

The French trains that ply between the coast and Paris are of an excellent standard. On the other hand changing trains at the 'black hole' of the Gare du Nord sharply focuses travellers' attention on a whole subculture of human beings who exist in and around a number of European railway stations. My favourite example of this little known branch of the human race is the 'bag-shuffler' – usually a middle-aged lady. The genus is initially recognisable by the multitudinous paper and plastic bags festooned about the person. Once at rest the contents are constantly and interminably shuffled from one bag to another, and back again, the ritual being accompanied by low mutterings.

French railway stations, which are heated to a temperature relating to gentle simmer on a domestic cooker, have perfected a waiting room seating arrangement that precludes any but a drunk contortionist stretching out for a nap. In common with most other railway stations, food and drink are expensive and credit cards impossible to use, even at the swanky station restaurants.

The Metro connection between the railway stations of Gare du Nord and Gare de Lyon is not straightforward and involves a walk. The Gare de Lyon springs a minor trap for the unwary in that the inter-continental trains depart from platforms reached by a long walk up the far left platforms (facing the trains). Don't some of the French trains now resemble children's rocket drawings?

The station's toilet facilities are miniscule and men are charged for other than the use of a urinal and washbasin. Ladies have to pay about 2 Francs (F), a private closet costs 6F and a shower 12F. Potential users must not imagine they will be able to sneak in for a crafty stand-up wash – the toilets are intently watched over by attendants.

Although it may appear to an optional extra, it is obligatory to purchase a couchette ticket for the train journey. This is a Catch 22 situation brought about by the rule that only couchette ticket holders have the right to a seat! Yes, well, not so optional. It is also necessary to pack food and drink, at least for the French part of the journey, as usually there are no refreshment services. In Italy most trains are met, at the various station stops, by trolley pushing vendors of (expensive) sustenance.

Venice station is signed Stazione St Lucia and is most conveniently sited bang-on the edge of the Grand Canal waterfront with shops and restaurants to the left. Some of the cake shops sell slabs of pizza pie for about 800 lira (L) which furnishes good standby nourishment. The scheduled stopover here will have to be adjusted for any (inevitable) delay in arrival. Venice (on the outward journey) is the watershed where Greek, and the occasional Yugoslavian, carriages are coupled up and passengers can be guaranteed to encounter a number of nasties. These replacement compartments are seedier and dirtier than their more Western European counterparts, and the lavatories vary between bad to unspeakable. Faults include toilets that won't flush (sometimes appearing to mysteriously fill up); Greek toilet paper (which apart from other deficiencies lacks body and – please excuse the indelicacy – through which fingers break); no toilet paper at all (which is worst?); no soap dispenser; a lack of coat hooks; water taps that don't and the whole rather grimy.

From Venice the term 'Express' should be ignored as the train's progress becomes slower and slower and slower with long unscheduled stops and quite inordinate delays at the Yugoslavian frontiers. During the Yugoslavian part of the journey it is necessary for passengers to lock themselves into the compartments as some of the locals have an annoying habit of entering and determinedly looting tourists' luggage. There were even totally unsubstantiated rumours, in the 1986 summer, of locals spraying an aerosol knockout gas through the keyholes, breaking in and relieving passengers of their belongings, at their leisure. I must stress I have not actually met victims and the story may be apocryphal. It is inadvisable to leave the train at Belgrade for a stopover as the accommodation available to tourists is extremely expensive, costing in the region of £60 for a double room per night, and it is almost impossible to renegotiate a couchette for the remainder of the onward journey. There are trolley attendants at the major Yugoslavian railway stations but the contents of the rolls proffered are of an 'interesting' nature resembling 'biltong' or 'hardtack' burgers. Certainly when poked by the enthusiastic vendors I'm sure their fingers buckle. Another item of nutriment on offer are large, cheese curd pies and a railway employee wanders round twice a day with a very large aluminium teapot ostensibly containing coffee. Nobody appears to be interested in payment with Yugoslavian dinars, but American dollars or English pounds sterling almost cause a purr of satisfaction. Travellers lucky enough to have the services of a Greek attendant may well find he keeps a cache of alcoholic drinks for sale. An aside is that the Yugoslavians are obsessed by wheel-tapping and at all and every stop, almost at the drop of a sleeper, appear and perform. Much of the journey beyond Belgrade is on a single line track and should, for instance, a cow break into a trot the animal might well overtake the train. At the frontier passengers may be reminded of the rigours of Iron Curtain countries, as they will being subjected to rigorous, lengthy baggage and documents checks by a swamp of officials, whose numbers include stern faced, unsmiling, gun-toting police.

In stark contrast the friendly Greek frontier town of Idomeni is a tonic. Even late at night the station's bank is open as is the taverna/snackbar with a scattering of tables on the platform and a buzz of brightly lit noise and activity.

To avoid the Yugoslavian experience a very pleasant alternative is to opt for the railway route that travels the length of Italy to Brindisi port. Here international ferry-boats can be caught to the mainland Greek port of Igoumenitsa or Patras from either of which buses can be used to make the connection with Athens, whilst Patras offers the possibility of another train journey to Athens.

Brindisi (Italy), contains several traps for the unwary. Unfortunately the railway station and quay for the Italy-Greek ferry-boats are some 200m apart, which on a hot day.... The railway station has no formal ticket office or barrier. It is only necessary to dismount, turn left along the platform, left again, beside the concrete wall supporting the first floor concourse (which stretches over and above the platforms), across the railway lines and left again down the sterile dockland street to the ferry-boat complex. The road, hemmed in by a prefabricated wall on the right, curves parallel to the seawall on the left, from which it is separated by a high chain link fence, a number of railway lines and tarmacadam quay. But, before leaving the station, stop, for all the ticket offices and necessary officials are situated in the referred to upper storey buildings and in the 'Main Street'. My favourite tour office is across the road from the station, alongside a bank on the corner formed by the 'Main St' and the 'Ferry-Boat' street. The staff are very helpful and most informative. Diagonally across the bottom of this end of the 'Main St' is a small, tree edged square which, as it is well endowed with park benches, has become an unofficial waiting room with travellers and backpackers occupying most of the available seating. Do not forget when booking rail tickets to ask for Brindisi Maritime as the town railway station is some kilometres inland.

The international ferry-boats on this route are, in the main, luxurious, beautifully appointed and expensive. Possible trappings include a sea-water swimming pool, a ladies' hairdresser and beauty salon, a number of restaurants and a self-service cafeteria, a coffee bar and a disco. Unfortunately the cafeteria dishes are out-rageously expensive with, for instance, a meal for two of veal and potatoes, a spinach pie, lettuce salad and a ½ bottle of emasculated retsina costing about 1750 drs with a coffee hovering on the 100 drs mark. Moral, try not to eat on board. A splendid but expensive two berth cabin with a generous en suite bathroom sets a traveller back some 4000 drs. Prices everywhere are in American dollars and the change desk, even when on the Greece to Italy leg, does not change currency into Italian lira....?

Travellers under 26 years of age can take advantage of British Rail's *Inter-Rail pass* while American and Canadians may obtain a *Eurorail pass* prior to reaching Europe by applying to *Victoria Travel Centre*. There is also the *Transalpino ticket* available from the London office of the firm of the same name and all these offers hold out a substantial discount on standard train and ferry fares, but are subject to various terms and conditions. Another student outfit offering cut-price train, coach and airline flights is **London Student Travel** (& *Eurotrain*).

Certainly it must be borne in mind that the Greek railway system is not extensive and, unless travelling around other European countries, a concessionary pass might not represent much of a saving. On the other hand discounts in respect of the Greek railways includes travel on some of the state railway buses (OSE).

Examples of the various tickets, costs and conditions are as follows:

Inter-Rail ticket	Under 26 years of age, valid one month for use in 21 countries (and also allows half-fare travel in the UK on Sealink and B+I ships as well as P&O ferries via Southampton and Le Havre).	£139	
Transalpino ticket	Under 26, valid for two months, allows stop-over en route to the destination. London to Athens via Brindisi or Yugoslavia from	Single £99.99	Return £189.80

Other ticket options include B.I.G.E., Eurotrain and 'Athens Circle'.

Timetables & routes (Illustration 1)

This section caused me as much work as whole chapters on other subjects. *British Rail*, whose timetable I had the greatest difficulty deciphering and *Thomas Cook*, whose timetable I could understand, were both helpful.

(1) London (Victoria Station), Dover (Western Docks), (jetfoil), Ostend, Brussels, Liege, Aachen, Cologne (change train, ¾ hr delay); Mainz, Mannheim, Ulm, Munich (change train ¾ hr delay), Salzburg, Jesenice, Ljubljana, Zagreb, Belgrade (Beograd), Skopje, Gevgelija, Idomeni, Thessaloniki to Athens.
An example of the journey is as follows:
Departure: 1300 hrs, afternoon sea crossing, evening on the train, late night change of train at Cologne, night on the train, morning change of train at Munich, all day and night on the train arriving Athens very late some 2½ days later at 2314 hrs.

(2) London (Charing Cross/Waterloo East stations), Dover Hoverport, (hovercraft), Boulogne Hoverpoint, Paris (du Nord), change train (and station) to Paris (de Lyon), Strasbourg, Munich, Salzburg, Ljubljana, Zagreb, Belgrade (change train 1¾ hrs delay), Thessaloniki to Athens.
An example:
Departure: 0955 hrs and arrive 2½ days later at 2315 hrs.
Second class single fares from £128 and return fare from £251.30.

(3) London (Victoria), Folkestone Harbour, (ferry-boat), Calais, Paris (du Nord), change train (and station) to Paris (de Lyon), Venice, Ljubljana, Zagreb, Belgrade, Thessaloniki to Athens.
An example:
Departure: 1415 hrs and arrive 2¾ days later at 0840 hrs.

(4) London (Liverpool St), Harwich (Parkeston Quay), ferry-boat, Hook of Holland, Rotterdam, Eindhoven, Venio, Cologne (change train), Mainz, Mannheim, Stuttgart, Ulm, Munich, Salzburg, Jesenice, Ljubljana, Zagreb, Belgrade, Nis, Skopje, Gevgelija, Idomeni, Thessaloniki to Athens.

An example:
Departure: 1940 hrs, night ferry crossing, change train at Cologne between 1048 and 1330 hrs, first and second nights on the train and arrive at Athens middle of the day at 1440 hrs.

An alternative is to take the more pleasurable train journey through Italy and make a ferry-boat connection to Greece:

(5) London (Victoria), Folkestone Harbour, Calais, Boulogne, Amiens, Paris (du Nord), change train and station to Paris (de Lyon), Dijon, Vallorbe, Lausanne, Brig, Domodossala, Milan (Central), Bologna, Rimini, Ancona, Pescara, Bari to Brindisi.

    (5a) Brindisi to Patras sea crossing.

    (5b) Patras to Athens.

    An example:
Departure: 0958 hrs, day ferry crossing, change of train at Paris to the Parthenon Express, one night on the train and arrive at Brindisi at 1850 hrs. Embark on the ferry-boat departing at 2000 hrs, night on the ferry-boat and disembark at 1300 hrs the next day. Take the coach to Athens arriving at 1600 hrs.

    The second class single fare costs from £149.90.

On all these services children benefit from reduced fares, depending on their age. Couchettes and sleepers are usually available at extra cost and Jetfoil sea crossings are subject to a surcharge.

    Details of fares and timetables are available from *British Rail Europe* or *The Hellenic State Railways (OSE)*. The most cogent, helpful and informative firm through whom to book rail travel must be *Victoria Travel Centre.* I have always found them to be extremely accommodating and it is well worth contacting *Thomas Cook Ltd,* who have a very useful range of literature and timetables available from their Publications Department.

The above are only a guide and up-to-date details must be checked with the relevant offices prior to actually booking.

From the Continent & Scandinavia to Athens
Pick up one of the above main lines by using the appropriate connections detailed in Illustration 1.

    Departure terminals from Scandinavia include Helsinki (Finland); Oslo (Norway); Gothenburg, Malmo and Stockholm (Sweden); Fredrikshavn and Copenhagen (Denmark).

BY COACH
This means of travel is for the more hardy voyager and/or young. If the description of the train journey has caused apprehension, the tales of passengers of the less luxurious coach companies should strike terror into the listener/reader. Common 'faults' include lack of 'wash and brush up' stops, smugglers, prolonged border custom investigations, last minute changes of route and breakdowns. All this is on top of the forced intimacy with a number of widely disparate companions, some wildly drunk, in cramped, uncomfortable surroundings.

    For details of the scheduled *Euroways Supabus* apply *c/o Victoria Coach Station* or to the *National Express Company.* A single fare costs from £79 and a return ticket from £140. This through service takes 4 days plus, with no overnight layovers but short stops at Cologne, Frankfurt and Munich where there is a change of coach. Fares include ferry costs but exclude refreshments. Arrival and departure in Greece is at the Peloponissou Railway Station, Athens. The timetable is as follows:

Departure from London, Victoria Coach Station, Bay 20: Friday and Saturday at 2030 hrs arriving at 1100 hrs 4½ days later.

Return journey
Departure from Filellinon St, Syntagma Sq, Athens: Wednesday and Friday at 1300 hrs arriving London at 0800 hrs, 4 days later.

Express coach companies include *Consolas Travel*. This well-established company runs daily buses during the summer months, except Sunday, and single fares start at about £35 with a return ticket costing from £69. Other services are run by the various 'pirate' bus companies, the journey time is about the same and, again, prices, which may be slightly cheaper, do not include meals. On a number of islands, travel agents signs still refer to the *Magic Bus*, or as a fellow traveller so aptly put it – the *Tragic Bus*, but the company that ran this renowned and infamous service perished some years ago. Imitators appear to perpetuate the name.

In the United Kingdom it is advisable to obtain a copy of the weekly magazine *Time Out*, wherein the various coach companies advertise. For return trips from Athens, check shop windows in Omonia Sq, the American Express office in Syntagma Sq, or the Students Union in Filellinon St, just off Syntagma Sq. *Eurolines Intercars (Uniroute)* runs a national coach service that shuttles between Athens and Paris on a three day journey. The buses depart twice a week at 1030 hrs, Wednesday and Saturday, at a cost of 12,000 drs but note that baggage costs an extra 200 drs. The French end of the connection is close by the Metro station Porte Vincennes and the Athens terminus is alongside the Stathmos Larissis railway station.

These buses are comfortable with air conditioning but no toilet so the leg-stretching stops are absolutely vital, not only to purchase victuals but for passengers to relieve themselves. It is a problem that the standard of the 'way-station' toilets and snackbars varies from absolutely awful to luxurious. And do not forget that the use of the lavatories is usually charged for in Greece and Yugoslavia. To help make the journey acceptable passengers must pack enough food and drink to tide them over the trip. There are sufficient stops in Greece at, for instance, Livadia, Larissa and Thessaloniki as well as the frontier, which takes up to some 2¾ hrs. The Yugoslavian part of the route passes through Belgrade and at about two-thirds distance there is a lunchtime motorway halt. At this sumptuous establishment even Amex credit cards are accepted and the lavatories are free – a welcome contrast to the previous, 'mind boggling' stop where even the Greeks blanched at the sight of the toilets! The bus and driver change at Trieste which is probably necessary after the rigours of the Yugoslavian roads. Use of the lavatories in the bus station has to be paid for and they are very smelly with a 'lecher' in the ladies. One of the two Italian stops is at a luxurious motorway complex. The route between Italy and France over the Alps takes a tediously long time on winding, narrow moutain roads with an early morning change of driver in France. It may well be necessary to 'encourage' the driver on this section to make an unscheduled halt in order to save burst bladders. The bus makes three Paris drop-offs, at about midday three days later, and the best disembarkation point depends on a traveller's plans.

Devotees of the Le Havre channel crossing must make for the Gare St Lazaire railway station. The Metro, with one change, costs about 5 francs (F) each and the coach's arrival time allows passengers to catch a Paris to Le Havre train. This departs on the three hour journey at 1630 hrs and the tickets cost some 100 F each. No information in respect of cross channel ferries is available at the railway station, despite the presence of a number of tourist information desks.

Incidentally the walk from the Le Havre railway terminus to the ferry-boat quay is a long haul but there are reasonably priced taxis between the two points. The superb restaurant *Le Southampton*, conveniently across the street from the dock, may well compensate for the discomfort of the trudge round, especially as they accept payment by Amex.

BY CAR (Illustration 2)

Usually only a worthwhile alternative method of travel if there are at least two adults and travellers are planning to stay for longer than three weeks, as the journey from England is about 1900 miles and takes approximately 50 hrs nonstop driving.

One of the shortest routes from the United Kingdom is via car-ferry to Ostend (Belgium), on to Munich, Salzburg (Germany), Klagenfurt (Austria) and Ljubljana (Yugoslavia). There the Autoput E94 is taken on to Zagreb, Belgrade (Beograd) and Nis on the E5, where the E27 and E55 are taken via Skopje to the frontier town of Gevgelija/Evzonoi. Note that due to major rebuilding works, the Yugoslavian road between Zagreb and Nis can be subject to lengthy delays.

The very large intercontinental lorries are rather more dangerous in Yugoslavia where they appear to regard the middle of the sometimes narrow roads as their own territory.

Drivers through France have a number of possible routes but those choosing to skirt Switzerland will have to cross over into Italy, usually angling down through Lyon and heading in the general direction of Turin. Once over the border into Italy, bypass Turin (Torino) and proceed to Piacenza, Brescia, Verona, Padua (Padova), Venice and cut up to Trieste. I say bypass because the ordinary Italian roads are just 'neat aggravation' and the cities are almost impossible to circumnavigate. Although motorways involve constant toll fees they are much quicker and less wearing on the nerves. Note that Italian petrol stations have a nasty habit of closing for a midday siesta between 1200 and 1500 hrs. An alternative route is via Turin, Milan, Bergamo, Brescia, Verona and on to Trieste which leads around the southern edge of a few of the lakes, in the area of Brescia. Excursions to Padua and Venice are obvious possibilities.

From Trieste the most scenic (and winding) route is to travel the Adriatic coast road via Rijeka, Zadar and Split to Dubrovnik. The lovely medieval inner city of Dubrovnik is well worth a visit. At Petrovac the pain starts as the road swings up to Titograd around to Kosovska Mitrovika, Pristina, Skopje and down to the border at Gevgelija. The stretch from Skopje to the Greek frontier can be rather unnerving. Signposting in Yugoslavia is usually very bad; always obtain petrol when the opportunity crops up and lastly but not least city lights are often turned off during the hours of darkness (sounds a bit Irish to me!), making night driving extremely hazardous. To save the journey on from Petrovac, it is possible, at the height of the season, to catch a ferry from Dubrovnik (or take the pretty coastal road on to the port of Bar) to Igoumenitsa or Patras on the Greek mainland.

Detailed road reports are available from the *Automobile Association* but I would like to stress that in the Yugoslavian mountains, especially after heavy rain, landslips can (no will!) result in parts of the road disappearing at the odd spot as well as the surface being littered with rocks. There you go!

The main road through Greece, to Athens via Pirgos, Larissa and Lamia, is wide and good but the speed of lorries and their trailer units can still prove disquieting. Vehicles being overtaken are expected to move right over and tuck well into the hard shoulder. From Evzonoi to Athens, via Thessaloniki, is 340 miles (550 kms) and some of the major autoroute is a toll road.

Personally my favourite choice of route involves crossing the Channel to Le Havre, cutting down through France, which holds few perils for the traveller, via Evreux, Chartres, Pithiviers, Montargis, Clamecy, Nevers, Lyon and Chambery to the Italian border at Modane. Here the fainthearted can take the tunnel whilst the adventurous wind their way over the Col du Mont Cenis.

In Italy, at say Verona or Padua, it is worth considering, as for the alternative train journey, cutting down the not all that attractive Adriatic seaboard to one of the international Italian ferry-boat ports of Ancona, Bari, Brindisi or Otranto where boats connect to Igoumenitsa or Patras on the Greek mainland (*See* BY FERRY-BOAT).

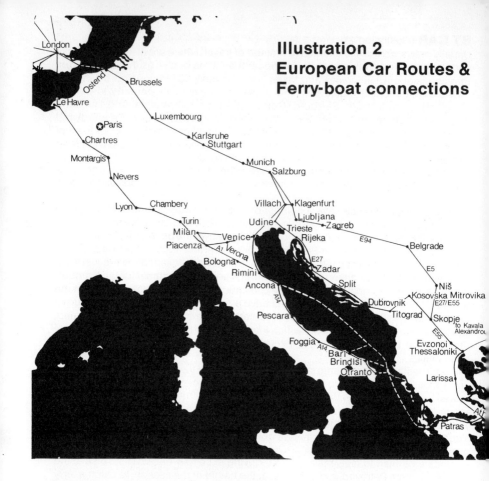

Illustration 2
European Car Routes & Ferry-boat connections

General Vehicle & Personal Requirements

Documents required for travel in any European country include an *International Driving Licence,* and a *Carnet de Passages en Douanes* (both issued by the AA and valid for one year) as well as a *Green Insurance Card.* It is recommended to take the vehicle's registration documents as proof of ownership and the vehicle must have a nationality sticker of the approved pattern and design.

Particular countries' requirements include:

Italy Import allowances are as for Greece but the restriction on the importation of Italian currency equals about £100.

All cars entering Italy must possess both right and left hand external driving mirrors.

Switzerland If intending to drive through Switzerland remember that the Swiss require the vehicle and all the necessary documents to be absolutely correct. (They would.) The authorities have a nasty habit of stopping vehicles some distance beyond the frontier posts in order to make thorough checks.

Yugoslavia A valid passport is the only personal document required for citizens of, for example, Denmark, West Germany, Finland, Great Britain and Northern Ireland, Republic of Southern Ireland, Holland and Sweden. Americans and Canadians must have a visa and all formalities should be checked with the relevant Yugoslavian Tourist Office.

It is compulsory to carry a warning triangle, a first aid kit and a set of replacement vehicle light bulbs. The use of spotlights is prohibited and drivers planning to travel during the winter should check the special regulations governing the use of studded tyres.

Visiting motorists cannot obtain fuel without petrol coupons, which are available at the frontier and, supposedly, from travel agents *Kompass* or *Putnik*. Carefully calculate the amount of coupons required for the journey and pay for them in foreign currency at the frontier as the rate allowed is very advantageous compared to that if the coupons are paid for in Yugoslavian dinars. Petrol stations are often far apart, closed or out of petrol, so fill up when possible.

Photographers are only allowed to import five rolls of film; drinkers a bottle of wine and a quarter litre of spirits and smokers 200 cigarettes or 50 cigars. Each person may bring in unlimited foreign currency but only 1500 dinars.

Fines are issued on the spot and the officer collecting one should issue an official receipt.

To obtain assistance in the case of accident or breakdown dial 987 and the *SPI* will come to your assistance.

Greece It is compulsory to carry a first aid kit as well as a fire extinguisher in a vehicle and failure to comply may result in a fine. It is also mandatory to carry a warning triangle and it is forbidden to carry petrol in cans. In Athens the police are empowered to confiscate and detain the number plates of illegally parked vehicles. The use of undipped headlights in towns is strictly prohibited.

Customs allow the importation of 200 cigarettes or 50 cigars, 1 litre of spirits or 2 litres of wine and only 3000 drs but any amount of foreign currency. Visitors from the EEC may import 300 cigarettes or 75 cigars, 1½ litres of spirits or 4 litres of wine.

Speed Limits
See table below – all are standard legal limits which may be varied by signs

	Built-up areas	Outside built-up areas	Motorways	Type of vehicle affected
Greece	31 mph (50 kph)	49 mph (80 kph)	62 mph (100 kph)	Private vehicles with or or without trailers
Yugoslavia	37 mph (60 kph) 62 mph* (100 kph)*	49 mph (80 kph)	74 mph (120 kph)	Private vehicles without trailers

*Speed on dual carriageways

BY FERRY-BOAT (Illustration 2)
Some of the descriptive matter under the heading BY TRAIN in this chapter refers to inter-country, ferry-boat travel.

Due to the popularity of the ferry port of Brindisi, height of the season travellers must be prepared for crowds, lengthy delays and the usual ferry-boat scrum (scrum not scum). Other irritants include the exas-perating requirement to purchase an embarkation pass, with the attendant formalities which include taking the pass to the police station on the second floor of the port office to have it punched! Oh, by the way, the distance between the railway station and the port is about 200m and it is absolutely necessary to 'clock in' at least 3 hrs before a ferry's departure otherwise passengers may be 'scratched' from the fixture list, have to rebook and pay again. That is why the knowledgeable head for the other departure ports, more especially Otranto.

If making this trip on the return journey from Greece, great care must be taken when purchasing the ferry-boat tickets, especially at Igoumenitsa (Greek mainland). The competition is hot and tickets may well be sold below the published price. If so and a traveller is amongst the 'lucky ones' it is best not to count one's drachmae until on board. The port officials carefully check the tickets and if they find any that have been sold at a discount then they are confiscated and the purchaser is made to buy replacements at the full price. Ouch!

Do not forget that the availability of ferry-boat sailings must be continually checked, as must airline and bus timetables. This is especially necessary during the months of October through to the beginning of May when the services are usually severely curtailed. So be warned.

USEFUL NAMES & ADDRESSES

The Automobile Association, Fanum House, Basingstoke, Hants RG21 2EA
Tel. (0256) 20123
The Greek National Tourist Organization, 195-197 Regent St.,
London W1R 8DL   Tel. (01)-734 5997
The Italian State Tourist Office, 1 Princes St, London W1R 8AY.
Tel. (01)-408 1254
The Yugoslav National Tourist Office, 143 Regent St, London W1R 8AE.
Tel. (01)-734 5243
British Rail Europe, PO Box 303, London SW1 1JY.
Tel. (01)-834 2345 (keep ringing).
The Hellenic State Railways (OSE), 1-3 Karolou St, Athens, Greece
Tel. 01.5222-491
Thomas Cook Ltd, Publications Dept, PO Box 36, Thorpewood, Peterborough
PE3 6SB.   Tel. (0733)-63200

Other useful names & addresses mentioned in the text include:
Time Out, Southampton St, London WC2E 7HD.
Courier Flights/Inflight Courier, 45 Church St, Weybridge, Surrey KT13 8DG.
Tel. (0932) 57455/56
Owners Abroad Ltd, Valentine House, Ilford Hill, Ilford, Essex ICI 2DG.
Tel. (01)-514 8844
Olympic Airways, 164 Piccadilly, London W1   Tel. (01)-846 9080
ref. 'Love-a-Fare'   Tel. (01)-846 9966
Aegina Club Ltd, 25A Hills Rd, Cambridge CB2 1NW   Tel. (0223) 63256
Ramblers Holidays, 13 Longcroft House, Fretherne Rd, Welwyn Garden City,
Herts AL8 6PQ.   Tel. (07073) 31133
Small World, Old Stone House, Judges Terrace, East Grinstead, Sussex RH19 1AQ
Tel. (0342) 27272
Martyn Holidays, West Leigh House, 390 London Rd, Isleworth, Middlesex,
TW7 5AD.   Tel. (01)-847 5855
Greek Sun Holidays, 23 Haymarket, London, SW1 4DG.   Tel.(01)-839 6055/6
Worldwide Student Travel, 39 Store St, London WC1E 7BZ.   Tel.(01)-580 7733
Victoria Travel Centre, 52 Grosvenor Gdns, London SW1.   Tel.(01)-730 8111
Transalpino, 214 Shaftesbury Ave, London WC2H 8EB.   Tel.(01)-836 0087/8
London Student Travel, (Tel. (01)-730 3402/4473) (**& Eurotrain,**
Tel. (01)-730 6525) both at 52 Grosvenor Gdns, London SW1N 0AG.
Euroways Supabus, c/o Victoria Coach Station, London SW1.   Tel.(01)-730 0202
or c/o National Express Co.
The Greek address is: 1 Karolou St, Athens.   Tel. 5240 519/6
Eurolines Intercars (Uniroute), 102 Cours de Vincennes, 75012 Paris (Metro
Porte Vincennes)
National Express Co, Westwood Garage, Margate Rd, Ramsgate CT12 6SI.
Tel. (0843) 581333
Consolas Travel, 29-31 Euston Rd, London NW1   Tel. (01)-278 1931
The Greek address is: 100 Eolou St. Athens.   Tel. 3219 228

Amongst others the agencies and offices listed above have, over the years and in varying degrees, been helpful in the preparation of the guides and I would like to extend my sincere thanks to all those concerned. Some have proved more helpful than others!

Olympic Airways overseas office addresses are as follows:
America: 647 Fifth Ave, New York, NY 10022, USA.
Tel. (0101-212) (Reservations) 838 3600 (Ticket Office) 735 0290
Canada: 1200 McGill College Ave, Suite 1250, Montreal, Quebec H3B 4G7
Tel. (0101 418) 878 9691
: 80 Bloor St West, Suite 406, Toronto ONT M55 2VI, Canada.
Tel. (0101 416) 920 2452
Australia: 44 Pitt St, 1st Floor, Sydney, NSW 2000, Australia.
Tel. (01061 2) 251 2044
South Africa: Bank of Athens Buildings, 116 Marshall St, Johannesburg, S. Africa.
Tel. (01027 11) 836 5951
Denmark: 4 Jernbanegade DK 1608, Copenhagen, Denmark.
Tel. (010451) 126-100
Sweden: 44 Birger Jalsgatan, 11429 Stockholm, Sweden.
Tel. (010468) 113-800

More useful overseas names & addresses include:
Let's Go Travel Services, Harvard Student Agencies, Thayer Hall B, Harvard University, Cambridge, MA02138 USA.   Tel. 617 495 9649
Canadian Universities Travel Service, 187 College St, Toronto ONT M5T 1P7 Canada   Tel. 417 979 2406
Automobile Association & Touring Club of Greece (ELPA), 2 Messogion Street, Athens.   Tel. (01) 7791 615

Paleochora Beach

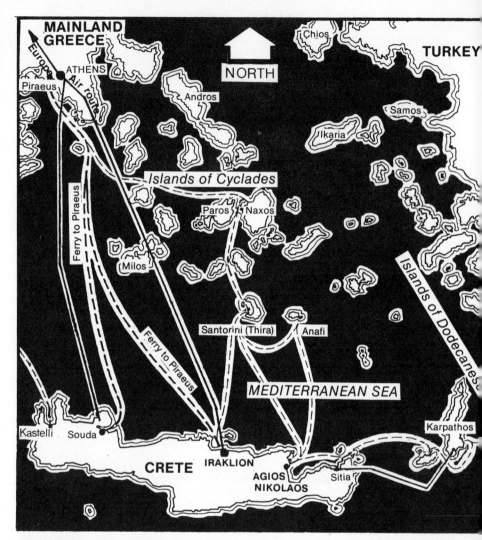

Illustration 3   Greek Mainland to Crete connections

3 Travel between Athens & Crete

I see land. I see the end of my labour. Diogenes

The Greek islands are very thick on the water, numbering between 1000 and 3000, depending upon which authority you wish to believe. Approximately 100 are inhabited of which Crete is the largest. (Illustration 3.)

Over the years a specialised and efficient system of waterborne travel developed and, in the past, the only way of setting foot on an island was to make for the relevant port and board a ferry-boat. Apart from the advent of international air flights direct to the larger islands, including, naturally, Crete, the opening up of a number of smaller airfields to take domestic flights has made it possible to fly to Athens and take an interisland flight to a scattering of island aerodromes.

BY AIR

Greeks now utilise the service extensively, so it can prove difficult to get a seat for domestic flights on the spot, especially at the height of the tourist season, and it may be preferable to forward book through a local Olympic office prior to arrival.

Travellers arriving in Athens other than by aircraft and wanting a domestic flight from the West airport can catch one of the Olympic coaches to the airport. These depart from the Olympic terminal and offices, 96-100 (Leoforos) Sygrou, between 0600 hrs and midnight at a cost of 45 drs, compared to the 350/400 drs odd charged by a taxi. An irate reader has taken me to task for not pointing out that approximately an hour must be allowed between catching the airline bus and the relevant plane check-in time. There are also city buses, details of which are listed in CHAPTER 9 (ATHENS), amongst the bus timetables. Many travellers do not wish to stop over in Athens. If this is the case, and arriving other than on an Olympic flight, they can travel directly, after landing, from the East to the domestic, West, airport using the connecting bus service.

The staff of Olympic, the Greek airline, are usually very helpful and their English good, although occasionally it is possible to fall foul of that sporadic Greek characteristic, intransigence. I remember arriving, heavily laden and tired, at the Olympic offices very early one morning. On asking for advice about the location of any suitable hotel, I was politely directed, by the girl at the enquiries desk, to the Tourist police, which would have involved an uphill walk of at least 1½ km, weighed down by an assortment of bags. There was a hotel, in which we stayed, immediately around the corner from the terminal!

It is well worth considering utilising internal flights on one leg of a journey, especially if Athens is the point of arrival or departure. The possible extra cost of the flight, over and above the overland and ferry fares, must be balanced against the time element. For instance, Athens to Iraklion by air takes some 50 mins whilst the ferry takes about 12 hours. One other advantage of domestic air travel is that the fares can be paid for by the use of American Express, Diners or Access Mastercard, possibly saving precious drachmae, especially towards the end of a holiday.

Cretan towns served by airports include Iraklion, Chania and Sitia.

NOTE that already in 1987 the cost of domestic flights has risen by a staggering 28%, on average.

BY BUS

There are daily scheduled bus services to the mainland ports of Gythion and Piraeus (CHAPTER 10) that connect by ferry-boat to Crete. Please refer to CHAPTER 9 (ATHENS) for full details of bus timetables.

BY FERRY

In the following comments I am calling on my experience of travelling third and tourist class on any number of ferry-boats.

In general, if sleeping arrangements are available they will prove satisfactory if certain basic rules are followed. First claim a bunk by depositing luggage on the chosen berth, it will be quite safe as long as money and passports are removed. The position of a berth is important and despite the labelling of 'Men' and 'Women' sleeping areas, a berth can usually be selected in either. But try to choose one adjacent to stern deck doors to ensure some ventilation as, due to the location of the third and tourist class accommodation, it can get very hot and stuffy beneath decks. A last tip is to lay a towel over plastic bunk covering to alleviate what otherwise would prove to be a sticky, uncomfortable night.

The third class lavatories are often in an unsightly condition, even prior to a craft's departure. To help enjoy reasonable surroundings and have the use of a shower, quietly trip into the next class and use their facilities (but don't tell everybody). Both the toilets and the showers suffer from the usual deficiencies listed under Greek bathrooms in CHAPTER 4, so be prepared.

Important points to take into account when ferry-boating include the following:
1. The ferries are owned by individual steamship companies and an employee of one line will be unable or unwilling to give enquirers information in respect of another company's timetable. Incidentally, this individual ownership can lead to a wide disparity in quality of service and general comfort between different ferry-boats.
2. The direct Piraeus to Crete ferry-boat links do not suffer from the scheduled timetable slippage that occurs on those voyages making a large number of 'pit-stops'. On the other hand the Piraeus-Gythion-Kastelli ferry-boat service does incur delays that can run into hours.
3. There are usually four basic fare classes: first, second, tourist and third/deck class. The published fares on scheduled ferries are government controlled and the third/deck class option represents extremely good value. Purchasers must ensure that they state the fare class required as failure to do so may well result in a more expensive, tourist ticket being bought instead of the cheaper, deck class. Apart from the aforementioned four categories, there can be a variety of first and second-class sleeping accommodation, including private and shared cabins.
4. Food and drink on the ferries used to be comparatively expensive, but price rises on the land have not been mirrored at sea. On the other hand the service is often discourteous and inefficient so it may be advantageous to pack provisions for a long voyage.

Wholesome and inexpensive ferry-boat picnic food includes: tomatoes, cucumber, bread, salami, ham, Sunfix orange juice and a bottle of wine (or two!). Take some bottled water. Greek chocolate (especially with nuts) is very good but does not keep well in the ambient daytime temperatures.
5. The state of the toilets and the lack of basic supplies makes it mandatory that one or two lavatory rolls are packed, easily to hand as it were. The usual lack of washroom facilities commends the stowage of a pack of 'wipes'.

Quite frankly, on some occasions it will be necessary to stand on the rim of the toilet bowl as the only way of using the facility. Sorry!
6. Tickets should be purchased from a ticket agency prior to a voyage, as they can cost more when purchased on board. Ticket agency offices vary from 'the plush' to boxed-in back stairs. Clients are advised to check the scheduled prices and they should not go wrong. On the other hand they must be sure their price list is up to date as fare increases over recent years have been very large. For instance the 3rd class Piraeus to Iraklion charge increased from 1246 drs to 1719 drs between April 1985 and October 1986.
7. At the height of the season, the upper deck seats are extremely hot during the day and uncomfortably chilly at night. It is advisable to stake a claim to a seat as early as

possible because the ferries are usually very crowded during the summer months. Voyagers who intend to lay out a sleeping bag and sleep the night away on the deck would do well to remember to occupy a seat, not the deck itself which is more often than not sluiced down in the night hours.
8. Travellers should ensure they have a good, fat book and a pack of cards to while away the longer sea voyages. Despite the awesome beauty of the islands and the azure blue sea, there are often long, unbroken periods of Mediterranean passage to be endured, interrupted only by the occasional passing ship and the dramatic activity and ructions that take place during a port call.
9. Travellers sensitive to discordancy, and who find disagreeable a cacophony, a clamour of sound, may well find unacceptable the usual raucous mix experienced in the average 3rd class lounge. This is made up of two televisions, tuned to different programmes (the picture constantly flickering, suffering a snowstorm or horizontally high jumping in a series of stills) accompanied by an overlaying wail of Greco-Turkish music piped over the ship's tannoy system. Best to fly!

One delight is to keep a weather eye open and hope to observe some dolphins diving and leaping in the ship's wake. Their presence is often made discernible by the loud slapping noise they make when re-entering the water.

Ferry-boaters must take care when checking connections, schedules and time-tables as they can, no do, change during the year, especially outside the inclusive months of May to September, as well as from one year to another. So be warned.

Do not forget, when the information is at it's most confusing, the Port police are totally reliable, but often a little short of English. Their offices are almost always on, or adjacent to the quayside.

Other holiday-makers should note that the large influx of this 'genus' of fun loving tourist, can have quite an impact on an island, and the cognoscenti normally vacate the particular port of call for that day.

CRUISE SHIPS
Fly-cruise packages on offer are usually rather up-market and in the main are based on seven days or multiples thereof. The cruise ships call in at selected islands for a part or full day, with excursions where applicable.

Other holiday-makers should note that the large influx of this 'genus' of fun loving tourist can have quite an impact on an island, and the *cognoscenti* normally vacate the particular port of call for that day.

GREEK ISLAND PLACE NAMES
This is probably the appropriate place to introduce the forever baffling problem which helps to bedevil the traveller – Greek pla .e names. For instance, Crete is also designated Kriti or Kreta.

The reason for the apparently haphazard nomenclature lies in the long and complicated territorial ownership of Greece and its islands, more especially the islands. The base root may be Greek, Latin, Turkish or Venetian. Additionally the Greek language has three forms – Demotic (spoken), Katharevousa (literary) and Kathomiloumeni (compromise), of which the Demotic and Katharevousa have each been the official linguistic style. Even as recently as 1967-74 the Colonels made Katharevousa, once again, the authorised form, but Demotic is now the approved language. Help!

Street names can be equally confusing and I have plumped for my personal choice and stated the alternatives, but where this is not possible, well, there you go! I mean how can Athens' main square, Syntagma be spelt Syntagina, Sintagma or Syntagmatos?

Hotel and pension titles give rise to some frustration as can Guides using Greek script names, with two or three alternatives, including a similar meaning, Roman scripted appellation.

Street names are subject to some obscurity as the common noun Odhos (street) is often omitted, whilst Leoforos (avenue) and Plateia (square) are usually kept in the name. The prefix Saint or St is variously written as Agios, Aghios, Ayios, Ag or Ai.

Due to scholastic critical comments I must defend my habit of mixing Roman and Greek script when referring to establishment and street names. For example, I have written the Greek **AKTH EΘNIKHΣ ANTIΣTAΣHΣ** which translates to the Roman *Akti Ethnikis Antistasis*. My only defence is that 99.9% of readers will transmit that which they see to the brain without being able to make the mental gymnastics necessary to substitute the different letters, more especially those that have no easy or direct equivalent. Will my more erudite friends excuse the rest of us dyslectic Grecophiles!

A *nome* approximates to a small English county, a number of which make up a province such as the Peloponnese or Thessaly.

At this stage, without apologies, I introduce my own definition to help identify an unspoilt Greek town as follows: *where the town's rubbish is collected by donkey, wooden panniers slung across its back, slowly clip clopping up a stepped hillside street, the driver, not even in sight but probably languishing in a stray taverna!*

Map nomenclature	Greek	Translation
Agios/Ag/Ayios/Aghios	Αγιος	Saint
Akra/Akrotiri	Ακρωτήρι	Cape/Headland
Ano	Ανω	Upper
Archeologikos (horos)	Αρχαιολογικός	Ancient (site)
Chora/Horo/Horio/Khorio	Χωριό	Village
Kato	Κάτω	Lower
Kolpos	Κολποζ	Gulf
Leoforos	Λεωφόροζ	Avenue
Limni	Λίμνη	Lake/Marsh
Limin	Λιμάνι	Port harbour
Moni/Monastiri	Μοναστήρι	Monastery
Naos	Ναόζ	Temple
Nea/Neos	Νέο	New
Nissos	Νήσοζ	Island
Odhos/Odos	Δρόμοζ (Οδος)	Street
Ormos	Ορμοζ	Bay
Oros	Οροζ	Mountain
Plateia	Πλατεια	Square
Palios/Palaios	Παλιόζ	Old
Potami	Ποτάμι	River
Spilia	Σπηλιά	Cave
Vuno	Βουνό	Mountain

Useful Greek

English	Greek	Sounds like
Where is...	Που είναι	Poo eene...
...the Olympic Airways office	τα γραφεία τηζ Ολυμπιακήζ	...ta grafia tis Olimbiakis
...the railway station	ο σιδηροδρομικόζ σταθμόζ	...sidheerothromikos stathmos
...the bus station	ο σταθμόζ των λεωφορειων	...stathmos ton leoforion
...the boat	το πλοίο	...to plio
...the nearest underground station	ο πλησιέοτεροζ σταθμόζ του ηλεκτρικοο	...o pleessiestehros stathmos too eelektrikoo
...the ticket office	το εκδοτήριο των εισιτηρίων	...to eckdhoterio ton eessitirion
...the nearest travel agency	το πλησιέστεπο πρακτορεον ταξιδίων	...to pleessiestehro praktorion taxidion
I'd like to reserve...	Θέλω να κρατήσω	Thelo na kratiso
...seat/seats on the	θέση/θέση για	...thessee/thessis ghia

...to	για	...ghia
...plane	αεροπλάνο	...aeroplano
...train	τραίνο	...treno
...bus	λεωφορείο	...leoforio
...ferry-boat	πλοίο	...plio
When does it leave/arrive	Πότε φεύγει/φθάνει	Poteh fehvghi/fthanee
Is there...	Υπάρχει	Eeparhee...
...from here to	απ εδώστο	...Apetho sto
...to	στον	...ston
Where do we get off	Που κατεβαίνομε	Poo katevenomhe
I want to go to	Θέλω να πάω στουζ	Thelo na pao stoos...
I want to get off at	Θέλω να κατέβω στο	Thelo na katevo sto...
Will you tell me when to get off	Θα μου πείτε που να κατέβω	Thah moo peete poo nah kahtevo
I want to go to...	Θέλω να πάω στουζ	Thelo na pao stoos
Stop here	Σταμάτα εδώ	Stamata etho
How much is it	Πόσο είναι	Posso eene
How much does it cost	Πόσο κάνει η μεταφορά	Posso kani i metafora
...to	στο	...sto
Do we call at	Θα σταματήσωμε στην	Tha stamatissome stin

Signs often seen affixed to posts & doors

Greek	English
ΑΦΙΞΙΣ	ARRIVAL
ΑΝΑΧΩΡΗΣΙΣ	DEPARTURE
ΣΤΑΣΙΣ	BUS STOP
ΕΙΣΟΔΟΣ	ENTRANCE
ΕΞΟΔΟΣ	EXIT
ΚΕΝΤΡΟ	CENTRE (as in town centre)
ΕΙΣΟΔΟΣ ΕΛΕΥΘΕΡΑ	FREE ADMISSION
ΑΠΑΓΟΡΕΥΕΤΑΙ Η ΕΙΣΟΔΟΣ	NO ENTRANCE
ΕΙΣΙΤΗΡΙΑ	TICKET
ΠΡΟΣ ΤΑΣ ΑΠΟΒΑΘΡΑΣ	TO THE PLATFORMS
ΤΗΛΕΦΩΝΟΝ	TELEPHONE
ΑΝΔΡΩΝ	GENTLEMEN
ΓΥΝΑΙΚΩΝ	LADIES
ΑΠΑΓΟΡΕΥΕΤΑΙ ΤΟ ΚΑΠΝΙΣΜΑ	NO SMOKING
ΤΑΜΕΙΟΝ	CASH DESK
ΤΟΥΑΛΕΤΕΣ	TOILETS
ΑΝΟΙΚΤΟΝ	OPEN
ΚΛΕΙΣΤΟΝ	CLOSED
ΩΘΗΣΑΤΕ	PUSH
ΣΥΡΑΤΕ	PULL

4 Island Accommodation

How oft doth man by care oppressed, find in an inn a place of rest. Combe

Package, villa and tour organised holiday-makers have accommodation arranged prior to arrival in Greece. If travelling around, then the most important matter is undoubtedly the procurement of lodgings, especially the first overnight stay on a new island or at an untried location.

The choice of accommodation is bewildering, varying from private houses (usually clean but with basic bathroom facilities) to luxury class hotels able to hold their own with the most modern European counterpart. The deciding factor must be the budget and a person's sensibilities. My comments in respect of standards reflect comparisons with Western European establishments. Those referring to prices are usually in comparison with other Greek options. The standard of accommodation in Crete naturally varies from place to place. For instance, even in the established tourist resort of Ag. Nikolaos, it can range from the indecently plush to extremely simple, island Rooms.

Travellers stepping off a ferry-boat are usually part of a swarming throng made up of Greeks, tourists and backpackers engulfed by a quayside mass of Greeks, tourists and backpackers struggling to get aboard the ferry-boat. Visitors may well be approached by men, women and youngsters offering rooms. It is a matter of taking potluck there and then, or searching around the town oneself. The later in the day, the more advisable it is to take an offer, unseen but it is obligatory to establish the price, if the rooms are with or without shower and how far away they are located. It can prove unnerving to be 'picked up' and then commence on an ever-lengthening trudge through the back streets of a strange place, especially as Greek ideas of distance are rather optimistic.

Any accommodation usually requires a traveller's passport to be relinquished. As a passport is also required to change money and to hire a car or a scooter, it is a good idea, if married or travelling with friends, to have separate documents. Then, if necessary, one passport can be left at the abode and another kept for other purposes, as required.

Official sources and many guidebooks lay much emphasis on the role of the Tourist police in finding accommodation, but this cannot be relied upon as the offices may well be closed on arrival. Moreover recent changes in the structure of the various police forces is resulting in the once separate and independent Tourist police being integrated into the offices of the Town police. I regret that this may well be a very retrograde step. Such a pity that the Greeks, the innovators of this excellent service, should now abandon the scheme, more especially in the light of the ever increasing numbers of tourists. Perhaps having achieved their goal of ensuring Greece is a number one holiday spot, the authorities are allowing the tour guides and couriers (that go 'hand in sand' with the ever increasing number of package tourists), to take over the Tourist police role in an *ex officio* capacity? Preposterous! I hope so.

A fruitful source of accommodation leads are convenient tavernas, which, more often than not, result in an introduction to a room or pension owner. Failing that, they usually send out for someone.

BEDROOMS

Greek bedrooms tend to be airy, whitewashed and sparsely furnished. The beds are often hard, as are the small pillows, and unyielding mattresses may well be laid directly on to bed-boards and not springs.

It is advisable to inspect bedroom walls for blood-red splats of flattened, but once gorged, mosquitoes resulting from a previous occupant's night-time vigil. Well designed rooms usually have a top-opening window screened off with gauze so that they can be left ajar without fear of incursions by winged creepy-crawlies. Where no gauze is in evidence, it is best to keep the windows tightly closed at night, however alien this may seem. Those not in possession of a proprietary insect repellent may well have to reconcile themselves to a sleepless night, any tell-tale buzzing echoing in the ears indicating one has already been bitten. It is comparable to being attacked by Lilliputian Stuka night-fighters.

Hanging points are noticeable by their absence. Often there will be no wardrobe but if present, there is unlikely to be any hangers, not even the steel-wire type, and the cupboard doors may be missing. A rather idiosyncratic feature is that clothes hooks, when present, are often very inadequate, looking as if they have been designed, and are only suitable for, hanging coffee mugs by the handles.

Even more maligned and even more misunderstood than Greek food is:

THE GREEK BATHROOM

I use the descriptive word bathroom, rather than refer simply to the toilets, because the total facility requires some elucidation. The following will not apply to luxury, Class A or B hotels – well, it should not!

The plumbing is quite often totally inadequate and instead of the separate wastes of the bath, shower and sink being plumbed into progressively larger soil pipes, thus achieving a 'venturi' effect, they are usually joined into a similar diameter tube to that of the individual pipes. This inevitably causes considerable back pressure with inescapable consequences. The toilet waste is almost always insufficient in size and even normal, let alone excessive, use of toilet paper results in dreadful things happening, not only to your bathroom, but probably to a number of bathrooms in the building, street and possibly the village. If this were not enough.....the header tank rarely delivers sufficient 'flush'. The Greeks have had, for many years, to be economic in the use of water and some islands ration it, turning off the supply for a number of hours per day, in the height of the summer.

Common faults are to find the lavatory without a seat; flooded to a depth of some inches; the bathroom light not working; no toilet roll; door locks not fitted as well as dirty WC pans and or any combination of the above. Furthermore, the wash basin may well be without a drain plug. Amongst other reasons, the lack of a plug is to stop flooding if a sink tap is accidently left turned on when the mains water is switched off, and not turned off when the water supply is resumed!

The most common type of en suite bathroom is an all purpose lavatory and shower room. Beware! Years of research reveals that the shower head is usually positioned in such a way as to not only wash down the occupant but to drench the (amazingly) absorbent toilet roll as well as the bathers clothes, towel and footwear. Incidentally the drain point is usually located in such a way as to ensure that the bathroom is kept awash to a depth of between 1" and 3"..... and the resultant pool invariably lies where a toilet sitter's feet fall – if you read my meaning.

It is not unusual for there to be no hot water, even if a heating system is in evidence. Government energy conservation methods, the comparatively high cost of electricity and the use of moderately sized solar heating panels, all contribute to this state of affairs. Where solar panels are the means of heating the water, remember to beat the rush and shower as early as possible, for the water soon loses its heat. Why not share with a friend? If hot water is available, but it is not heated by solar energy, then it will be necessary to locate the relevant electric switch. This is usually a 4 way position, ceramic knob hidden away behind a translucent panel door. On the other hand.... To

ACCOMMODATION

be fair to owners of accommodation, it is standard practice to charge for the use of hot water showers so it pays the landlord to have the switch out of sight and reach. Room charges may well be increased by 50 to 100 drs per day for the use of a shower, but this will be detailed on the Government controlled price list that should be displayed, and is usually suspended on the back of the bedroom door.

One stipulation on water-short islands that really offends the West European (and North American?) sense of delicacy, is the oft present, hardly legible sign, requesting guests to put their 'paper' in the wastebin supplied, and not down the pan! I must own up to not always obeying this dictum and have had to make a hurried departure from a number of islands, let alone a pension or village, when the consequences of my profligate use of toilet paper have become apparent.

THE BEACH
Some backpacking youngsters utilise the shore for their night's accommodation. In fact all island ferry-boaters must be prepared to consider the beach as a standby at the more crowded locations during the months of July and August, although I have only had to spend two or three nights on the beach in the eight or nine years of island excursions. Certainly the weather could not be more ideal for sleeping under the stars, the officials are generally not too fussed and may well direct travellers to a suitable spot. Beware of mosquitoes and tar.

CAMPING
In direct contrast to *ad hoc* sleeping out on the beach, camping, except on approved sites, is strictly forbidden, but the law is not always rigorously applied. The restriction comes about from a wish to improve general hygiene, to prohibit and discourage abuse of private property and as a precaution against forest fires. The NTOG operate most of the licensed sites, some of which are spectacularly located, but there are some authorised, privately run camping grounds, which are also price controlled. There are quite a few campsites on Crete. A *Carnet-Camping International*, although not normally requested, affords campers worldwide, third-party liability cover and is available to United Kingdom residents from the AA and other, similar organisations.

If moved on by any official for sleeping out on the beach or illegally camping, it is advisable not to argue and go quietly. The Greek police have fairly wide and autonomous powers and it is preferable not to upset them unnecessarily.

A guide to overnight campsite fees is as follows:
Adults 200-300 drs; children ½ adult rate and tent hire 150-250 drs.

YOUTH HOSTELS (ΞΕΝΩΝΑΣ ΝΕΩΝ)
Establishments include **YMCA** (XAN), **YWCA** (XEN) in Athens as is the **YHA**, which also has one or three outposts on the islands.

Greek Youth Hostels are rather down-at-the-heel and tend to be operated in a somewhat slovenly manner. None of the old get-up-and-go familiar to members of some other countries – morning ablutions in ice-cold water and placing used razor blades in disused tobacco tins nailed to the wall.

It is preferable to have YHA membership, taking the Association's card along. Approximate prices per night at the YMCA and YWCA are 700 drs and in a Youth Hostel 300-350 drs.

ROOMS
The story goes that as soon as a tourist steps off the ferry, he (or she) is surrounded by women crying *Rooms* ('*Dhomatio*'), and whoops, within minutes he is ensconced in some wonderful Greek family's private home.

33

History may well have been like that, and in truth the ferries are still met at almost every island, the inhabitants offering not only rooms but pensions and the lower category hotels. Rooms are the cheapest accommodation and are generally very clean, sometimes including the option of breakfast, which is ordinarily charged extra. Prices reflect an island's popularity and the season, but usually the mid-season cost on Crete is between 800-1000 drs for a double room, depending upon the classification.

Apart from a prospect being approached leaving the ferry, the Tourist police would, in the past, advise of rooms to let but their role is being drastically reduced in their planned amalgamation with the Town police. The Tourist police offices were signed, if at all, 'ΤΟΥΡΙΣΤΙΚΗ ΑΣΤΥΝΟΜΙΑ'. Householders display the sign 'ΕΝΟΙΚΙΑΖΟΝΤΑΙ ΔΩΜΑΤΙΑ' or simply 'ΔΩΜΑΤΙΑ', when they have a room to rent. Government approved and categorised rooms are subject to an official tariff, and are slightly more expensive than the free-lance householders. A general point relates to a cautionary tale told to us by a delightful French couple. They were in the habit of replying to a room owner's enquiry as to how many nights they wished to stay by saying *"Tonight"*. One lady room owner interpreted this to mean two nights! Beware the inaccurate translation.

At the more tourist popular island resorts a new, unwelcome phenomena has reared 'his' ugly head. This is the long stay, layabout who rents a large double or triple bedroom for the summer season from a hapless, unsuspecting owner of accommodation. The entrepreneur, a species to be avoided, then sublets out the room, cramming in some 5 or 6 a night.

PENSIONS ('PANSION, ΠΑΝΣΙΟΝ')

This type of lodging was a natural progression from *Rooms* and now represents the most easily found and reasonably priced accommodation on offer.

The older type of pension is rather reminiscent of those large Victorian English houses, split up into bed-sits. In the main though they have been purpose built, usually during the Colonels' regime (1967-74) when government grants were freely available for the construction of tourist quarters. The owner often lives on one floor and acts as concierge. The rooms are functional and generally the guests on each level share a bathroom and shower and (a rather nice touch when provided) a communal refrigerator in which visitors can store their various provisions and drinks. Mid-season charges on Crete vary between 1000 and 1500 drs for a double room.

Sometimes a breakfast of coffee, bread and jam, perhaps butter and a boiled egg, is available for about 150 drs and represents fair value compared with the cost of a cafe breakfast.

TAVERNAS (ΤΑΒΕΡΝΑ)

Tavernas are, first and foremost, eating places. Some tavernas, especially those situated by, or near, beaches, have Rooms available. The only drawback is that the more popular the taverna, the less likely guests are to get a full night's sleep, but of course the more involved they will be with the taverna's social life which will often continue on into the small hours. Charges are similar to those of a pension.

HOTELS (ΞΕΝΟΔΟΧΕΙΟΝ)

Shades of difference and interpretation can be given to the nomenclature by variation of the bland, descriptive noun hotel. For instance ΞΕΝΟΔΟΧΕΙΟΝ ΥΠΝΟΥ indicates a hotel that does not serve meals and ΠΑΝΔΟΧΕΙΟΝ a low grade hotel.

Many backpackers don't consider hotels their first choice. The higher classification ones are more expensive than pensions and the lower grade hotels often cost the same, but may well be rather seedy and less desirable than the equivalent class pension. Greek hotels are classified L (Luxury) A, B, C, D and E and the prices charged within these categories (except L) are controlled by the authorities.

It is unfortunately difficult to differentiate between hotels and their charges as each individual category is subject to fairly wide standards, and charges are subject to a multitude of possible percentage supplements and reductions as detailed below:

Shower extra (C, D and E hotels); number of days stayed less than three: plus 10 per cent; air conditioning extra (A and B hotels); out of season deduction (ask); high season extra (ie the months of July, August and the first half of September: plus 20 per cent); single occupancy: about 80 per cent of a double room rate. The higher classification hotels may well insist on guests taking demi-pension terms, especially in high season.

The following table must be treated as a guide only but is based on 1987 prices.

Class	Comments	Indicated mid-season, double-bedroom price
L	All amenities, a very high standard and price. Probably at least one meal in addition to breakfast will have to be purchased. Very clean. Very hot water.	
A	High standard and price. Most rooms have en suite shower or bath. Guests may well have to accept demi-pension terms. Clean. Hot water.	6000 drs.
B	Good standard. Many rooms have en suite shower or bath. Clean. Hot water.	3000 drs.
C	Usually an older hotel. Faded elegance, shared bathroom. Cleanish. Possibly hot water.	2500 drs.
D	Older, faded hotel. Shared bathroom, which may well be 'interesting'. A shower, if available will be an 'experience', and the water cold.	2000 drs.
E	Old, faded and unclean. The whole stay will be an 'experience'. Only very cold water.	1500 drs.

The prices indicated include government taxes, service and room occupancy until noon. Where in the text reference is made to 'official rates', these are the prices listed in the *Guide to the Greek Hotels*. Generally prices listed are those applicable to 1986.

THE XENIAS
Originally government owned and promoted to ensure the availability of high-standard accommodation at important tourist centres but now often managed by private enterprise. Only A, B and C rated categories and they are of a better standard than hotels in a similar class.

FLATS & HOUSES
During the summer months this type of accommodation, referred to by travel agents and package tour operators as villas, is best booked prior to arriving in Greece. Not only will pre-booking be easier but, surprisingly, works out cheaper than flying out and snooping around.

The winter is a different matter, but probably not within the scope of most of our readers.

Further useful names & addresses
The Youth Hostel Association, 14 Southampton St, London WC2E 7HY.   Tel. (01) 836 8541.

Useful Greek

English	Greek	Sounds like
I want...	Θέλω	Thelo...
...a single room	ένα μονό δωμάτιο	...enna mono dhomatio
...a double room	ένα διπλό δωμάτιο	...enna thiplo dhomatio
...with a shower	με ντουζ	...me doosh
We would like a room	Θα θέλαμε ένα δωμάτιο	Tha thelame ena dhomatio
for...	για	ghia...
two/three days/a week/	δύο/τρείζ μέρεζ/μια	thio/trees meres/meea
until	εβδομαδα/μεχρι	evthomatha/mekhri
Can you advise of another...	Ξέρετε κανένα άλλο...	Xerete kanena alo...
house with rooms	σπιτι με δωμάτιο	speeti meh dhomatio
pension	πανσιόν	panseeon
inn	πανδοχείο	panthokheeo
hotel	ξενοδοχείο	ksenodhokheeo
youth hostel	ξενώναζ νέων	xenonas neon
How much is the room	Πόσο κάνει το δωμάτιο	Poso kanee dho dhomatio ghia
for a night?	για τη νύχτα	ti neektah
That is too expensive	Είναι πολύ ακριβά	Eene polee akriva
Have you anything cheaper?	Δεν έχετε άλλο πιό φθηνό	Dhen ekhete ahlo pio ftheeno
Is there...	Υπάρχει	Eeparkhee
a shower	ένα ντουζ	doosh
a refrigerator	ένα ψυγείο	psiyeeo
Where is the shower?	Που είναι το ντουζ	Poo eene dho doosh
I have to leave...	Πρέπει να φύγω	Prepee na feegho...
today	σήμερα	simera
tomorrow	αύριο	avrio
very early	πολύ νωρίς	polee noris
Thank you for a	Ευχαριστώ για την	Efkareesto ghia tin
nice time	συμπαθητική ώρα*	simpathitiki ora

*This is the exact translation, which would never be used, however, in Greek. An expression meaning rather: 'thanks for the fun' is:

	Ευχαριστώ για την	Efkaristo ghia
	διασκέδαση	tin thiaskethasi

5 Travelling around an island

A man is happier for life from having once made an agreeable tour   Anon

A few introductory remarks may well be apposite in respect of holiday-makers' possessions and women in Greece. The matter will also be discussed elsewhere but it is not out of place to reiterate one or two points (Rosemary calls it 'carrying on').

PERSONAL POSSESSIONS
Do not leave airline tickets, money, travellers' cheques and or passports behind at the accommodation. A man can quite easily acquire a wrist-strap handbag in which to conveniently carry these items. The danger does not, even today, lie with the Greeks, but with fellow tourists, down-and-outs and professional thieves working a territory.

WOMEN
There has been, in recent years, a movement towards the 'Spanish-Costa' percentage ploy. Young Greek men, in the more popular tourist areas, have finally succumbed and will now sometimes try it on. It's up to you girls, there is no menace, only opportunities.

Now back to the main theme of the chapter but before expanding on the subject, a few words will not go amiss in respect of:

BEACHES
A surprisingly large number of beaches are polluted in varying degrees, mainly by seaborne plastic and some tar.

Jellyfish and sea urchins can occasionally be a problem in a particular bay, jellyfish increasingly so. One of my Mediterranean correspondents advises me that cures for the jellyfish sting include, ammonia, urine (ugh) and a paste of meat tenderiser (it takes all sorts I suppose).

The biggest headache (literally) to a tourist is the sun, or more accurately, the heat of the sun at the height of the summer season. The islands benefit from the relief of the prevailing wind, the *Meltemi*, but to give an example of the extreme temperatures sometimes experienced, in Athens a few years ago birds were actually falling out of the trees, and they were the feathered variety! Every year dozens of holiday-makers are carted off, suffering from acute sunburn. A little often, (sun that is), must be the watchword.

It is very pleasant to observe more and more middle-aged Greek ladies taking to the sea, often in all enveloping black costumes and straw hats. Some, to preserve their modesty, appear to swim in everyday clothes.

Despite the utterly reasonable condemnation of modern day advances in technology by us geriatrics, one amazing leap forward for all travelling and beach bound mankind is the Walk-Master personal stereo-cassettes. No more the strident, tinny beat of the transistor (or more commonly the 'ghetto-blaster'), now simply the jigging silence of ear-muffed and transfixed faces. Splendid!

It may well be that a reader is a devoted sun worshipper and spends every available minute on the beach, patio or terrace; if so there is no need to read any further. On the other hand when a holiday-maker's interests range beyond conversion of the sun's very strong rays into painful, peeling flesh, and there is a wish to travel around an island, then the question of *modus operandi* must be given some thought.

First, purchase an island map and one of the colourful and extremely informative tourist guides available on the larger islands. An excellent general map of Crete that can be purchased prior to departure is produced by **Clyde Surveys** of Maidenhead.

Having purchased the maps and guides it is necessary to consider the alternative methods of travel and appraise their value.

ON FOOT

Owing to the hilly terrain of the islands and the daytime heat encountered, readers may well have had enough walking without looking for trouble. A quick burst down to the local beach, taverna, shop or restaurant, and the resultant one hundred or so steps back up again, may well go a long way to satiating any desire to go 'walkies'. If needs be, walking is often the only way to negotiate the more rugged donkey tracks and the minimum footwear is a solid pair of sandals or 'trainers'.

HITCHING

The comparative paucity of privately owned cars makes hitchhiking an unsatis-factory mode of travel. On the other hand, if striking out to get to, or return from, a particular village on a dead end road, most Greek drivers stop when thumbed down. It may well be a lift in the back of a Japanese pickup truck, possibly sharing the space with some chickens, a goat or sheep or all three!

DONKEY

Although once a universal 'transportation module', now usually only available for hire on specific journey basis in particular locations. A personal prejudice is to consider donkey rides part of the unacceptable face of tourism, added to which it is now exorbitantly expensive.

BUSES

Buses (and taxis) are the universal method of travel in Greece, so the services are widespread if, naturally enough, a little Greek in operation. Generally they run approximately on time and the fares are, on the whole, extremely reasonable. Passengers must expect to share the available space with fairly bulky loads and, occasionally, live-stock.

The trick is to first find the square on which the buses terminus and then locate the bus office where the tickets are pre-purchased and on the walls or windows of which is stuck the timetable and the fares structure. On some bus routes the fares are collected by a conductor, although this is unusual. Be available well prior to the scheduled departure times as buses have a 'nasty habit' of departing early. Ensure any luggage is placed in the correct storage compartment, otherwise it may go missing.

Buses are often crowded, especially when a journey coincides with a ferry-boat disgorging its passengers. The timetables are usually scheduled so that a bus or buses await a ferry-boat's arrival, except perhaps very early or late arriving craft. A bus rarely leaves a potential client standing, they just encourage everyone in. The real fun starts if the bus is not only 'sardine packed', but fares are collected by the conductor who has to somehow make his way through, round and over the passengers.

Do not fail to observe the decorations, festooned around and enveloping the driver. Often these displays resemble a shrine, which taking account of the way some of the drivers propel their bus, is perhaps not so out of place. Finally do have some change available as coins are always in short supply. It is helpful to know that local buses maybe labelled TOPIKO (ΤΟΠΙΧΟ).

A critic recently took me to task for not stressing that the summer bus schedules listed throughout the text are the subject of severe curtailment, if not total termination, during the winter months from October through to May. So, smacked hand Geoffrey and readers please note.

TAXIS

As indicated in the previous sub-heading, taxis are the 'other' mode of island travel. They are usually readily available and can be remarkably modern and plush. On the other hand....

Ports and towns nearly always have a main square on which the taxis rank but come the time of a Ferry-boat's arrival they usually queue on the quayside. Fares are governed by law and, at the main rank, are often displayed giving examples of the cost to various destinations. Charges are reasonable by European standards, but it is essential to establish the cost prior to hiring.

It may come as a shock for a 'fare' to have his halting pidgin Greek answered in 'pure' Australian or American. But this is not surprising when one considers that many island Greeks have spent their youth on merchant ships or emigrated to the New World for 10 to 15 years. On their return home, with a relatively financially secure future, many take to taxi driving to supplement their income (and possibly to keep out of the little woman's way?).

BICYLE, SCOOTER & CAR HIRE

Be very careful to establish what (if any) insurance cover is included in the rental fee, and that the quoted hire charge includes the various compulsory taxes.

On the whole, bicycles are very hard work and poor value in relation to, say, the cost of hiring a Lambretta or Vespa scooter – an option endorsed when the mountainous nature of most islands, and the midday heat, is taken into considera-tion. The ubiquitous Italian machines are progressively being replaced by semi-automatic Japanese motorcycles which, although they do away with the necessity to fight the gears and clutch, are not entirely suited to transporting two heavyweights. I have had the frightening experience, when climbing a steep mountainside track, of the bike jumping out of gear, depositing my passenger and I on the ground leaving the scooter whirling round like a crazed mechanical catherine-wheel.

It is amazing how easy it is to get a good tan while scootering. The moderate wind draws the sun's heat, the air is laden with the smell of wild sage and oleanders and with the sun on one's back...marvellous!

Very rarely is a deposit requested when hiring a bike or motorbike but a passport is required. Always shop around to check out various companies' charges: the nearer to a port, town or city centre a hirer is, the more expensive the machines will be. A short walk towards the unfashionable quarters can be very rewarding. Take a close look over the chosen mode of transport before settling up, as maintenance of any mechanical unit in Greece is poor to non-existent. Bicycles and scooters, a few years old, will be 'pretty clapped out'. A client must check the brakes, they will be needed, and should not allow the hirer to fob him off without making sure there is a spare wheel.

Increasingly, the owners of two wheeled vehicles are hiring out dubious looking crash helmets. Flash young Greek motorbike riders usually wear their 'Space Age' headgear on the handlebars, where no doubt it will protect them (that is the handlebars) from damage.

A useful tip when hiring a scooter is to take along a towel! It doubles up as useful additional padding for the pillion passenger's bottom on rocky roads and saves having to sit on the painfully hot plastic seating should a rider forget to use the squab when parked up. Sunglasses are necessary to protect the rider's eyes from airborne insects. Out of the height-of-season and early evening it becomes very chilly so a sweater or jumper is a good idea and females may well require a head scarf, whatever the time of day or night.

Fuel is served in litres and five litres of two-stroke costs about 320-340 drs. Fill up as soon as possible as fuel stations are in fairly short supply outside the main towns. Increasingly the gap between the scooter and the car is being filled with more sophisticated machinery which include moon-tyred and powerfully engined Japanese motorbikes and beach-buggies.

Typical daily hire rates are: for a bicycle 150 drs; a scooter/Lambretta 1000-1500 drs; a car from 5000 drs including full insurances and taxes but mileage may cost extra, calculated at so much per kilometre. Out of season and period hire for all forms of conveyance can benefit from 'negotiation'.

Car hire companies require a daily deposit, which now starts off at 10,000 drs per day, as well as a hirer's passport and driving licence details. It is noticeable that I and many readers regard car hire as a legalised rip-off. Another subject that causes unpleasant disputes is the increasing habit of the hire companies to charge comparatively expensively for any damage incurred, and I mean any damage however slight. A hirer's detailed reasons for the causes of an accident, the damage and why it should not cost anything falls on deaf ears. Furthermore it is no use threatening to involve the police as they will not be at all interested in the squabble.

Several other words of warning might not go amiss. Taking into account the state of the roads, do not hire a two-wheeled conveyance if not thoroughly used to handling one. There are a number of very nasty accidents every year, involving tourists and hired scooters. Additionally the combination of poor road surfaces and usually inadequate to non-existent lights should preclude any night-time scootering. A hirer must ensure he (or she) is fully covered for medical insurance, including an unscheduled, Medicare flight home, and check, before leaving the homeshores, that a general holiday policy does not exclude accidents incurred on hired transport.

The glass fronted metal framed shrines mounted by the roadside are graphic reminders of a fatal accident at this or that spot. Incidentally, on a less macabre note, if the shrine is a memorial to a man, the picture and bottle often present (more often than not of Sophia Loren and whisky) represent that person's favourite earthbound desires.

But back to finger-wagging. The importance of the correct holiday insurance cover cannot be over-stressed. The tribulations I have encountered in obtaining inclusive insurance, combined with some readers' disastrous experiences, have resulted in the inclusion in the guide of an all embracing scheme. This reminder should be coupled with the strictures in CHAPTER 1 drawing attention to the all-inclusive policy devised for readers of the *Candid Guides*, for details of which *See* Page ii. Enough said!

ROADS
The main roads of most islands are passable but asphalted country lanes often degenerate alarmingly, becoming nothing more than heavily rutted and cratered tracks. Much road building and reconstruction is under way. Beware as not all roads, indicated as being in existence on the official maps, are anything more than, at the best, donkey tracks or are simply non-existent. Evidence of broken lines marking a road on the map must be interpreted as meaning there is no paved highway at all.

Further useful names and addresses
Clyde Surveys Ltd., Reform Road, Maidenhead, Berks SL6 8BU   Tel. (0628) 21371
Efstathiadis Group, 14 Valtetsiou St, Athens.   Tel. 3615 011

Useful Greek

English	Greek	Sounds like
Where can I hire a...	Που μπορώ να νοικιάσω ένα	Poo boro na neekeeaso enna...
...bicycle	ποδήλατο	...pothilato

...scooter	σκούτερ	...sckooter
...car	αυτοκίνητο	...aftokinito
I'd like a...	Θα ηθελα ένα	Tha eethela enna...
I'd like it for...	Θα το ήθελα για	Tha dho eethela ghia...
...a day	μία μέρα (or: μιά)	...mia mera
...days	μέρες	...meres
...a week	μία εβδομάδα	...mia evthomadha
How much is it by the...	Πόσο κάνει την	Poso kanee tin...
...day	μέρα	...mera
...week	εβδομάδα	...evthomadha
Does that include...	Συμπεριλαμβάνονται σαυτό	Simberilamvanonte safto
...mileage	τα χιλιόμετρα	...tah hiliometra
...full insurance	μικτή ασφάλεια	...meektee asfaleah
I want some	Θέλω	Thelo
...petrol (gas)	βενζίνης	...vehnzini
...oil	λάδι	...lathi
...water	νέρο	...nero
Fill it up	Γεμίστε το	Yemiste to
...litres of petrol (gas)	λίτρα βενζίνης	...litra vehnzinis
How far is it to...	Πόσο απέχει	Poso apechee
Which is the road for...	Ποιός είναι ο δρόμος για	Pios eene o thromos ghia
Where are we now	Που είμαστε τώρα	Poo eemaste tora
What is the name of this place	Πώς ονομάζεται αυτό το μέρος	Pos onomazete afto dho meros
Where is...	Που είναι	Poo eene...

Road Signs

ΑΛΤ	STOP
ΑΠΑΓΟΡΕΥΕΤΑΙ Η ΕΙΣΟΔΟΣ	NO ENTRY
ΑΔΙΕΞΟΔΟΣ	NO THROUGH ROAD
ΠΑΡΑΚΑΜΠΤΗΡΙΟΣ	DETOUR
ΕΛΑΤΤΩΣΑΤΕ ΤΑΧΥΤΗΤΑΝ	REDUCE SPEED
ΑΠΑΓΟΡΕΥΕΤΑΙ Η ΑΝΑΜΟΝΗ	NO WAITING
ΕΡΓΑ ΕΠΙ ΤΗΣ ΟΔΟΥ	ROAD REPAIRS
ΚΙΝΔΥΝΟΣ	BEWARE (Caution)
ΑΠΑΓΟΡΕΥΕΤΑΙ ΤΟ ΠΡΟΣΠΕΡΑΣΜΑ	NO OVERTAKING
ΑΠΑΓΟΡΕΥΕΤΑΙ Η ΣΤΑΘΜΕΥΣΙΣ	NO PARKING

41

They had tried the hotel menu but......

6 Island Food & Drink

Let us eat and drink for tomorrow we die. Corinthians

It is a pity that many tourists, prior to visiting Greece, have, in sundry restaurants throughout Europe and North America, 'experienced' the offerings masquerading as Greek food. Greek food and drink does not appear to cross its borders very well and I do not think it is possible to recreate the unique quality of Greek cooking in foreign lands. Perhaps this is because they owe much of their taste to, and are in sympathy with, the very air laden with the scent of the flowers and herbs, the very water, clear and chill, the very soil of the plains and scrubclad mountains, the ethereal and uncapturable quality that is Greece. Incidentally many critics would postulate that it was impossible to create Greek food, full stop, but be that as it may....

Salad does not normally send me into ecstasy but, after a few days in Greece, the very thought of a peasant salad, consisting of endive leaves, sliced tomatoes and cucumber, black olives, olive oil and vinegar dressing, all topped off with feta cheese and sprinkled with oregano, parsley or fennel, sends me salivating to the nearest taverna.

Admittedly, unless you are lucky enough to chance across an outstanding taverna, the majority are surprisingly unadventurous and the choice of menu limited. Mind you there are one or two restaurants serving exciting and unusual meals, if the spelling mistakes are anything to go by. For instance I have observed over the years the following no doubt appetising dishes: *omeled, spachetti botonnaise, shrings salad, bowels entrails, lump cutlets, limp liver, mushed pot, shrimps, crambs, kid chops, grilled meat bolls, spar rips, wine vives, fiant oven, sward fish, pork shops, staffed vine leaves, wild greens, string queens, wildi cherry, bater honi, gregg goti (!), mate with olive oil, bruised meat, forced meat balls and Creek salad* – don't they sound interesting.

On a more positive note, whilst the usual dishes will be known to readers, a recommendation, a mention of a dish I haven't seen before and a 'musing' may not go amiss. As to the recommendation, where an eating house serves up a good, creamy tzatziki and a Greek salad it makes a very refreshing dish to combine the two. This year I came across a meal I have not encountered previously, **ΜΠΟΥΡΕΚΑΚΙΑ** or *bourekakia*. These are long, thin tubes of battered ham filled with feta cheese and are very, very tasty. The ruminative, brown study relates to the humble potato. Why, oh why, taking into account the copious plates of patatas available (thus proving the existence in quantity of the aforesaid tuber) are there no variations on the theme? Where are, oh where are mashed, roast or creamed potatoes to, once in a while, usurp the omnipresent, universal chip?

A FEW HINTS & TIPS

Do not insist upon butter, the Greek variant is not very tasty to the European palate, is expensive and in the heat tends to dissolve into greasy pools.

Sample the retsina wine and after a bottle or two a day for a few days there is every chance you will enjoy it. Moreover, retsina is beneficial (well that's what I tell myself), acting as a splendid anti-agent to the comparative oiliness of some of the food.

Bread is automatically served with a meal – and charged for – unless a diner indicates otherwise but it is very useful for mopping up any excessive olive oil and requires no butter to make it more greasy. It has become a noticeable, and regrettable, feature in recent years that the charge for bread has increased to between 10 and 30 drs per head, and I have seen it as high as 40 drs. Naughty!

Greek food tends to be served on the 'cool' side and even if the meal started out hot, and by some mischance is speedily served, it will arrive on a thoroughly chilled plate.

The selection of both food and drink is almost always limited and unenterprising, unless diners elect to frequent the more international restaurants (but why go to Greece?). On the other hand the choice of establishments in which to eat and/or drink is unlimited, in fact the profusion is such that it can prove very confusing. If in doubt about which particular restaurant or taverna to patronise, use the well tried principle of picking one frequented by the locals. It will inevitably serve good quality food at reasonable prices. It is generally a waste of time to ask a Greek for guidance in selecting a good taverna or restaurant as he will be reluctant to give specific advice in case the recommendation proves unsatisfactory.

Especially in the more rural areas, do not be shy, ask to look over the kitchen to see what's cooking. If denied this traditional right, be on your guard as the food may well be precooked, tasteless and plastic, particularly if the various meals available are displayed in a neon-lit showcase. Do not order the whole meal all at once, as would be usual at home. If you do it will be served simultaneously and/or in the wrong sequence. Order course by course and take your time, everyone else does.

Diners are not being ignored if the waiter does not approach the table for anything up to 20 minutes, he is just taking his time and is probably overworked. At first the blood pressure does tend to inexorably rise as the waiter appears to continue to studiously disregard your presence. It makes a visitor's stay in Greece very much more enjoyable if all preconceived ideas of service can be forgotten. Lay back and settle into the glorious and indolent timelessness of the locals' way of life. If in a hurry, pay when the order arrives for if under the impression that it took a disproportionate time to be served, just wait until it comes to settling up. It will probably take twice as long to get the bill (*logariasmo*), as it did to receive the food.

Fish, contrary to expectations, is very expensive, even in comparison with European prices, so you can imagine the disparity with the cost of other Greek food. When ordering fish it is normal to select the choice from 'the ice' and, being priced by weight, it will be put on the scales prior to cooking. This is the reason that fish is listed at so many drachmae per kilo, so is not so outrageously costly as may at first appear.

Government price lists are a legal necessity for most drinking and eating places, and should state the establishment's category and the price of every item served. Two prices are shown, the first being net is not really relevant, the second, showing the price actually charged, includes service and taxes.

Food is natural and very rarely are canned or any frozen items used, even if available. When frozen foods are included in the meal the fact must be indicated on the menu by addition of the initials *KAT*. The olive oil used for cooking is excellent, as are the herbs and lemons, but it can take time to become accustomed to the different flavours imparted to food. Before leaving the subject of hints and tips, remember that olive oil can be pressed into service for removing unwanted beach-tar from clothes.

A most enjoyable road, quayside or ferry-boat breakfast is to buy a large yoghurt and a small pot of honey, mix the honey into the yoghurt and then relish the bitter-sweet delight. If locally produced, natural yoghurt (usually stored in cool tubs and spooned into a container) cannot be purchased, the brand name *Total* is an adequate substitute being made from cow's or sheep's milk. I prefer the sheep derived product and, when words fail, break into a charade of 'baa-ing'. It keeps the other shoppers amused if nothing else. The succulent water melon, a common and inexpensive fruit, provides a juicy lunchtime refreshment.

Apart from waving the tablecloth in the air, or for that matter the table, it is usual to call *parakalo* (please). It is also permissible to say *gharkon* or simply 'waiter'.

THE DRINKS

Non-alcoholic beverages

Being a cafe (and taverna) society, coffee is drunk at all times of the day and night. Greek coffee (*kafe*) is in fact a leftover from the centuries long Turkish influence, being served without milk in small cups and always with a glass of deliciously cool water. Unless specified otherwise, it will be served sickly sweet or *varigliko*. There are many variations but the three most usual are *sketto* (no sugar), *metrio* (medium) or *glyko* (sweet). Beware not to completely drain the cup, the bitter grains will choke you. Except in the most traditional establishments (*kafeneions*), you can ask for *Nes-kafe* or simply *Nes* which, as you would think, is an instant coffee but this Greek produced version has a comparatively muddy taste. If you require milk with your coffee it is necessary to ask for *meh gala*. A most refreshing version is to have Nes chilled or *frappe*. French coffee (*ghaliko kafe*), served in a coffee pot with a separate jug of hot milk, espresso and cappucino are found in the larger, provincial cities, ports and international establishments. However, having made a detailed request, you may well receive any permutation of all the possibilities listed above, however carefully you think you have ordered.

Tea, (*tsai*), perhaps surprisingly, is quite freely available, made of course with the ubiquitous teabag, which is not so outrageous since they have become so universally commonplace. In more out of the way places herbal tea may be served.

Purchasing bottled mineral waters is not always necessary as, generally, island water is superb but should you wish to have some stashed away in the fridge, brand names include *Loutraki, Nigita,* and *Sariza*. *Sprite* is fizzy and *lemonada/lemonatha* a stillish lemonade. Orangeade (*portokaladha*), cherry soft drink (*visinatha*) and fruit juices are all palatable and sold, as often as not, under brand names, as is the universal *Koka-Kola*.

A word of warning comes from a reader who reported that, in the very hot summer months, some youngsters drink nothing but sweet, fizzy beverages. This can result in mouth ulcers caused by fermenting sugar, so drink some water every day. day.

Alcoholic beverages

They are generally sold by weight. Beer comes in 330g tins, very occasionally a small bottle or more usually the large 500g bottles – have the 500g, it is a good measure. Wine is sold in 340/430g (half bottle), 680/730g (1.1 pints) and 950g (1¾ pints) sized bottles.

Beer Greek brewed or bottled beer represents very good value except when served in cans, which are the export version and, I regard, a 'swindle'. This European habit should be resisted for no other reason than it means the cost, quantity for quantity, is almost doubled. Now that *Fix Hellas* is rarely if ever obtainable, due to the founder's death, the only other, widely available, bottled beers are *Amstel* and *Henninger*. Draught lager is insidiously creeping in to various resorts and should be avoided, not only for purist reasons, but because it is comparatively expensive, as are the imported, stronger bottled lagers. No names, no pack drill but *Carlsberg* is one that springs to mind. A small bottle of beer is referred to as a *mikri bira* and a large one, *meghali bira*.

Wine Unresinated (*aretsinoto*) wine is European in style, palatable and popular brands include red and white *Demestika* and *Cambas*. More refined palates will approve of the whites (*aspro*) and the reds (*kokino*). Greek wine is not so much known for its quality but if quantity of brands can make up for this then Greece will not let you down.

Resinated wine is achieved, if that can be considered the expression, by the barrels, in which the wine is fermented, being internally coated with pine tree resin. The resultant liquid is referred to as retsina, most of which are white, with a *kokkineli* or rose version, being available. Some consider the taste to be similar to chewing wet, lead pencils but this is patently obviously a heresy. Retsina is usually bottled, but some tavernas serve 'open' retsina in metal jugs and when purchased for personal consumption it can be found being dispensed from large vats, buried in side-street cellars, into any container a client might like to press into service. The adjective 'open' is used to describe locally brewed retsina available on draught or more correctly from the barrel. Asking for a *Kortaki* ensures being served the traditional, small bottle of retsina rather than a full sized bottle. Rumour has it that the younger retsinas are more easily palatable, but that is very much a matter of taste. A good 'starter' kit is to drink a bottle or two twice a day for three or four days and if the pain goes....

Spirits & others As elsewhere in the world, sticking to the national drinks represents good value.

Ouzo, much maligned and blamed for other excesses, is, in reality, of the aniseed family of drinks (which include Ricard and Pernod) and, taken with water, is a splendid 'medicine'. Ouzo is traditionally served with *mezethes* (or *mezes*) (the Greek equivalent of Spanish tapas) which is a small plate of, for instance, a slice of cheese, tomato, cucumber and possibly smoked eel, octopus and an olive. When served they are charged for, costing some 20 to 30 drs, but the tradition of offering them is disappearing in many tourist locations. If you specifically do not wish to be served mezes then make the request *ouzo sketto*. *Raki* is a stronger alternative to Ouzo, often 'created' in Crete.

Metaxa brandy, available in three, five and seven star quality, is very palatable but with a certain amount of 'body', whilst *Otys* brandy is smoother. Greek aperitifs include *Vermouth*, *Mastika* and *Citro*.

DRINKING PLACES

Prior to launching into the various branches of this subject, I am at a loss to understand why so many cafe-bar and taverna owners select chairs that are designed to cause the maximum discomfort, even suffering. They are usually too small for any but a very small bottom, too low and made up of wickerwork or rafia that painfully impresses it's pattern on the sitter's bare (sun-burnt?) thighs.

Kafeneion (ΚΑΦΕΝΙΟΝ) Greek cafe, serving only Turkish coffee. Very Greek, very masculine and in which women are rarely seen. They are similar to a British working man's club, but with backgammon, worry beads and large open windows giving a dim view of the smoke-laden interior.

Ouzeries (ΟΥΖΕΡΙ) As above, but the house speciality is (well, well) Ouzo.

Cafe-bar (ΚΑΦΕ ΜΠΑΡ) As above, but serving alcoholic beverages as well as coffee and women are to be seen.

Pavement cafes French in style, with outside tables and chairs sprawling over the road as well as the pavement. Open from mid-morning, throughout the day, to one or two o'clock the next morning. Snacks and sweet cakes are usually available.

Inside any of the above, the locals chat to each other in that peculiar Greek fashion which gives the impression that a full-blooded fight is about to break out at any moment. In reality, they are probably just good friends, chatting to each other over the blaring noise of a televised football match, a plastic, sickly American soap opera or a ghastly English 'comic' programme with Greek subtitles.

Drinks can always be obtained at a taverna or restaurant, but you may be expected to eat, so read on.
It is of course possible to drink at hotel cocktail bars, but why leave home!

EATING PLACES

At the cheapest end of the market, and more especially found in Athens, are pavement-mounted stands serving doughnut-shaped bread which make for an inexpensive nibble.

Pistachio nut & ice-cream vendors They respectively push their wheeled trolleys around the streets, selling a wide variety of nuts in paper bags for 20 drs or so and good value ice-cream in a variety of flavours and prices.

Galaktopoleio (ΓΑΛΑΚΤΟΠΩΛΕΙΟ). Shops selling dairy products including milk (*gala*), butter, yoghurt (*yiaorti*), bread, honey and sometimes omelettes and fritters with honey (*loukoumades*). A traditional but more expensive alternative to a restaurant/bar in which to purchase breakfast.

Zacharoplasteion (ΖΑΧΑΡΟΠΛΑΣΤΕΙΟΝ) Shops specialising in pastries, cakes (*glyko*), chocolates (which are comparatively expensive) and soft drinks as well as, sometimes, a small selection of alcoholic drinks.

Galaktozacharoplasteion A combination of the two previously described establishments.

Snackbar (ΣΝΑΚ-ΜΠΑΡ, Souvlatzidika & Tyropitadika) Snackbars are not so numerous in the less touristy areas, and are often restricted to one or two in the main town. They represent marvellous value for a stand-up snack and the most popular offering is *souvlaki* – pita bread (or a roll) filled with grilled meat or kebab, (*doner kebab* – slices off the rotating vertical spit of an upturned cone of meat also called *giro*), a slice of tomato, chopped onion and a dressing. Be careful, as souvlaki is not to be muddled with *souvlakia* which, when served at a snackbar, consists of pieces of lamb, pork or veal meat grilled on a wooden skewer and is indistinguishable from *Shish-kebab*, or (guess what) souvlakia when served at a sit-down meal where the metal skewered meat pieces are interspersed with vegetables. Other goodies include *tiropites* – hot flaky pastry pies filled with cream cheese; *boogatsa* – a custard filled pastry; a wide variety of rolls and sandwiches (*sanduits*) with cheese, tomato, salami and other spiced meat fillings as well as toasted sandwiches (*tost*).

This reminds me to point out to readers that if 'toast' is ordered as part of a breakfast it is odds on that a toasted cheese sandwich will be served.

Pavement cafes Serve snacks and sweets.

Pizzerias Seem to be on the increase and are restaurants specialising in the imported Italian dish which prompts one to ask why not go to Italy? To be fair they usually represent very good value and a large serving often feeds two.

Tavernas (ΤΑΒΕΡΝΑ), Restaurants (ΕΣΤΙΑΤΟΡΙΟΝ), Rotisserie (ΨΗΣΤΑΡΙΑ) & Rural Centres (ΕΞΟΧΙΚΟΝ ΚΕΝΤΡΟΝ) Four variations on a theme. The traditional Greek taverna is a family concern, frequently only open in the evening. More often than not, the major part of the eating area is outside, under a vine trellis covered patio, along the pavement and/or on a roof garden.

Restaurants tend to be more sophisticated, possibly open all day and night, but the definition between the two is rather blurred. The price lists may include a chancy English translation, the waiter might be smarter and the tablecloth and napkins could well be linen, in place of the taverna's paper table covering and serviettes.

As tavernas often have a spit-roasting device tacked on, there is little, discernible difference between a rotisserie and a taverna. A grilled meat restaurant may also be styled ΨΗΣΤΑΡΙΑ.

The Rural Centre is a mix of cafe-bar and taverna in, you've guessed it, a rural or seaside setting.

Fish tavernas (ΨΑΡΟΤΑΒΕΡΝΑ) Tavernas specialising in fish dishes.

Hotels (ΞΕΝΟΔΟΧΕΙΟΝ). ΞΕΝΟΔΟΧΕΙΟΝ ΥΠΝΟΥ is a hotel that does not serve food, ΠΑΝΔΟΧΕΙΟΝ a lower category hotel and **XENIA**, a Government-owned hotel. Xenias are usually well run, the food and drink international, the menu written in French and the prices reflect all these 'attributes'.

An extremely unpleasant manifestation, to old fogeys like me, is illustrated by one or two menus spotted in the more popular holiday resorts, namely Greek bills of fare set out Chinese restaurant style. You know, set 'Meal A' for two, 'Meal B' for three and 'C' for four and more.....!

THE FOOD
Some of the following represents a selection of the wide variety of menu dishes available.

Sample menu

Ψωμί (Psomi)	Bread
ΠΡΩΙΝΟ	BREAKFAST
Αυγά τηγανιτα με μπέικον και τομάτα	Fried egg, bacon & tomato
Τοστ βούτυρο μαρμελάδα	Buttered toast & marmalade
Το πρόγευμα (to pro-ye-vma)	English (or American on some islands) breakfast
ΑΥΓΑ	EGGS
Μελάτα	soft boiled
Σφικτά	hard boiled
Τηγανιτά	fried
Ποσσέ	poached
ΤΟΣΤ ΣΑΝΤΟΥΙΤΣ	TOASTED SANDWICHES
Τοστ με τυρί	toasted cheese
Τοστ (με) ζαμπόν και τυρί	toasted ham & cheese
Μπούρκερ	burger
Χαμπουρκερ	hamburger
Τσίσμπουρκερ	cheeseburger
Σάντουιτς λουκάνικο	hot dog
ΟΡΕΚΤΙΚΑ	APPETIZERS/HORS D'OEUVRES
Αντσούγιες	anchovies
Ελιές	olives
Σαρδέλλες	sardines
Σκορδαλιά	garlic dip
Τζατζίκι	tzatziki (diced cucumber & garlic in yoghurt)
Ταραμοσαλάτα	taramasalata (a fish roe pate)
ΣΟΥΠΕΣ	SOUPS
Σούπα φασόλια	bean
Αυγολέμονο	egg & lemon
Ψαρόσουπα	fish
Κοτόσουπα	chicken
Ντοματόσουπα	tomato
Σούπα λαχανικών	vegetable
ΟΜΕΛΕΤΕΣ	OMELETTES
Ομελέτα μπέικον	bacon
Ομελέτα μπέικον τυρί τομάτα	bacon, cheese & tomato
Ομελέτα τυρί	cheese
Ομελέτα ζαμπόν	ham
Ομελέτα ουκωτάκια πουλιών	chicken liver

ΣΑΛΑΤΕΣ	SALADS
Ντομάτα Σαλάτα	tomato
Αγγούρι Σαλάτα	cucumber
Αγγουροτομάτα Σαλάτα	tomato & cucumber
Χωριάτικη	Greek peasant village salad

ΛΑΧΑΝΙΚΑ (ΛΑΔΕΡΑ*)	VEGETABLES
Πατάτες	potatoes
Πατάτες Τηγανιτές	chips (french fries)
φρέσκα φασολάκια	green beans
Σπαράγκια	asparagus
Κολοκυθάκια	courgettes
Σπανάκι	spinach

*indicates cooked in oil.

Note various methods of cooking include:
Baked – στο φούρνο; boiled – βραστά; creamed – με ασπρη σαλτσα; fried – τηγανιτα; grilled – στη σχαρα; roasted – ψητά; spit roasted – σούβλας.

ΚΥΜΑΔΕΣ	MINCED MEATS
Μουσακάς	moussaka
Ντομάτες Γεμιστές	stuffed tomatoes (with rice or minced meat)
Κεφτέδες	meat balls
Ντολμαδάκια	stuffed vine leaves (with rice or minced meat)
Παπουτσάκια	stuffed vegetable marrow (rice or meat)
Κανελόνια	canelloni
Μακαπόνια με κυμά	spaghetti bolognese (more correctly with mince)
Παστίτσιο	macaroni, mince and sauce
Σουβλάκι	shish-kebab

ΡΥΖΙ	RICE
Πιλάφι	pilaff
Πιλάφι (με) γιαούρτι	with yoghurt
Πιλάφι συκωτάκια	with liver
Σπανακόριζο	with spinach
Πιλάφι κυμά	with minced meat

ΠΟΥΛΕΡΙΚΑ	POULTRY
Κοτόπουλο	chicken, roasted
Πόδι κότας	leg of chicken
Στήθος κότας	chicken breast
Κοτόπουλο βραστό	boiled chicken
Ψητο κοτοπουλο στη σούβλα	spit-roasted chicken

ΚΡΕΑΣ	MEAT
Νεφρά	kidneys
Αρνϊ	lamb†
Αρνίσιες Μπριζόλες	lamb chops
Παιδάκια	lamb cutlets
Συκώτι	liver
Χοιρινδ	pork†
Χοιρινές Μπριζόλες	pork chops
Λουκάνικα	sausages
Μπιφτέκι	steak (beef)
Μοσχαρίσιο	veal
Μοσχαρίσιες Μπριζολες	veal chops
Μοσχάρι	grilled veal
Ψητό Μοσχαράκι	roast veal

† often with the prefix suffix to indicate if roasted or grilled as above.

ΨΑΡΙΑ	FISH
Σκουμπρί	mackerel
Συναγρίδα	red snapper
Μαρίδες	whitebait
Οκταπόδι	octopus
Καλαμάρια	squid
Μπαρμπούνι	red mullet
Κέφαλος	mullet
Αυθρίνι	grey mullet

ΤΥΡΙΑ	CHEESE
Φετα	feta (goat's-milk based)
Γραβιέρα	gruyere-type cheese
Κασέρι	cheddar-type (sheep's-milk based)

ΦΡΟΥΤΑ	FRUITS
Καρπούζι	water melon
Πεπόνι	melon
Μήλα	apple
Πορτοκάλι	oranges
Σταφύλια	grapes
Κομπόστα φρούτων	fruit compote

ΠΑΓΩΤΑ	ICE-CREAM
Σπέσιαλ	special
Παγωτό βανίλλια	vanilla
Παγωτό σοκολάτα	chocolate
Παγωτό λεμονι	lemon
Γρανίτα	water ice

ΓΛΥΚΙΣΜΑΤΑ	DESSERTS
Κέικ	cake
φρουτοσαλάτα	fruit salad
Κρέμα	milk pudding
Κρεμ καραμελέ	cream caramel
Μπακλαβας	crisp pastry with nuts & syrup or honey
Καταίφι	fine shredded pastry with nuts & syrup or honey
Γαλακτομπούρεκο	fine crispy pastry with custard & syrup
Γιαούρτι	yoghurt
Μέλι	honey

ΑΝΑΨΥΚΤΙΚΑ	COLD DRINKS/SOFT DRINKS
Πορτοκάλι	orange
Πορτοκαλάδα	orangeade
Λεμονάδα	lemonade made with lemon juice
Γκαζόζα (Gazoza)	fizzy lemonade
Μεταλλικό νερό	mineral water
Κόκα κολα	Coca-cola
Πέψι κολα	Pepsi-cola
Σέβεν-απ	Seven-Up
Σόδα	soda
Τονικ	tonic
Νερό (Nero)	water

ΚΑΦΕΔΕΣ	COFFEES
Ελληνικός (Καφές)	Greek coffee (sometimes called Turkish coffee ie. Τουπκικος Καφε)
σκέτο (skehto)	no sugar
μετριο (metrio)	medium sweet

FOOD & DRINK

γλυκό (ghliko)   sweet (very)
(Unless stipulated it will turn up 'ghliko'. Do not drink Turkish coffee before the grouts have settled.)
Νες καφέ   Nescafe
Νες (με γαλα) (Nes me ghala)   Nescafe with milk
Εσπρέσσο   espresso
Καπουτσίνο   cappucino
φραπέ   chilled coffee is known as 'frappe'
Τσάι   tea
Σοκαλάτα γάλα   chocolate milk

ΜΠΥΡΕΣ   BEERS
  ΦΙΞ (ΕΛΛΑΣ) Μπύρα   Fix (Hellas) beer
    φιάλη   bottle
    κουτί   can
  ΑΜΣΤΕΛ (Αμστελ)   Amstel
  ΧΕΝΝΙΝΓΕΡ (Χέννινγκερ)   Henninger
                                          (300g usually a can
                                          500g usually a bottle)

ΠΟΤΑ   DRINKS
  Ούζο   Ouzo
  Κονιάκ   Cognac
  Μπράντυ   Brandy
  Μεταξά   Metaxa
    3 ΑΣΤ   3 star
    5 ΑΣΤ   5 star
  Ουίσκυ   Whisky
  Τζιν   Gin
  Βότκα   Vodka
  Καμπάρι   Campari
  Βερμούτ   Vermouth
  Μαρτίνι   Martini

ΚΡΑΣΙΑ   WINES
  Κόκκινο   red
  Ασπρο   white
  Ροζε Κοκκινέλι   rose
  Ξηρό   dry
  Γλυκό   sweet
  Ρετσίνα   resinated wine
    e.g. Θεόκριτος   Theokritos
  Αρετσίνωτο   unresinated wine
    e.g. Δεμέστιχα   Demestica
                                          340g is a ½ bottle
                                          680g is a bottle
                                          950g is a large bottle

Useful Greek

English	Greek	Sounds like
Have you a table for...	Εχετε ένα τραπέζι για	Echete enna trapezee ghia...
I'd like...	Θέλω	Thelo...
We would like...	Θέλουμε	Thelome...
a beer	μιά μπύρα	meah beerah
a glass	ένα ποτήρι	ena poteeree
a carafe	μιά καράφα	meea karafa
a small bottle	ένα μικρό μπουκάλι	ena mikro bookalee
a large bottle	ένα μεγάλο	ena meghalo bookalee

51

bread	ψωμί	psomee
tea with milk	τσάι με γάλα	tsai me ghala
with lemon	τσάι με λεμόνι	me lemoni
Turkish coffee (Greek)	Τούρκικος καφές	Tourkikos kafes
sweet	γλυκός	ghleekos
medium	νέτριος	metreeo
bitter (no sugar)	πικρό	pikro
Black coffee	Nescafe xwpis γάλα	Nescafe horis ghala
Coffee with milk	Nescafe με γάλα	Nescafe me ghala
a glass of water	ενα ποτήρι νερό	enna poteeree nero
a napkin	μιά πετσέτα	mia petseta
an ashtray	ένα σταχτοδοχείο	enna stachdothocheeo
toothpick	μιά οδοντογλυφίδα	mea odontoglifidha
the olive oil	το ελαιόλαδο	dho eleolatho
Where is the toilet?	Που είναι η τουαλέττα	Poo eene i(ee) tooaleta?
What is this?	Τι είναι αυτό	Ti ine afto
This is…	Αυτό είναι	Afto eene
cold	κρύο	kreeo
bad	χαλασμένο	chalasmeno
stale	μπαγιάτικο	bayhiatiko
undercooked	άψητο	apseeto
overcooked	παραβρασμένο	paravrasmeno
The bill please	Το λογαριασμό παρακαλώ	To loghariasmo parakalo
How much is that?	Πόσο κάνει αυτό	Poso kanee afto?
That was an excellent meal	Περίφημο γέυμα	Pereefimo yevma
We shall come again	Θα ξανάρθουμε	Tha xanarthoume

His and Hers

7 Shopping & Public Services

Let your purse be your master   Proverb

Purchasing items in Greece is still quite an art form or subject for a degree course. The difficulties have been compounded by the rest of the western world becoming nations of supermarket shoppers, whilst the Greeks have stayed traditionally and firmly with their individual shops, selling a fixed number of items and sometimes only one type of a product.

Shopping for a corkscrew, for instance, might well involve calling at two or three seemingly look-alike ironmongers, but no, they each specialise in certain lines of goods and do not stock any items outside those prescribed, almost as if by holy writ.

Bakers usually have to be diligently searched for and when found are frequently located, tucked away in or behind other shops. A pointer to their presence may well be a pile of blackened, twisted olive wood, stacked up to one side of the entrance, and used to fuel the oven fires.

Cake shops (*Zacharoplasteion*) may sell bottled mineral water (ask for a cold bottle).

The question of good and bad buys is a rather personal matter but the items listed below are highlighted on the basis of value of money and quality. Clothing and accessories that are attractive and represent good value include embroidered peasant dresses, leather sandals, woven bags and furs. Day-to-day items that are inexpensive take in Greek cigarettes, drinks including Ouzo, Metaxa brandy and selected island wines. Suitable gifts for family and friends embraces ceramic plates, sponges, Turkish delight and worry beads (*komboloe*). Disproportionately expensive items include camera film, toiletries, books and playing cards. Do not forget to compare prices and preferably shop in the streets and markets, not in airport and hotel concessionary shops, which are often more expensive.

Try not to run short of change. Everybody else does, including bus conductors, taxi drivers and shops.

Opening Hours
Strict or old fashioned summer shop hours are:
Monday, Wednesday and Saturday: 0830-1400 hrs; Tuesday, Thursday and Friday: 0830-1330 hrs & 1730-2030 hrs.

Generally, during the summer months, shops in tourist areas are open Monday to Saturday from 0800-1300 hours. Then they close until 1700 hours, after which they open again until at least 2030 hours, if not 2200 hours. Sundays and Saints' days are more indeterminate, but there is usually a general shop open, somewhere. In very popular tourist resorts and busy ports, shops often open seven days a week.

Drink
Available either in the markets from delicatessen meat/dairy counters or from 'off-licence' type shops.

Smokers
Imported French, English and American cigarettes are inexpensive, compared with European prices, at between 100 and 120 drs for a packet of 20. Greek cigarettes, which have a distinctive and different taste, are excellent. Try *Karellia*, which cost about 68 drs for a packet of 20 and note that the price is printed around the edge of the packet. Even Greek cigars are almost unheard of on the islands, while in Athens, they cost 10 drs and Dutch cigars work out at about 25 drs each. So, if a cigar-smoker, take along your holiday requirements.

Newspapers & Magazines
The *Athens News* is published daily except Mondays in English and costs 50 drs.
Overseas newspapers are available up to 24 hours after the day of publication, but
note that all printed matter is comparatively expensive.

Photography (Fotografion – ΦΩΤΟΓΡΑΦΕΙΟΝ)
Photographers should carry all the film possible as, being imported, it is comparatively expensive. To counter the very bright sunlight, when using colour film, blue
filters should be fitted to the lens.

Tourist Guides & Maps
Shop around before purchasing, as the difference in price of the island guides can
be as much as 150 drs, ie from 200-350 drs. Island maps cost between 80-100 drs.
  Some major ports and towns have one authentic, well stocked bookshop, usually
positioned a little off the town centre. The proprietor often speaks adequate English
and courteously answers most enquiries.

SHOPS
Bakers & Bread Shops (ΑΡΤΟΠΟΙΕΙΟΝ, ΑΡΤΟΠΩΛΕΙΟΝ or ΠΡΑΤΗΡΙΟΝ ΑΡΤΟΥ)
For some obscure reason bakers are nearly always difficult to locate, being hidden
away, and bread shops tend to be few and far between. Bakers may also sell cheese
and meat pies. They are almost always closed on Sundays and all holidays, despite
the ovens often being used by the local community to cook their Sunday dinners.
  The method of purchasing bread can prove disconcerting, especially when sold
by weight. Sometimes the purchaser selects the loaf and then pays but the most
bewildering system is where it is necessary to pay first then collect the goods.
Difficult if the shopper's level of Greek is limited to grunts, "thank you" and "please"!
  Greek bread also has another parameter of measure, that is a graduation in hours –
1 hour, 4 hours and so on. After the period is up, it is usually completely inedible,
having transmogrified into a rock-like substance.

Butcher (ΚΡΕΟΠΩΛΕΙΟΝ)
Similar to those at home but the cuts are quite different (surely the Common Market
can legislate against this deviation!).

Galaktopoleio *et al.*
See CHAPTER 6

Markets
The smaller ports and towns may have a market street and the larger municipalities
often possess a market building. This is thronged with locals and all the basic
necessities can be procured inexpensively. Fruit and vegetable stalls are interspaced by butchers and dairy delicatessen shops. During business hours, the
proprietors are brought coffee and a glass of water by waiters carrying the cups and
glasses, not on open trays, but in round, aluminium salvers with a deep lid, held
under a large ring handle, connected to the tray by three flat arms.

Supermarkets (ΥΠΕΡΑΓΟΡΑ/ΣΟΥΠΕΡΜΑΡΚΕΤ)
Very much on the increase and based on smalltown, self-service stores but not to
worry, they inherit all those delightful, native Greek qualities including quiet chaos.

Speciality Shops
Found in some big towns and Athens while pavement browsing. The little basement shops are espied down flights of steps, specialising, for instance, in dried fruit, beans, nuts and grains.

Street Kiosks (Periptero/ΠΕΡΙΠΤΕΡΟ)
These unique, pagoda-like huts stay open remarkably long hours, often from early morning to after midnight. They sell a wide range of goods including newspapers, magazines (surprisingly sometimes pornographic literature), postcards, tourist maps, postage stamps, sweets, chocolates, cigarettes and matches. Additionally they form the outlet for the pay phone system and, at the cost of 5 drs, a local call may be made. It is rather incongruous, to observe a Greek making a possibly important business call, in amongst a rack of papers and magazines, with a foreground of jostling pedestrians and a constant stream of noisy traffic in the background.

Alternate Ways of Shopping
Then there are the other ways of shopping: from handcarts, their street-vendor owners selling respectively nuts, ice-cream, milk and yoghurt; from the back of a donkey with vegetable-laden panniers or from two wheeled trailers drawn by fearsome sounding, agricultural rotovator power units. Often the donkey or powered trailer has an enormous set of scales mounted on the back end, swinging like a hangman's scaffold.

If the vegetable/fruit is being sold by 'gypsy-types' then it is advisable to only purchase from those who have their prices written up, usually on a piece of cardboard. Even Anne admits to being ripped off by a roadside banana seller and advises that they are frequently prosecuted for breaking the law.

Frequently the shops used include:
ΒΙΒΛΙΟΠΩΛΕΙΟΝ – Bookshop; ΙΧΘΥΟΠΩΛΕΙΟΝ – Fishmonger; ΟΠΩΡΟΠΩΛΕΙΟΝ – Greengrocer; ΠΑΝΤΟΠΩΛΕΙΟΝ – Grocer; ΚΑΠΝΟΠΩΛΕΙΟΝ – Tobacconist. Readers may observe that the above all have a similar ending and it is worth noting that shop titles that terminate in 'ΠΩΛΕΙΟΝ/Πωλειο' are selling something, if that's any help.

SERVICES
The Banks (ΤΡΑΠΕΖΑ)
The minimum opening hours are 0800 to 1330 hrs, Monday to Thursday and 0800 to 1300 hrs on Friday. Some banks, in the most tourist ravaged spots, open on Saturday and a very few on Sunday. Smaller towns, villages or for that matter islands do not have a bank in which case there may be a local money changer acting as agent for this or that National Bank. Do not forget that a passport is almost always required to change travellers' cheques. In the larger cities, personal cheques may be changed at a selected bank when backed by a Eurocheque (or similar) bank guarantee card. A commission charge of between 50 and 150 drs is made, depending on the size of the transaction. Whereas Eurocheques used to be changed in sums up to £50, English sterling, the arrangement now is that a cheque can be cashed in drachmae, up to 17,000 drs. As the charges for changing cheques are based on a sliding scale weighted against smaller amounts, this new arrangement helps save on fees.

The service is generally discourteous and only one employee, if at all, reluctantly speaks English so make sure the correct bank is selected to carry out a particular transaction (such as changing a personal cheque). Each bank displays a window sticker giving an indication of the tourist services transacted. There is nothing worse, after queuing for half an hour or so, than to be rudely told to go away. I once chose the wrong bank to change a personal cheque, only to receive a loud blast of abuse about some long-departed foreigner's bouncing cheque. Most embarrassing.

The larger hotels transact traveller's cheques, but naturally enough at a disadvantageous rate compared with the banks.

Another interesting source of taking currency abroad, for United Kingdom residents, is to use National Giro Post Office cheques which can be cashed at any Post Office in Greece. This is a very useful wheeze, especially on busy tourist islands where foreign currency desks are usually subject to long queues. Detailed arrangements have to be made with the International branch of Giro.

Whilst discoursing on the subject of Post Offices, they now offer a surprisingly wide variety of banking services, for which see below. This is exceptionally helpful on an island where there are no banking services.

The basis of Greek currency is the drachmae. This is nominally divided into 100 lepta and occasionally price lists show a price of, say 62.60 drs. As prices are rounded up (or down), in practice the lepta is not now encountered. Notes are in denominations of 50, 100, 500, and 1000 drs and coins in denominations of 1 and 2 drs (bronze), 5, 10 and 20 and 50 drs (nickel). Do not run out of change, it is always in demand. Repetitious I know, but well worth remembering.

Museums

The following is a mean average of the information to hand but each museum is likely to have its own peculiarities. In the summer season (1st April – 31st October) they open daily 0845-1500/1900 hrs, Sundays and holidays 0930-1430/1530 hrs and are closed Mondays or Tuesdays. They are closed 1st January, 25th March, Good Friday, Easter holiday and 25th December. Admission costs range from free to 100/150 drs, whilst Sundays and holidays are very occasionally free.

The Post Office (ΤΑΧΥΔΡΟΜΕΙΟΝ/ΕΛΤΑ)

Stamps can be bought from kiosks (at a commission) and shops selling postcards as well as from the Post Offices. Post boxes are scattered around, are usually painted yellow, are rather small in size and often difficult to find, being fixed, high up, on side-street walls. In 1986 postage rates for cards to the United Kingdom were 27 drs for a small card and 35 drs for a large one.

Most major town Post Offices are modern and the service received is only slightly less rude than that handed out by bank staff. When confronted by two letter-box openings, the inland service is marked ΕΣΩΤΕΡΙΚΟΥ/Εσωτερικου and the overseas ΕΞΩΤΕΡΙΚΟΥ/Εξωτερικου. Letters can be sent for poste restante collection, but a passport will be required for them to be handed over.

Post Offices are usually only open Monday to Friday between 0730-2030 hrs for stamps, money orders and registered mail; 0730-2000 hrs for poste restante and 0730-1430 hrs for parcels. Parcels have to be collected.

In recent years the range of Post Office services has been expanded to include cashing Eurocheques and Travellers' cheques as well as changing currency. All but the most out of the way island offices now offer these facilities. *See* **Banks.**

Telephone Office (OTE)

A separate organisation from the Post Office and to accomplish an overseas or long-distance call it is necessary to go to the OTE office. Here there are separate booths from which to make calls but busy offices usually suffer from long queues. The counter clerk indicates which compartment is to be used and, in a bank, alongside him are mounted the instruments to meter the cost. Payment is made after completion of the call at a current rate of 3½ drs per unit so ensure that the meter is zeroed prior to making a connection. Opening days and hours vary enormously. Smaller offices may only open weekdays for say 7 hours between 0830-1530 hrs whilst the larger city offices open 24 hours a day, seven days a week.

Overseas dialling codes		Inland services	
Australia	0061	Directory enquiries	131
Canada & USA	001	Provincial enquiries	132
New Zealand	0064	General Information	134
South Africa	0027	Time	141
United Kingdom & Ireland	0044	Medical care	166
Other overseas countries	161	City police	100
		Gendarmerie	109
		Fire	199
		Tourist police	171
		Roadside assistance	104
		Telegrams/cables	165

To dial England, drop the '0' from all four figure codes. Thus making a call to, say Portsmouth, for which the code is 0705, dial 00 44 705 ....

The internal service is both very good and reasonably priced. Local telephone calls cost 5 drs and can be made from some bars and the pavement kiosks (periptero). The presence of a telephone is often indicated by the sign ΕΔΩ ΤΗΛΕΦΩΝΕΙΤΕ, a blue background denotes a local phone, and an orange one, an inter-city phone. Another sign, Εδω Τηλεφωνειτε (the lower case equivalent), signifies 'telephone from here'. The method of operation is to insert the coin and dial. If a connection cannot be made, place the receiver back on the cradle and the money is returned.

Telegrams may be sent from either the OTE or Post Office.

Useful Greek

ΓΡΑΜΜΑΤΟΣΗΜΑ – stamps; ΔΕΜΑΤΑ – parcels.

English	Greek	Sounds like
Where is...	Που είναι	Poo eenne...
Where is the nearest...	Που είναι η πλησιέστερη	Poo eenne i pleesiesteri
baker	ο φούρναρης/ψωμάς	foornaris/psomas
bakery	Αρτοποιείον	artopieeon
bank	η τράπεζα	i(ee) trapeza
bookshop	το βιβλιοπωλείο	to vivleeopolieo
butchers shop	το χασάπικο	dho hasapiko
chemist shop	το φαρμακείο	to farmakio
dairy shop	το γαλακτοπωλείο	galaktopolieon
doctor	ο γιατρός	o yiahtros
grocer	το μπακάλης	o bakalis
hospital	το νοσοκομείο	to nosokomio
laundry	το πλυντήριο	to plintirio, (plintireeo, since i = ee)
liquor store	το ποτοπωλείο	to potopolio (potopoleeo)
photographic shop	το φωτογραφείο	to fotoghrafeeo
post office	το ταχυδρομείο	to tahkithromio
shoe repairer	το τσαγκαράδικο	to tsangkaradiko
tailor	ο ραπτης	o raptis
Have you any...	Εχετε	Ekheteh...
Do you sell...	Πουλάτε	Poulate...
How much is this...	Πόσο κάνει αυτό	Posso kanee afto...
I want...	Θέλω	Thelo...
half kilo/a kilo	μισό κιλό/ένα κιλό	miso kilo/ena kilo
aspirin	η ασπιρίνη	aspirini
apple(s)	το μήλο/μήλα	meelo/meela
banana(s)	η μπανάνα/μπανάνες	banana/bananes
bread	το ψωμί	psomee
butter	το βούτυρο	vutiro

cheese	το τυρί	tiree
cigarettes (filter tip)	το τσιγάρο (με φίλτρο)	to tsigharo (me filtro)
coffee	καφές	cafes
cotton wool	το βαμβάκι	to vambaki
crackers	τα κρακεράκια	krackerakia
crisps	τσιπς	tsseeps
cucumbers	το αγγούρι	anguree
disinfectant	το απολυμαντικό	to apolimantiko
guide book	ο τουριστικός οδηγός	o touristikos odhigos
ham	το ζαμπόν	zambon
ice-cream	το παγωτό	paghoto
lemons	το λεμόνια	lemonia
lettuce	το μαρούλι	to marooli
map	το χάρτης	o khartis
a box of matches	ενα κουτί σπίρτα	ena kuti spirta
milk	το γάλα	to ghala
pate	πατέ	pate
(ball point) pen	το μπικ	to bik
pencil	το μολύβι	to molivi
pepper	το πιπέρι	to piperi
(safety) pins	μια παραμάνα	mia (meea) paramana
potatoes	οι πατάτες	patates
salad	η σαλάτα	i salatah
salami	το σαλάμι	salahmi
sausages	το λουκάνικα	lukahniko
soap	το σαπούνι	to sapooni
spaghetti	σπαγγέτο	spayehto
string	ο σπαγκος	o spangos
sugar	η ζάχαρη	i zakhahree
tea	το τσάι	to tsai
tomatoes	η ντομάτες	domahdes
toothbrush	η οδοντόβουρτσα	odhondovourtsa
toothpaste	η οδοντόκρεμα	odhondokrema
writing paper	το χαρτι γραψίματος	to kharti grapsimatos

Iraklion Harbour

8 Greece: History, Mythology, Religion, Present-day Greece, Greeks & their Holidays

All ancient histories, as one of our fine wits said, are but fables that have been accepted. Voltaire

HISTORY

Excavations have shown the presence of Palaeolithic man up to 100,000 years ago. Greece's history and mythology are, like the Greek language, formidable to say the least, with legend, myth, folk tales, fables and religious lore often inextricably mixed up. Archaeologists are now finding that some mythology is in fact based on historical fact. For instance the great Minoan civilisation centred on Crete, which may well have been the fabled Atlantis of pre-history, was mysteriously and suddenly destroyed. Recent, informed speculation leads to the conclusion that about 1700 BC a vast volcanic eruption, presumed to be centred on the island of Santorini (Thira) in the Cyclades, destroyed this flourishing and far reaching culture.

Historically Greeks fought Greeks, Phoenicians and Persians. Under Alexander the Great they conquered Egypt and vast tracts of Asia Minor. Then they were in turn conquered by the Romans. After the splitting of the Roman Kingdom into Western and Eastern Empires, the Greeks, with Constantinople as their capital, were ruled by the Eastern offshoot, only to fall into the hands of the Franks about AD 1200, followed by the Turks. The Venetians, Genoese and finally the Turks ruled most of the islands.

In 1821 the War of Independence commenced, which eventually led to the setting up of a Parliamentary Republic in 1928. Incidentally, Thessaly, Crete and the Dodecanese islands remained under Turkish rule. By the time the Dodecanese islanders had thrown out the Turks, the Italians had taken over. If you are now confused, give up, because it gets even more difficult to follow.

The Greek monarchy, which had come into being in 1833, and was related to the German Royal family, opted in 1913 to side with the Axis powers. The chief politician Eleftherios Venizelos, disagreed, was dismissed and set up a rival government, after which the King, under Allied pressure, retired to Switzerland. In the years following the end of the First World War, the Turks and Greeks agreed, after some fairly bloody fighting, to exchange a total of one and a half million people.

In 1936 a General Metaxas became dictator. He achieved immortal fame by booting out Mussolini's representative, when in 1940, Mussolini demanded permission for Italy's troops to traverse Greece, and received the famous *Ochi* (No). (This day has become a national festival known as *Ochi Day*, celebrated on 28th October.) The Italians demurred and marched on Greece, the soldiers of whom, to the surprise of everybody including themselves, reinforced the refusal by routing them. The Italians were only saved from total humiliation by the intervention of the Germans, who then occupied Greece for the duration of the Second World War. At the end of hostilities, all the Italian held Greek islands were reunited with mainland Greece.

As German ascendancy declined, the Greek freedom fighters split into royalist and communist factions and proceeded to knock even more stuffing out of each other than they had out of the Germans. Until the British intervention, followed by large injections of American money and weapons, it looked as if Greece would go behind the Iron Curtain. A second civil war broke out between 1947 and 1949 and this internal strife was reputed to have cost more Greek lives than were lost during the whole of the Second World War.

In 1951, Greece and Turkey became full members of NATO, but the issue of the ex-British colony of Cyprus was about to rear its ugly head, with the resultant, renewed estrangement between Greece and Turkey.

The various political manoeuvrings, the involvement of the Greek monarchy in domestic affairs and the worsening situation in Cyprus, led to the *coup d'etat* by the Colonel's Junta in 1967, soon after which King Constantine II and his entourage fled to Italy. The Colonel's extremely repressive dictatorship was, seemingly, actively supported by the Americans and condoned by Britain. Popular countrywide feeling and, in particular, student uprisings between 1973-1974, which were initially put down in Athens by brutal tank attacks, led to the eventual collapse of the regime in 1974. In the death-throes of their rule, the Colonels, using the Cyprus dream to distract the ordinary people's feeling of injustice, meddled and attempted to overthrow the vexatious priest, President Makarios. The net result was that the Turks invaded Cyprus and made an enforced division of that unhappy, troubled island.

In 1974, Greece returned to republican democracy and in 1981 joined the EEC.

RELIGION

The Orthodox Church prevails everywhere but there are small pockets of Roman Catholicism as well as very minor enclaves of Muslims on the Dodecanese islands and mainland western Thrace. The schism within the Holy Roman Empire, in 1054, caused the Catholic Church to be centred on Rome and the Orthodox Church on Constantinople.

The Turkish overlords encouraged the continuation of the indigenous church, probably to keep their bondsmen quiet, but it had the invaluable side effect of keeping alive Greek customs and traditions during the centuries of occupation.

The bewildering profusion of small churches, scattered 'indiscriminately' all over the islands, is not proof of the church's wealth, although the Greek people are not entirely convinced of that fact. It is evidence of the piety of the families or individuals who paid to have them erected, in the name of their selected patron saint, as thanksgiving for God's protection. The style of religious architecture changes between the island groups.

Many churches only have one service a year, on the name day of the particular patron saint, and this ceremony is named *Viorti* or *Panayieri*. It is well worth attending one of these self-indulgent extravaganzas to observe and take part in celebratory village religious life and music. One and all are welcome to the carnival festivities which include eating and dancing in, or adjacent to, the particular churchyard.

The words Byzantine and Byzantium crop up frequently with especial reference to churches and appertain to the period between the forth and fourteenth centuries AD. During this epoch Greece was, at least nominally, under the control of Constantinople (Instanbul), built by the Emperor Constantine on the site of the old city of Byzantium. Religious paintings executed on small wooden panels during this period are called ikons. Very, very few original ikons remain available for purchase, so beware if offered an apparent 'bargain'.

When visiting a church, especially noticeable are the pieces of shining, thin metal, placed haphazardly around or pinned to wooden carvings. These *tamata* or *exvotos* represent limbs or portions of the human body and are purchased by worshippers as an offering, in the hope of an illness being cured and/or limbs healed.

GREEKS

In making assessment of the Greek people and their character, it must be remembered that, perhaps even more so than the Spaniards or the Portuguese, Greece has only recently emerged into the twentieth century. Unlike other countries 'discovered' in the 1960s by the holiday industry they have not, in the main, degraded or debased their principles or character, despite the onrush of tourist wealth. For a people to have had so little and to face so much demand for European 'necessities', would have strained a less hardy and well-balanced people.

Greece's recent emergence into the western world is evidenced by the still patriarchal nature of their society, a view supported, for instance, by the oft-seen spectacle of men lazing in the tavernas whilst their womenfolk work in the fields (and why not?).

Often the smallest village, on the remotest island, has an English-speaking islander who lived abroad at some time in his life, earning a living through seafaring, as a hotel waiter, or as a taxi driver. Thus, while making an escape from the comparative poverty at home, for a period of good earnings in the more lucrative world, a working knowledge of English, American or Australian will have been gained. *Greek strine*, or as usually contracted *grine*, simply has to be heard to be believed.

The greatest hurdle to understanding is undoubtedly the language barrier, especially if it is taken into account that the Greeks appear to have some difficulty with their own language in its various forms. Certainly, they seem, on occasions, not to understand each other and the subject matter has to be repeated a number of times. Perhaps that is the reason for all the shouting!

There can be no doubt that the traditional Greek welcome to the *xenos* or *singrafeus*, now increasingly becoming known as *touristas* has, naturally, become rather lukewarm in the more 'besieged' areas. It is often difficult to reconcile the shrugged shoulders of a seemingly disinterested airline official or bus driver, with being stopped in the street by a gold-toothed, smiling Greek proffering some fruit. But remember the bus driver may realise the difficulty of overcoming the language barrier, it is very hot, he has been working long hours earning his living and he is not on holiday.

Sometimes a drink appears mysteriously at one's taverna table, the donor being indicated by a nod of the waiter's head, but a word of warning here. Simply smile and accept the gift graciously. Any attempt to return the kindness by 'putting one in the stable' for your new found friend only results in a 'who buys last' competition which will surely be lost. I know, I am speaking from battle-weary experience. Greeks are very welcoming and may well invite a tourist to their table. But do not expect more, they are reserved and have probably had previous unhappy experiences of ungrateful, rude, overseas visitors.

To look over churches or monasteries visitors must ensure they are adequately covered, including legs and arms, and should note that many religious establishments strictly apply the rules. It seems a pity for a tourist to have made a special excursion, sometimes involving arduous walking, only to be turned away at the gate. Men must wear a shirt and trousers, not shorts, and women a modest blouse, skirt and take a head scarf, it might be required.

Women tourists can travel quite freely in Greece without fear, except from other tourists. On the other hand females should not wear provocative attire or fail to wear sufficient clothing when in close social contact with Greek men, who might well be inflamed into action, or Greek women, whom it will offend, probably because of the effect on their men! Certainly all the above was the case until very recently but the constant stream of 'available' young tourist ladies on the more popular islands, has resulted in the local lads taking both a 'view' and a chance. It almost reminds one of the Costa Brava in the early 1960s. The disparate moral qualities of the native and tourist females is resulting in a conundrum for young Greek wormen. To compete for their men's affections they have to loosen their principles with an unheard of and steadily increasing number of speedily arranged marriages, if you know what I mean.

Do not miss the *Volta* (Βολτα), the traditional family evening walkabout on city, town and village square. Dressed for the event, an important part of the ritual is for the family to show off their marriageable daughters. Good fun and great watching, but the Greeks are rather protective of their family and all things Greek... you may comment favourably, but keep adverse criticism to yourself.

It is interesting to speculate on the influence of the early Greek immigrants on American culture, especially when considering the American habit of serving water with every meal, the ubiquitous hamburger (which is surely a poorly reproduced and inferior souvlaki) and some of the official uniforms, more particularly the flat peaked hats of American postmen and policemen.

THE GREEK NATIONAL HOLIDAYS

Listed below are the national holidays and on these days many areas and islands hold festivals, but with a particular slant and emphasis.

1st January	New Year's Day/The Feast of Saint Basil
6th January	Epiphany/Blessing of the Waters – a cross is immersed in the sea, lake or river during a religious ceremony
The period 27th Jan to 17th February	The Greek Carnival Season
25th March	The Greek National Anniversary/Independence Day
April – Movable days	Good Friday/Procession of the 'Epitaph'; Holy Week Saturday/Ceremony of the Resurrection; Easter Sunday/open air feasts
1st May	May/Labour Day/Feast of the Flowers
1st to 10th July	Greek Navy Week
15th August	Assumption Day/Festival of the Virgin Mary, especially in the Cycladian island of Tinos (beware travelling at this time, anywhere in the area)
28th October	National Holiday/'Ochi' Day
24th December	Christmas Eve/carols evening
25th December	Christmas Day
26th December	St Stephen's Day
31st December	New Year's Eve carols, festivals

In addition to these national days, each island has its own particular festivals and holidays which are listed individually under each island description. Many island churches only have one service a year.

A word of warning to ferry-boat travellers will not go amiss here – DO NOT travel to an island immediately prior to one of these festivals NOR off the island immediately after the event. It will be almost impossible to do other than stand, that is if one has not already been trampled to death in the various stampedes to and from the ferry-boats.

PART TWO

9 ATHENS CITY (ATHINA, AΘHNAI)

There is no end of it in this city, wherever you set your foot, you encounter some memory of the past. Marcus Cicero

Tel. prefix 01

The capital of Greece and major city of Attica. Previously the springboard for travel to most of the Greek islands, but less so since a number of direct flights have become available to the larger islands. Experienced travellers flying into Athens airport, often try to arrange their arrival for early morning and head straight for either West airport (for a domestic flight), Piraeus port, the railway station or bus terminal, so as to be able to get under way immediately.

ARRIVAL BY AIR
International flights other than Olympic Airways land at the:

East airport
Public transport facilities include:
Bus No. 18:   East airport to Leoforos Amalias. Every 20 mins from 0600-2400 hrs. Fare 80 drs. Yellow express bus.
Bus No. 121:   East airport to Leoforos Olgas. 0650-2250 hrs. Fare 80 drs.
Bus No. 19:   East airport to Plateia Karaiskaki/Akti Tselepi, Piraeus. Every hour from 0800-2000 hrs. Fare 80 drs. Yellow express bus.
Bus No. 101:   East airport via Leoforos Possidonos (coast road) to Klisovis/Theotoki St, Piraeus. Every 20 mins from 0500-2245 hrs. Fare 30 drs.

Domestic and all Olympic flights land at the:

West airport
Public transport facilities include:
Bus No. 133:   West airport to Leoforos Square, Leoforos Amalias, Filellinon & Othonos Streets (Syntagma Sq). Every ½ hour from 0530-0030 hrs. Fare 30 drs. Blue bus.
Bus No. 122:   West airport to Leoforos Olgas. Every 20 mins. Fare 30 drs. Blue bus.
Buses No.   West airport via Leoforos Possidonos (coast road) to Klisovis St, Piraeus.
107 & 109:

In addition there are Olympic buses connecting West and East airports as well as Olympic buses from the West airport to the Olympic offices (*Tmr* 12C6) on Leoforos Sygrou and Syntagma Square. Every 20 mins between 0600-2000 hrs. Fare 100 drs.

ARRIVAL BY BUS
International coaches usually decant passengers at Syntagma Sq (*Tmr* 1D/E4/5), Stathmos Larissis Station (*Tmr* B/C1), or close to one of the major city bus terminals.

ARRIVAL BY FERRY
See **Piraeus**, CHAPTER 10

ARRIVAL BY TRAIN
See **Trains, A to Z.**

GENERAL (Illustrations 4 & 5)
Even if a traveller is a European city dweller, Athens will come as a sociological and cultural shock to the system. In the summer it is a hot, dusty, dry, crowded, traffic-bound, exhaust polluted bedlam, but always friendly, cosmopolitan and ever on the move.

On arrival in Athens, and planning to stay over, it is best to select the two main

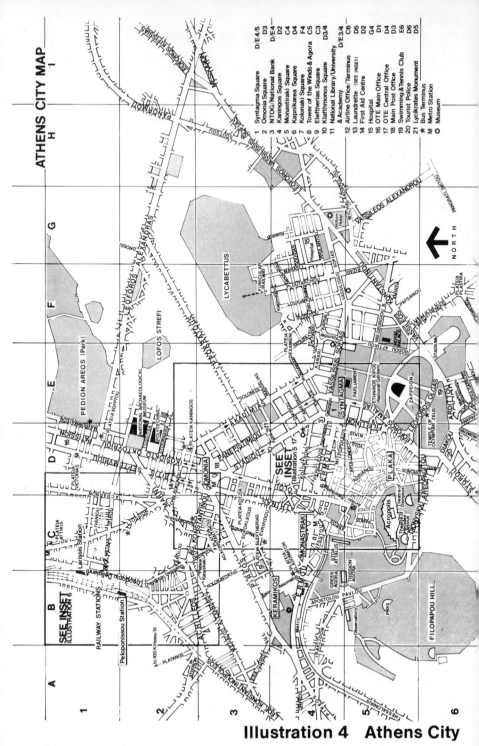

ATHENS CITY MAP

1 Syntagma Square — D/E4,5
2 Omonia Square — D3
3 NTOG/National Bank — D/E4
4 Kaningos Square — D2
5 Monastiraki Square — C4
6 Kapnikarea Square — D4
7 Kolonaki Square — F4
8 Tower of the Winds & Agora — C5
9 Eleftherias Square — C3
10 Klafthmonos Square — D3/4
11 National Library/University & Academy — D/E3,4
12 Airline Office/Terminus — C6
13 Laundrette (SEE INSET) — D5
14 First Aid Centre — D2
15 Hospital — G4
16 OTE Main Office — D1
17 OTE Central Office — L4
18 Main Post Office — D3
19 Swimming & Tennis Club — E6
20 Tourist Police — D6
21 Lycikrates Monument — D5
★ Bus Terminus
M Metro Station
○ Museum

Illustration 4   Athens City

squares of Syntagma (*Tmr* 1D/E4/5) and Omonia (*Tmr* 2 D3). These can be used as centres for the initial sally and from which to radiate out to the other squares or plateias.

There is no substitute for a city map which is issued free (yes free) from the Tourist Board desk in the National Bank of Greece on Syntagma Sq (*Tmr* 3, D/E4). *See* **NTOG, A to Z.**

Syntagma Square (Constitution or Parliament Square) (*Tmr* 1D/E4/5). The airport and many other buses stop off here. It is the city centre with the most elite hotels, airline offices, international companies, including the American Express headquarters, smart cafes and the Parliament building all circumscribing the central, sunken square. In the bottom right-hand (or south-east) corner of the plateia, bounded by Odhos Othonos and Leoforos Amalias, are some very clean, attendant minded toilets. There is a charge for the use of the 'squatties'.

To orientate, the Parliament building and Monument to the Unknown Warrior lie to the east of the square. To the north-east, in the middle distance, is one of the twin hills of Athens, Mt Lycabettus (Lykavittos). The other hill is the Acropolis, to the south-west, and not now visible from Syntagma Sq due to high-rise buildings. On the west side of the square are the offices of American Express and a battery of pavement cafes, with Ermou St leading due west to Monastiraki Sq. To the north are the two parallel, main avenues of Stadiou (a one-way street down to Syntagma) and Venizelou or Panepistimiou (a one-way street out of Syntagma) that both run north-west to:

Omonia Square (Concorde or Harmony Square) (*Tmr* 2D3) The 'Piccadilly Circus' or 'Times Square' of Athens but rather tatty really, with a constant stream of traffic bludgeoning its way round the large central island crowned by an impressive fountain. Visitors trying to escape the human bustle on the pavements by stepping out into the kerbside should beware that they are not mown down by a bus, taxi or private car.

Constant activity night and day, with seemingly every nationality cheek by jowl, lends the square a cosmopolitan character all of its own. On every side are hotels, varying from the downright seedy to the better-class tawdry, housed in rather undistinguished, 'neo-city-municipal' style, nineteenth century buildings, almost unique to Athens.

Various Metro train entrance/exits emerge around the square, similar to air raid shelters, spewing out and sucking in travellers. The Omonia underground concourse has a Post Office, telephones, a Bank and, by the Dorou St entrance, a block of 'squatty' toilets for which the attendant charges 10 drs for 2 sheets of paper.

Shops, cafes and booths fill the gaps between the hotels and the eight streets that converge on the Square.

To the north-east side of Omonia, on the corner of Dorou St, is a taxi rank and beyond, on the right, a now rather squalid, covered arcade brimful of reasonably priced snackbars. Through this covered passageway, and turning to the left up 28 Ikosiokto Oktovriou (28th October St)/Patission St, and then right down Veranzerou St, leads to:

Kaningos Square (*Tmr* 4D2) Serves as a Bus terminal for some routes.

To the south of Omonia Sq is Athinas St, the commercial thoroughfare of Athens. Here every conceivable item imaginable, including ironmongery, tools, crockery and clothing, can be purchased, and parallel to which, for half its length, runs Odhos Sokratous, the city street market during the day and the red-light district by night.

Athinas St drops due south to:

Monastiraki Square (*Tmr* 5C4) This marks the northernmost edge of the area known as the **Plaka** (*Tmr* D5) bounded by Ermou St to the north, Filellinon St to the east, and to the south by the slopes of the Acropolis.

Many of the alleys in this area follow the course of the old Turkish streets, most of the houses are mid-nineteenth century and represent the 'Old Quarter'.

Climbing the twisting maze of streets and steps of the lower north-east slopes of the Acropolis requires the stamina of a mountain goat. The almost primitive, island-village nature of some of the houses is very noticeable, due, it is said, to a Greek law passed after Independence. This was enacted to alleviate a housing shortage and allowed anyone who could raise the roof of a building, between sunrise and sunset, to finish it off and own the dwelling. Some inhabitants of the Cyclades island of Anafi (Anaphe) were reputed to have been the first to benefit from this new law and others followed to specialise in restoration and rebuilding, thus bringing about a colony of expatriate islanders within the Plaka district.

From the south-west corner of Monastiraki Sq, Ifestou St and its associated byways house the Flea Market, which climaxes on Sunday into stall upon stall of junk, souvenirs, junk, hardware, junk, boots, junk, records, junk, clothes, junk, footwear, junk, pottery and junk. Where Ifestou becomes Odhos Astigos and curves round to join up with Ermou St, there are a couple of extensive secondhand bookshops with reasonably priced (for Greece that is), if battered, paperbacks for sale. From the south-east corner of Monastiraki, Pandrossou St, one of the only enduring reminders of the Turkish Bazaar, contains a better class of antique dealer, sandal and shoe makers, and pottery stores.

Due south of Monastiraki Sq is Odhos Areos, unfortunately the first 100m or so of which is now host to a raggle-taggle band of European and Japanese drop-outs selling junk trinkets from the pavement kerb. They seem to have driven out the original stallholders and shop keepers on this stretch. Climbing Odhos Areos skirts the Roman Agora, from which various streets lead upwards, on ever upwards, containing a plethora of stalls and shops, specialising in leather goods, clothes and souvenirs. The further you climb, the cheaper the goods become. This interestingly enough does not apply to the tavernas and restaurants which seemingly become more expensive as one ascends.

The 'chatty' area known as the **Plaka** is 'littered' with eating places, a few good, some bad, some tourist rip-offs. The liveliest street, Odhos Kidathineon, is jam-packed with cafes, tavernas and restaurants and at night is bestrewn with music-playing layabouts. The class, tone and price of the establishments improves proceeding in a north-eastwards direction. I have to admit to gently knocking the Plaka over the years but it must be acknowledged that the area offers the cheapest accommodation and eating places in Athens and generally appears to have been cleaned up in recent times. In fact, since the 1986 'Libyan' downturn in American tourists, the area has become positively attractive. Early and late in the year the Plaka returns to being a super place to visit. The shopkeepers become human, shopping is inexpensive and the tavernas revert to being 'Greek' and lively. In the last 3 weeks of February the *Apokria Festival*, a long running 'Halloween' style carnival, is centred on the Plaka. The streets are filled with dozens of revellers dressed in fancy dress, masks and funny hats wandering about, throwing confetti, and creating a marvellous atmosphere. For this event all the tavernas are decorated.

To the east of Monastiraki Sq is Ermou St which is initially lined by clothes and shoe shops. One third of the way towards Syntagma Sq and Odhos Ermou opens out into a small square on which there is the lovely Church of Kapnikarea (*Tmr* 6D4). Continuing eastwards, the shops become smarter with a preponderance of fashion stores whilst parallel to Ermou St is Odhos Ploutonos Kteka, which becomes Odhos Mitropoleos. Facing east, on the right is the city's Greek Orthodox Cathedral, Greek

Mitropolis. The Church was built about 1850, from the materials of 70 old churches, to the design of four different architects resulting, not unnaturally, in a building of a rather 'strange' appearance. Alongside and to the south is the diminutive medieval Church, Little Mitropolis or Agios Eleftherios, dating back to at least the twelfth century but which has materials, reliefs and building blocks probably originating from the sixth century AD. A little further on is the intriguing and incongruous site of a small Byzantine church, built over and around by a modern office block, the columns of which tower above and beside the tiny building.

Leaving Syntagma Sq by the north-east corner, along Vassilissis Sofias, and turning left at Odhos Irodou Attikou, runs into:

Kolonaki Square (*Tmr* 7F4) The most fashionable square in the most fashionable area of Athens, around which most of the foreign embassies are located. *The British Council* is located on the square, as are some relatively expensive cafes, restaurants and boutiques.

To the north of Kolonaki, across the pretty orange tree planted Dexameni Sq, is the southernmost edge of **Mt Lycabettus** (*Tmr* F/G3). Access to the summit can be made on foot, by a number of steep paths, the main one of which, a stepped footpath, advances from the north end of Loukianou St, beyond Odhos Kleomenous. A little to the east, at the top of Ploutarchou St, which breaks into a sharply rising flight of steps, is the cable car funicular railway. This runs in a 700ft long tunnel, emerging near to the nineteenth-century chapel, which caps the fir tree-covered mountain, alongside a modern and luxuriously expensive restaurant. There are also some excellent toilets. The railway service runs continuously as follows:
Winter: Wednesday, Saturday, Sunday 0845-0015 hrs; Thursday 1030-0015 hrs; Monday, Tuesday, Friday 0930-0015 hrs.
Summer: As for winter but opening hours extend to 0100 hrs every day. The trip costs 65 drs one-way and 100 drs for a return ticket.

A more relaxed climb, passing the open air theatre, can be made from the north end of Lycabettus.

The topmost part of the mountain, where the funicular emerges, is surprisingly small if not doll-like. The spectacular panorama that spreads out to the horizon, the stupendous views from far above the roar of the Athens traffic, is best seen in the early morning or late afternoon. Naturally the night hours are the time to see the city's lights.

Leaving Plateia Kolonaki from the south corner and turning right at Vassilissis Sofias, sally's forth to the north corner of:-

The National Garden (Ethnikos Kipos) (*Tmr* E5) Here peacocks, waterfowl and songbirds blend with a profusion of shrubbery, subtropical trees, ornamental ponds, various busts and cafe tables through and around which thread neat gravel paths.

To the south of the gardens are the Zappeion Exhibition Halls. To the north-west, the Greek Parliament buildings, the old Royal Palace and the Tomb or Monument to the Unknown Warrior, guarded by the traditionally costumed Evzones, the Greek equivalent of the British Buckingham Palace Guards (*See* **Places of Interest, A to Z**). South-east of the National Gardens is the Olympic Stadium erected in 1896, on the site of the original stadium, built in 330 BC, and situated in a valley of the Arditos Hills. South-west across Leoforos Olgas are the Olympic swimming pool and the Tennis and Athletic Club. To the west of these sporting facilities is the isolated gateway known as the Arch of Hadrian overlooking the busy traffic junction of Leoforos Olgas and Leoforos Amalias. Through the archway, the remains of the

Temple of Olympian Zeus are outlined, 15 only of the original 104 Corinthian columns remain standing.

Leaving Hadrian's Arch, westwards along Odhos Dionysiou Areopagitou leads to the south side of:-

The Acropolis (Akropoli) (Tmr C5) A 10-acre rock rising 750 ft above the surrounding city and surmounted by the Parthenon Temple, built in approximately 450 BC, the Propylaia Gateway, the Temple to Athena Nike and the triple Temple of Erechtheion. Additionally, there has been added the modern Acropolis Museum, discreetly tucked away, almost out of sight.

At the bottom of the southern slope are the Theatre of Dionysos, originally said to seat up to 30,000 but more probably 17,000, and the smaller, second century AD, Odeion of Herodes Atticus, which has been restored and is used for plays and concernts during the summer festival. It is thought provoking to consider that the Dionysos Odeion is the original theatre where western world drama, as we know it, originated.

The west slope leads to the Hill of Areopagos (Areios Pagos) where, in times of yore, a council of noblemen dispensed supreme judgements. Across Apostolou Pavlou St lie the other tree covered hills of Filopapou (Philopappos/Mouseion), or Hill of Muses, from whence the views are far-reaching and outstanding; Pnyx (Pnyka), where The Assembly once met and a *son et lumiere* is now held, and the Asteroskopeion (Observatory), or the Hill of Nymphs, whereon stands, surprise, surprise, an observatory.

Descending from the Asteroskopeion towards and across Apostolou Pavlou St is:-

The (Greek) Agora (Tmr B/C4) The gathering place from whence the Athenians would have approached the Acropolis. This marketplace cum civic centre is now little more than rubble, but the glory that once was is recreated by a model.

Nearby the Temple of Hephaistos or Thission (Theseion) sits on a small hill overlooking the Agora and to one side is the reconstructed marketplace, Stoa Attalus, the cost of which was met from private donations raised by American citizens.

A short distance to the east of the Greek Agora is the site of:-

The Roman Forum (or Agora) (Tmr C5) Close by is the Tower of the Winds (Tmr 8C5) a remarkable octagonal tower, probably built in the first century BC and which served as a combination water clock, sundial and weather vane. Early descriptions say the building was topped off with a bronze weather vane represented by the mythological Triton complete with a pronged trident. The carved eight gods of wind can be seen, as can traces of the corresponding sundials, but no interior mechanism remains and the building is now used as a store for various stone antiquities.

A short distance to the north-west is an area known as **The Keramikos** (Tmr B4), a cemetery or graveyard, containing the Street of the Tombs, a funeral avenue laid out about 400 BC.

In a north-easterly direction from Keramikos along Pireos St, via Eleftherias Sq Bus terminal (Tmr 9C3), turning right down Evripidou St, across Athinas and Eolou Streets, leads to:-

Klafthmonos Square (Klathmonos)(Tmr 10D3/4) Supposedly the most attractive Byzantine Church in Athens, Aghii Theodori, is positioned in the west corner of the square.

Looking north-east across Stadiou St, up Korai St and across Panepistimiou Ave, reveals an imposing range of neo-classical buildings (*Tmr* 11D/E3/4), fronted by formal gardens. These comprise the University flanked by, to the left (facing), the National Library, and to the right, the Academy. Behind and running parallel to Stadiou and Panepistimiou, is Akadimias St, on which is another Bus terminal. Just off Akadimias St, in Massalias St, is the Hellenic-American Union, many of whose facilities are open to the general public. These include an English and music library, as well as a cafeteria.

North-west of Klafthmonos Sq, to the left of Eolou St, is:-

Kotzia Square(*Tmr* D3) A very large plateia around which, on Sunday at least, a profusion of flower sellers' stalls circle the square.

The once paved area has now been dug up by archaeologists who have unearthed a veritable treasure trove of ancient Athens city walls. At the time of writing the fate of the site is in the hands of the opposing and seemingly irreconcilable tugs of the modernists, who have a vision of a vast underground car park, and the traditionalists, who, quite rightly, wish to see the dig preserved for posterity.

Fokionos Negri Actually a street, if not an avenue, rather than a square but somewhat distant from the city centre almost in the suburbs to the north, and usually just off the street plans of Athens. To reach Fokionos Negri from Omonia Sq, proceed up 28 (Ikosiokto) Oktovriou, which runs into Patission St, on past the National Archaeological Museum and Green Park (Pedion Areos), both on the right, to where Agiou Meletiou St runs across Patission St. Fokionos Negri starts as a fairly narrow sidestreet to the right, but widens out into a tree lined, short, squat avenue with a wide, spacious, centre pedestrian way once gravelled but now subject to extensive resurfacing. Supposedly the *Dolce Vita* or *Via Veneto* of Athens but not out of the ordinary, if quiet wealth is normal. Extremely expensive cafes edge the square halfway up on the right and it certainly becomes extremely lively after nightfall.

Numbers 5, 11, 12 or 13 trolley-bus, going north, trundle past the turning.

THE ACCOMMODATION & EATING OUT
The Accommodation On the islands the haul of accommodation includes even 'E' Class hotels but in Athens I have erred on the side of caution and stuck with 'B', 'C' and some better 'D' class hotels and pensions. No doubt there are some acceptable Class 'E' hotels but....

On Adrianou St (*Tmr* D5) (Plaka district) are a few very cheap dormitories and students' hostels, where a certain amount of rooftop sleeping is allowed, costing upwards of 350 drs per night. Unless set well back from the main road, a set of earmuffs or plugs is almost obligatory to ensure a good night's sleep.

On a cautionary note, since the end of 1981 the Greek authorities have been closing a number of the more 'undesirable', unlicensed hotels, so a particular favourite overnight stop from years gone by may no longer be in business.

Most of the hotel charges listed in this book are priced at the 1986 rates but these will average out for 1987 as follows:

Class	Single	Double	
A	5200-7200	7500-9500	en suite bathroom
B	3300-6700	4600-8700	& breakfast included
C	2200-4300	3500-5650	sharing bathroom and
D	900-1300	1400-2000	room rate only

SYNTAGMA AREA (*Tmr* 1D/E4/5)
Festos Guest House (*Tmr* D/E5) 18 Filellinon St   Tel. 323-2455
Directions: From Syntagma Sq, walk up the rise of Odhos Filellinon past a number of cut-price ticket joints and very nearly opposite Ag Nikodimos Church, on the right.

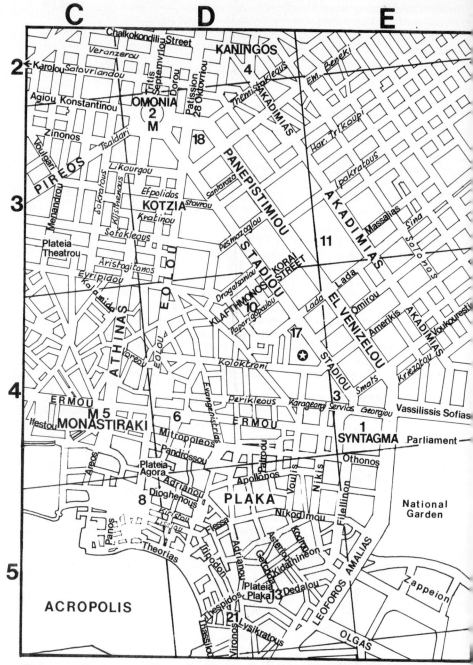

Illustration 5   Athens City Inset – The Plaka

Ethnic guest house with dormitories, triples and quadruplet rooms working out at between 350 and 500 drs per person. For the indiscriminately young at heart!

Hotel Cleo (Cleopatra)*(Tmr* D4) 3 Patroou St   Tel 322-9053
Directions: Leaving Syntagma Sq, walk down Mitropoleos St, towards Monastiraki Sq and take the fourth turning left.
   Well recommended if threadbare. Ground floor dormitory, free baggage store. Double rooms from 1600-2500 drs.
NB. The owners also have a guest house nearby in 18 Apollonos St.

Pension John's Place *(Tmr* D4) (Class C) 5 Patroou St   Tel 322-9719
Directions: As for *Hotel Cleo* above.
   Not surprisingly, the affable old Papa is named John. Well looked after accommotion with singles from 900 drs and doubles from 1300 drs, naturally sharing bathroom facilities.

George's Guest House *(Tmr* D4) (Class B) 46 Nikis St.   Tel 322-6474
Directions: From Syntagma Sq, walk west along Mitropoleos St and turn down the first left-hand turning and the Guest House is on the right, beyond the first sidestreet.
   Calls itself a *Youth Hostel with student prices*. Recommended by four Texas college girls, met on the train to Patras some years ago now and whose first stop in Greece was this guest house. Shared bathroom and hot water in the evening, if you are quick. Doubles from 1200 drs.

Hotel Kimon *(Tmr* D5) (Class D) 27 Appollonos   Tel 323-5223
Directions: Midway on Appollonos St, one block down from Mitropoleos St.
   Old but renovated with all rooms sharing the bathrooms. Single rooms start off at 800 drs increasing to 1000 drs whilst double rooms start at 1000 drs rising to 1200 drs.

YMCA (XAN) *(Tmr* E4) 28 Omirou St   Tel 362-6970
Directions: From the north-east corner of Syntagma Sq proceed up Panepistimiou St, take the third turning right and across Akadimias Avenue, on the right.
   Closed for some years for renovations and may open in 1987..... then again it may not.

YWCA (XEN) *(Tmr* E4) 11 Amerikis St   Tel 362-4291
Directions: All as above but second turning off Panepistimiou St and on the left.
   Apart from accommodation there is a cafe serving sandwiches, a hairdressing salon, library and laundry facilities. Singles from 780 drs and shared rooms 700 drs per head.

OMONIA AREA *(Tmr* 2D3)
Any hotel or pension rooms facing Omonia Square must be regarded as very noisy.
Hotel Omonia *(Tmr* D3) (Class C) 4 Omonia Sq   Tel 523-7210
Directions: Just stand on Omonia Sq, swivel on your heels and on the north side of the Square.
   The reception is on the first floor, as is a cafe-bar and terrace, overlooking the square and its action. Modern but 'worn international' look to the place. Clients may well have to take demi-pension terms. A double room en suite costs from 1500 drs, breakfast 200 drs and a meal from 900 drs.

Hotel Banghion *(Tmr* D3) (Class C) 18b Omonia Sq.   Tel 324-2259
Directions: As for *Hotel Omonia*, but south side of the square.
   Elegant and ageing. From 1950 drs for a double room sharing a bathroom, increasing to 2400 drs (16th July - 30th Sept), with breakfast available at 230 drs.

Hotel Carlton (*Tmr* D3) (Class C) 7 Omonia Sq. Tel 522-3201
Directions: As for *Hotel Omonia*.
    Very Greek provincial and old fashioned. Single rooms cost 900 drs and double rooms 1100 drs, both sharing a bathroom.

Hotel Europa (*Tmr* D2) (Class C) 7 Satovriandou St. Tel 522-3081
Directions: North of Omonia Sq and the second main street up, lying east/west. This if often listed as Chateaubriandou St but the local authorities either have, or have not, been notified of the change. Whatever, the street is now a pedestrian precinct.
    Another 'Greek provincial' hotel, the remarkably ancient lift of which creaks its way up and down to the various floors. The rooms are adequate, there is even a wardrobe and the floors are covered with brown linoleum. To use the shower the concierge must be asked for the relevant key, in mime if a guest's Greek is sketchy as the staff's knowledge of English is very limited. When produced, the key might well be adjudged large enough to open the doors of the Bastille. Weighed down by this instrument, the moment of truth is about to dawn, for when the door is opened, sheer disbelief may well be the first reaction, especially if it is the first ever stopover in Athens, as it was mine years ago. A cavernous and be-cobwebbed room reveals plumbing that beggars description. Enough to say the shower is most welcome, even if the lack of a point to anchor the shower head, whilst trying to soap oneself down, requires interesting body contortions. The rate for a single room is 900 drs and for a double is 1400 drs with shared bathrooms.

Hotel Alma (*Tmr* D2/3) (Class C) 5 Dorou Tel 524-0858
Directions: Dorou St runs north from the north-east corner of Omonia Sq.
    Modern and the rooms with a balcony are on the seventh and eighth floors. From 2200 drs for a double room with breakfast costing 200 drs.

Hotel Parnon (*Tmr* D2) (Class C) 20 Tritis Septemvriou/21 Chalkokondili
Tel. 523-0014
Directions: North of Omonia Sq on the junction of Tritis Septemvriou and Chalkokondili St.
    Modern and noisy. A double room with bath and room service costs 2500 drs (April-October) and a breakfast 350 drs.

Hotel Eva (*Tmr* C2) (Class D) 31 Victoros Ougo Tel. 522-3079
Directions: West of Omonia, parallel to and two blocks back from Ag. Konstantinou.
    Well recommended with single rooms from 1000 drs and double rooms 1700 drs, both with en suite bathrooms. Breakfast costs 200 drs.

Hotel Marina (*Tmr* C3) (Class C) 13 Voulgari Tel. 523-7832/3
Directions: South-west from Omonia along Odhos Pireos and 4th turning to the right.
    Single rooms cost from 800 drs, double rooms 1200 drs, both sharing the bathroom, while rooms with en suite bathrooms cost 1100 drs and 1500 drs respectively. Breakfast is charged at 200 drs.

Hotel Vienna (*Tmr* C3) (Class C) 20 Pireos Tel. 524-9143
Directions: South-west of Omonia Sq.
    New, clean and noisy, at about 2800 drs for a double room en suite, in the early summer, and a breakfast costs 200 drs.

Hotel Athinea (*Tmr* C2) (Class C) 9 Vilara Tel. 523-3884
Directions: Westwards along Ag. Konstantinou and situated on one side of the small square of Agiou Konstantinou.
    Old but beautifully positioned although cabaret night life may intrude. A restaurant and cake shop are close by as is a taxi rank. A single room starts off at 1600 drs and a double 2100 drs en suite. Breakfast is priced at 250 drs.

Hotel Pythagorion (*Tmr* C2/3) (Class C) 28 Ag. Konstantinou   Tel. 524-2811
Directions: West of Omonia Sq.
A single room from 1300 drs and a double room from 1800 drs, both with bath. Breakfast costs 200 drs and lunch/dinner from 700 drs.

Hotel Florida (*Tmr* C3) (Class C) 25 Menandrou   Tel. 522-3214
Directions: Third turning left, south-west along Pireos St.
Single rooms from 950 drs and doubles 1500 drs both without a bathroom, whilst en suite cost 1140 drs and 1690 drs respectively. Breakfast 180 drs.

Hotel Alcestis (Alkistis) (*Tmr* C3) (Class C) 18 Plateia Theatrou   Tel. 321-9811
Directions: From Pireos St, south down either Sokratous or Menandrou Streets and across Odhos Sofokleous St.
Only open March to October. Despite its chromium-plated appearance, all glass and marble with a prairie-sized lobby awash with Americans, it is a Class C hotel in a commercial square. Popular, with double rooms from 2750 drs, breakfast 250 drs and lunch/dinner from 1000 drs.

MONASTIRAKI AREA (*Tmr* 5C4)
Hotel Tembi/Tempi (*Tmr* C/D4) (Class D) 29 Eolou (Aiolu/Aeolou)   Tel. 321-3175
Directions: A main street north of Ermou St, opposite the Church of Ag. Irini.
Pleasant rooms with singles sharing the bathroom start at 950 drs rising to 1200 drs (1st June - 30th Sept). Double rooms sharing cost from 1200 drs and en suite 1400 drs advancing to 1400 drs and 1600 drs respectively.

Hotel Ideal (*Tmr* C/D4) (Class D) 39 Eolou/2 Voreou Sts.   Tel. 321-3195
Directions: On the left of Eolou, walking up from Odhos Ermou, and on the corner with Voreou St.
A perfect example of a weather-worn, 19th century, Athens neo-classical building complete with an old fashioned, metal and glass canopy entrance and matchbox sized, wrought iron balconies. The accommodation lives up to all that the exterior promises. The management are helpful, there is a telephone, TV room, a bar and luggage can be stored. Tourist information is freely available as are battered paperbacks for guests. The bathroom facilities are shared but there is 24 hour hot water – promise!

Hotel Hermion (*Tmr* C/D4) (Class C) 66c Ermou St   Tel. 321-2753
Directions: East of Monastiraki, adjacent to Kapnikarea Church and Square (*Tmr* 6D4).
Old but clean with the reception up the stairs. All rooms share bathrooms with the single room rate starting off at 900 drs and the double rooms 1800 drs.

Hotel Attalos (*Tmr* C3/4) (Class C) 29 Athinas   Tel. 321-2801
Directions: North from Monastiraki Sq.
Recommended to us by a splendidly eccentric English lady artist who should know – she has been visiting Greece for some 20 years. Between 16th March - 30th June singles cost 1485 drs and doubles, with a shower, 1815 drs rising to 1600 drs and 2000 drs (1st July - 30th Sept). Breakfast is charged at 230 drs.

Hotel Cecil (*Tmr* C3/4) (Class D) 39 Athinas   Tel. 321-7079
Directions: North from Monastiraki Sq and two buildings up from the Kalamida St turning on the left-hand side. This is the other side of the road from a very small chapel, incongruously stuck on the pavement. The 'informative' sign outside the hotel is no help.
Clean looking with a single room costing 1100 drs and a double 1600 drs. The bathrooms are shared.

PLAKA/METZ STADIUM AREAS (*Tmr* D5 & D/E6)
The Plaka is rich in accommodation, as it is in most things!
Hotel Phaedra (*Tmr* D5) (Class D) 4 Adrianou/16 Herephontos   Tel. 323-8461
Directions: Situated close by a multi-junction of various streets including Lysikratous, Galanou, Adrianou and Herephontos, opposite the Byzantine Church of Ag. Aikaterini and its small, attractive gardens.

Pretty area by day, noisy by night. Family hotel with a ground floor bar. Double rooms start off at 1400 drs and rise to 3000 drs. Breakfast costs 200 drs.

Students' Inn (*Tmr* D5) 16 Kidathineon St   Tel. 324-4808
Directions: On the left of Kidathineon St, walking up from the Adrianou St junction, and almost opposite the garden of the Japanese eating house.

Hostelish but recommended as good value with hot showers 'on tap' (sorry) and an English-speaking owner. There is a roof-top, a passable courtyard, a snackbar, the use of a washing machine (which does not always work) and a baggage store costing 50 drs per day. The clean but basic rooms are complete with a rickety oil-cloth covered table and mug. Singles cost between 1200 drs and 1300 drs and doubles from 1500 drs to 1600 drs. The doors are locked at 0200 hrs.

Left off Kidathineon Street, climbing towards Syntagma Sq, is Odhos Kodrou on which are two clean pleasant hotels in a very pleasant area, the:
Hotel Adonis (*Tmr* D5) (Class B) 3 Kodrou   Tel. 324-9737
Directions: As above and on the right.

Actually a pension so the rates are not outrageous. All rooms have en suite bathrooms with singles starting off at 1450 drs and doubles 1600 drs. rising respectively to 1750 drs and 2150 drs (1st July - 30th Sept).

Acropolis House (*Tmr* D5) (Class B) 6-8 Kodrou   Tel. 322-2344
Directions: As above and on the left.

Highly recommended and once again officially classified as a pension with a choice of rooms sharing or complete with en suite bathrooms. Single room rates commence at 1520 drs and doubles 1840 drs rising to 2100 drs and 2540 drs (16th June - 30th Sept).

Closer to Kidathineon St, and on the right is the:
Kouros Pension (*Tmr* D5) (Class C) 11 Kodrou   Tel. 322-7431
Directions: As above.

Rather more provincial than the two establishments detailed above, which lack of sophistication is reflected in the lower prices (and standards). All rooms share the bathrooms and the single room rate starts at 800 drs and a double 1110 drs climbing to the dizzy heights(!) of 1020 drs and 1600 drs (1st May - 30th Sept).

Hotel Solonion (*Tmr* D5) (Class E) 11 Sp Tsangari/Dedalou   Tel. 322-0008/3080
Directions: To the right of Kidathineon St (facing Syntagma Sq) between Dedalou St and Leoforos Amalias. Odhos Tsangari is a continuation of Asteriou St.

Run by a rather stern faced lady who is assisted by a varied collection of part time assistants to run the old, faded but refurbished building. If a guest strikes lucky the night porter will be a delightful old boy who was once a merchant in the Greek community resident in Turkey, and was caught up in the huge population resettlement of 1922/23. The accommodation is 'student provincial', the rooms being high ceilinged and the rather dodgy floorboards are hidden beneath brown linoleum. The bathrooms are distinctly ethnic and Victorian in style but hot water is promised all day. On a fine day......it is possible to espy the Acropolis... well a bit of it. No single rooms are available, a double room sharing the bathroom costs from 1200 drs, including one bath a day, rising to 1400 drs (1st April - 15th Oct).

Close by the *Hotel Solonion* are the:-

Hotel Kekpoy (Cecrops) (*Tmr* D5) (Class D) 13 Tsangari   Tel. 322-3080
Directions: On the same side as and similar to the *Solonion* but a building or two towards Leoforos Amalias.

All rooms share the bathroom with singles costing 950 drs and doubles 1200 drs.

Hotel Phoebus (Fivos) (*Tmr* D5) (Class C) Asteriou/12 Peta   Tel. 322-0142
Directions: Back towards Kidathineon, on the corner of the Asteriou and Peta Streets.

Rather more up-market than the 3 previously listed hotels. A double room en suite costs 2400 drs rising to 2900 drs (1st June - 30th Sept) and breakfast 250 drs.

A few side streets towards the Acropolis is the:-

Hotel Ava (*Tmr* D5) 9 Lysikratous St   Tel. 323-6618
Directions: As above.

I have no personal experience but the establishment has been mentioned as a possibility and is in an excellent, central but quiet situation although it is rather expensive. All rooms have en suite bathrooms, are heated and air conditioned. Single rooms cost from 2000 drs and doubles from 3000 drs. There are family suites complete with kitchen and regrigerator (sic).

New Clare's House (*Tmr* E6) (Class C Pension) 24 Sorvolou St   Tel. 922-2288
Directions: Rather uniquely, the owners have had a large compliments slip printed with a pen and ink drawing on the face, and on the reverse side, directions in Greek saying: *Show this to the taxi driver*. This includes details of the location, south of the Stadium, on Sorvolou St between Charvouri and Voulgareos Streets. The pension is on the right, halfway down the reverse slope with the description *white building with the green shutters*. From Syntagma proceed south down the sweep of Leoforos Amalias keeping to the main avenues hugging the Temple of Olympian Zeus and along Odhos Diakou. Where Diakou makes a junction with Vouliagmenis and Ardittou Avenues, Odhos Anapafseos leads off in a south-east direction and Sorvolou St 'crescents' off to the left. Trolley buses 2, 4, 11 & 12 drop travellers off by the Stadium. It is quite a steep climb up Sorvolou St, which breaks into steps, to the pretty and highly recommended area of Metz (highly regarded by Athenians that is). Plus points are that the narrow nature of the lanes, which suddenly become steps, keeps the traffic down to a minimum and the height of the hill raises it above the general level of smog and pollution.

The pleasant, flat fronted pension is on the right and has a marble floor entrance hall. Inside, off to the left, is a large reception/lounge/bar/breakfast/common room and to the right, the lift. The self confident English speaking owner presides over matters from a large desk in the reception area and is warily helpful. The lady staff receptionists do not exactly go wild in an orgy of energy sapping activity, tending to indulge in a saturnalia of TV watching. Guests in the meantime can help themselves to bottles of beer (80 drs) and Coke from the bar, paying when convenient to them and the receptionist. Despite the inferred aura of excellence the usual collection of faults crop up from time to time including: cracked loo seats; no hot water, despite being assured that there is 24 hours hot water (and for longer no doubt were there more hours in the day!); missing locking mechanism on the lavatory door; toilets having to be flushed using a piece of string and the television on the blink. I do not mean to infer that these irritating defects occur all at once – just one or two, every so often. Single rooms sharing a bathroom cost 2000 drs and en suite 2500 drs while double rooms sharing cost 2500 drs and en suite 3300 drs. Incidentally where the well appointed bathrooms are shared, the pleasant rooms only have to go fifty-fifty with one other room. The charges, which include breakfast 'with warm bread every day', may at first impression (and for that matter second and third impression) appear on the expensive side. The 'pain' might be eased by the realisation that the 4th floor has a balcony and a self-catering kitchen, complete with cooker and a fridge, and the 5th floor a laundry room with an iron and 2 rooftop clothes lines. These facilities must of course be taken into account when weighing up comparative prices. The management create an atmosphere that will suit the young, very well behaved student and the older traveller but not exuberant rowdies. Hands are smacked if guests lay around eating a snack on the front steps, hang washing out of the windows or make a noise, especially between the hours of 1330 and 1700 and after 2330 hrs. You know, lights out boys and no smoking in the dorms. *Clare's House* was originally recommended by pension owner Alexis on the island of Kos but in recent years has been included in one or two of the smaller tour companies' brochures for the Athens overnight stop. Certainly an old friend of ours, Peter, who 'has to put up with yachting round the Aegean waters during the summer months', almost always spends some of his winter Athens months at Clare's and swears by the place.

Before leaving the area there is an intriguing possibility, accommodation that is, in a very quiet street edging the west side of the Stadium.
Joseph's House Pension (*Tmr* E6) (Class C) 13 Markou Moussourou   Tel. 923-1204
Directions: From the region of Hadrian's Arch/the Temple of the Olympian Zeus (*Tmr* D6) proceed up Avenue Ardittou in a north-easterly direction towards the Stadium. Odhos Markou Moussourou climbs steeply off to the right, immediately prior to the wooded hillside Arditos. The pension is on the left, beyond Meletiou Riga St. On the other hand it is just as easy to follow the directions to *Clare's House* and proceed east along Charvouri St until it bumps into Markou Moussourou.
   The bathrooms are shared with single rooms charged at 700 drs and doubles at 950 drs.

THISSION AREA (THESION) (*Tmr* B/C4/5)
First south-bound Metro stop after Monastiraki and a much quieter area.
Hotel Phedias (*Tmr* B4) (Class C) 39 Apostolou Pavlou   Tel. 345-9511
Directions: South of the Metro station.
   Modern and friendly with double rooms from 2200 drs and breakfast 250 drs per head.

OLYMPIC OFFICE AREA (*Tmr* C6)
Hotel Karayannis (*Tmr* C6) (Class C) 94 Leoforos Sygrou   Tel. 921-5903
Directions: On the corner of Odhos Byzantiou and Leoforos Sygrou, opposite the side exit of the Olympic terminal office.
   'Interesting', tatty and noisy, but very necessary for travellers arriving really late at the terminal. Rooms facing the main road should be avoided. The Athenian traffic, which appears to roar up and down non-stop round the clock, gives every appearance of making the journey along Leoforos Sygrou via the hotel balconies, even three or four storeys up. There are picturesque views of the Acropolis from the breakfast and bar rooftop terrace, even if they are through a maze of television aerials. Single rooms with en suite bathroom cost 1310 drs, a double room sharing 1650 drs, and a double room en suite 1780 drs. Breakfast for one costs 220 drs. Best to splash out for the en suite rooms as the hotel's shared lavatories are of a 'thought provoking' nature with a number of the unique features detailed under the general description of bathrooms in CHAPTER 4.

Whilst in this area it would be inappropriate not to mention the:-
Super-Bar Restaurant Odhos Faliron
Directions: As for the *Hotel Karayannis* but behind the Olympic office.
   Now not inexpensive but very conveniently situated, even if it is closed on Sundays. Snackbar food with 2 Nes meh gala, a toasted cheese and ham sandwich and boiled egg costing 280 drs. On this occasion I actually wanted toast....

Youth Hostel 57 Kypselis St and Agiou Meletiou 1   Tel. 822-5860
Directions: Located in the Fokionos Negri area of North Athens. Proceed along 28 (Ikosiokto) Oktovriou/Patission Street from Omonia Sq, beyond Pedion Areos Park to Ag Meletiou St. Turn right and follow until the junction with Kypselis St. Trolley buses No. 3, 5, 11, 12 & 13 make the journey.

This is *The Official Youth Hostel* and does fulfil the requirements of those who require very basic, cheap accommodation, albeit in dormitories. The overnight charge is 300/500 drs.

Taverna Youth Hostel (*Tmr* G2) 1 Drossi St & 87 Leoforos Alexandra Tel. 646-3669
Directions: East of Pedion Aeros Park along Leoforos Alexandras almost as far as the junction with Ippokratous St. Odhos Drossi is on the left. It is possible to catch trolley-bus No. 7 from Panepistimiou Avenue or No. 8 from Kanigos Sq (*Tmr* 4D2) or Akadimias St.

Actually a taverna that 'sprouts' an 'unofficial Youth Hostel' for the summer months only.

If only to receive confirmation regarding the spurious Youth Hostels, it may be worth visiting the:-
YHA Head Office (*Tmr* D3/4) 4 Dragatsaniou   Tel. 323-4107
Directions: The north side of Plateia Klafthmonos in a street on the left-hand side of Stadiou St.

Only open Monday - Friday, 0900 - 1500 hrs. They advise of vacancies in the youth hostels and issue international youth hostel cards.

LARISSIS STATION AREA (*Tmr* B/C1)
See **Trains, A to Z.**

CAMPING
Sample daily site charges per person vary between 200-300 drs (children half-price) and the hire of a tent between 150-300 drs.
Sites include the following:-

Distance from Athens	Site name	Amenities
8 km	**Athens Camping.** 198 Athinon Ave. On the road to Dafni (due west of Athens). Tel. 581-4113	Open all year, 25 km from the sea. Bar, shop and showers.
10 km	**Dafni Camping.** Dafni. On the Athens to Corinth National Road. Tel. 581-1562	Open all year. 5 km from the sea. Bar, shop, showers and kitchen facilities.

For the above: Bus 853, Athens - Elefsina, departs Koumoundourou Sq/Deligeorgi St (*Tmr* C2/3) every 20 mins between 0510 - 2215 hrs.

14.5 km	**Patritsia.** Kato Kifissia, N. Athens. Tel. 801-1900 Closed 'temporarily' for 1986, query 1987?	Open June-October. Bar, shop, showers, laundry and kitchen facilities.
16 km	**Nea Kifissia.** Nea Kifissia, N. Athens. Tel. 807-5544	Open April - October. 20 km from the sea. Bar, shop, showers, swimming pool and laundry.
18 km	**Dionyssiotis.** Nea Kifissia, N. Athens. Tel. 807-1494	Open all year.
25 km	**Papa-Camping.** Zorgianni Ag. Stefanos. Tel. 803-3446	Open June-October. 25 km from the sea. Laundry, bar and kitchen facilities.

For the above (sited on or beside the Athens National Road, north to Lamia): Lamia bus from 260 Liossion St (*Tmr* C1/2), every hour from 0615 to 1915 and at 2030 hrs.

35 km	**Marathon Camping.** Kaminia, Marathon. NE of Athens. Tel. 0294-55577	On a sandy beach, Open March to 31st October. Showers, bar, restaurant and kitchen facilities.
35 km	**Nea Makri.** 156 Marathonos Ave, Nea Makri. NE of Athens just south of Marathon. Tel. 0294-92719	Open April - October. 220m from the sea.. Sandy beach, laundry, bar and shop.

For the above: The bus from Odhos Mavrommateon, Plateia Egyptou (*Tmr* D1), every ½ hour from 0530 to 2200 hrs.

26 km	**Cococamp.** Rafina. East of Athens. Tel. 0294-23413	Open all year. On the beach, rocky coast. Laundry, bar, showers, kitchen facilities, shop and restaurant.
29 km	**Kokkino Limanaki Camping.** Kokkino Limanaki, Rafina. Tel. 0294-31602	On the beach. Open April - October.
29 km	**Rafina Camping.** Rafina. East of Athens. Tel. 0294-23118	Open May - October. 4 km from the sandy beach. Showers, bar, laundry, restaurant and shop.

For the above: The Rafina bus from Mavrommateon St, Plateia Egyptou (*Tmr* D1). Twenty-nine departures from 0550 to 2200 hrs.

20 km	**Voula Camping.** 2 Alkyonidon St, Voula. Just below Glyfada and the Airport. Tel. 985-2712	Open all year. On the sandy beach. Showers, laundry, shop and kitchen facilities.
27 km	**Varkiza Beach Camping.** Varkiza. Coastal road Athens-Vouliagmenis-Sounion. Tel. 897-3613	Open all year. By a sandy beach. Bar, shop, supermarket, taverna, laundry and kitchen facilities.
60 km	**Sounion Camping.** Sounion. Tel. 0292-39358	Open all year. By a sandy beach. Bar, shop, laundry, kitchen facilities and a taverna.
76 km	**Vakhos Camping.** Assimaki near Sounion. On the Sounion to Lavrion road. Tel. 0292-39263	Open June - September. On the beach.

For the above: Buses from Mavrommateon St, Plateia Egyptou (*Tmr* D1) every hour from 0630 to 1730 hrs. Note to get to *Vakhos Camping* catch the Sounion bus via Markopoulo and Lavrion.

The Eating Out Where to dine out is a very personal choice and in a city the size of Athens there are so many restaurants and tavernas to choose from that only a few recommendations are made. In general, steer clear of Luxury and Class A hotel dining rooms, restaurants offering international cuisine and tavernas with Greek music and/or dancing* which may be very good but are usually on the expensive side.

Note the reference to Greek dancing and music is not derogatory – only an indication that it is often the case that standards of cuisine may not be any better and prices often reflect the 'overheads' attributable to the musicians. But See **Palia & Xynou Tavernas**.

In Athens and the larger, more cosmopolitan, provincial cities, it is usual taverna practice to round off prices, which proves a little disconcerting at first.

In despair it is noted that some restaurants and tavernas climbing the slopes of the Acropolis up Odhos Markou Avrilou, south of Eolou St, are allowing 'Chinese menu' style collective categories (A, B, C etc) to creep into their Greek menu listings.

PLAKA AREA (*Tmr* D5)
A glut of eating houses ranging from the very good and expensive, the very expensive and bad, to some inexpensive and very good.

Taverna Thespis 18 Thespidos St   Tel. 323-8242
Directions: On the right of a lane across the way from Kidathineon St, towards the

bottom or south-east end of Adrianou St.

Recommended and noted for its friendly service. The house retsina is served in metal jugs. A two hour slap-up meal of souvlaki, Greek salad, fried zucchini, bread and two carafes of retsina will cost in excess of 1600 drs for two.

Plaka Village 28 Kidathineon
Directions: In the block edged by the streets of Adrianou and Kidathineon.

An excellent souvlaki snackbar but to sit down costs an extra 16 drs per head. Price lists do not make this plain and the annoying habit can cause, at the least, irritation. This practice is also prevalent in the Omonia Square 'souvlaki arcade'. A large bottle of beer costs 80 drs, the home-made tzatziki is good, the service is quick and they even remain open Sunday lunchtimes.

ΟΥΖΕΡΙ Ο ΚΟΥΚΛΗΣ 14 Tripodon St   Tel. 324-7605
Directions: Up the slope from the Thespidos/Kydathineon junction, one to the left of Adrianou (facing Monastiraki Sq), and on the left. Distinguishing the establishment is not difficult as the 1st floor balcony is embellished with a large, stuffed bird and two big, antique record player horns mounted on the wrought iron balustrade.

The taverna, standing on its own, evokes a provincial country atmosphere. It is necessary to arrive early as the ouzerie is well patronised by the locals, which patronage is not surprising considering the inexpensive excellence of one or two of the standard dishes. One of these is the 'flaming sausages' which cook away on stainless steel plates set in front of the diner and are served up with a large bowl full of hors d'oeuvres at a cost of 1000 drs for two. Great value, very filling indeed but watch the napkins don't go up in flames!

Eden Taverna 3 Flessa St
Directions: Off Adrianou St, almost opposite Odhos Nikodimou, and on the left.

Mentioned because their menu includes many offerings that excellently cater (sorry) for vegetarian requirements. Open 1200 hrs to 0100 hrs every day except Tuesdays.

Stamatopoulos Palia Plakiotiki Taverna 26 Lissiou/Flessa Sts   Tel. 322-8722
Directions: Beyond the *Eden Taverna* on the right of the corner of Flessa and Lissiou Streets.

Claims to be one of Athens' oldest tavernas. Anne whose strong recommendation the Palia is, and taking my prejudices to heart, concedes that there is music. But here it is a major attraction in the shape of a huge, spherical man, with a name to match, Stavros Balagouras. He is the resident singer/accordionist/electric pianist and draws tourists and 'real' Greeks alike with his dignified and heartfelt performance. Besides traditional, old national songs there is year-round dancing, if customers feel like it, on the 1 square metre floor space! The taverna is particularly Greek and lively at festival times, added to which the food is good and much cheaper than similar establishments. Cheese and meat dishes with salad and wine for two costs just 1500 drs.

Platanos Taverna 4 Dioghenous St
Directions: Dioghenous St runs parallel to Odhos Adrianou St, at the Monastiraki Square end.

A conventional taverna serving inexpensive lunch and dinner. Closed Sundays.

Michiko Restaurant 27 Kidathineon St   Tel. 324-6851
Directions: On the right, beyond the junction with Asteriou St proceeding in a north-east direction (towards Syntagma Sq), close to a small square and church.

Japanese, if you must, and extremely expensive.

Xynou/Xynos 4 Arghelou Geronda (Angelou Geronta)   Tel. 322-1065
Directions: Left off the lower Plaka Square end of Kidathineon St (facing Syntagma Sq) and on the left, towards the far end of the pedestrian way. The unprepossessing entrance door is tucked away in the corner of a recess and can be missed.

One of the oldest, most highly rated Plaka tavernas and well patronised by Athenians. Evenings only and closed on Saturdays and Sundays. A friend advises me that it is now almost obligatory to book in advance although I have managed to squeeze a table for two early on in the evening.

Mention of its popularity with Athenians prompts me to stress these are well-heeled locals – you know shipowners, ambassadors and ageing playboys. Xynou is definitely on the 'hotel captains' list of recommended eateries and the tourists who eat here tend to look as if they have stepped off the stage-set of Dallas. But it is not surprising that the *cognoscente* gather here. Despite being in the heart of Athens, the single storey, shed like, roof tiled buildings evoke a rural ambience. The buildings edge two sides of the high wall enclosed gravel area, on which the chairs and tables are spread. The food is absolutely excellent and considering the location the prices are not that outrageous. A meal of two dolmades in lemon sauce, a plate of moussake, a lamb fricassee in lemon sauce, a tomato and cucumber salad, a bottle of kortaki retsina and bread for two costs 1530 drs. It seems a pity that the bread has to be charged at 50 drs but then the ample wine list does include an inexpensive retsina. Three guitarists serenade diners, the napkins are linen, and the service is first class. Readers are recommended to save up and try Xynou's at least once, an experience that will not be easily forgotten.

Plateia Agora is a lovely, elongated, chic Plaka Square formed at the junction of the bottom of Eolou and the top of Adrianou and Kapnikarea Streets. The square spawns a number of cafe-bar restaurants and these include the *Possidion* and *Appollon*, the canopied chairs and tables of which edge the street all the way round the neat, paved plateia. There is a spotless public lavatory at the top (Monastiraki) end. The *Appollon* has a particularly wide range of choice and clients can sit at the comfortable tables for an (expensive) hour or so over a coffee (100 drs), a fried egg breakfast (300 drs) or a full blown meal. Hope your luck is in and the organ grinder wanders through.

From the little square formed by a 'junction of the ways', adjacent to the Lycikrates Monument (*Tmr* 21D5), Odhos Vironos falls down towards the south Acropolis encircling avenue of Dionysiou/Areopagitou.

Snackbar Odhos Vironos
Directions: As above and on the right (Plaka behind one) of the street.
More a small 'doorway' souvlaki pita shop but small is indeed splendid.

Restaurant Olympia 20 Dionysiou Areopagitou
Directions: Proceed along Dionysiou Areopagitou from the junction with Odhos Vironos in a clockwise direction. The restaurant is on the right, close to the junction with Thassilou Lane (that incidentally climbs and bends back up to the top of Odhos Thespidos) hard up against the foot of the Acropolis. Between Thassilou Lane and the sun-blind-shaded lean-to butted on to the side of the restaurant, is a small grassed area and an underground Public toilet.

The prices seem reasonable and the place appears to portend good things but.... I can only report the promise was in reality disappointing. The double Greek salad (185 drs) was in truth only large enough for one, the moussaka (161 drs) was 'inactive', the kalamares were unacceptable and the roast potatoes (yes roast potatoes) were in actuality nothing more than dumpy wedges. Oh dear! They do serve a kortaki retsina for 92 drs.

STADIUM (PANGRATI) AREA (*Tmr* E/F6)
Karavitis Taverna (ΚΑΡΑΒΙΤΗΣ) 4 Pafsaniou (Paysanioy)
Directions: Beyond the Stadium (*Tmr* E/F6) going east (away from the Acropolis)
along Vassileos Konstantinou, and Pafsaniou is 3rd turning to the right. The taverna
is on the left.

A small, leafy tree shaded gravel square fronts the taverna which is so popular that
there is an extension across the street, through a pair of 'field gates'. Our friend Paul
will probably berate me (if he was less of a gentleman) for listing this gem. Unknown
to visitors but extremely popular with Athenians, more especially those who, when
college students, frequented this jewel in the Athens taverna crown. A meal for 4 of a
selection of dishes including lamb, beef in clay, giant haricot beans, garlic flavoured
meat balls, greens, tzatziki, 2 plates of feta cheese, aubergines, courgettes, bread
and 3 jugs of retsina from the barrel for some 2400 drs. Beat that. But some
knowledge of Greek is an advantage and the taverna is only open in the evening.

Instead of turning off Vassileos Konstantinou at Odhos Pafsaniou, take the next right
proceeding further eastwards.

ΜΑΓΕΜΕΝΟΣ ΑΥΛΟΣ (The Magic Flute) Odhos Aminda (Amynta)
Directions: As above and the restaurant is 20m up on the right.

Swiss dishes including fondue, schnitzels and salads. Despite being rather more
expensive than its near neighbours it is well frequented by Athenians including the
composer Hadzithakis (so Anne advises me).

Virinis Taverna, Archimedes St.
Directions: Before the side streets to the two restaurant/tavernas detailed above, the
2nd turning to the right off Vassileos Konstantinou, after the Stadium (*Tmr* E/F6)
proceeding in an easterly direction, is Odhos Eratosthenous which climbs up to
Plateia Plastira. To the right of the square is Archimedes Street. The taverna is about
a 100m along on the left. Incidentally, if returning to the centre of Athens it is possible
to continue along this street and drop down Odhos Markou Moussourou back to
Vassileos Konstantinou.

A good selection of bistro dishes at reasonable prices, including, for instance,
beef in wine sauce at a cost of 350 drs. Anne indicated I might find the place rather
'up market' as there were no souvlaki pitas on offer. Cheeky thing! It's only that I have
learnt through expensive experience over the years that in Greece gingham
tablecloths and French style menus tend to double the prices!

SYNTAGMA AREA (*Tmr* 1D/E4/5)
Corfu Restaurant 6 Kriezotou St   Tel. 361-3011
Directions: North of Syntagma Sq and first turning right off Panepistimiou (El.
Venizelou).

Extensive Greek and European dishes in a modern, friendly restaurant.

Delphi Restaurant 15 Nikis St   Tel. 323-4869
Directions: From the south-west corner of Syntagma Sq, east along Mitropoleos and
the first turning left.

Modern, reasonably priced food and friendly service. Extensive menu.

Sintrivani Restaurant 5 Filellinon St
Directions: South-west corner of Syntagma Sq and due south.

Garden restaurant serving a traditional menu at reasonable prices.

Vassillis Restaurant 14A Voukourestiou
Directions: North of Syntagma Sq and the second turning off Panepistimiou St to the
right along Odhos Smats and across Akadimias St.

Variety, in traditional surroundings.

Ideal Restaurant 46 Panepistimiou St.
Directions: Proceed up Panepistimiou from the north-east corner of Syntagma Sq and the restaurant is on the right.
Good food at moderate prices.

YWCA 11 Amerikis St
Directions: North-west up either Stadiou or Panepistimiou St and second or third road to the right, depending which street is used.
Cafeteria serving inexpensive sandwiches.

There are many cafes in and around Syntagma Square. Recommended, but expensive, is the:
Brazilian Coffee Cafe
Directions: Close by Syntagma Sq in Voukourestiou St.
Serves coffee, tea, toast, butter and jam, breakfast, ice-creams and pastries.

OMONIA AREA (*Tmr* 2D3)
Elliniki Taverna On the corner of Dorou and Satovriandou Streets.
Directions: North of Omonia Sq, along Dorou St and almost immediately on the left.
Good value, if a little showy.

Taverna Kostoyannus 37 Zaimi St
Directions: Leave Omonia northwards on 28 (Ikosiokto) Oktovriou, turn right at Odhos Stournara to the near side of the Polytechnic School, and Zaimi St is the second road along. The taverna is to the left approximately behind the National Archaeological Museum.
Good food, acceptable prices and comes well recommended. As in the case of many other Athenian tavernas, it is not open for lunch or on Sundays.

Snackbars
Probably the most compact, reasonably priced 'offerings' but in grubby surroundings, lie in the arcade between Dorou St and 28 (Ikosiokto) Oktovriou, off Omonia Sq. Here are situated cafes and stalls selling almost every variety of Greek convenience fast food. A 'standard'* souvlaki costs 70 drs and a 'spezial'*, or deluxe, 90 drs BUT do not sit down unless you wish to be charged an extra 15-20 drs per head. A beer costs 80 drs.
Note the 'standard' is a preheated slab of meat whilst the 'spezial' is the traditional, giro meat-sliced offering.

Cafes
Everywhere of course, but on Omonia Sq, alongside Dorou St and adjacent to the *Hotel Carlton*, is a magnificent specimen of the traditional kafeneion.
Greek men sip coffee and tumble their worry beads, as they must have done since the turn of the century.

Bretania Cafe
Directions: On Omonia Square beside the junction with Athinas St.
An excellent, very ethnic, very old fashioned Greek 'sticky' sweet shop which is more a galaktozacharoplasteion than a cafe. Renowned for its range of sweets, yoghurt and honey, cream and honey, rice puddings and so on, all served with sugar sweet bread and drinks until 0200 hrs every day.

Continuing on down Athinas St, beyond Plateia Kotzai, leads past the covered meat market building on the left and the:
'Meat Market' Tavernas
Directions: As above and towards the rear of the building. It has to be admitted it is necessary to pick one's way through piles of bones and general market detritus after dark.

Open 24 hours a day and a find for those who like to slum it in a less expensive establishment of some note.

LYCABETTUS (LYKAVITOS) AREA (*Tmr* F/G4)
As befits an expensive area, these listings are very expensive.

Je Reviens Restaurant 49 Xenokratous St
Directions: North-east from Kolonaki Sq, up Patriachou Ioakim St to the junction with and left on Marasli St, up a flight of steps until it crosses Xenokratous St.
French food. Creditable but expensive. Open midday and evenings.

L'Abreuvoir 51 Xenokratous St
Directions: As for *Je Reviens* as are the comments, but even more expensive.

Al Convento Restaurant (*Tmr* G4) 4 Anapiron   Tel. 723-9163
Directions: North-east from Kolonaki Sq along Patriarchou Ioakim to Marasli St. Turn left and then right along Odhos Souidias and Anapiron St is nearly at the end.

Bonanza Restaurant 14 Voukourestiou
Directions: From the north-west corner of Plateia Kolonaki, take Odhos Skoufa, which crosses Voukourestiou St.
Once known as the *Stage Coach*. Not only Wild West in decor, air-conditioned and serving American style food but very expensive with steaks as a house speciality. Why not go to the good old US of A? Lunch and evening meals, open 1200 to 1600 hrs and 1900 to 0100 hrs.

THE A TO Z OF USEFUL INFORMATION
AIRLINE OFFICES & TERMINUS (*Tmr* 12C6) Referred to in the introductory paragraphs, as well as under **The Accommodation**, the busy offices are to the left (facing Syntagma Sq), of the frantic Leoforos Sygrou. As with other Olympic facilities the office doubles as a terminus for airport buses arriving from and departing to the East and West Airports. Passengers who land up here should note that the most convenient, combined bus stop to, say Syntagma Square, the centre of Athens, is, (with the building behind one), across the busy thoroughfare and some 50m up the incline of Leoforos Sygrou. This 'hosts' any number of buses and trolley-buses while the stop directly across the road serves only one or two buses and no trolley-buses.

Aircraft Timetables. *See* CHAPTER 3 for general details of the airports described in this guide that are serviced from Athens and the individual chapters for details of the actual timetables.

BANKS (Trapeza – ТРАПЕΖА) Note that if a bank strike is under way (apparently becoming a natural part of the tourist season 'high jinks'), the **National Bank** on Syntagma Sq stays open and in business. However, it becomes more than usually crowded in these circumstances. Banks include the:
National Bank of Greece (*Tmr* 3D/E4) 2 Karageorgi Servias, Syntagma Sq.
All foreign exchange services: Monday to Thursday 0800 - 1400 hrs; Friday 0800 - 1330 hrs; Saturday, Sunday & holidays 0900 - 1600 hrs. Travellers' cheques & foreign cash exchange services: weekdays 0800 - 2000 hrs; Saturday, Sunday & holidays 0900 - 1600 hrs.
Ionian & Popular Bank (*Tmr* D/E4/5) 1 Mitropoleos St
Only open normal banking hours.
Commercial Bank of Greece (*Tmr* E4) 11 Panepistimiou (El. Venizelou)
Only open normal banking hours.
American Express (*Tmr* 1D/E4/5) 2 Ermou St, Syntagma Sq.   Tel. 324-4975/9
Carries out usual Amex office transactions and is open Monday to Thursday 0830 - 1400 hrs; Friday 0830 - 1330 hrs and Saturday 0830 - 1230 hrs.

BEACHES Athens is not on a river or by the sea, so to enjoy a beach it is necessary to leave the main city and travel to the suburbs by the sea. Very often these beaches are operated under the aegis of the NTOG, or private enterprise in association with a hotel. The NTOG beaches usually have beach huts, cabins, tennis courts, a playground and catering facilities. Entrance charges vary from 25-100 drs.

There are beaches and/or swimming pools at:

Paleon Faliron/ Faliro	A seaside resort	Bus No. 126: Departs from Odhos Othonos, south side of Syntagma Sq (*Tmr* E5).
Alimos	NTOG beach	Bus No. 133: Departs from Odhos Othonos, south side of Syntagma Sq (*Tmr* E5).
Glyfada (Glifada)	A seaside resort	Bus No. 129: Departs from Leoforos Olgas, south side of the Zappeion Gardens (*Tmr* E5/6).
Voula	NTOG beach Class A	Bus No. 122: Departs from Leoforos Olgas, south side of Zappeion Gardens (*Tmr* E5/6).
Voula	NTOG beach Class B	Bus No. 122: Adults 60 drs, children 40 drs.
Vouliagmeni	A luxury seaside resort and yacht marina. NTOG beach.	Bus No. 118: Departs from Leoforos Olgas, south side of the Zappeion Gardens (*Tmr* E5/6). Adults 70 drs, children 50 drs, cabin 150 drs.
Varkiza	A seaside resort and yacht marina. NTOG beach.	Bus No. 115: Departs from Leoforos Olgas, south side of the Zappeion Gardens (*Tmr* E5/6). Adults 100 drs, children 50 drs.

There are beaches all the way down to Cape Sounion (Sounio) via the coast road. Buses terminus at 14 Mavrommateon St (*Tmr* D/E1) west of Pedion Areos Park and north of Omonia Sq. The Athens/Cape Sounion bus departs every hour from 0630 hrs and leaves Sounion for Athens every hour from 0800 - 1900 hrs. The one-way fare costs 350 drs and the journey takes 1½ hours.

BOOKSELLERS Apart from the secondhand bookshops in the Plaka Flea Market (*See* **Monastiraki Square, Introduction**), there are three or four on Odhos Nikis (west of Syntagma Sq) and Odhos Amerikis (north-west of Syntagma Sq) as well as one on Lysikratous St, opposite the small church (*Tmr* 21D5). Of all the above it is perhaps invidious to select one but here goes....
The Compendium Bookshop (& Computers) 28 Nikis St.   Tel. 322-6931
Well recommended for a wide range of English language publications. **The Transalpino** travel office is in the basement.

BREAD SHOPS In the more popular shopping areas. Descending along Odhos Adrianou, in the Plaka (*Tmr* D5), from the Odhos Thespidos/Kidathineon end, advances past many shops, general stores and a bread shop (or two). They make way for souvenir and gift shops on the way towards Monastiraki.

BUSES AND TROLLEY-BUSES These run variously between 0500 and 0030 (half an hour past midnight) and are usually crowded, but excellent value with a 'flat rate' charge of 30 drs. Travel between 0500 and 0800 hrs is free, not only on the buses but the Metro as well.

Buses The buses are blue (and green) and bus stops are marked Stasis (ΣΤΑΣΙΣ). Some one-man-operated buses are utilised and a few have an honesty box for fares.

Trolley-Buses Yellow coloured vehicles and bus stops. Entered via a door at the front marked Eisodos (ΕΙΣΟΔΟΣ), with the exit at the rear, marked Exodus (ΕΞΟΔΟΣ).

Have the correct money to put into the fare machine as there are no tickets or change disgorged.

Major city terminals & turn-round points (*See* footnote at the end of this section)
Kaningos Sq: (*Tmr* 4D2) North-east of Omonia Sq.
Stadiou/Kolokotroni junction: (*Tmr* D/E4). This has replaced the Korai Sq terminus now that Korai has been pedestrianised.
Liossion St: (*Tmr* C2) North-west of Omonia Sq.
Eleftherias Sq: (*Tmr* 9C3) North-west of Monastiraki Sq.
Leoforos Olgas (*Tmr* D/E5/6) South of the National Garden's Mavvrommateon St:* (*Tmr* D/E1) West of Pedion Areos Park north of Omonia Sq.
* *The tree shaded north-south street is lined with bus departure points.*

Egyptou Place (Aigyptou/Egiptou): (*Tmr* D1) Just below the south-west corner of Pedion Areos Park, alongside 28 (Ikosiokto) Oktovriou.
Ag. Asomaton Square: (*Tmr* B/C4) West of Monastiraki Sq.
Koumoundourou St: (*Tmr* C2/3) West of Omonia Sq, third turning right off Ag. Konstantinou.

Trolley-bus timetable
Some major city routes include
No. 1:   Plateia Attikis (Metro station) (*Tmr* C1), Stathmos Larissis (railway station) Karaiskaki Place, Ag. Konstantinou, Omonia Sq, Syntagma Sq, Kallithea suburb (SW Athens). Every 10 mins from 0505 - 2350 hrs.
No. 2:   Pangrati (*Tmr* G6), Leoforos Amalias (Central), Syntagma Sq, Omonia Sq, 28 Ikosiokto Oktovriou/Patission St, Kipseli (N. Athens). From 0630 - 0020 hrs.
No. 10: N. Smirni (S. Athens), Leoforos Sygrou, Leoforos Amalias, Syntagma Sq, Panepistimiou St, Stadiou/Kolokotroni junction (*Tmr* D/E4). From 0500 - 2345 hrs.
No. 12: Leoforos Olgas (*Tmr* D/E5/6), Leoforos Amalias, Syntagma Sq, Omonia Sq, 28 Ikosiokto Oktovriou/Patission St (N. Athens). From 0630 - 2235 hrs.
Other routes covered by trolley-buses include:
No. 3:   Patissia to Erythrea (N. to NNE Athens suburbs). From 0625 - 2230 hrs.
No. 4:   Odhos Kypselis (*Tmr* E1) (North of Pedion Areos park), Omonia Sq, Syntagma Sq, Leoforos Olgas to Ag Artemios (SSE Athens suburbs). From 0630 - 0020 hrs.
No. 5:   Patissia (N. Athens suburb), Omonia Sq, Syntagma Sq, Filellinon St, Koukaki (S. Athens suburb). From 0630 - 0015 hrs.
No. 6:   Ippokratous St (*Tmr* E3), Panepistimiou St, Omonia Sq to N. Filadelfia (N. Athens suburb). Every 10 mins from 0500 - 2320 hrs.
No. 7:   Panepistimiou St (*Tmr* D/E3/4), 28 Ikosiokto Oktovriou/Patission St to Leoforos Alexandras (N. of Lycabettus). From 0630 - 0015 hrs.
No. 8:   Plateia Kaningos (*Tmr* 4D2), Odhos Akadimias, Vassilissis Sofias, Leoforos Alexandras, 28 Ikosiokto Oktovriou/Patission St. From 0630 - 0020 hrs.
No. 9:   Odhos Kypselis (*Tmr* E1) (North of Pedion Areos park), 28 Ikosiokto Oktovriou/Patission St, Stadiou St, Syntagma Sq, Petralona (W. Athens suburb – far side of Filopapou). Every 10 mins from 0455 - 2345 hrs.
No. 10: Stadiou/Koloktoroni junction (*Tmr* D/E4), Stadiou St, Syntagma Sq, Filellinon St, Leoforos Sygrou, Nea Smirni (S. Athens suburb). Every 10 mins from 0500 - 2345 hrs.
No. 11: Koliatsou (NNE Athens suburb), 28 Ikosiokto Oktovriou/Patission St, Stadiou St, Syntagma Sq, Filellinon St, Plastira Sq, Eftichidou St, N. Pangrati (ESE Athens suburb). Every 5 mins from 0500 - 0010 hrs.
No. 13: 28 Ikosiokto Oktovriou/Patission St, Akadimias St, Vassilissis Sofias, Papadiaman-topoulou St, Leoforos Kifissias, Labrini (just beyond Galatsi suburb) (NE Athens suburb). Every 10 mins from 0500 - 2400 hrs.
No. 14: Leoforos Alexandras, 28 Ikosiokto Oktovriou/Patission, Patissia (N. Athens suburb).

Bus timetable
Bus numbers are subject to a certain amount of confusion, but here goes! Some of the routes are as follows:
No. 022: Kaningos Sq (*Tmr* 4D2), Akadimias, Kanari, Patriarchou Ioakim, Marasli, Genadiou St (SE Lycabettus). Every 10 mins from 0520 - 2330 hrs.
No. 024: Leoforos Amalias (*Tmr* D/E5), Syntagma Sq, Panepistimiou St, Omonia Sq, Tritis

Septemvriou, Stournara, Sourmeli, Acharnon, Liossion St. Every 20 mins from 0530 - 2400 hrs.

NB This is the bus that delivers passengers to 260 Liossion St (Tmr *C2*), *one of the main bus terminals.*

No. 040: Filellinon St (close to Syntagma Sq – *Tmr D/E4/5*), Leoforos Amalias, Leoforos Sygrou to Vassileos Konstantinou, Piraeus. Every 10 mins, 24 hours a day. Green bus.

No. 045: Kaningos Sq (*Tmr* 4D2), Akadimias St, Vassilissis Sofias, Leoforos Kifissias to Kefalari and Politia (NE Athens suburb). Every 15 mins from 0600 - 0100 hrs.

No. 049: Athinas St (*Tmr* C/D3), (S. of Omonia Sq), Sofokleous, Pireos, Sotiros, Filonos St, Plateia Themistokleous Piraeus. Every 10 mins, 24 hours a day. Green bus.

No. 051: Off Ag. Konstantinou (*Tmr* C2/3), W of Omonia Sq, Kolonou St, Platonos St (W. Athens suburb). Every 10 mins from 0500 - 2400 hrs.

NB This is the bus that connects to the 100 Kifissou St (Tmr *A2*), *a main bus terminal.*

No. 115: Leoforos Olgas (*Tmr* D/E5/6), Leoforos Sygrou, Leoforos Possidonos (coast road) to Varkiza. Every 20 mins, 24 hours a day.

No. 118: Leoforos Olgas, Leoforos Sygrou, Leoforos Possidonos (coast road) to Vouliagmeni. Every 20 mins from 1245 - 2015 hrs.

No. 122: Leoforos Olgas, Leoforos Sygrou, Leoforos Possidonos (coast road) to Voula. Every 20 mins from 0530 - 2400 hrs.

No. 132: Othonos St (Syntagma Sq, *Tmr* 1D/E4/5), Filellinon St, Leoforos Amalias, Leoforos Sygrou to Edem (SSE Athens suburb). Every 20 mins from 0530 - 1900 hrs.

No. 224: Polygono (N. Athens suburb), 28 Okosiokto Oktovriou/Patission St, Kaningos Sq, Vassilissis Sofias, Democratias St (Kessariani, E. Athens suburb). Every 20 mins from 0500 - 2400 hrs.

No. 230: Ambelokipi (E. Athens suburb), Leoforos Alexandras, Ippokratous St, Akadimias St, Syntagma Sq, Leoforos Amalias, Dionysiou Areopagitou, Apostolou Pavlou, Thission. Every 10 mins from 0500 - 2320 hrs.

No. 510: Kaningos Sq (*Tmr* 4D2), Akadimias St, Ippokratous St, Leoforos Alexandras, Leoforos Kifissias to Dionyssos (NE Athens suburb). Every 20 mins from 0530 - 2250 hrs.

No. 527: Kaningos Sq, (*Tmr* 4D2) Akadimias St, Leoforos Alexandras, Leoforos Kifissias to Amaroussion (NE Athens suburb). Every 15 mins from 0615 - 2215 hrs.

NB The Athens-Attica bus services detailed above cover the city and its environs. The rest of Greece is served by:

1) **KTEL** A pool of bus operators working through one company from two terminals. 260 Liossion St* and 100 Kifissou St**

2) **OSE** (the State Railway Company) Their buses terminus alongside the main railway stations of Stathmos Peloponissou and Larissis. Apart from the domestic services, there is a terminal for other European capitals, including Paris, Instanbul and Munich, at Stathmos Larissis Station.

* **Liossion St** (*Tmr* C2) is to the east of Stathmos Peloponissou Railway Station. The terminus serves Halkida, Edipsos, Kimi, Delphi, Amfissa, Kamena Vourla, Larissa, Thiva, Trikala (Meteora) Livadia, Lamia. **Refer to bus route No. 024 to get to this terminus.**

** **Kifissou St** (*Tmr* A2) is to the west of Omonia Sq, beyond the 'steam railway' lines, across Leoforos Konstantinoupoleos and up Odhos Platonos. The terminus serves Patras, Pirgos (Olympia), Nafplio (Mikines), Adritsena (Vasses), Kalamata, Sparti (Mistras), Githio (Diros), Tripolis, Messolongi, Igoumenitsa, Preveza, Ioanina, Corfu, Zakynthos, Cephalonia, Lefkas, Kozani, Kastoria, Florina, Grevena, Veria, Naoussa, Edessa, Seres, Kilkis, Kavala, Drama, Komotini, Korinthos, Kranidi, Xilokastro. **Refer to bus route No. 051 to get to this terminus.**

For any bus services connecting to the islands detailed in this guide, refer to the relevant Mainland Ports and Island chapters.

CAMPING *See* **The Accommodation.**

CAR HIRE As any other capital city, numerous offices, the majority of which are lined up in the smarter areas and squares, such as Syntagma Sq and Leoforos Amalias. Typical is:

Pappas, 44 Leoforos Amalias   Tel. 322-0087

There are any number of car hire (and travel) firms on the right of Leoforos Sygrou, descending from the 'spaghetti junction' south of the Temple of Olympian Zeus (*Tmr* D6).

CAR REPAIR Help and advice can be obtained by contacting:
The Automobile & Touring Club of Greece (ELPA), 2 Messogion St (*Tmr* I. 3)
Tel. 779-1615
For immediate, emergency attention dial 104.
There are dozens of backstreet car repairers, breakers and spare part shops parallel and to the west of Leoforos Sygrou, in the area between the Olympic office and the Temple of Olympian Zeus.

CHEMIST *See* **Medical Care**

CINEMAS There are a large number of outdoor cinemas. Do not worry about a language barrier as the majority of the films have English (American) dialogue with Greek subtitles.
Aigli in the Zappeion is a must and is situated at the south end of the National Garden. Other cinemas are bunched together on the streets of Stadiou, Panepistimiou and 28 Ikosiokto Oktovriou/Patission.
Anne notes that the cinemas in Athens, of which there are vast numbers, generally show poor quality films with scratches, hisses, jumps, long black gaps and or loss of sound especially between reels. However her recommendation is the:
Radio City 240 Patission St
Large screen, good sound and knowledgeable operators.

CLUBS, BARS & DISCOS Why leave home? But if you must, there are enough to satiate the most voracious desires.

COMMERCIAL SHOPPING AREAS During daylight hours a very large street market ranges up Odhos Athinas (*Tmr* C3/4), Odhos Sokratous and the associated side streets from Ermou St, almost all the way up to Omonia Sq. After dark the shutters are drawn down, the stalls canvassed over and the 'ladies of the night' appear.
Plateia Kotzia (*Tmr* C/D3) spawns a flower market on Sundays whilst the Parliament Building side of Vassilissis Sofias (*Tmr* E4) is lined with smart flower stalls that open daily.
Monastiraki Sq (*Tmr* 5C4) and the various streets that radiate off are abuzz, specialising in widely differing aspects of commercial and tourist trade. Odhos Areos contains a plethora of leather goods shops; the near end of Ifestou lane is edged by stall upon stall of junk and tourist 'omit-abilia' (the forgettable memorabilia); Pandrossou Lane contains a better class of shop and stall selling sandals, pottery and smarter 'memorabilia' while the square itself has a number of handcart hawkers.
The smart department stores are conveniently situated in or around Syntagma Sq, and the main streets that radiate off the square, including Ermou, Stadiou and Panepistimiou.
See **Bread Shops** & **Trains** for details of other markets and shopping areas.

DENTISTS & DOCTORS *See* **Medical Care**

EMBASSIES
Australia: 15 Messogion Av. Tel. 775-7651
Canada: 4 Ioannou Gennadiou St Tel. 723-9511
Great Britain: 1 Ploutarchou & Ypsilantou Sts. Tel. 723-6211
Ireland: 7 Vassileos Konstantinou Tel. 723-2771

New Zealand: 5-17 Tsoha St.	Tel. 641-0311
South Africa: 124 Kifissias/Iatridou	Tel. 692-2125
USA: 91 Vassilissis Sofias	Tel. 721-2951
Denmark: 15 Philikis Etairias Sq.	Tel. 724-9315
Finland: 1 Eratosthenous & Vas. Konstantinou Streets	Tel. 751-5064
Norway: 7 Vassileos Konstantinou St	Tel. 724-6173
Sweden: 7 Vassileos Konstantinou St	Tel. 722-4504
Belgium: 3 Sekeri St	Tel. 361-7886
France: 7 Vassilissis Sofias	Tel. 361-1663
German Federal Republic: 3 Karaoli/Dimitriou Streets	Tel. 369-4111
Netherlands: 5-7 Vassileos Konstantinou	Tel. 723-9701

HAIRDRESSERS No problems with sufficient in the main shopping areas.

HOSPITALS *See* **Medical Care**

LAUNDRETTES There may be others but a good, central recommendation must be:
Coin-op *(Tmr* 13D5) Angelou Geronda
Directions: From Kidathineon St (proceeding towards Syntagma Sq), at the far end of
Plateia Plaka turn right down Angelou Geronda, towards Dedalou, and the laundrette
is on the right-hand side.
   A machine load costs 200 drs, 9 mins of dryer time 20 drs and a measure of powder
30 drs. In respect of the detergent, why not pop out to Kidathineon St and purchase a
small packet of Tide for 38 drs. The staff carry out the wash and dry operation at a cost
of 400 drs for customers who are busy and are prepared to leave the laundry behind.
Open in the summer daily 0800 - 2100 hrs.
   The more usual Athens style is for customers to leave their washing at any one of
the countless laundries and collect it next day dry, stiff and bleached (if necessary).
   Note that my lavatorial obsession would not be satisfied without mentioning the
Public toilet sited on Plateia Plaka.

LOST PROPERTY The main office is situated at: 33 Ag Konstantinou (Tel. 523-
0111), the Plateia Omonia end of Ag. Konstantinou. The telephone number is that of
the Transport police who are now in charge of lost property (or *Grafio Hamenon
Adikimenon*). It is still true to say that you are far more likely to 'lose' personal
belongings to other tourists, than to Greeks.

LUGGAGE STORE There is one at No. 26 Nikis St *(Tmr* D5) advertising the service at
a cost of 50 drs per day per piece; 250 drs per week and 750 drs per month.

MEDICAL CARE
Chemists/Pharmacies (Farmakio – ΦΑΡΜΑΚΕΙΟ) Identified by a green or red
cross on a white background. Normal opening hours and a rota operates to give a
'duty' chemist cover.
Dentists & Doctors Ask at the **First Aid Centre** for the address of the School of
Dentistry where free treatment is available. Both dentists and doctors advertise
widely and there is no shortage of practitioners.
First Aid Centre (KAT) *(Tmr* 14D2) 21 Tritis Septemvriou St, beyond the Chalkokon-
dili turning and on the left.   Tel. 150
Hospital *(Tmr* 15G4) Do not proceed direct to a hospital but initially attend the **First
Aid Centre.** If necessary they direct patients to the correct destination.
Medical Emergency: Tel. 166

METRO/ELEKTRIKOS (ΗΣΑΜ) The Athens underground or subway system, which
operates below ground in the heart of the city and overground for the rest of the

journey. It is a simple one track layout from Kifissia (north-east Athens suburb) to Piraeus (south-west of Athens), and represents marvellous value with two rate fares of 30 and 60 drs. Passengers must have the requisite coins to obtain a ticket from the machine, prior to gaining access to the platforms. Everyone is most helpful and will, if the ticket machine 'frightens' a chap, show how it should be operated. Take care, select the ticket value first, then put the coins in the slot and keep the ticket so as to be able to hand it in at the journey's end. The service operates between 0505 and 0015 hrs (the next morning) and travel before 0800 hrs is free. Keep an eye open for the old-fashioned wooden carriages.

Station Stops There are 21 which include Kifissia (NE suburb), Stathmos Attiki (for the main railway station), Plateia Victorias (N. Athens), Omonia Sq, Monastiraki Sq (Plaka), Plateia Thission (for the Acropolis) and (Piraeus) Port. From the outside, the Piraeus terminus is rather difficult to locate, the entrance being in the left-hand corner of what appears to be an oldish waterfront building. There used to be 20 stations but the new 'Peace Stadium' has acquired a stop called Irene.

MUSIC & DANCING *See* **Clubs, Bars & Discos & The Eating Out**

NTOG (EOT) The headquarters of the National Tourist Organisation (NTOG) or, in Greek, the EOT (Elinikos Organismos Tourismou – ΕΛΛΗΝΙΚΟΣ ΟΡΓΑΝΙΣΜΟΣ ΤΟΥΡΙΣΜΟΥ) is on the 5th floor at 2 Amerikis St (*Tmr* E4) close by Syntagma Sq. But this office does not normally handle the usual tourist enquiries although the commissionaires manning the desk do hand out bits and pieces of information.

The information desk, from whence the free Athens map, advice, information folders, bus and boat schedules and hotel facts may be obtained, is situated inside and on the left of the foyer of the:
National Bank of Greece (*Tmr* 3D/E4) 2 Karageorgi Servias, Syntagma Sq
Tel. 322-2545
Directions: As above.

Do not hope to obtain anything other than pamphlets and a snatch of guidance as it would be unrealistic to expect personal attention from staff besieged by wave upon wave of tourists of every creed, race and colour. The hotel information sheets handed out now include a list of Athens Class D & E hotels. Open Monday - Friday, 0800 - 2000 hrs, Saturdays 0900 - 1400 hrs.

There is also an NTOG office conveniently situated at the East Airport.

OPENING HOURS (Summer months) These are only a guideline and apply to Athens (as well as the larger cities). Note that in country and village areas, it is more likely that shops are open from Monday to Saturday inclusive for over 12 hours a day, and on Sundays, holidays and Saints days, for a few hours either side of midday. The afternoon siesta is usually taken between 1300/1400 hrs and 1500/1700 hrs.
Trade Stores & Chemists Monday, Wednesday and Saturday 0800 - 1430 hrs. Tuesday, Thursday and Friday 0900 - 1300 hrs and 1700 - 2000 hrs.
Food Stores Monday, Wednesday and Saturday 0800 - 1500 hrs. Tuesday, Thursday and Friday 0800 - 1400 hrs and 1730 - 2030 hrs.
Art & Gift Shops Weekdays 0800 - 2100 hrs. Sundays (Monastiraki area) 0930 - 1445 hrs.
Restaurants, Pastry Shops, Cafes & Dairy Shops Seven days a week.
Museums *See* **Museums, Places of Interest.**
Public Services (including Banks) Refer to the relevant **A to Z** heading.

OTE There are offices at: No. 85, 28 Ikosiokto Oktovriou/Patission St (*Tmr* 16D1) (open 24 hrs a day); 15 Stadiou St (*Tmr* 17D4) (open Monday to Friday 0700-2400 hrs, Saturday and Sunday 0800 - 2400 hrs); 53 Solonos (*Tmr* E3) and 7 Kratinou

(Plateia Kotzia) (*Tmr* C/D3) (open between 0800 and 2400 hrs). There is also an office at 45 Athinas St (*Tmr* C/D3).

PHARMACIES *See* Medical Care

PLACES OF INTEREST
Parliament Building (*Tmr* E4/5) Syntagma Sq. Here it is possible to watch the Greek equivalent of the British 'changing the Guard at Buckingham Palace'. The special guards (Evzones) are spectacularly outfitted with tasselled red caps, white shirts (blouses do I hear?), coloured waistcoats, a skirt, white tights, knee-garters and boots topped off with pom-poms. The ceremony officially kicks off at 1100 hrs on Sunday morning but seems to falter into action at about 1045 hrs. Incidentally there is a band thrown in for good measure.

Museums The seasons are split as follows: Winter, 1st November - 31st March; Summer, 1st April - 31st October. Museums are closed on: 1st January, 25th March, Good Friday, Easter Day and Christmas Day. Sunday hours are kept on Epiphany, Ash Monday, Easter Saturday, Easter Monday, 1st May, Whit Sunday, Assumption Day, 28th October and Boxing Day. They are only open in the mornings on Christmas Eve, New Year's Eve, 2nd January, Easter Thursday and Easter Tuesday. Museums are closed on Tuesdays unless otherwise indicated. Students with cards will achieve a reduction in fees.

Acropolis (*Tmr* C5). The museum exhibits finds made on the site. Of special interest are the sixth century BC statues of Korai women. Entrance charges are included in the admission fee to the Acropolis, which costs 400 drs per head and is open in the Summer: 0730 - 1930 hrs; Sunday and holidays 0800 - 1800 hrs. The museum hours are 0730 - 1930 hrs; Tuesdays 1200 - 1800 hrs; Sundays and holidays 0800 - 1800 hrs.

Benaki (*Tmr* E/F4) On the corner of Vassilissis Sofias and Koubari (Koumbari) St, close by Plateia Kolonaki. A very interesting variety of exhibitis made up from private collections. Particularly diverting is a display of national costumes. Summer hours: daily 0830 - 1400 hrs, Sundays and holidays 0930 - 1430 hrs. Entrance 100 drs.

Byzantine (*Tmr* F4/5) 22 Vassilissis Sofias. As one would deduce from the name – Byzantine art. Summer hours: daily 0845 - 1500 hrs; Sunday and holidays, 0930 - 1430 hrs; closed Mondays. Entrance costs 200 drs.

Goulandris 13 Levidou St, Kifissia, N. Athens. Natural History. Summer hours: daily 0900 - 1400 hrs; Sunday and holidays 1000 - 1600 hrs; closed Fridays. Entrance costs 30 drs.

Goulandris (*Tmr* F4) 4 Neophitou Douka St (off Vassilissis Sofias). The second or 'other' Goulandris Museum. The situation is not helped by the little quirk of some people referring to the Natural History Museum as 'Goulandris'. Help! This Goulandris, that is the Cycladic and Ancient Greek Art Goulandris Museum is open daily in the summer 1000 - 1600 hrs; closed Tuesday, Sunday and holidays. Entrance costs 150 drs.

Kanelloupoulos (*Tmr* C5) On the corner of Theorias and Panos Sts. (Plaka). A smaller version of the Benaki Museum and located at the foot of the northern slope of the Acropolis, at the Monastiraki end. Summer hours: daily 0845 - 1500 hrs; Sunday and holidays 0930 - 1430 hrs. Entrance costs 100 drs (and is charged Sundays and holidays).

Keramikos (Tmr B4) 148 Ermou St. Finds from Keramikos cemetery. Summer hours: daily 0845 - 1500 hrs; Sunday and holidays 0930 - 1430 hrs. The museum is (apparently) open every day. Entrance to the site and museum costs 100 drs.

National Gallery & Alexandros Soutzos (Tmr G4), 46 Vassileos Konstantinou/ Sofias. Mainly 19th and 20th century Greek paintings. Summer hours: 0900 - 1500 hrs; Sunday and holidays 1000 - 1400 hrs; closed on Mondays. Entrance costs 30 drs.

National Historical & Ethnological (Tmr D4) Kolokotroni Square, off Stadiou St. Greek history and the War of Independence. Summer hours: 0900 - 1400 hrs; Sunday and holidays 0900 - 1300 hrs; closed Mondays. Entrance costs 100 drs.

National Archaeological (Tmr D/E2), 1 Tossitsa St, off 28 Ikosiokto Oktovriou/ Patission St. The largest and possibly the most important Greek museum, covering a wide variety of exhibits. A must if you are a museum buff. Summer hours: 0800 - 1700 hrs; Sunday and holidays 0800 - 1700 hrs; closed on Mondays. Entrance costs 300 drs which includes entrance to the Santorini and Numismatic exhibitions (*See* below).

Numismatic In the same building as the National Archaeological and displaying, as would be imagined, a collection of Greek coins, spanning the ages. Summer hours: 0930 - 1330 hrs; Sunday and holidays 0900 - 1400 hrs; closed on Tuesdays. Admission is free.
Also housed in the same building are the:
Epigraphical Collection: Summer hours: 0830 - 1330 hrs; Sunday and holidays 0900 - 1400 hrs.
Santorini Exhibits: Summer hours: 0930 - 1500 hrs every day, closed on Mondays. and
The Casts and Copies Exhibition: Summer hours: 0900 - 1400 hrs daily; closed Sunday and Mondays.

Popular (Folk) Art (Tmr D5) 17 Kidathineon St, The Plaka. Folk art, folklore and popular art. Summer hours: 1000 - 1400 hrs; Sunday and holidays 1000 - 1400 hrs; closed on Mondays. Entrance free.

War (Tmr F4/5) 2 Rizari St, off Leoforos Vassilissis Sofias. Warfare exhibits covering a wide variety of subjects. Summer hours: daily 0900 - 1400 hrs; Sunday and holidays 0930 - 1400 hrs; closed on Mondays. Entrance is free.

Theatres & Performances For full, up-to-date details enquire at the NTOG office (*Tmr* 3D/E4). They should be able to hand out a pamphlet giving a precise timetable for the year. As a guide the following are performed year in and year out:
Son et Lumiere. From the Pnyx hillside, a *Son et Lumiere* features the Acropolis. The English performance starts at 2100 hrs every evening, except when the moon is full, and takes 45 minutes. There are French versions at 2215 hrs daily except Tuesdays and Fridays when a German commentary is provided at 2200 hrs. Tickets are available for 300 drs (students 120 drs) at the entrance of the Church, Ag Dimitros Lombardiaris, on the way to the show. Catch a No. 230 bus along Dionysiou Areopagitou St getting off one stop beyond the Odeion (Theatre) of Herodes Atticus and follow the signposted path on the left-hand side.

Athens Festival. This prestigious event takes place in the restored and beautiful Odeion of Herodes Atticus, built in approximately AD 160 as a Roman theatre, seating about 5000 people and situated at the foot of the south-west corner of the Acropolis. The festival lasts from early June to the middle of September, and consists of a series of plays, ballet, concerts and opera. The performances usually commence at 2100 hrs and tickets, which are on sale up to 10 days before the event, are obtainable from the Theatre or from the *Athens Festival booking office* (*Tmr* D/E4), 4 Stadiou St, Tel. 322-1459.

Dora Stratou Theatre. (*Tmr* A6) A short stroll away on Mouseion or Hill of Muses. On the summit stands the Monument of the Filopapou (Philopappos) and nearby the Dora Stratou Theatre, where an internationally renowned troupe of folk dancers, dressed in traditional costumes, perform a series of Greek dances and songs. Performances are timed to coincide with the ending of the *Son et Lumiere,* on the Pnyx. The show, produced from early May up to the end of September, costs between 450-750 drs per head (students 350 drs), starts at about 2215 hrs, lasts approximately one hour, and is well worth a visit. Tickets are available from the Theatre (Tel. 314-4395) between 0900 - 1400 hrs.

Lycabettus Theatre. On the north-east side of Lycabettus Hill (Lykavitos, Likavittos, Lykabettos, etc. etc.). Concerts and theatrical performances take place in the hillside open-air theatre between the middle of June and the first week of September from 2100 hrs. Tickets can be purchased from the theatre box office, one hour before the event, or from the *Athens Festival booking office*, referred to above under *Athens Festival.*

POLICE *See* **Tourist police.**

POST OFFICES (Tachidromio – ΤΑΧΥΔΡΟΜΕΙΟΝ) Weekday opening hours, as a guide, are 0800 to 1300 hrs. The Central Post Office at 100 Eolou St (*Tmr* 18D3), close by Omonia Sq, is open Monday - Saturday, 0730 - 1500 hrs. Branch offices are situated on the corner of Othonos and Nikis Streets (Syntagma Sq); at the Omonia Sq underground Metro concourse and on Dionysiou Areopagitou St, at the corner of Tzireon St (*Tmr* D6).

The telephone and telegraph system is run by a separate state organisation. *See* **OTE.**

PHOTOGRAPHY (Fotografion ΦΩΤΟΓΡΑΦΕΙΟΝ) Visitors requiring photographs for various membership cards can use the instant photo booth in the Metro underground concourse, Omonia Sq (*Tmr* 2D3).

SHOPPING HOURS *See* **Opening Hours.**

SPORTS FACILITIES
Golf. There is an 18 hole course, the Glifida Golf Club close by the East(ern) Airport. Changing rooms, restaurant and refreshment bar.
Swimming. There is a Swimming (and Tennis) Club on Leoforos Olgas (*Tmr* 19E6), across the way from the Zappeion, National Gardens. The Hilton Hotel (*Tmr* G 4) has a swimming pool but, if you are not staying there, use of it costs the price of an (expensive) meal. *See* **Beaches.**
Tennis. There are courts at most of the NTOG beaches (*See* **Beaches**) as well as at the Ag. Kosmas athletics centre, close by the West airport.

TAXIS (ΤΑΞΙ). Used extensively and, although they seem to me to be expensive, they are 'officially' the cheapest in Europe. The Athens drivers are, now, generally without scruples. Fares are metered and costed at about 23 drs per kilometre. But they are subject to various surcharges including 15 drs for each piece of baggage, 240 drs per hour of waiting time and 30 drs for picking up at, or delivering to, public transport facilities. There is also an extra charge for the hours between midnight and daylight.

When standing at a taxi rank drivers must pick up a fare, but are not obliged to do so when cruising, for which there is an extra 'flag falling' charge of 25 drs. The sign ΕΛΕΥΘΕΡΟΝ indicates a cab is free for hire. The minimum fare is 110 drs and approximate sample fares include: Syntagma/Omonia Squares to the East airport 500 drs and to the West airport 400 drs; the East airport to Piraeus 500 drs and the West airport to Piraeus 350 drs.

TELEPHONE *See* **OTE.**

TOURIST OFFICE/AGENCIES *See* **NTOG** & **Travel Agents.**

TOURIST POLICE *(Tmr* 20D6) I understand, despite the reorganisation of the service, that the Athens headquarters is to remain in operation. This is situated at 7 Leoforos Sygrou (Sygrou/Syngrou/Singrou Av). Open daily 0800 - 2200 hrs. Tel. 923-9224. Tourist information in English is available from the Tourist police on the telephone number 171.
    There are also Tourist police offices close by and just to the north of Larissis Railway station (open 0700 - 2400 hrs, tel. 821-3574) and the East airport (open 0730 - 2300 hrs, tel. 981-4093).

TOILETS Apart from the various bus termini and the railway stations, there is a super Public toilet on the south-east corner of Syntagma Sq, as there is a pretty grim 'squatty' in the Omonia Sq Metro concourse. The Plaka is well 'endowed' with one at Plateia Plaka, (on Odhos Kidathineon) and another on the Plateia Agora at the other end of Odhos Adrianou. Visitors to Mt Lycabettus will not be 'caught short' and the toilets there are spotless.

TRAINS (Illustration 6) They arrive at (or depart from) either (a) Larissis Station (Stathmos No. 1) or (b) Peloponissou Station (Stathmos No. 2).

(A) **LARISSIS STATION (STATHMOS No. 1)** *(Tmr* B/C1)   Tel. 821-3882
The main, more modern station of the two. Connections to the Western European services and the northern provinces of Central Greece, Thessaly, Macedonia and Thrace. The bus stop to the centre of Athens is to the right of the station, with the building behind one. Refer to Buses below.
    Services in and around the building include:
The National Bank of Greece. A branch opens Monday to Thursday 0830 - 1400 hrs and Friday 0830 - 1330 hrs.
Post Office. Open Monday to Saturday 0700 - 2000 hrs and Sunday 0900 - 1400 hrs. They transact money exchange and cash travellers' cheques.
Tourist police. There is an office just to the north of the station building. *See* **Tourist police.**
    To the front of the station is a pavement cafe-bar (a coffee 56 drs) and an elongated square, well more a widening of the road.

The Accommodation
Even early and late in the summer a number of the hardier stretch out on the pavements around and about the stations (and at the *Hotel Oscar's* rates I'm not surprised). Arrivals, even whilst on the train, are bombarded with offers of accommodation, so much so that the touts are a nuisance.
    With the station behind one, to the right, across the concourse and on the corner, is the:
Hotel Lefkos Pirgos *(Tmr* C1) (Class E) 27 Leof. Metaxa/Deligianni   Tel. 821-3765
Directions: as above.

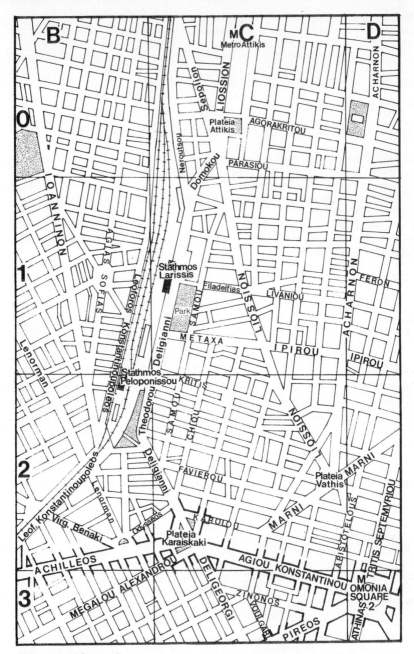

Illustration 6
Athens City Inset – The Railway Stations

Seedy looking with double rooms sharing bathroom starting at 1100 drs, rising to 1300 drs.

Hotel Nana (*Tmr* C1) (Class C), 29 Leof. Metaxa   Tel. 884-2211
Directions: Alongside the *Hotel Lefkos Pirgos*
Smarter (well it is C class) with the charges reflecting this eminence. A double room en suite starts off at 2600 drs rising to 3300 drs (16th March - 31st Oct).

Directly opposite the main station entrance is the:
Hotel Oscar (*Tmr* C1) (Class B), 25 Samou/Filadelfias   Tel. 883-4215
Directions: As above.
I hardly dare detail the room rates which for a double room kicks off at 3860 drs rising to 4000 drs, en suite naturally. Breakfast costs 280 drs. I must own up to staying at the *Oscar*. But it was at the end of a long stint on the Greek islands added to which there were a couple of other (good) reasons. Firstly they accept payment by American Express which, as I have written before, may be of great assistance in eking out dwindling funds and secondly the hotel is conveniently close to the railway and the inter-country coach station. Thus the comforts of this hotel, or similar, can be put to good use in order to build up the bodily reserves prior to a planned long distance bus or railway journey! That is not to say that even this luxurious establishment does not escape some of the common faults oft experienced as a 'norm' when staying at its lower classified 'cousins'. The en suite bathroom of our room had a loose lavatory seat, the bath plug had no chain attached (there was a chain but it was not attached), and the small bathroom window was tied up with string. The bedroom sliding balcony window would not completely shut – there was no locking mechanism and the air conditioning didn't. Mind you I must admit to making a reservation without Rosemary, who guarded our backpacks whilst I sorted out the formalities. It may have been the sight of the two towering, afore-mentioned packs backing through the swing doors into reception that resulted in our being allocated this particular 'downtown' room, at the rear of the hotel, overlooking and overlooked by towering blocks of flats.

Hotel Elena (Helena) (*Tmr* B/C1) (Class C) 2 Psiloriti/Samou   Tel. 881-3211
Directions: Along Samou St, south from Leof. Metaxa St, and on the right.
Single rooms sharing the bathroom cost 850 drs and en suite 1250 drs; double rooms sharing 1400 drs and en suite 1700 drs.

Hotel Louvre (*Tmr* C2) (Class D) 9 Chiou/Favierou Sts   Tel. 522-9891
Directions: Next street back from and parallel to Samou St, towards the south end of Chiou St.
Greek provincial in outward appearance despite the grand and evocative name. Single rooms sharing cost 850 drs; double rooms sharing 1220 drs and en suite 1550 drs.

Joy's Hotel (*Tmr* D1) 38 Feron St   Tel. 823-1012
Directions: Proceed up Odhos Filadelfias, almost directly opposite the main station, across Odhos Liossion continuing along Livaniou St as far as Odhos Acharnon. Turn left and then first right on to Feron St.
Reputedly a good value 'Youth Hostel' style establishment offering accommodation ranging from the roof (300 drs) to quadruples. A single bed starts off at 900 drs and a double 1400 drs.

Street Market Whilst in this area it is worth noting that Odhos Chiou, between Kritis and Favierou Sts, is host to an extensive street market where almost everything is sold from fish to meat and hardware to clothing.

Bread Shop & Supermarket (*Tmr* B/C1/2) On the corner of Samou St and Eratyras St. A bit disorganised but very useful.

Snackbar (*Tmr* B/C1) Odhos Samou
Directions: Across the street from the Park on the stretch of Odhos Samou between Filadelfias and Leof. Metaxa Sts.

A small, convenient souvlaki pita snackbar, run by a very friendly chap, with a souvlaki and bottle of beer costing 125 drs.

Buses: Trolley-bus No. 1 pulls up to the right of the station as do the No's 2 and 4. The fare to Syntagma Sq is 30 drs.

(B) **PELOPONISSOU STATION (STATHMOS NO 2)** (*TMR* B1/2)   Tel. 513-1601
The station for trains to the Peloponnese, the ferry connections for some of the Ionian islands and international ferries to Italy from Patras.

TRAINS (General)
Tickets: The concept behind the acquisition of a ticket is similar to that of a lottery. On buying a ticket, a compartment seat is also allocated. In theory this is a splendid scheme, but in practice the idea breaks down in a welter of bad tempered argument over who is occupying whose seat. Manners and quaint old-fashioned habits of giving up one's seat to older people and ladies are best avoided. I write this from the bitter experience of offering my seat to elderly Greek ladies only for their husbands to immediately fill the vacant position. Not what one had in mind! Find your seat and stick to it like glue and if you have made a mistake feign madness, admit to being a foreigner, but do not budge.

At Peloponissou Station the mechanics of buying a ticket take place in organised bedlam. The ticket office 'traps' open half an hour prior to the train's departure. Scenes reminiscent of a Cup Final crowd develop, with prospective travellers pitching about within the barriers of the ticket hatch, and all this in the space of about 10m by 10m. To add to the difficulty, there are two hatch 'slots' and it is anybody's guess which one to select. It really is best to try and steal a march on this 'extra-curricula' activity, diving for a hatch whenever one opens up.

Travellers booking a return journey train ticket to Europe, and routing via Italy, must ensure the ticket is from Patras, not Athens. (Yes, Patras.) Then purchase a separate Athens to Patras ticket thus ensuring a seat. A voyager boarding the train with an open ticket will almost surely have to stand for almost the whole of the 4 hour journey. Most Athens - Patras journeys seem to attract an 'Express' surcharge of between 100-150 drs which is charged by the ticket collector.

Incidentally, the general architecture of the Peloponissou building is delightful, especially the ceiling of the booking office hall, centrally located, under the main clock face. To the left, on entering the building, is a glass-fronted information box with all the train times listed on the window. The staff manning this desk are extremely helpful and speak sufficient English to pose no problems in communication (the very opposite of the disinterest shown at the NTOG desk in the National Bank of Greece, on Syntagma Sq).

Advance Booking Office. Information and advance booking for both stations is now handled at:
No. 6, Sina (*Tmr* E3) off Akadimias St (Tel. 363 4402/4406); No. 1, Karolou (Satovriandou) (*Tmr* C2) west of Omonia Sq. (Tel. 524 0647/8) and No. 17, Filellinon (*Tmr* D/E5) (Tel. 323 6747/6273).

Toilets The station toilets usually, well always, lack toilet paper.

Sustenance (on the train) An attendant brings inexpensive drinks and snacks around from time to time and hot snacks are available from platform trolleys at the major railway stations.

Railway Head Office (*Tmr* C2) Hellenic Railways Organisation (OSE) 1-3 Karolou St.
Tel. 522-2491
Directions: One back from the far end of Ag. Konstantinou west from Omonia Sq.

Provisions Shopping in the area of the railway stations is made easy by the presence of the Street Market on Odhos Chiou (*See* **Larissis Station, Trains**).

Access to the stations
Bus/Trolley-bus. From the Airport, travel on the Olympic bus to the terminal at 96-100 Leoforos Sygrou (which at a cost of 45 drs is extremely good value). Then catch a bus (Nos. 133, 040, 132, 155, 903 and 161 amongst others) across the street from the terminus to Syntagma Sq and then a No. 1 trolley-bus via Omonia Sq to the station. Instead of making a change of bus at Syntagma Sq it is also possible to walk west from the terminal on Leoforos Sygrou across Falirou and Odisseos Androutsou Streets to the parallel street of Odhos Dimitrakopoulou and catch a No. 1 trolley-bus all the way to the stations. From Piraeus Port catch the No. 40 (green) bus on Leoforos Vassileos Konstantinou (parallel to the quay) to Syntagma Sq, or the No. 049 from Plateia Themistokleous to Athinas St, close by Omonia Sq. *See* **Arrival by Air, Introduction; Airline offices & terminus** & **Buses & Trolley-Buses, A to Z.**

Metro The metro station for both railway stations is Attiki, close to Plateia Attikis. From the platform, assuming a traveller has come from the south, dismount and turn right down into the underpass to come out the far or west side of the station on Odhos Liossion. Turn left and walk to the large irregular Plateia Attikis (with the *Hotel Lydia* on the right). Proceed down Domokou St, (the road that exits half-right on the far side of the square), which spills into Plateia Deligianni edged by Stathmos Larissis. A more long-winded alternative is to get off the Metro at Omonia Sq, walk west along Ag. Konstantinou to Karaiskaki Sq and then up Odhos Deligianni, or why not catch a No. 1 trolley-bus.

Taxi A reasonable indulgence, if in a hurry, although it must be noted that in the crowded traffic conditions of Athens it is often quicker to walk than catch a cab. *See* **Taxis.**

Station to Station To get from one to the other, say Stathmos Larissis to Peloponissou, it is necessary to turn right out of the station and climb the steps over the railway line turning left at the bottom of the far side of the steps and walk some 100m to the forecourt in front of Stathmos Peloponissou. Almost, but not quite, adjacent, as some guides put it, if 150m on a very hot day, laden down with cases seems contiguous.

TRAIN TIMETABLES
Peloponissou Station It is easy to read the Peloponissou timetable and come to the conclusion that a large number of trains are leaving the station at the same time. On seeing the single-line track, a newcomer cannot be blamed for feeling apprehensive that it may prove difficult to select the correct carriages. The mystification arises from the fact that the trains are detailed separately from Athens to say Corinthos, Mikines, Argos, Tripolis, Pirgos and etc, etc. There is no mention that the railway line is a circular layout, with single trains circumscribing the route and that each place name is simply a stop on the journey.

Making changes for branch lines can be 'exciting'! Stations are labelled in demotic script and there is no comprehensible announcement from the guard, thus it is easy to fail to make an exit on cue!

Athens to Patras:
Depart   0640, 0826, 1020, 1305, 1542, 1820, 2139 hrs.
Arrive   1055, 1206, 1430, 1653, 2005, 2153, 0149 hrs.

Patras to Athens:
Depart   0630, 0811, 1105, 1350, 1705, 1842, 2013, 0210 hrs.
Arrive   1002, 1257, 1457, 1832, 2118, 2239, 0010, 0636 hrs.
One way fare: Athens to Patras : B class 540 drs, A class 811 drs.

TRAVEL AGENTS There are offices selling tickets for almost anything to almost anywhere which include:
ABC 58 Stadiou St. Tel. 321-1381
CHAT 4 Stadiou St. Tel. 322-2886
Key Tours 5th Floor, 2 Ermou St. Tel. 323-3756
Viking* 3 Filellinon St. Tel. 322-9383
* *Probably the agency most highly regarded by students for prices and variety.*
International Student & Youth Travel Service (SYTS) 11 Nikis St. Tel. 323-3767
For FIYTO membership. Second floor, open Monday - Friday 0900 - 1900 hrs. and Saturday from 0900 - 1200 hrs.

Filellinon and the parallel street of Odhos Nikis, to the west of Syntagma Sq, are jam packed with tourist agencies and student organisations including one or two express coach and train fare companies. A sample, going up the rise from Syntagma Square, includes:
Budget Student Travel On the right opposite a church.
Stafford Travel On the corner of Filellinon and Kidathineon Sts.

YOUTH HOSTEL ASSOCIATION *See* **The Accommodation**

A souvlaki snackbar owner – Iraklion actually, and the boots are a give-away

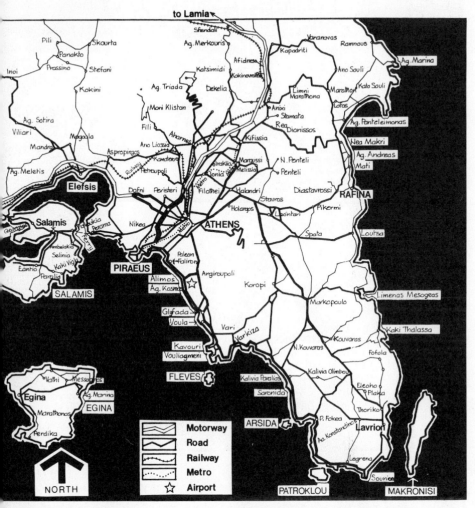

Illustration 7
Athens Environs, Suburbs, Bus & Metro Routes

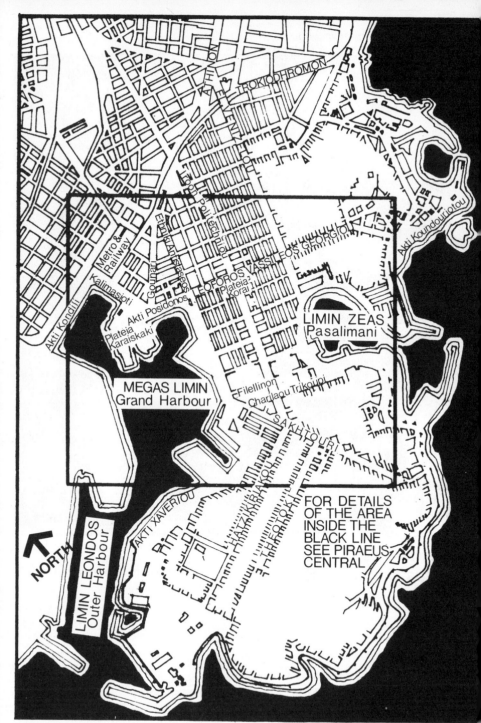

Illustration 8   Piraeus

10 PIRAEUS (Pireas, Pireefs)

Fortune and hope farewell! I've found the port you've done with me; go now with others sport   From a Greek epigram

Tel prefix 01
Piraeus is the port of Athens (Illustrations 8, 9 & 10) and the usual ferry-boat departure point for Crete and, incidentally, most other Aegean islands. A confusing town
on first acquaintance, but very unlike the old Piraeus portrayed in the film *Never on
Sunday.* The bawdy seaport cafes, tavernas and seedy waterfront have been
replaced by smart shipping offices, respectable banks and tree planted thorough-
fares, squares and parks.
 Arrival at Piraeus will usually be by Metro or bus if coming from inland, or by ferry-
boat if arriving by sea. (Well, it would be a long tiring swim, wouldn't it?).

ARRIVAL BY BUS
From Syntagma Sq (Athens), Bus No. 40 arrives at Plateia Korai (*Tmr* C3) but in truth
that is rather an over simplification. For a start the bus is absolutely crammed early
morning and it is very difficult to know one's exact whereabouts which is germane as
the bus hurtles on down to the end of the Piraeus peninsula. The first indicator that
the end of the ¾ hour journey is imminent is when the bus runs parallel to the Metro
lines. The second is crossing a wide avenue at right-angles (Leoforos Vassileos
Georgiou) after which signs for the Archaeological Museum indicate that it is time to
bale out.
 From Plateia Korai, north-west along Leoforos Vassileos Georgiou (Yeoryiou)
leads to the Main (Grand or Central) Harbour (*Tmr* D2); south-east progresses
towards Limin Zeas (Pasalimani) (*Tmr* C/D4) and east towards Limin Mounikhias
(Tourkolimano) (*Tmr* B5), the latter two being the marina harbours.
 From Omonia Sq (Athens) Bus No. 49 arrives at Ethniki Antistaseos (*Tmr* C2); from
the East airport, (a yellow) Bus No. 19 (but often numberless), arrives at Karaiskaki Sq
(*Tmr* C/D2). Karaiskaki or Akti Tzelepi Square is a main bus terminal. The brackets
note regarding the No. 19 bus should be expanded to point out that all the other
buses are blue.
 Another service (Bus No. 101) arrives at Theotoki St (*Tmr* E/F3/4) from whence
head north-east towards Sakhtouri St and turn left in a northerly direction to reach
the southern end of the Main Harbour quay front.

ARRIVAL BY METRO
Piraeus Metro station (*Tmr* 1C1/2), the end of the line, is hidden away in the corner of
a large but rather inconspicuous building, flanked by Plateia Roosevelt. It could well
be a warehouse, an empty shell of an office block, in fact almost anything but a Metro
terminus. Passengers emerge opposite the quayside, at the north end of the
waterfront.
 If catching a ferry almost immediately, it is probably best to make a temporary
headquarters by turning right out of the entrance, following the quay round to the left
and 'falling' into one of the three or so cafe-bars set in the harbour facing side of a
sizeable quayside block of buildings. The importance of establishing a shorebase,
or bridgehead, becomes increasingly apparent whilst attempts are made to locate
the particular ferry-boat departure point.
 To obtain tickets turn to the left (*Fsw*) out of the Metro station and follow the
quayside round. First major landmark is Karaiskaki (or Akti Tzelepi) Sq (*Tmr* C/D2),
fronted by large shipping office buildings which are surmounted by a number of
neon lit signs. These advertising slogans change from year to year but the point is

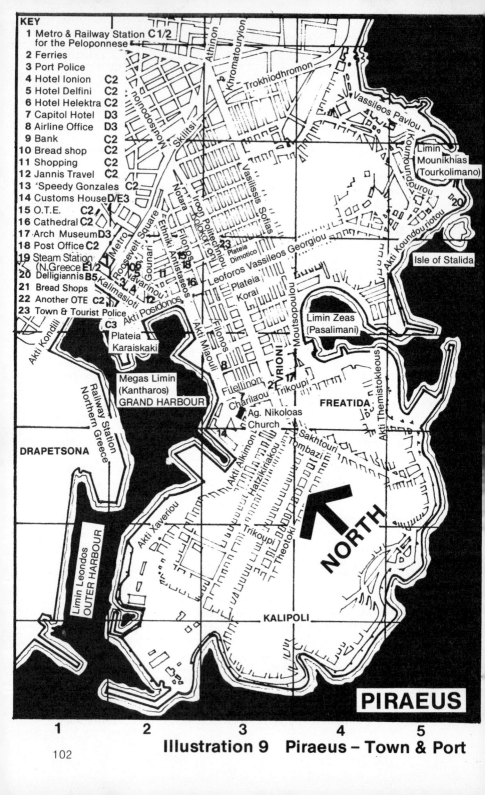

KEY

1 Metro & Railway Station **C1/2**
 for the Peloponnese
2 Ferries
3 Port Police
4 Hotel Ionion **C2**
5 Hotel Delfini **C2**
6 Hotel Helektra **C2**
7 Capitol Hotel **D3**
8 Airline Office **D3**
9 Bank **C2**
10 Bread shop **C2**
11 Shopping **C2**
12 Jannis Travel **C2**
13 'Speedy Gonzales' **C2**
14 Customs House **D/E3**
15 O.T.E. **C2**
16 Cathedral **C2**
17 Arch Museum **D3**
18 Post Office **C2**
19 Steam Station **E1/2**
 (N.Greece)
20 Delligiannis **B5**
21 Bread Shops
22 Another OTE **C2**
23 Town & Tourist Police

PIRAEUS

Illustration 9   Piraeus – Town & Port

that they are a noticeable landmark. Proceed along the quay road (Akti Posidonos), between the Streets of Gounari and Ethniki Antistaseos, (*Tmr* C2), keeping the waterfront to the right. Reference to **Ferry-Boat Ticket Offices, A to Z** gives details of various ticket offices. The port police are located in a quayside shed and must be regarded as favourites to dispense fairly accurate information about ferry-boats. Any information received though is best tucked away for future comparison with the rest of the advice acquired.

ARRIVAL BY FERRY
Reorientate using the above information, but bearing in mind that ferries dock all the way round the Grand Harbour, from the area of the Metro station (*Tmr* 1C1/2) as far down as the Olympic office (*Tmr* 8D3).

ARRIVAL BY TRAIN
If passengers have not alighted at Athens, Peloponnese trains pull up at the same terminus building as the Metro (*Tmr* 1C1/2) and the Northern Greece trains on the far (north-west) side of the Grand Harbour (*Tmr* 19D/E1/2).

THE ACCOMMODATION & EATING OUT
The Accommodation General remarks for Athens also apply here. Although I have never had to doss (or camp) out in Piraeus, I am advised that it is not to be recommended. There are just too many disparate (desperate?) characters wandering about. Anne acidly pointed out that it was not entirely safe for lone females walking round revising a guide book – and requested danger money!

Close by the Metro Station are the:
Hotel Ionion (*Tmr* 4C2) (Class C) 10 Kapodistrion   Tel. 417-0992
Directions: Turn left from the Metro station and/or Roosevelt Sq (*Fsw*) down the quay road, Kalimasioti St, and left again at the first turning.
    The hotel, halfway up on the right, is noticeable by the prominent sign promising *Family Hotel and from now on Economical Prices*. But is it with doubles from 2000 drs?
The Delfini (*Tmr* 5C2) (Class C) 7 Leoharous St   Tel. 412-3512
Directions: As above, but the second turning left.
    Doubles with shower from 2200 drs.
Hotel Helektra (*Tmr* 6C2) (Class E) 12 Navarinou   Tel. 417-7057
Directions: At the top of Leoharous St, turn right on to Navarinou St and the hotel is at the end of the block.
    During the season doubles sharing the bathroom cost 1100 drs.

Following the quay road of Akti Posidonos round to the right along the waterfront of Akti Miaouli towards the Custom's office (*Tmr* 14D/E3), and close by the Church of Ag Nikolaos, advances to the bottom of Leoforos Charilaou Trikoupi (*Tmr* D3). This street runs south-east and is amply furnished with cheaper hotels including the following:
Capitol Hotel (*Tmr* 7D3) (Class C) Ch. Trikoupi/147 Filonos Sts   Tel. 452-4911
Directions: As above
    A double en suite costs 1650 drs.
Glaros Hotel (Class C) 4 Ch. Trikoupi   Tel. 452-7887
Double rooms start at 1400 drs sharing and 1650 drs en suite. Breakfast costs 180 drs.
Serifos Hotel (Class C) 5 Ch. Trikoupi.   Tel. 452-4967
A double room en suite from 1650 drs.
Santorini Hotel (Class C) 6 Ch. Trikoupi.   Tel. 452-2147
Prices as for the *Serifos Hotel*.

Homeridion Hotel (Class B) 32 Ch. Trikoupi.　　　　　Tel. 451-9811
Rather expensive with a double room starting off at 1710 rising during the season to 2250 drs.

Forming a junction with Leoforos Charilaou Trikoupi is Notara St up which turn left. On this street is sited the:
Faros Hotel (Class D) 140 Notara St　　　　　Tel. 452-6317
Directions: As above.
　More down-to-earth with a double room en suite from 1465 drs.

Again at right angles to Leoforos Charilaou Trikoupi, is Kolokotroni St on which are situated the following hotels:
Park House (Class B) 103 Kolokotroni St　　　　　Tel. 452-4611
Directions: As above.
　Double rooms en suite from 3790 drs including a shower and breakfast.
Aris Hotel (Class D) 117 Kolokotroni St　　　　　Tel. 452-0487
　A double room sharing from 1250 drs and en suite 1400 drs.

Also leading off to the left is Iroon Politechniou (once Vassileos Konstantinou) whereon:
Noufara Hotel (Class B) 45 Iroon Politechniou　　　　　Tel. 411-5541
Directions: As above.
　Doubles start at 3200 drs complete with shower. (Phew!)
Savoy Hotel (Class B) 93 Iroon Politechniou　　　　　Tel. 413-1102
Guests will have to be flush with a double room en suite costing 4905 drs including breakfast.

Up Iroon Politechniou, turning right, or south-east, at Plateia Korai along Leoforos Vassileos Georgiou (Vassileos Yeoryiou) proceeds, on the left, to:
Diogenis Hotel (Class B) 27 Leoforos Vassileos Georgiou　　　　　Tel. 412-5471
Directions: As above.
　A few hundred drachmae less than the *Savoy* at 4020 drs. The prices include breakfast.

The Eating Out For eating out read the Athens comments as a general guide. Piraeus is not noted for outstanding rendezvous around the Grand Harbour and its encircling terrain, despite the numerous restaurants, tavernas and cafes along the quayside roads. On the other hand there are some excellent eating places in the area bordering the eastern coastline of the Piraeus peninsula, bounded by Akti Moutsopoulou (*Tmr* C/D3/4) and Akti Koumoundourou (*Tmr* B5) encircling (respectively) the Zeas and Mounikhias harbous.
　Especially recommended by Anne is the classy:
Delligiannis (*Tmr* 20B5) 1 Akti Koundouriotou　　　　　Tel. 413-2013
Directions: A very pleasant setting of the 'pretty' part of Piraeus up on the hill to the south-west of Limin Mounikhias. This overlooks a few million pounds worth of private yachts lying to anchor in the most attractive harbour.
　Apart from the position, the selection of food is excellent and there is outside seating while the inside resembles a high-class saloon bar. The service is quick, friendly and honest. For instance, enquirers will be advised that the 'souvlaki flambe' is nothing more than souvlaki on fire! 'Inside information' advises that the 'birds liver in wine' is delicious, despite being listed as a starter. Costing 450 drs, the portions are larger than most main courses at other tavernas.

On Plateia Karaiskaki, a number of cafe-bar/restaurants stretch along the quayside of the large building that dominates the square. A white van sometimes parks up, early in the day, on the edge of the square, selling small pizzas and feta cheese pies for 70 drs from the back of the vehicle.

THE A TO Z OF USEFUL INFORMATION
AIRLINE OFFICE & TERMINUS *(Tmr* 8D3) The Olympic office is halfway down the Esplanade of Akti Miaouli, at the junction with Odhos II Merarkhias.

BANKS The most impressive is a vast, imposing emporium situated opposite the corner of the Esplanade roads of Posidonos and Miaouli *(Tmr* 9C2).

BEACHES Between Zeas and Mounikhias harbours, opposite Stalida island. Also *See* **Beaches, A to Z, Athens.**

BREAD SHOPS One on Roosevelt Sq *(Tmr* 10C2) and others on Odhos Kolokotroni *(Tmr* 21C2/3) and Charilaou Trikoupi *(Tmr* 21D3).

BUSES Two buses circulate around the peninsula of Piraeus. One proceeds from Roosevelt Sq to Limin Mounikhias, and on to Neon Faliron, and the other from Korai Sq *(Tmr* C3) via the Naval Cadets College to Limin Zeas.

COMMERCIAL SHOPPING AREA *(Tmr* 11C2) There is a flourishing and busy Market area behind the Bank mentioned above, hemmed in by the streets of Gounari and Ethniki Antistaseos. There is an excellent supermarket on the corner of Odhos Makras Stoas, if a shopper cannot be bothered to visit the various shops and stalls of the market. Prices in Piraeus are generally higher than elsewhere in Greece and shop hours are as for Athens.

FERRY-BOATS Most island ferry-boats leave from the area encompassed by Akti Kondili, to the north of the main harbour, Karaiskaki Sq, Akti Posidonos and Akti Miaouli, to the west of the main harbour. As a general rule the ferries for Crete depart from the more southerly part of the Esplanade road, Akti Miaouli *(Tmr* D2/3). For timetables and further details *See* **Iraklion** (CHAPTER 12) and **Chania** (CHAPTER 13). Note that ferry-boats also dock at **Kastelli** (CHAPTER 15), **Ag. Nikolaos** (CHAPTER 17) and **Sitia** (CHAPTER 18).

FERRY-BOAT TICKET OFFICES Yes well, at least they lie extremely thick on the waterfront. It is probably best to make enquiries about the exact location of the particular ferry's departure point when purchasing the tickets. Ticket sellers 'lie in wait' all the way down the quayside streets of Kalimasioti and Akti Posidonos, that is, from the Metro Station, past the Gounari St turning to the bottom of Ethniki Antistaseos. They tend to refer to a ship's point of departure with an airy wave of the hand.
     My favourite offices lie at opposite ends of the spectrum, as it were, and are:
Jannis Stoulis Travel *(Tmr* 12C2) 2 Gounari St.   Tel. 417-9491
Directions: Situated on the right at Gounari St *(Sbo).*
     The owner, who wears a rather disinterested air, is extremely efficient and speaks three languages, including English.

His fast talking, 'speedy Gonzales', counterpart occupies a wall-to-wall stairway on Kalimasioti St *(Tmr* 13C2). My regard for the latter operator may be coloured by the fact that he was the man who sold me my first ever Greek island ferry-boat ticket.

There are two ticket offices on the harbour side of the large building on Plateia Karaiskaki, beyond the cafes, two of almost dozens of ticket offices spaced around

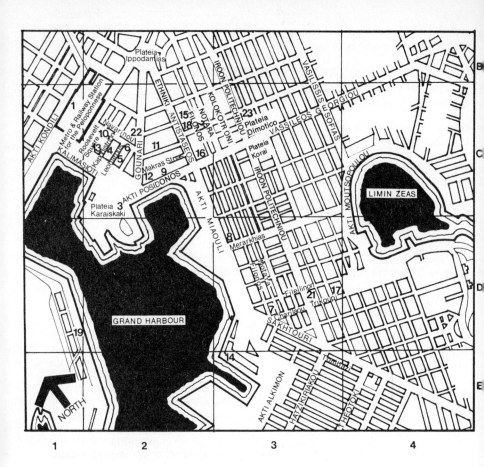

Tmr = Town map reference
Fsw = Facing seawards
Sbo = Sea behind one

Illustration 10   Piraeus Inset

this edifice. An enterprising vendor of tickets lurks, from early morning, amongst the ferry-boat stalls on Akti Posidonos.

When searching the quayside for the correct ferry-boat, do not go beyond the Port Offices and Custom house (*Tmr* 14D/E3), towards the south end of the harbour, as these berths are for cruise ships only.

NTOG Somewhat inconveniently situated on Zeas Harbour (*Tmr* C/D4) and only open weekdays between 0700 - 1500 hrs.

OTE The main office (*Tmr* 15C2) is north of the Post Office and another is on Odhos Navarinou (*Tmr* 22C2).

PLACES OF INTEREST

Archaeological Museum (*Tmr* 17D3) Situated between Filellinon and Leoforos Charilaou Trikoupi Sts and reopened in the last few years. Reportedly well laid out, with easy to identify exhibits. Opening hours Monday to Saturday, 0845 - 1500 hrs, Sunday 0930 - 1430 hrs and closed Tuesdays. Only Greeks are allowed free admission here, as elsewhere in Greece, foreigners having to pay 100 drs.

Ag Triada (*Tmr* 16C2) The Cathedral was rebuilt in the early 1960s, having been destroyed in 1944. Distinctive, mosaic tile finish.

Zea Theatre Adjacent to the Archaeological Museum, the remains date from about the second century BC.

Limin Zeas (Pasalimani) (*Tmr* C/D4) This semicircular harbour is of great antiquity. Now it shelters fishing boats and caiques, provides a yacht basin for larger, modern yachts, is the location for the Naval Museum of Greece, contains a Flying Dolphin (hydrofoil) terminal as well as a base for yacht charterers. Excavations have shown that, in ancient times, several hundred boat sheds radiated out around the edge of the harbour housing the Triremes, the great, three-banked warships of antiquity.

The Naval Museum of Greece Adjacent to Zeas Harbour with a varied and interesting series of exhibits down through the ages.

Limin Mounikhias (Tourkolimano or Mikrolimano) (*Tmr* B5) Continuing on round the coast cliff road from Limin Zeas, past the bathing beach (facing the tiny island of Stalida) and the Royal Yacht Club of Greece, leads to the renowned, 'chatty', picturesque and again semicircular harbour of Mounikhias. From here racing yachts are believed to have departed for regattas in Saroniko Bay as far back as the 4th century BC, as they do now. The quayside is ringed with tavernas, cafes and restaurants forming a backcloth to the multi-coloured sails of the assembled yachts crowded into the harbour.

The Hill of Kastela overlooks the harbour and has a modern, open-air, marble amphitheatre, wherein theatre and dance displays are staged, more especially during the Athens Festival (*See* **Places of Interest, A to Z, Athens**).

Filonos Street (*Tmr* B/C/D2/3) The 'Soho' of Piraeus, espousing what's left of the old *Never on Sunday* atmosphere of the town.

POLICE
Port On the quay bounded by Akti Posidonos.
Tourist & Town (*Tmr* 23C3) Dimotico Square.

POST OFFICE (*Tmr* 18C2) On Filonos St, north-west of the Cathedral.

RAILWAY STATIONS
Metro (Underground) (*Tmr* 1C1/2). *See* **Arrival by Metro.**
'Steam' Station (*Tmr* 1C1/2) The Peloponnese terminus is alongside and the far side of the Metro Station.
'Steam' Station (*Tmr* 19D/E1/2) The terminus for Northern Greece is situated on the far, north-west side of the Grand Harbour.

SWIMMING POOL Adjacent to Limin Zeas Harbour.

TELEPHONE NUMBERS & ADDRESSES
NTOG (*Tmr* C/D4) Zeas Marina   Tel. 413-5716
Port authorities   Tel. 451-1311

OTHER MAINLAND PORTS

GITHION (Gythion). For details of this mainland Peloponnese port *See* **Kastelli** (CHAPTER 15).

Chania Old Quarter

PART THREE
11 Introduction to Crete (Kriti)

There is a land called Crete in the midst of the wine dark sea.   Homer in The Odyssey

VITAL STATISTICS
The island is approximately 264 km long, and averages some 55 km in width with an area estimated at 8,200 sq km and a population of just below 500,000.

SPECIALITIES
Yoghurt (from a tub); tighanites – pancakes covered with honey and sesame seeds; Cretan wines of note, include Minos, Gortinos and Kissamos; Mandareeni – a tangerine liquer; raki or tsikoudhia – a (more) lethal ouzo; herbal tea; honey; embroidery; Nikos Kazantzakis (author of amongst other books, *Zorba the Greek*) the Cretan men's mountain 'uniform' of headscarf, black shirt, old fashioned jodhpurs and riding boots.

RELIGIOUS HOLIDAYS AND FESTIVALS
These include, (in addition to the Greek national celebrations) two weeks before Lent, a carnival celebrated throughout the island; 25th March at the Churches of Prasas (Iraklion County) and Apokorona (Chania County) – Annunciation of Our Lady; First Sunday after Easter at the Monasteries of Vrondisi and Zaros (Iraklion County) and Neo Chorio and Apokorona (Chania County) – St Thomas; 23rd April at the Monastery of Ag. Georgios Epanosifi (between Archanes and Charakas, Iraklion County) – a religious feast and celebratory mass; 20-27th May, Chania City – anniversary of the Battle of Crete; 26-27th May, Chora Sfakion – anniversary of the Declaration of the 1821 Revolution; 24th June – island-wide bonfires – birthday of St John the Baptist; Falasarna (Nr Kastelli, Chania County) – a moveable Tomato fiesta (dependent on when they ripen, of course!); 1st-15th July, Dafnes (Iraklion County) – wine festival, folk art exhibition; 2nd-10th July, Sitia and Kornaria – cultural and artistic festivities; 13th-18th July, Voukolies (Chania County) – cultural and artistic events; 15th-30th July, Rethymnon – wine festival; 16th-31st July, Rethymnon – handicraft exhibition; 15th-17th July, Voni (Nr Thrapsano, Iraklion County) – religious fair; 19th-22nd July, Sitia – raisin festival; 29th-31st July, Archanes – painting and handicraft exhibition; 28th July-10th August, Vamos – cultural and artistic events; 13th-15th August, Archanes – festival; 12th-15th August, Anogia (Rethymnon County) – cultural and artistic festivities; 13th-20th August, Perama (Rethymnon County) – raisin festival; 15th August, religious fairs in many villages, including Mochos (Iraklion County), Neapolis, Meskla (Chania County), Alikampos near Vryses (Chania County), Armeni (Rethymnon County), Chrysoskalitissa near Stomio (Chania County), Spili (Rethymnon County) and Akoumia near Melambes (Rethymnon County) – Assumption of Virgin Mary; 13th-15th August, Neapolis – festivities; 25th August, Amari (Rethymnon County) – religious fairs, St Titus day; 27th August, Vrondisi Monastery (Iraklion County) and Vryses (Chania County) – religious fair, St Fanourios; 29th August, Kournas and Ghionna site (both in Chania County) – religious fair, St John the Baptist; 1st-10th September, Gavalochori (Chania County) – folklore manifestations; 14th September, Alikianos, Varypetro (Chania County) and villages around Mount Idha – religious fairs, Raising of the Holy Cross; 7th October, Monastery of Gouverneto (Chania County) – St John the Hermit; third Sunday of October, Elos (Chania County) – chestnut festival; 8th November, Arkadhi Monastery (Rethymnon County) – anniversary of the 1866 holocaust, folklore dancing in Rethymnon town; 11th November, Iraklion – religious procession for patron saint of the town (St Menas); 4th December, Ag. Varvara (Iraklion County) – St Barbara; 6th December, Agios Nikolaos (Lasithi County) – St Nicholas.

GENERAL

Crete is not so much an island, more a land in its own right. It is very much what you make it, with extreme contrasts offering almost every type of scenery and terrain imaginable: from the date palm clad, sandy beach shore of Vai in the north-east to the winter-snow clad mountains in the south-west; from the modernity of the National Highway, that skirts most of the north coastline, to the uncertain, almost indistinguishable donkey tracks that penetrate the interior vastness; from the lowland, polythene covered greenhouse squalor that edges some of the vast Messara Plain to the simple, agricultural simplicity of the Omalos mountain plain; from the dusty, urbane, worldly-wise city of Iraklion to the country town of Kastelli; from the quiet, orderly, business-like Neapolis to the industrial squalor of Timbaki; from the relatively peaceful, seaside charm of Rethymnon to the package tourist frenzy of Agios Nikolaos; from fly-blown, bedraggled Lendas to the simple, native charm of Keratokambos; from the over-exploited cave dwellings of Matala to the almost idyllic fishing village of Loutro; from the disjointed sprawl of Ierapetra to the bustling, beautiful alpine mountain town of Spili and the simple Minoan remains of Kato Zakros to the heavily restored, ancient city of Knossos.

Due to the extremely clement weather, the island has a long tourist season stretching from the beginning of April to the end of October. A number of areas have been subject to massive exploitation by the holiday industry, but whatever the requirements, Crete, perhaps more than any other situation in Greece, if not Europe, can surely fulfill every person's wishes. Be they for a sophisticated, self-contained luxury dream hotel or the rural simplicity of a small pension situated on a craggy, granite mountainside or edging a sun drenched beach. Activities can, for instance, encompass the extremes of hedonistic sunbathing, the quiet bustle of investigating archaeological sites to brisk mountain walking.

Crete's complicated and convoluted past is matched by an almost embarrassing wealth of archaeological remains and historical sites. Both require a lot more than a passing and light hearted enquiry to even scratch the surface.

Much is made of the Cretan's independant, steadfast, fiery nature and the exuberance of their welcome but it is expecting too much, in the comparatively short time available to most travellers to experience more than the usual reception afforded to the vast majority of holiday-makers. These now number some 1,000,000 per year, mostly concentrated in the summer months. Certainly Cretans suffer fools less gladly than most of their fellow countrymen on the other islands and often do not take kindly to being the subject of prying eyes, more especially photographic curiosity.

Visitors' requirements must vary considerably from a two week package holiday, an independant traveller, wishing to break loose of the fetters usually associated with 'organised' tourism, and the 'dedicated' drop-out planning on eking out a summer on one or other of the beaches, where the authorities turn a blind eye to this unlawful pursuit.

Most travellers arrive on Crete at the airports or harbours of the northern cities of Iraklion or Chania while some more intrepid voyagers may dock at the ports of Kastelli in the north-west, or Agios Nikolaos, in the north-east.

Due to the geographical spread and spacing of the major northern towns of Ag. Nikolaos, Chania, Iraklion and Rethymnon, and taking into account the mountain ranges that form east to west barriers, it is more comprehensible to split the guide up into a number of regions based on the aforementioned places. Obviously the more adventurous may cover all of one of these areas, or maybe several. The time available to a great majority of tourists will not allow more than a detailed visit to some selected locations or a more cursory inspection of rather more places. Time is not the only controlling factor and account must be taken of the available lines of communication. The first time visitor may well not appreciate that with no trains, a bus service that only radiates out from the various town centres on the north coast and many roads that were not really constructed with modern day traffic in mind, daily distances covered can be comparatively small. Added to these strictures are the extremely mountainous nature of much of the land and the fact that many of the minor roads are in an appalling condition, all of which only further undermines all but the most determined traveller's ability to attain widely spaced objectives.

Due to the extent and diffuse aspects of Crete, I have had to amend the accustomed *Candid Guide* format and style usually followed. For instance, recording the 'First Impressions' of each island in a group has been altered to one of listing these for each significant place covered in any detail. Crete has sufficient accommodation to cope with all but the height of season influx, unlike many small islands where rooms may be at a premium for much of the year. The sheer size and amount of accommodation available makes it physically impossible to stay in, or even call on, more than a percentage of them in the larger towns. I have, therefore, only listed those places that caught my fancy (for some reason or another) as well as noting the frequency of accommodation in locations, where it is less easily available. The same reasoning and approach applies to eating out.

Crete, once extensively forested, is now only lightly wooded, which may well be something to do with the islands comparative shortage of fresh water. There is an abundance of flora, seen at its best after the spring rains, some of which are indigenous to Crete, including the 'all healing' Cretan 'dittany', from the mint family of plants. Wild life includes the very interesting 'Kri-Kri' (Agrimi) but no other creature of note although there are supposed to be scatterings of scorpions, but no snakes. The bird life makes Crete an ornothologist's delight, the most impressive of the species surely being the majestic birds of prey.

Symbols, Keys & Definitions

Below are some notes in respect of the few initials and symbols used in the text as well as an explanation of the possibly idiosyncratic nouns, adjectives and phrases that are to be found scattered throughout the book.

Where and when inserted, a star system of rating indicates my judgement of an island and possibly it's accommodation and restaurant standards by the inclusion of one to five stars. One star signifies bad, two basic, three good, four very good and five excellent. I must admit the ratings are carried out on whimsical grounds and are based purely on personal observation. For instance where a place, establishment or island receives a detailed critique I may consider that sufficient unto the day.... The absence of a star or any mention at all has no detrimental significance and might, for instance, indicate that I did not personally inspect the establishment.

Keys

The key *Tmr* is used as a map reference to aid easy location on port and town maps. Other keys used include *Sbo* – 'Sea behind one'; *Fsw* – 'Facing seawards'; *Fbqbo* – 'Ferry-boat quay behind one' and OTT – 'Over The Top'.

GROC's definitions, 'proper' adjectives & nouns: They definitely require some elucidation as follows:

Backshore: the furthest strip of beach from the sea's edge. The marginal rim edging the shore from the surrounds. *See* **Scrubbly**

Benzina: a small fishing boat.

Chatty: with pretensions to grandeur or sophistication.

Dead: an establishment that appears to be 'terminally' closed and is not about to open for business.

Donkey-droppings: as in 'two donkey-droppings' indicating a very small, 'one-eyed' hamlet.

Doo-hickey: an Irish based colloquialism suggesting an extreme lack of sophistication and or rather 'daffy' (despite contrary indications in the authoritive *Patridges Dictionary of Slang!*).

Downtown: a rundown/derelict area of a settlement – the wrong side of the railway tracks.

Ethnic: very unsophisticated, Greek indigenous and as a rule applied to hotels and pensions. *See* **Provincial.**

Greasy spoon: a dirty, unwholesome taverna or restaurant.

Great unwashed: the less attractive, modern day mutation of the 1960s hippy. Western European, 'by choice', inactive loafers, layabouts, and or unemployed drop-outs. Once having located a desirable location, often a splendid beach, they camp out usually under plastic and in shabby tents, thus ensuring the spot is made totally unattractive to anyone else. The 'men of the tribe' tend to trail a mangy dog on a piece of string. The women, more often than not with a grubby child or two in train, pester cafe-bar clients to purchase items of jewelry.

Note the above genre appears to be incurably penniless (but then who isn't?).

Hillbilly: another adjective or noun, similar to 'ethnic', often applied to describe countryside or a settlement, as in 'backwoods'.

Hippy: those who live outside the predictable, boring (!) mainstream of life and are frequently genuine if sometimes impecunious travellers. The category may include students or young professionals taking a sabbatical and who are 'negligent' of their sartorial appearance.

Icons: naturally, a religious painting of a holy person or personages, usually executed on a board. During the Middle Ages the Mediterranean would appear to have been almost awash with unmanned rowing boats and caiques ferrying icons hither and thither.

Independents: vacationers who prefer to step off the package holiday carousel and make their own way.

Krifo Scholio: illegal, undercover schools operated during the Turkish occupation, generally run by the inmates of religious orders to educate Greek children in the intricacies of the Orthodox religion and the traditional ways of life.

Mr Big: a local trader or pension owner, an aspiring tycoon, a small fish trying to be a big one in a smaller pool. Flashy with shady overtones.

One-eyed: small

Poom: a descriptive noun borrowed after sighting on Crete, some years ago, a crudely written sign advertising accommodation that simply stated POOMS! The accommodation on offer was crude, low-ceilinged, raftered, earth-floored, window-less rooms simply equipped with a truckle bed and rickety oil-cloth covered washstand – very reminiscent of typical Cycladean cubicles of the 1950/60s period.

Provincial: usually applied to accommodation and is an improvement on *Ethnic.* Not meant to indicate, say, dirty but should conjure up images of faded, rather gloomy establishments with a mausoleum atmosphere; high ceilinged Victorian rooms with worn, brown linoleum; dusty, tired aspidistras; bathrooms of unbelievable antiquity.

Richter scale: borrowed from earthquake seismology and employed to indicate the (appalling) state of toilets, on an 'eye-watering' scale.

Rustic: unsophisticated, unrefined.

Schlepper: vigorous touting for customers by restaurant staff. It is said of a good schlepper, in a market, that he can 'retrieve' a passer-by from up to 30 or 40 metres.

Scrubbly: often applied to a beach and indicating a rather messy, shabby area – often the 'backshore'.

Squatty: A Turkish (French) style ablution arrangement. None of the old familiar lavatory bowl and seat. Oh no, just two moulded footprints edging a dirty looking hole set in a porcelain surround. Apart from the unaccustomed nature of the exercise, the Lord simply did not give us enough limbs to keep ones shirt up and control wayward trousers that constantly attempt to flap down on to the floor, which is awash with goodness knows what! All this has to be enacted whilst gripping the toilet roll in one hand and wiping one's 'botty' with the other hand. Impossible! Incidentally the ladies should perhaps substitute blouse for shirt and skirt for trousers, but then it is easier (I am told) to tuck a skirt into one's waistband!

Way-station: mainly used to refer to an office or terminus stuck out in the sticks and cloaked with an abandoned, unwanted air.

A taxi, Chania Harbourside

Tmr

1 Ferry-boat terminal B4
2 Hotel Dedalos C2
3 Hotel Hellas B/C2
4 Pension Lions C2
5 Hotel Astoria C3
6 Hotel Kretan Sun C2
7 Hotel Olympic D2
8 Hotel Palladion B/C2
9 Hotel Hania B2
10 Youth Hostel B1/2
11 Hotel Xenia A/B1
12 Pension Mary's B1
13 Pension Karpathos B1/2
14 Rooms Vergina B1
15 Rooms Mary B1
16 Hotel Rea B1
17 Hotel Ionia C2
18 Pension Ilion C3/4

19 Restaurant Kostas C2
20 Victoria Pizza Bar C2/3
21 Fotiou Lane C2
22 Airline Office D3
23 National Bank of Greece B2
24 Bread Shops C2
25 Ferry-boat Bus terminal B4
26 Chania Bus terminal C1
27 Xenia Bus terminal A/B1/2
28 Town Police C2/3
29 Tourist shop A/B1/2
30 Laundrette B/C3
31 Laundry B/C2
32 N.T.O.G. C3
33 O.T.E. B/C2
34 Basilica of St. Mark C2

35 Agias Ekaterini C1
36 Agios Titos Church B2/3
37 Venetian Fort A3
38 Venetian Arsenals B2/3
39 Plateia Venizelos/ Morosini Fountain C2
40 Archaeological Museum C3
41 Venetian Loggia B/C2
42 Kainouria Gate D2/3
43 Post Office C/D2
44 Tourist Police C2
45 Port Police A/B3/4
46 Tennis Club B/C4
47 Plateia Kallergon/ El Greco Park B/C2
48 Plateia Eleftherios C3
49 Plateia Kornarou/ Bembo Fountain D2

Tmr = Town map refe
Fsw = Facing seawa
Sbo = Sea behind or

IRAKLION

Illustration

114

12 IRAKLION (Heraklion, Iraklio, Heracleion) **
Largest city, main port and airport

FIRST IMPRESSIONS
A dusty, bustling, cosmopolitan city port; a mix of Cretan and Western European worlds; one-way traffic systems, traffic police, traffic lights and parking meters.

VITAL STATISTICS
Tel. prefix 081. Population about 85,000.

HISTORY
Iraklion surfaces historically in the Roman era as Herakleium, the port of Knossos. The Arabs took over the town (and island) in AD824 and named it Khandak after which, in 961, Phokas liberated the town and renamed it Khandax. In 1210 the Venetians made the city their capital and named it (and the island) Candia. The Venetians heavily fortified the city over the next 400 years but the Turks finally wore down the inhabitants, after a 22-year seige, in 1669. This was despite various relief forces being sent from Europe. The Venetian commander at the surrender was Francesco Morosini (honoured and recalled in the present-day name for the Fountain Square). Under the Turks the city was named Megalo Kastro, only assuming its present name after the end of Turkish rule, in 1898.

GENERAL
Iraklion can be a disappointing starting point. It has all the basic features that should ensure a satisfactory mix, including a Venetian harbour and other fine buildings, a walled city, a lively street market and a cosmopolitan fountain square, as well as a convenient commercial port and airport. Somehow the ingredients have been incorrectly added to the blender. Perhaps it is the lack of a self-respecting beach and a comprehensible grid layout to the town but I suspect the root of the problem is that the Venetian harbour is not sited in such a way as to act as an attractive focal point. Admittedly as the foremost administrative and commercial city of the island, as well as the centre of the tourist comings and goings, it would probably be asking too much to expect more charm and less frenetic activity. Buildings are coming down and going up all over the place, parking is impossible and the traffic is controlled by traffic lights, policemen and parking meters. Well, well!

There are a number of central cafe-bar gathering places. The most important, interesting and expensive is Plateia Venizelos (*Tmr* 39C2) formed by the pedestrian-precinct part of Chandakos St, where it butts on to the Main Street of (25th) Ikosipende Avgoustou. This irregular-shaped square surrounds the impressive and magnificent Morosini Fountain. Others include Plateia Kallergon/El Greco Park (*Tmr* 47B/C2) and Eleftherios Sq (*Tmr* 48C3) but both are rather disjointed. The former acts as a meeting place for the genus 'space man' (the 'laid back' variety) and drop-outs, and the latter is too large and spread out to provide a satisfactory venue.

Confinement of much of the new development within the old city walls has probably resulted in an uneasy feel to the layout but where Iraklion has spread outside the constraints of the Venetian fortifications, the resultant growth is of a totally unsatisfactory nature. To the west, row upon row of ugly, unfinished, concrete high-rise apartments and hotels are interspaced by poorly asphalted and unmade roads, barren waste areas littered with untidy heaps of rubble, scrap cars and the inevitable piles of blue plastic wrapped rubbish. To the east, 'concrete boxes' and relatively low-rise imitators of some of the worst of Western European sprawl lie thick on the ground. Perhaps the proximity of the airport has restricted the builders' towering ambitions in a heavenly direction!

It would be churlish to end the preamble on this sour note for many will find Iraklion to be full of interest and fascination: the unexpected and narrow side streets rambling almost drunkenly from one part of the City to another; the sheer excitement of Plateia Venizelos, (the fountain square), thronged with a cosmopolitan society; the throbbing street market that fills Odhos 1866 (*Tmr* C2), and its associated side lanes, that spills on to Kornarou Sq, close by the exquisite Bembos Fountain (*Tmr* 49D2); the Archaeological Museum and its outstanding collection of exhibits (*Tmr* 40C3); the rebuilt Venetian Arsenal (*Tmr* 38B2/3); Byzantine and Venetian churches including Agios Ekaterini (*Tmr* 35C1) and its outstanding collection of icons; finally the night-time bustle of the pedestrian street of Dhedhalou (*Tmr* C2/3) with rows of restaurant chairs and tables lining one side of the wide passageway.

ARRIVAL BY AIR
The airport is fairly close to the City centre, and can be reached by taxi, a 4 km walk or a 10 minute bus ride. The bus, No. 1, stops 700 m from the airport and the City end of the journey is very conveniently sited on Plateia Eleftherios, opposite the *Hotel Astoria* (*Tmr* 5C3) at the NTOG and Museum end of the square. The bus runs every 10 minutes until 2300 hrs and at 40 drs must be good value. Olympic Airways also run a bus service from the airport to their office (*Tmr* 22D3) at the south end of Eleftherios Sq.

ARRIVAL BY BUS
Buses arrive by ferry, so the information below applies.

ARRIVAL BY FERRY
The Piraeus boats storm into the Ferry-boat terminal (*Tmr* 1B4), throw out the bow anchor, reverse on to the quay wall, and, with a 'squeal of the brakes', the ramps seem to be down and vehicles thundering off before the ship is finally moored up. (In stark contrast to the pussy-footing about of their Italian counterparts). The ferries arrive in the early morning so there is plenty of time to take one's bearings before deciding on any particular course of action.

If moving straight out of town, the main Bus terminal (*Tmr* 25B4) is directly across the dual carriageway and the information sheet obtainable from the office is excellent.

To stay in Iraklion, consider turning right out of the Ferry-boat terminal gates along the Esplanade. Leave the Venetian Arsenal (*Tmr* 38B2/3) on the left, proceed up the rise past the small Venetian harbour on the right and turn left on to and up Odhos Ikosipende Avgoustou. At the top of this street, by the traffic lights on Plateia Nikiforos Phokas, turn left along Odhos Dikaiossinis which opens out on to Plateia Eleftherios. The point of this roundabout route is that it takes in most of the useful points that a traveller may wish to visit, ending up at the NTOG offices (*Tmr* 32C3), opposite the Archaeological Museum on the left of Eleftherios Sq.

THE ACCOMMODATION & EATING OUT
The Accommodation Bearing in mind the introductory remarks regarding the general abundance of accommodation, Iraklion is no exception to the rule but is rather more expensive in comparison to other major centres such as Chania and Rethymnon. The City is bursting with quarters of every class and type, but here are details of a few from the wide choice available.

There is an excellent organisation called *Filoxenia*, The Association of Rooms to Rent (Pensions) in the Iraklion Prefecture. Phew! The address is 1 Giamalaki St (2nd floor), Iraklion, Crete. Tel. 081-224260 (*Tmr* B/C1). Their plaque is stuck on the door of all members and ensures that the accommodation is clean and reasonably priced. The President is Achilleas Tsixlis who also runs the *Pension Achilleas* of the same address.

Anne whom readers will note has carried out much of the follow up research for the second edition, is of the opinion that travellers wishing to nose out inexpensive accommodation are best served by heading directly for the Chandakos area (*Tmr* B/C1/2). See below.

Hotel Dedalos (*Tmr* 2C2) (Class C) 15 Dhedhalou (Dedalou).   Tel. 224391
Directions: Dhedhalou St, a pedestrian precinct, is a left-hand turning off Ikopsipende Avgoustou opposite Plateia Venizelos (Fountain).

All rooms are en suite with a single room costing 1685 drs and a double room 2025 drs. Between 1st July and 15th October the rates rise to 1090 drs and 2490 drs. Breakfast may be mandatory, depending on occupancy, and costs 240 drs.

Pension Hadjidakis (Class C) 22 Dhedhalou.   Tel. 242446
Directions: Opposite the *Hotel Dedalos* (above).

Clean, sparse accommodation at 1500 drs for a double room sharing the bathroom.

Pension Lions (*Tmr* 4C2) (Class C) 9 Odhos Androgeo (ΑΝΔΡΟΓΕΟ)   Tel. 226510
Directions: Odhos Androgeo is east off Ikosipende Avgoustou St opposite Plateia Kallergon.

The owner is the secretary of the *Filoxenia* organisation and the pension is very clean if a little dingy but reasonably furnished. A high season double room costs 1500 drs sharing the bathroom.

Hotel Selena (Class C) 7 Odhos Androgeo   Tel. 226377
Directions: Close to the above pension.

A pleasant hotel with en suite bathrooms. On the other hand it is pleasing to report that they do not let us down, displaying a few of the intriguing little defects that make Greek accommodation such a 'joy'. One particular bathroom had the 'lavatory' positioned so that neither the lid nor seat could be fully raised, requiring males to utilise all the hands God issued; the lavatory flush mechanism emerged through a hole in the ceiling but obstructed the window and, despite there being a wall mounted shower point, the shower head did not possess a reciprocal hanging point. Thank goodness chaps do not have to 'wee' at the same time as they shower! Single rooms from 1760 drs and doubles 2200 drs rising to 2100 drs and 2650 drs (1st June - 30th Sept.).

Hotel Hellas (*Tmr* 3B/C2) (Class D) 11 Kantanoleon.   Tel. 225121
Directions: From Plateia Kallergon proceed past Odhos Minotavrou to the right and the hotel is on the left.

The proprietor, Mr. John, is a strong, engaging, helpful man. The hotel, which is more a pension, even a hostel, is a very useful and good value establishment to have up one's sleeve with a pleasant garden patio bar. It is true to say that the longer the stay the more apparent is the seediness with hot water being an 'off and on' commodity. Rooms are detailed as sharing the bathrooms but there are a few double rooms with bathroom en suite (1300 drs). Single rooms cost 800 drs and double rooms 900 drs rising respectively to 900 drs and 1015 drs (20th June - 19th Oct.). There is also a multi-bed dormitory.

Continuing round the block to the left are two downbeat Guest Houses offering basic accommodation:

Georgias on the left and **Atlas** on the right. I do not think they are members of *Filoxenia*! Anne assures me that the Atlas is okay, well basic with clean double rooms sharing the bathroom costing 1250 drs per night. Breakfast is available on the roof garden.

The side street now runs into Odhos Chandakos. To the left is the bottom of Plateia Venizelos but turning right, downhill, blazes the trail to more accommodation.

Hotel Palladion (*Tmr* 8B/C2) (Class D) 16 Chandakos St.   Tel. 282563
Directions: Half-way down Chandakos St, on the right.
    A truly ethnic, old fashioned, Greek provincial town hotel. All rooms share the bathrooms with singles costing 600 drs per night and doubles 900 drs rising to 750 drs and 1210 drs respectively (1st July - 30th Sept.).

Hotel Hania (*Tmr* 9B2) (Class E) 19 Kydonias St.   Tel. 284282
Directions: Continue on down Chandakos St and turn right along Odhos Kydonias. The hotel sits in a recess in the line of the street. *See* note below.
    George Thiakakis runs the lodgings not so much as a hotel, more as a cheap, cheerful and colourful hostel for the young. The entrance and courtyard are liberally covered in murals and instructions (which are only disobeyed if you wish to incur George's wrath). Try not to be put off by his 'couldn't care less', 'take it or leave it' attitude and bear in mind his understanding of English is often relative to his interest in the matter under discussion. Attentive readers will realise that I regard George as an irascible, middle-aged man but Anne's report says "George was very nice to me"! So take your choice - probably I am an unreasonable, geriatric travel writer! Keep an eye out for the three mannequins up the (private) stairs to the right and the massed plants in named and dated pots presented by past guests. A single bed costs 350 drs; double rooms 700 - 1000 drs and triples 1000 - 1400 drs.
N.B. Unfortunately George is scheduled to move and open a new establishment at CHERSONISOS (*See* ROUTE THREE), possibly as early as 1987. Let us hope the *Hania's* style lives on otherwise Chersonisos' gain will be Iraklion's loss.

Rooms Kristakos (Class E) 1 Vlaston (ΕΥΓΕΝΙΚΟ).
Directions: In the lane opposite Kydonias St. Despite still being signposted the *Hotel Regina* the establishment is *Rent Rooms Kristakos*, the hotel having vanished.
    Very ethnic, almost awful. The lady may well be in an emotional state and asks 1000 drs for a double room with shared bathroom.

Further on down Odhos Chandakos, to the right, leads to:

The Youth Hostel (*Tmr* 10B1/2) No 24, Chandakos   Tel. 286281
Directions: As above but note the establishment is closed between 1000 and 1330 hrs for cleaning.
    A bed costs about 320 drs with free showers. Sheets can be rented; luggage store in the manager's office costs 40 drs a day and there are mopeds for hire.

Beyond, on the left is:

Pension Marys (*Tmr* 12B1) (Class C) 48 Chandakos St   Tel. 281135
Directions: Despite the Pension being signed 44 further up the street, it is at No 48. BUT this pleasant building, with a tiny courtyard covered by trellis trained vines is due for demolition. The owners have already acquired a new place up the road on the left at No 37.

Not only inexpensive but very pleasant. Double rooms sharing the bathroom cost 980 drs in the high season and triples 1360 drs. The larger rooms have a washbasin and 'assorted' furniture.

Continuing down Chandakos St leads from the sublime to the ridiculous. By turning right at the bottom of the road on to the coastal thoroughfare of Sophocles Venizelou, leads to:

The Xenia (*Tmr* 11A/B1) (Class A) Sophocles Venizelou   Tel. 284000
Directions: As above, diagonally opposite the Historical Museum situated in downtown west Iraklion.
    The setting belies the hotel's excellence (Xenias are usually of a good, if expensive quality). This Xenia is comparatively inexpensive for its class and a double room with shower costs 2800 drs, the mandatory breakfast from 280 drs and lunch or dinner from 850 drs.

Not all is lost in the pursuit of inexpensive accommodation as this area is rich in outcrops of the acceptable including the:-

Pension Karpathos (*Tmr* 13B1/2) 4 Gazi St
Directions: The street is behind the Bus terminal, to the left of Odhos Grevenon (*Sbo*) and on the left.

Rooms Vergina (*Tmr* 14B1) 32 Odhos Chortaton (Chortatson)   Tel. 242739
Directions: On Chortaton St, close to the junction with Gazi St.

Rooms Mary (*Tmr* 15B1) 25 Odhos Chortaton
Directions: The other side of the street from *Rent Rooms Vergina*, and up the street away from the seafront.

Hotel Rea (*Tmr* 16B1) (Class D) 4 Kalimeraki St   Tel. 223638
Directions: On a street laterally connecting Chortaton and Grevenon Sts, one up from Gazi Street (*Sbo*).
    A modern building with garden. Double rooms only, sharing the bathroom for which the inclusive rate per night, including the use of the shower, is 1100 drs.

In the area of Plateia Nikiforos Phokas, at the top of Odhos Ikosipende Avgoustou, is another area from which to radiate.

Hotel Kretan Sun (*Tmr* 6C2) (Class E) 10 Odhos 1866   Tel. 243794
Directions: At the top of Ikosipende Avgoustou St, overlooking Nikiforas Phokas Sq. The entrance is immediately to the right on entering Odhos 1866. The street gets fairly crowded (to say the least) during market hours.
    Every roster of accommodation should list a downbeat, typically ethnic Greek hotel in a noisy area (should it not?) The Kretan is clean and basic and the owner a humourist. When asked for double room rates he quotes 1140 drs then quickly adds a further 200 drs for 2 showers which are charged with or without use! The pill is sweetened because, as Aliki Tsakiris puts it, guests, having paid the impost, may have as many free showers as they like! After the addition of tax the double room charge finally totals 1360 drs. This is against a listed 'official' double room rate, sharing the bathroom, of 1012 drs (20th June - 20th Oct.). Incidentally the 'official' rate for a single room for the same period is 900 drs.

Hotel Ionia (*Tmr* 17C2) (Class E) 5 Odhos Evans   Tel. 281795
Directions: On Evans St next along and parallel to Odhos 1866, in an easterly direction, opposite the connecting lane of Fotiou (*Tmr* 21C2).

All rooms share the bathrooms with singles starting off at 720 drs and doubles 750/880 drs rising to 880 drs for a single and 960/1125 drs for a double room (1st July - 30th Sept.). A shower costs an extra 80/100 drs.

Hotel Kritikon (*Tmr* C2) 26 Evans St   Tel.220211
Directions: From *Hotel Ionia*, on the other side of the street and 50 m to the south.
Double rooms only, sharing the bathroom, cost 1200 drs.

Pension Ilion (*Tmr* 18C3/4) 43 Ariadnis   Tel. 283867
Directions: From Pláteia Eleftherios turn down Odhos Xanthou Dhidhou, leaving the Museum (*Tmr* 40C3) to the right and the Tourist Office (*Tmr* 32C3) to the left. At the bottom turn right (on Odhos Merambellou) past the Coin-op laundrette (*Tmr* 30B/C3) where the lane narrows, and next right on to Odhos Ariadnis. The Pension is on the left.
A double room sharing the bathroom costs 1300 drs.

Hotel Olympic (*Tmr* 7D2) (Class C) Plateia Kornarou   Tel. 288861
Directions: Proceed up Odhos 1866 to the very top end which leads to the attractive square of Plateia Kornarou. The hotel is on the far left.
    The descriptive noun hotel is the same for previously described establishments, but there all similarity ends. Splendidly situated, but a double with en suite facilities costs 2205 drs, rising to 2710 drs in the high season. Breakfast costs 250 drs and is mandatory. The hotel notice boards have a lot of exceedingly useful tourist information.

Camping Iraklion   Tel. 286380
Directions: Take the main coast road out of Iraklion for about 5 km to the west. The No 1 Town Bus stops right outside, although, due to the siting of forecourt petrol pumps, the entrance looks more like a garage.
    Camping Iraklion is described in glowing terms by both the official camping guide, and Anne which is what really counts, with every facility including a private, sandy beach (and 'mixed saunas for the over 60s'?). Charges per night are adults 200 drs, children 100 drs and tent hire 200 drs. Despite being well laid out there is one Greek camping essential missing - shade.

The Eating Out
Generally a lot of establishments on offer which may be the reason why few are pre-eminent.
    There are a couple of cheese pie/tost bars on the Plateia Nikiforos Phokas crossroads (*Tmr* C2).
    Odhos Dhedhalou is packed with restaurants at the Morosini Fountain Sq end, but prices and offerings are much of a muchness except for:-

Kostas (*Tmr* 19C2) 6 Odhos Dhedhalou
Directions: On the right of the pedestrian way, walking up from Plateia Venizelos.
    Not as stylish as other caterers in this street, but they do serve up a reasonable choice of Greek food. Surprise, surprise the owner's name is Kostas. He is a very pleasant chap, but wears a permanently worried look between 8 pm and midnight if his establishment is not well patronised by tourists. Kostas has a theory that any shortfall in clientel is the result of a plot by UK & USA tourist firms, who advise their clients that Greece is full up, and because Greece has not aligned with those 'right-minded' Western European leaders who want to rid the world of both Col Ghadaffi and Libya. Seems a good reason to me to make sure one rewards the taverna with one's custom, doesn't it? Anne reported the moussaka to be delicious. A meal for two of moussaka, a large salad, retsina and bread costs 850 drs.

Klimataria. Odhos Dhedhalou
Directions: Almost next door to *Kostas*.
Possibly not such good value, although it is well frequented by locals.

The Victoria Pizza Bar (*Tmr* 20C2/3) Odhos Dhedhalou
Directions: Further on up the street from the two establishments detailed above, the pizza house is on the left with pavement tables across the street.
Advertises itself as *The Best Pizza in Town, 22 different kinds*, even if the sign is slightly more faded than it was some five years ago. I recall making derogatory comments on the lines that if tourists wished to eat pizzas then they should stay in Italy... but these pizzas are exceptionally good value. The house speciality is a whopping dish at 450 drs and if two of you are not famished, one dish will be sufficient.

However, they do have competition, because at the top end of Odhos Dhedhalou is a huge sign pointing around the corner into Eleftherios Sq. which reads, *Pizza Napoli, the most delicious pizza in the World - 20 different kinds*. Whow? But the *Victoria* is better value, their 'special' costing 450 drs compared to Napoli's 519 drs.

The Morosini Fountain Square restaurants are very expensive due to their location but fairly adjacent is:-

Fotiou Lane (*Tmr* 21C2)
Directions: A narrow covered lane between Odhos 1866 and Evans St.
There are a number of tavernas crammed along the length of this tiny, covered alley which used to offer very cheap food, but are now comparatively expensive, having been 'discovered' by free-spending tourists. 'C'est la vie'.
The Ionia around the corner, in Evans St, is well recommended.

To Mouragio (MOYPAYIO) (*Tmr* A2) Sophocles Venizelou
Directions: Situated on the waterfront Esplanade, Sophocles Venizelou, between the *Hotel Xenia* (*Tmr* 11A/B1) and the Old Harbour (*Tmr* A3).
Recommended by Yhanni, he of the *Hotel Hellas*. Mine host speaks excellent English and, even if the menu is of limited range, the portions are large. A meal for two of octopus, a plate-filling moussaka, a stuffed tomato and green pepper, a large helping of chips, and Greek salad, a big bottle of retsina (they do serve small ones) and bread for under 1000 drs.

THE A TO Z OF USEFUL INFORMATION
AIRLINE OFFICE & TERMINUS (*Tmr* 22D3) The Olympic Airways premises front on to the south end of Eleftherios Sq, adjacent to Odhos Averof Othonos.

Aircraft timetable
Iraklion to Athens
A minimum of six flights a day 0015, 0730, 1120, 1920, 2255, 2340 hrs.
Return
A minimum of six flights a day 0540, 0930, 1730, 1845, 2150, 2245 hrs.
One-way fare 3600 drs, duration 45 mins.
Iraklion to Mykonos island

Monday, Wednesday, Friday and Sunday	1040 hrs.
Tuesday, Thursday & Saturday	1440 hrs.
From 15th June additionally	
Monday	1655 hrs.
Return	
Monday, Wednesday, Friday & Sunday	0840 hrs.

Tuesday, Thursday & Saturday	1310 hrs.
From 15th June additionally	
Monday	1525 hrs.

One-way fare 3640 drs, duration 1 hr 10 mins.

Iraklion to Paros island
From 1st May

Tuesday, Thursday & Saturday	1510 hrs.
Return	
Tuesday, Thursday & Saturday	1405 hrs.

One-way fare 4180 drs, duration 45 mins.

Iraklion to Rhodes island

Daily	2015 hrs.
Return	
Daily	2135 hrs.

One-way fare 3510 drs, duration 40 mins.

Iraklion to Thessaloniki (M)

Tuesday, Saturday	1545 hrs.
Return	
Tuesday, Friday	1925 hrs.

One-way fare 5730 drs, duration 1¼ hrs.

Iraklion to Santorini island

Monday, Wednesday, Friday & Sunday	1040 hrs.
Return	
Monday, Wednesday, Friday & Sunday	0940 hrs.

One-way fare 2500 drs, duration 40 mins.

BANKS There are a number of banks on Odhos Ikosipende Avgoustou including the **National Bank of Greece** (*Tmr* 23B2) which accepts personal cheques, accompanied by a Eurocheque card, and changes travellers cheques. Be warned, in line with common practice, they will not willingly change notes into coins.

There is a 'porta-cabin' bank close to El Greco Park (*Tmr* B2) which I am advised offers a better exchange rate than the banks but suffers from long, slow moving queues. There is an **American Express** office alongside Creta Travel Bureau (*See* **Travel Agents**).

BEACHES None immediately to hand, it being necessary to travel either west or east.

To the west is **Almiros Lido**, about 5 km out of town. Keep to the old coast road, not The National Highway. If wishing to travel by bus take the No. 6 at a cost of 45 drs which leaves from the front of the *Astoria Hotel* (*Tmr* 5C3) every 20 minutes until 2015 hrs. Disembark at the sign for *Iraklion Camping*.

Alternatively, travel east to **Amnissos** (about 8 km), or beyond to **Vathianos Kampos**, both on the old road. Those using public transport should catch the No. 1 bus from Eleftherios Sq, under the trees opposite the *Hotel Astoria*. The area has a number of hotels and pensions strung out and fitted in between the old and new roads. I am never sure why anybody stays in this locality, it is not only unlovely but subject to a lot of traffic noise as well as the intermittent roar of incoming aircraft, being on the flight-path for Iraklion airport. On the other hand the beaches are satisfactory and sandy.

BICYCLE, SCOOTER & CAR HIRE Odhos Ikosipende Avgoustou, rising from the Venetian Harbour to the centre of the City, is the 'Rent-a-Wheels' and, incidentally, 'Travel Agent alley'. Scooters cost from 3500 drs for three days, including insurance and taxes, and cars the usual extortionate charges.

The other street with a concentration of powered vehicles for hire is Odhos

Chandakos and establishments include, unusually, the *Youth Hostel* (*Tmr* 10B1/2) for scooters and:

Ritz Rent-a-Car (*Tmr* 16B1)   Tel.223638
Competitive car rates with the office in the foyer of the *Hotel Rea*.
   Comparatively good value scooter hire is provided by:-
Cretan Summer (*Tmr* 47B/C2) 13 Akroleontos St   Tel.242515
Directions: North (or seawards) of Plateia Kallergon (*Tmr* 47B/C2).
Also *See* **Luggage Store**.

BOOKSELLERS Specialist shops on Plateia Venizelos and across the road, two up on the right, in Odhos Dhedhalou.

BREAD SHOP There is a good shop on the right towards the far end of the market in Odhos 1866 and another at No. 19 on the right of Agios Titoy (Titou) St (*Tmr* 24B3). There's an even better one at the very top of Odhos 1866, on the left very close to the *Hotel Olympic* (*Tmr* 7D2).

BUSES The major Bus terminal (*Tmr* 25B4) is opposite the Ferry-boat quay. Most unusually, the ticket office is able to hand over a (coloured) leaflet giving information about the various bus terminals and the timetables, but all is not lost as the leaflet is assuredly incomplete, not detailing one of the bus depots. After these derisive remarks let us hope I list the information correctly. A general KTEL telephone number is 288142/3.

Bus timetables
A THE FERRY-BOAT BUS TERMINAL (*Tmr* 25B4)   Tel. 282637

Iraklion to (Limin) Chersonisos, Malia
Daily   0630 – 2100 hrs, every 30 mins.
Return journey
Daily   0700 – 2200 hrs, every 30 mins.
One-way fare 180 drs; duration 1 hr; distance 37 km.
Note buses from Malia connect to:
Lasithi Plain
Daily   0830, 1400 hrs.
Return journey
Daily   1400, 1700 hrs.
One-way fare 290 drs; duration 1½ hrs; distance 60 km.

Iraklion to Ag. Nikolaos
Daily   0630, 0730, 0830, 0900, 0930, 1000, 1030,
                          1130, 1230, 1330, 1430, 1530, 1630, 1730,
                          1830, 1930, 2030 hrs.
Return journey
Daily   0630, 0730, 0810, 0900, 0930, 1030, 1100,
                          1130, 1230, 1300, 1330, 1430, 1530, 1630,
                          1730, 1800, 1830, 1900, 2000, 2100 hrs.
One-way fare 330 drs; duration 1½ hrs; distance 69 km.

Iraklion to Ierapetra
Daily   0730, 0830, 0930, 1030, 1130, 1330, 1430,
                          1530, 1630, 1830 hrs.
Return journey
Daily   0615, 0830, 1030, 1230, 1430, 1500, 1600,
                          1800, 1900 hrs.
One-way fare 510 drs; duration 2½ hrs; distance 105 km.

Iraklion to Sitia
Daily   0730, 0830, 0930, 1030, 1300, 1500, 1730 hrs.
Return journey
Daily   0630, 0915, 1115, 1215, 1415, 1430, 1615,
                             1715, 1915 hrs.
One-way fare 690 drs; duration 3½ hrs; distance 143 km.

Iraklion to Lasithi Plain
Daily   0830, 1400 hrs.
Sunday/holidays   0830, 1430 hrs.
Return journey
Daily   0700, 1400, 1700 hrs.
Sunday/holidays   1400, 1700 hrs.
One-way fare 340 drs; duration 2 hrs; distance 70 km.

Iraklion to Archanes
Daily   0730, 0800, 0900, 1000, 1100, 1200,
                             1300, 1400, 1500, 1700, 1830, 2030 hrs.
Sunday/holidays   0800, 0900, 1030, 1200, 1400, 1500,
                             1630, 1800, 2030 hrs.
Return journey
Daily   0645, 0730, 0800, 0830, 0900, 1000, 1100,
                             1200, 1300, 1400, 1500, 1600, 1745, 2000 hrs
Sunday/holidays   0730, 0830, 0945, 1115, 1300, 1400,
                             1545, 1715, 2000 hrs.
One-way fare 80 drs; duration ½ hr; distance 17 km.

Iraklion to Ag. Pelagia
Daily   0845, 0945, 1430, 1700 hrs.
Return journey
Daily   0930, 1030, 1515, 1745 hrs.
One-way fare 150 drs; duration ½ hr; distance 32 km.

Iraklion to Sisi, Milatos
Daily   0830, 1500 hrs.
Sunday/holidays   0830, 1500 hrs.
Return journey
Daily   0700, 1000, 1630 hrs.
Sunday/holidays   1000, 1630 hrs.
One-way fare 250 drs; duration 1½ hrs; distance 51 km.

Iraklion to Vianos, Myrtos, Ierapetra
Daily   0630 hrs.
Sunday/holidays   0630 hrs.
Return journey
Daily   1000, 1630 hrs.
Sunday/holidays   1630 hrs.
One-way fare 510 drs; duration 3 hrs; distance 106 km.

B THE CHANIA GATE BUS TERMINAL (*Tmr* 26C1)   Tel. 283073

Iraklion to Ag. Galini
Daily   0630, 0730, 0845, 1000, 1100, 1215, 1400,
                             1600, 1730 hrs.
Sunday/holidays   0730, 0830, 1030, 1215, 1500, 1700 hrs.
Return journey
Daily   0800, 0930, 1030, 1215, 1315, 1500, 1630,
                             1830, 2000 hrs.
Sunday/holidays   0800, 1030, 1230, 1500, 1730, 1930 hrs.
One-way fare 380 drs; duration 2½ hrs; distance 78 km.

Iraklion to Phaestos
Daily   0630, 0730, 0845, 1000, 1100, 1215,
1400, 1500, 1600, 1730 hrs.
Sunday/holidays   0730, 0830, 1030, 1215, 1500, 1700 hrs.
Return journey
Daily   0830, 1000, 1100, 1230, 1345, 1445, 1530,
1700, 1845 hrs.
Sunday/holidays   0830, 1100, 1300, 1530, 1600, 1700, 1800 hrs.
One-way fare 310 drs; duration 2 hrs; distance 63 km.

Iraklion to Matala
Daily   0730, 0845, 1000, 1215, 1300, 1500, 1630 hrs.
Sunday/holidays   0730, 0900, 1000, 1215, 1330, 1500, 1630 hrs.
Return journey
Daily   0700, 0930, 1100, 1215, 1430, 1700, 1830 hrs.
Sunday/holidays   0730, 1000, 1200, 1300, 1430, 1600, 1700 hrs.
One-way fare 340 drs; duration 2 hrs; distance 71 km.

Iraklion to Lendas
Daily   1000, 1330 hrs.
Sunday/holidays   1000 hrs.
Return journey
Daily   0630, 1445 hrs.
Sunday/holidays   1600 hrs.
One-way fare 390 drs; duration 3 hrs; distance 80 km.

Iraklion to Anoghia
Daily   0630, 0830, 1200, 1300, 1400, 1630 hrs.
Sunday/holidays   0830, 1400 hrs.
Return journey
Daily   0730, 0800, 1200, 1230, 1500 hrs.
Sunday/holidays   1200, 1500 hrs.
One-way fare 175 drs; duration 1 hr; distance 37 km.

Iraklion to Fodele
Daily   0630, 1400 hrs.
Return journey
Daily   0700, 1430 hrs.
Note there are no buses on Sunday/holidays either way.
One-way fare 165 drs; duration 1 hr; distance 34 km.

C THE 'XENIA' BUS TERMINAL (*Tmr* 27 A/B1/2)   Tel. 221765

Note this is not the official designation for the terminal.
The Bus office is in the corner of the square, hedged in by two snack bars.

Iraklion to Chania (via Rethymnon)
Daily   0530, 0630, 0730, 0815, 0900, 0930, 1000,
1030, 1115, 1145, 1215, 1230, 1245, 1315,
1345, 1430, 1515, 1545, 1615, 1645, 1715,
1745, 1815, 1845, 1930 hrs.
Return journey
Daily   0530, 0645, 0730, 0800, 0830, 0900, 0930,
1000, 1030, 1100, 1130, 1200, 1230, 1300,
1330, 1400, 1430, 1500, 1530, 1600, 1630,
1700, 1730, 1830, 1945 hrs.
Rethymnon: One-fare 375 drs; duration highway 1½ hrs; old road 2 hrs.
Chania: One-way fare 710 drs; duration highway 3 hrs; old road 5 hrs.

Iraklion to Omalos/Samaria Gorge
There is a bus for Omalos daily at 0530 hrs and a return bus from **Chora Sfakion** at 1600 hrs.

Note that baggage can be left in the office at the Xenia Bus station for 50 drs a day but the office closes at 1930 hrs.

D CITY BUSES (Sky blue in colour) Tel. 226065 (Knossos); Tel. 283915 (beaches). The information office for City Buses is at the west end of the Ferry-boat Bus terminal (*Tmr* 25B1) in a kiosk.
The Bus Stop (under the trees of Eleftherios Sq) opposite the *Hotel Astoria* (*Tmr* 5C3) serves the:
Airport: Bus No. 1, every 10 minutes until 2300 hrs at a one-way fare of 35 drs and **Amnissos** (beaches to the west): Bus No. 1, every 30 minutes until 2000 hrs at a one-way fare of 45 drs.
The Bus Stop (next to the Archaeological Museum) in front of the *Hotel Astoria* serves the:
Lido (beaches to the east): Bus No. 6, every 20 minutes until 2000 hrs at a one-way fare of 40 drs.
The Bus Stop on Ikosipende Avgoustou, or on the street next to the fruit market (read Evans Street), or opposite the Logia (read Plateia Venizelos) serves the:
Knossos Palace and the **Hospital**: Bus No. 2, every 20 minutes from 0630 – 2300 hrs at a one-way fare of 30 drs.

CINEMAS A number including one on Dikaiossinis St, opposite the Town police station (*Tmr* 28C2/3), and another on Eleftherios Sq, to the right of the *Astoria Hotel* (facing the square). Some only open for the summer and, as usual, offerings include American, English, French and German films with Greek subtitles. A list of film programmes, stuck on billboards, can be found in Dikaiossinis St.

COMMERCIAL SHOPPING AREA Odhos 1866, which connects Nikiforos Phokas Sq with Kornarou Square, is a 'pedestrianised' market and, when open (Monday - Saturday mornings until siesta time), is a throbbing, seething, bustling mass of stalls, shops and customers where almost everything can be purchased. There are good bread shops, several 'yogurterias', meat and vegetable shops, and ironmongers. From the Kornarou Sq end, Karterou St snakes off in a westerly direction and contains the fish market.
The 'Tourist Shop' or Mini Market (*Tmr* 29A/B1/2), situated opposite the *Xenia Hotel* (*Tmr* 11A/B1) alongside the Bus terminal, is a very, very, useful store, open seven days a week. It stocks nearly everything a traveller could conceivably require.
Idhomeneos St contains a concentration of shops selling souvenir lace, embroidery, shawls and Cretan dresses (*Tmr* C3).
General shop hours: Monday, Wednesday and Saturday, 0830 to 1400 hrs; Tuesday, Thursday and Friday 0830 to 1330 and 1730 to 2000 hrs.
Kiosks and tourist shops: On average open 0830 to 2000 hrs, including Sundays.

DISCOS Usually I do not specifically list them as they rarely require any advertisement but there is a recommended disco directly behind the *Hotel Astoria* (*Tmr* 5C3), 'next door', across from the NTOG office, called **The Piper Disco**. It proclaims it is air conditioned. There is another on the pedestrianised road which connects Odhos Dhedhalou and Androgeo, opposite the *Hotel Dedalos* (*Tmr* 2C2), called **Disco Esperides**.

ELPA The Iraklion office of the Greek equivalent of the British AA is off the map but well signposted from Plateia Eleftherios. The staff are extremely helpful but a phrase book is a necessity as, although their English is good and their wish to help unbounded, technicalities of automotive engineering is the rock on which many a good translation can founder. One of the problems (for anyone but a Greek to understand) is that one garage cannot carry out a full range of repairs and services. For example oil is changed by one business, brakes adjusted by another and engine tuning performed by a third and so on.

FERRY BOATS The ships dock at the Ferry-boat terminal (*Tmr* 1B4) opposite the main Bus station. Fortunately a fairly simple schedule is operated by the two firms (**Anek** and **Minoan Lines**) who slog it out overnight on the Crete to Piraeus journey. Both lines take about 11 hours and fares start at 1950 drs for third class and 2600 drs for second class with a bed.

For other daily mainland ferry-boat connections *See* CHANIA (CHAPTER 14), for details of weekly ferries KASTELLI (CHAPTER 15) and AG NIKOLAOS (CHAPTER 17) for interesting island connections. There is also a ferry-boat service that links Iraklion with Santorini island.

During the waking hours of the Iraklion/Piraeus ferry-boat journeys the 'captain and his crew' of the various boats exhort passengers to place their litter in the bins and bags provided in order to protect the indigenous Mediterranean sea fish, plant and animal life. Until very recently, in the early hours of the morning the crew could be observed throwing the bags of rubbish overboard!

Ferry-boat timetables

Iraklion to Piraeus (M) Overnight crossing.
1. **Minoan Lines**
Daily: CF Festos/Knossos. Departs 1830 hrs and arrives at about 0530 hrs.
Return journey
Daily: Departs 1830 hrs and arrives at about 0530 hrs.

2. **Anek Lines**
Daily: CF Candia/Rethymnon. Departs 1900 hrs and arrives at about 0600 hrs.
Return journey
Daily: Departs 1900 hrs and arrives at about 0600 hrs.

It appears that Cretans from the Iraklion area favour Minoan Lines and those from the west prefer Anek, both lauding the superior handling characteristics of the boats of their favourite company.

Iraklion to Santorini

Day	Departure time	Ferry-boat	Ports/Islands of Call
Tuesday	0800 hrs*	Portokalis Ilios	Santorini (Thira-Athinos port)
Wednesday	0730 hrs	Nearchos (Nearxos)	Santorini, Ios, Paros, Mykonos
Thursday	0800 hrs*	Portokalis Ilios	Santorini
Friday	0730 hrs	Nearchos (Nearxos)	Santorini, Ios, Paros, Mykonos
Saturday	0800 hrs*	Portokalis Ilios	Santorini
Sunday	0800 hrs*	Portokalis Ilios	Santorini

Return Journey
The **Portokalis Ilios** returns on the same day, departing from Athinos port, Santorini at 1730 hrs.

*Note this is a mean average (between 0745 & 0815 hrs).
One-way fare 1114 drs, duration 4¾ hrs.

This route is operated by the **MV Portokalis Ilios**, a smallish passenger ferry-boat. The main deck is short on loos, the ladies has 3 'sit downs', the gentlemens may be locked and the general shower room full of cleaning materials. One floor down there is one ladies' and one men's and a door marked *Under No Circumstances Leave This Door Open* which is nearly always tied wide open with rope! There is the usual mix of television and Greek music and, surprisingly, a money exchange at the Purser's Office, even if the rate of exchange is rather poor. A number of dishes are available from the self-service canteen.

Another ferry, the **Nearchos**, continues on from Santorini to 'one or three' of the other Cyclades islands.

FERRY BOAT TICKET OFFICES Most range along the harbour/bottom end of Ikosipende Avgoustou St, including the shipping company offices of **Anek** and **Minoan Lines**.

Zeis Travel. 48, Ikosipende Avgoustou St   Tel. 223214.
This office sells tickets for the **MV Portokalis Ilios**.
Eurocreta Travel. 19, Ikosipende Avgoustou St   Tel. 282814.
They handle the **FB Nearchos**.
Consolas Tourist Agency, *(Tmr* C/D2/3) Dhaskaloyiannis Sq,   Tel. 288847.
Advertise 'student offers' and competitively priced tickets.

    Naturally no information will be forthcoming from the 'wrong' office.

LAUNDRETTE There is a coin-op *(Tmr* 30B/C3). For directions *See Pension Ilion*, **The Accommodation**. A very welcome facility, the importance of which was best illustrated whilst watching a young American some years ago. He arrived, threw the total contents of his backpack into the machine and then stripped down to his underpants. Whilst putting his discarded garments into the washing machine he declared that, were there not such a crowd, he would dearly like to throw his underpants in as well. Only the rapturous encouragement decided him against the move. Open every day from 0800 - 2000 hrs. A wash costs 200 drs (4 x 50 drs), and use of the electric dryer 40 drs (2 x 20 drs). Remember to take plenty of loose coins as the banks do not give change without a considerable fuss. A sign indicates that the nearby **Mini Market Agfa** sells soap powder and will supply change. Once upon a time another sign pronounced *quins can be obtained at the motor car hire office*!

    There is a **Laundrette** *(Tmr* 31B/C2) but not self-service on Odhos Kantanoleon, by El Greco Park.

LUGGAGE STORE There is now a facility at:
Left Luggage No 48 Ikosipende Avgoustou
Directions: In a basement opposite the National Bank (*Tmr* 23B2).
 Charges 100 drs per day per item of luggage and the office is open daily 0630 -
2400 hrs.
 The bus and ferry-boat terminals are fairly safe and most owners of accommodation
help out. *See* **Xenia Bus Terminal, Buses**.

MEDICAL CARE
Chemists & Pharmacies Thick on the ground and a rota is in operation to give
round-the-clock cover.
Hospital The Benizelion Hospital is on the left of the Knossos road, some 4 km out of
town. For a bus *See*, **Buses (City)**.

NTOG (EOT) (*Tmr* 32C3) Conveniently situated in a smart office opposite the
Archaeological Museum. Some years ago I thought the staff rather offhand but Anne
assures me she found them very helpful. The office is open Monday - Saturday 0730 -
1930 hrs, and Sundays/holidays 0730 - 1430 hrs.

OTE (*Tmr* 33B/C2) Situated to one side of El Greco Park and open 0600 - 2400 hrs
daily. The tally machine for recording the number of charge units has a list of the
overseas exchange numbers.

PETROL Plentiful.

PLACES OF INTEREST
Cathedrals & Churches These include the following:
The Basilica of St Mark (*Tmr* 34C2). This is almost opposite Morosini Fountain Sq but
many visitors only remember the building from having sat on the steps whilst
consuming the odd snack. This is a pity, as the oft-restored church now houses
frescoes from the 13th to the 15th century, gathered from a wide variety of Cretan
churches. It also doubles as a lecture and concert hall. Built in 1240 by the
Venetians, it was rebuilt in 1303 and 1508 after earthquakes. The Turks converted it
into a mosque and finally it was restored in the late 1950s. The opening hours and
admission charges vary. Enough said!
Agia Ekaterini (St Katherine) (*Tmr* 35C1) On the edge of a self-named square, built in
the 15th century, altered in the 17th century and now a museum of religious art,
especially icons. The most renowned of these are six painted by one Mikhalis
Dhamaskinos, a contemporary of El Greco who, naturally, it is claimed studied here
when it was a monastery school and Renaissance centre. It is certain that a number
of famous Cretan artists, theologians and dramatists were students.
The Cathedral Of Agios Minas Built in the late 1850s and is only outstanding for its
size, dominating St Katherine's Sq. The Cathedral towers above:
The Church Of Agios Minas This is of uncertain age and the receptacle for various
antiquities.
Agios Titos Church (*Tmr* 36B2/3) Originally a Turkish mosque built in 1872 on the site
of a Byzantine church which had been destroyed by an earthquake. The building
reverted to the Orthodox faith in the late 19th century.

Koules Castle (*Tmr* 37A3) The Castle was built by the Venetians in the early 1500s
to guard the old harbour entrance, possibly on the site of an earlier structure. The
name it is known by is in fact the Turkish nomenclature. The structure has been
impressively restored and if visiting do not miss the sculptured Lions of St Mark.

Morosini Fountain (*Tmr* 39C2) This squats on the Plateia Venizelos which is more popularly known as Fountain Sq but no 'Brownie' points for guessing why. The lovely Venetian fountain was built by the then Governor, Francesco Morosini, in the early 1600s, but the lions probably date from the 14th century. The bas reliefs of the fountain basins have aquatic connections.

Museums

The Archaeological Museum (*Tmr* 40C3) I suggest that any visit is delayed until one or two Minoan sites have been visited, after which the exhibits can be viewed with the archaeological digs in the mind's eye. The museum is an impressive display and on the first floor are exhibited the Minoan frescoes. It is surprising that such exquisite exhibits should be shown off in such an ugly building added to which the labelling is poor, but the layout is simplicity itself. The water-colour paintings by Piet de Jong, executed to help the partial restoration work at Knossos, are very attractive. There is a most welcome cold drinking water machine behind the Museum. Open Tuesday - Saturday 0800 - 1900 hrs; Sundays/holidays 0800 - 1800 hrs and closed Mondays. Admission costs 250 drs but students are only charged 130 drs.

The Historical Museum Opposite the *Xenia Hotel* (*Tmr* 11A/B1) and contains exhibits from the early Christian period up to, and including, the Battle of Crete. There are also reconstructions of the Study of Nikos Kazantzakis (1883 - 1957), author of (amongst a number of renowned books) Zorba the Greek, and of Emanuel Tsouderos, the Greek statesman. Open Monday - Saturday 0900 - 1300 & 1500 - 1730 hrs; closed Sunday & holidays. Admission costs 150 drs.

Venetian Arsenals (*Tmr* 38B2/3) Built in the 16th century, those still standing are of a very large size and have been imaginatively restored in two arcaded and vaulted sections.

Venetian Loggia (*Tmr* 41B/C2) The building, which fronts on to the once Venetian Armoury, has been totally reconstructed and is now the City Hall.

Venetian Walls These are in an impressive state of preservation and were built in the 15th century. A testament to their solidity and effectiveness must be the 22 year seige that raged around them from 1648, when the Turks attempted to clean up the last outstanding bastion of Venetian rule on the island. After the inhabitants finally surrendered they were allowed to go scot free, an unusually generous and uncharacteristic act by the Turks. It was their customary practive to make an example of a chap in those days (you know burn or skin them alive, any other similar niceties). Two of the original gateways are well worth a visit, namely Kainouria (*Tmr* 42D2/3) and Chania (*Tmr* 26C1). A walk around the perimeter not only proves interesting but may work off any possible ill effects of too many ouzos. At the Martinengo Bastion, on the west of the Kainouria Gate, there is a zoo and the grave of the author Nikos Kazantzakis (**See Places of Interest - The Historical Museum**). Owing to a difference of opinion with the Orthodox Church in respect of his writings, he was not allowed to be buried in consecrated ground or with their blessing. The simple headstone, with an extract from one of his works, is inscribed *I hope for nothing. I fear nothing. I am free.*

POLICE

Port (*Tmr* 45A/B3/4) Where one would expect them to be I suppose, on the quayside.
Tourist (*Tmr* 44C2) Located on Dikaiossinis St between Nikiforos Phokas Sq and the large offices of the Town police. The officers are extremely helpful with some information available that is not handed out by the NTOG. There is a useful external noticeboard with plenty of informative leaflets pinned to it.
Town (*Tmr* 28C2/3) A large building on Dikaiossinis St.

POST OFFICE *(Tmr* 43C/D2) A modern building on Dhaskaloyiannis Sq. The service is rather brusque. In common with most Greek offices now, they exchange travellers' cheques and carry out Eurocheque transactions. Hours for this money business are between 0730 - 2000 hrs, whilst other business hours are the norm.

SPORTS FACILITIES There is a tennis club *(Tmr* 46B/C4) to the side of Beaufort St, (which swings down from Eleftherios Sq.) Payment is either by game fees or short-term membership.

TAXIS There are a number of ranks, including those on: Eleftherios Sq - all round the periphery; Dhaskaloyiannis Sq; by the NTOG office and on El Greco Park.

TELEPHONE NUMBERS & ADDRESSES

Tourist Police, *(Tmr* 44C2), Dikaiossinis St.	Tel. 283190
Hospital	Tel. 231931/237502
NTOG, *(Tmr* 32C3), 1 Xanthou Dhidhou	Tel. 228203/228225
Olympic Office, *(Tmr* 22D3), Eleftherios Sq.	Tel. 288866/229191
British Vice Consulate, 338 Dimokratias St *(Tmr* D3)	Tel. 224012/234127

TOILETS A rather rare public facility in Greece but the following are noteworthy. The Ferry-boat bus terminal *(Tmr* 25B4) 'sports' a pair as does El Greco Park *(Tmr* B2). The latter deserves a fuller description as they resemble a small zoo, well more an aviary. The fearsome woman attendant shares her unpleasant 'hole in the ground' with about 20 bedraggled birds which are not only caged in those unbearably tiny Greek cages but are even deprived of light. Despite all this they (the birds not the lady) sing incessantly even if the cream of the collection are 2 large, miserable cockatoos. Entrance to the toilets is 30 drs which seems a bit excessive. Perhaps it goes towards maintaining the aviary....! You have to see it to believe it.

TRAVEL AGENTS A number of the genre are detailed under **Ferry-boat Ticket Offices** and firms also range along Odhos Ikosipende Avgoustou.
Creta Travel Bureau *(Tmr* B2/3) 20-22 Epimenidhou   Tel. 243811
Directions: Walking up Odhos Ikosipende Avgoustou from the Venetian Harbour and Epimenidhou St is the first turning off to the left *(Sbo)*.

I have listed Creta because the American Express office is alongside. Card holders can arrange mail collection (daily 0900 - 2100 hrs) and money transactions (Monday - Friday 0900 - 1300 hrs).

ROUTE ONE
To Rethymnon via the National Highway (New Road, 78 km)
For many, travel on the National Highway will be interesting enough without venturing on to the byways of countryside Crete. Oddly enough the New Road quite often travels through more scenic and dramatic countryside than the Old Road. Not so remarkable is that it is a quicker route and nowhere is this better exemplified than on the journey between Iraklion and Rethymnon (or vice versa, if you will).

The immediate western environs of Iraklion are messy, trailing through an oil refinery with tanker buoys in the sea, but once on the adequately signposted highway, the scenery becomes *au naturel*.

AG. PELAGIA (21 km from Iraklion) Tel. prefix 081. Some 16 or 17 km from Iraklion, the seaside village of Ag. Pelagia is signposted to the right. The approach is by a steeply descending and winding road, which allows aerial views of the lovely bay encircled by the village. The road terminates in a car park to the near side of the beach, the backshore of which becomes an unofficial thoroughfare. The eastern

Illustration 12 Crete centred on Iraklion

horn of the bay is rocky with some dozen boats moored up, half of which are caiques. Small boat owners uniquely moor up their craft above water suspending them by framework supported slings. Vestiges of a concrete path lie gently shelving in the shallow water's edge (or are they Minoan remains?). This end of the very pleasant beach consists of large pebbles, followed by the aforementioned slabs of concrete or rock bedded into the surrounding sand, and then sand and very fine shingle.

The beach is edged by the high concrete patios of restaurants, tavernas, bars and shops pierced here and there by access steps. Halfway along the waterfront is a large unmade road to the left. This may be a dried-up river-bed and appears to head off into the foothills. Hereon are a pharmacy, money changer, scooter and car hire outfit and a boat-trip agency. Further along the beach an asphalted side street opens out and 'houses' a car hire firm, quality souvenir shops, a supermarket and travel businesses, all on the left-hand side, with fields and a parking lot on the right. On this area of the shore are beach umbrellas whilst at the far western end is a water-ski school and run, beyond which sun bathers have to put up with the whine of a swimming pool irrigation pump. This serves the *Capsis Beach Hotel and Bungalows,* a large complex straddling the headland. I write swimming pool (singular) but there are two and I must say that the Capsis Beach appears to be a superb hotel in a superb position. There is a very small, sandy beach cove around the headland which can only be reached from the hotel grounds. The 'Theatre on the Rocks' situated along the upward-climbing seafront road above the Capsis Beach Hotel is rather unique. This is a very small, pretty and beautifully sited outdoor theatre built into the rocks, similar to a miniature ancient Greek open-air odeion. The theatre puts on regular performances throughout the summer.

The taverna and restaurant prices at Ag. Pelagia are slightly higher than the average, which is not surprising as this is almost exclusively good quality, hotel holiday territory. Although I have not seen any signs for **Rooms**, there are four officially listed.

Back on the main road the mountains in this area are green and aromatic.

FODELE (29 km from Iraklion) Signposted to the left and set in a plain planted with orange groves. Famed as the birthplace of Dominikos Theotokopoulos, more popularly known in art circles as El Greco. A 16th century artist, he probably studied under Titian in Venice and became a resident of Toledo, Spain. He proclaimed his Cretan nationality but not where he was born, which had to be decided on by others. The selection of Fodele as the location was given the seal of approval, in 1934, when a Spanish university presented the village with a plaque inscribed in both Spanish and Greek. This reads *The History Faculty of the University of Valadolid gives this plaque made of Toledo rock to Fodele in memory of the immortal glory of Dominikos Theotokopoulos. July 1934.* The Church houses some El Greco momentos and there are at least two places offering accommodation.

SISE (33 km from Iraklion) This is just to one side of the Highway and has **Rooms**.

Beyond Sise are dramatic headland views after which the route plunges down to sea-level alongside an inlet, opposite which is a petrol station. At this point a turning off to the left leads under the road and doubles back to:

BALI (46 km from Iraklion) The partly unmade road winds past one unofficial and fairly squalid 'free camping' site that appears to be inhabited by 'the great unwashed'. Beyond the campsite the road deteriorates and leaving the *Bali Beach Hotel* on the right, peters out in a river-bed. From here, now on foot, a lane leads down to the very small seafront set in the once lovely bay but now lined with tavernas lapping the water's edge. Unfortunately the bay is now absolutely chock-a-block with pedaloes although the Bali Beach has its own, small, private beach round to the

right. A lane to the left, lined with the odd taverna, gift shop and store, leads up to the edge of the hillside. Trip boats from Rethymnon make Bali a day visit and there are **Rooms**, both in the village and on the approach road an example of which is:
Rooms Charlotte.
Built on to the beach and a double room with an en suite bathroom costs 1500 drs a night.

PANORMOS (55 km from Iraklion) Tel prefix 0834. The Highway skirts Panormos but consider making the detour as it is a pretty working village. There is just as likely to be a large caique under construction in, and towering over, the small village square, just off the beach. Taverna tables are scattered around the toiling (well, maybe not toiling) boat builders. There are tavernas on all the rocks overlooking the sea, at which the service is slow, very slow.

The small pebbly beach is to the left off the road into the village, down a very neat, steep, asphalted slope. A notice from the mayor and his electorate owns up to not minding tourists using the beach and village facilities as long as they leave the place clean - or words to that effect - and why not?
The Hotel Panorma (Class C)
Close by the beach with en suite rooms costing 1260 drs for a single and 2030 drs for a double rising to 1650 drs and 2660 drs (1st June - 30th Sept).
There are plenty of other **Rooms** available including the:
Captain's House
This is excellently sited right on the sea and has fully furnished apartments from 2000 drs upwards.

There is a Post Office and plenty of general stores as well as an olive factory to the west of the village.

From Panormos it is only a few kilometres to:
LAVRIS The long beach, beyond the pleasant headland, is sandy with large rocks scattered about. The small plain edging the beach is rather scrubbly, heavily cropped by sheep, and there are signs that 'the unwashed' have camped out amongst the stunted trees. There are many plastic greenhouses, much market gardening and general cultivation.

At **Stavromenos** it is worth taking the dusty Old Road where it crosses under the New Highway, almost parallelling the long, sandy beach, and scattered along the length of which is a disjointed, shabby, ribbon development spotted by a number of smart hotels.

In amongst this is the village of:
MISSERIA (4 km from Rethymnon)
and:
Camping Arkadia   Tel. (0831) 28825
A quite large 'provincial' but well shaded campsite, just off the main road, close by two petrol stations, and edging a sweep of beach with a single foreshore.

The facilities include a bar, restaurant, shop and public phone. The hot water often isn't! Daily charges are 240 drs for an adult, 120 drs for a child and 200 drs for tent hire. The management hire out two wheeled appliances with mopeds costing 500 drs per day and scooters between 750 - 2000 drs a day, depending on the engine size. The relevant Iraklion - Rethymnon bus is No. 115.

Some ½ km further on down the road is **Camping Elizabeth** (Tel 28694).

The outskirts of Rethymnon are disjointed and of a shanty nature (*See* CHAPTER 13).

ROUTE TWO

To Lasithi Plain via Potamies (57 km) The turning off the Iraklion to Ag.
Nikolaos Highway for Lasithi Plain is prior to Limin Chersonisos, after 23 km. The
narrow road that winds up to the circular route around the perimeter of the hidden
valley of Lasithi, has to endure a constant stream of tour buses. If for no other reason
this makes it surprising that the villages of **Potamies**, **Sfendili** and **Avdou** (*Rooms*)
have remained relatively unspoilt and pretty. Petrol is available at **Gonies** from
whence the tree lined road snakes up the mountainside of the Dikti range, through
massed olive groves via the various **Keras** villages, hanging on the cliff-face, to the
fertile:

LASITHI PLAIN In recent years rebuilding of the circular road has very nearly been
completed with, in 1986, only the 2 km section between **Plati** and **Kato Metochi**
remaining unsurfaced. Thus it is pleasant to tour the plain in a clockwise (or
anticlock if you must) direction. Note that the older sections of the road suffer from
potholes.

The almost kingdom-like plain is remarkable for its hundreds of skeletal water
windmills with their reefing sails. Interestingly, these are not some relic of a Cretan
industrial revolution, a flowering of latter-day metal working, but more a Chicago
export of the 1920 - 1930 era. It appears that expatriate Greeks resident in the USA
realised that the early oil well frames and borers could be adapted to pump water -
not oil! The highly cultivated nature of the land, the massed fruit trees and apple
orchards with many grazing cows and donkeys gives a Western European feel to the
locality.

TZERMIADON (57 km from Iraklion) Tel. prefix 0844. The long High Street (traffic-
jammed when the tour buses are in full flow) is lined with general and gift shops.
Although relatively unspoilt, the tourists often mass here despite (or maybe because)
a number of the locals possessing a somewhat piratical air. Shops and services
include banks, an OTE, petrol and a bread shop. Perhaps to control the bursts of
human and traffic activity, there are often a number of police cars in evidence;
although the policemen are usually to be found playing backgammon in one of the
cafe-bars.

Accommodation includes the:
Hotel Kourites (Class B)   Tel. 22194
Actually classified as a pension and a very pleasant one at that. A double room with
en suite bathroom and balcony overlooking the plain should cost 1250 drs but we
have been charged 1500 drs. Singles are listed at 850 drs.
The hotel has a brand new annexe called the:
Hotel Lasithi Class E)
The same telephone number but less expensive charges. All rooms share the
bathrooms with singles costing 500 drs and doubles 710 drs, but we were quoted
1060 drs. Breakfast is available for 140 drs.
There is also the *Hotel Cri-Cri* (Class E) Tel. 22170/31231

Marmaketo is a spacious village and from here to **Ag. Konstantinos**, which lies
next to a dried-up river-bed, is similar to driving down an English country lane.
Mesa Lasithi marks the junction with the turning off to Neapolis and Ag.
Nikolaos. Keeping right leads past Kroustalenia Monastery, a centre of Cretan
resistance to the Turks (more correctly the Turks razed the place to the ground once
or twice), and on to **Ag. Konstantinos**, which has *Rooms* and tourist shops.

The rather mucky village of **Ag. Georgios**, where the road surface disappears altogether, has a large church, petrol station, shops and accommodation including the E class *Hotels Dias* and *Rea* (which has a butcher's shop in the corner of the dining room - convenient if nothing else). There is also a Museum of Cretan Folklore.

The village of **Avrakontes** has a petrol station; there are **Rooms** at **Kaminaki** and the village of **Magoulas** hosts the *Hotel Zeus* as well as a tourist shop and cafe bar.

PSYCHRO (67 km from Iraklion) Tel. prefix 0844. Psychro has three listed hotels, the D Class *Zeus* and E Class *Dictaion Androu* and *Heleni*. Its claim to fame is the proximity of the Diktaion Cave, the supposed birthplace of Zeus, the mythological god of gods, for which turn off to the left up a 2 km track from the village.

At **Plati** village, pretty and squalid, the road proper comes to an end and from hereon the surface is adequate if unmetalled, to:

KATO METOCHI A big, old village, the route through which passes around the large trees in the square. The animals hereabouts look to be in splendid condition and the cows are muzzled.

To leave the plain, and save retracing one's footsteps, it is possible to turn off towards unlovely **Mochos**, but the road turns into a wide, unmade swathe tumbling down to the coast with much construction work in hand.

ROUTE THREE

To Ag. Nikolaos (69 km) The signposting and roads east of Iraklion are unclear, to say the least.

One way out is to stick to the seafront past the ferry-boat harbour, up the hill with a caique incongruously still being built on the roadside, (that is some three years now) into an eastern outpost of Iraklion. From here skirt the airport and proceed along the coast road.

It is interesting that the armed forces have an extensive base alongside the airport. Perhaps the authorities have read the insurgent's handbook for revolution, first seize the airport and radio station!

The road continues along the shore whilst the Highway marches on to the right, forming a long island of ground between the two roads which is scattered with hotels and pensions. Although the beach is very sandy in stretches, the area has little to commend it for, apart from being on the flight path of Iraklion airport, the surroundings are rather bedraggled. Despite, or because of this, there are a number of large, modern, package tour hotels each complete with swimming pool, cocktail bar and disco nightclub. Super!

AMNISOS (about 8 km from Iraklion) Reputedly the Minoan harbour for Knossos. Offshore is the **Island of Dia**, a haven for the Kri-Kri (Agrimi) or wild ibex, a big goat with large curved horns, indigenous to Crete. **Vachianos Kampos** beach is excellent but crowded, and at **Gournes**, wherein is a large Air Force base, the Old and New Highways link. The resultant road skirts Limin Chersonisos and Malia, which some may say is a good thing.

LIMIN CHERSONISOS (26 km from Iraklion) Tel. prefix 0897. Now that nearly everything is buried underneath hotels, pensions, restaurants, tavernas, bars and tourist shops, it is difficult to imagine or accept that this is the site of the ancient city of Chersonisos. The seafront is edged by a narrow quayside road which links a series of small, sandy coves. At the western end an access road to the front emerges near a small promontory, distinguished by the prominent *Taverna Pharos Restaurant* (the Lighthouse Taverna). The headland, which unequally divides the sweep of the large bay into two, has a small Cycladean style chapel, and a fishing-boat quay to the right-hand side (*Fsw*). In the lee of the headland there is a small sandy beach with a few small boats drawn up on the foreshore. It is in this area that the sunken remains of ancient Roman quays are supposed to be visible beneath the surface of the water. To the left of the promontory there is another crescent-shaped beach. Both beaches are clean and the sea clear with a gently shelving bottom. Proceeding eastwards for the next mile or so the rocky waterfront is bordered by the quayside road, edged by literally dozens of hotels, pensions and tavernas and their sheltered patios. Although there is little indigenous Greek surviving in Limin, at least the hotels are low rise with a maximum of four storeys.

As most, if not all, of the accommodation is very expensive it is only to be applauded that George, he of Iraklion's *Hotel Hania* (*See* **The Accommodation, Iraklion**) intends to open up an establishment in Chersonisos.

Leaving Limin a glance backwards from the main road shows up a decrepit, sprawling brick and tile works, which will no doubt be cleared out of the way to make room for more hotels, and an isolated chapel on a small rocky headland at the end of a diminutive causeway.

I suspect the land between Limin and Malia will eventually be infilled and a couple of villages on the route have expanded their 'attractions' in an effort to sidetrack some of the boom trade of:

MALIA (34 km from Iraklion) Tel. prefix 0897. A sweeping bay, sandy beach, pleasant vistas, agricultural activity and proximity to Iraklion airport have combined to popularise the once open-spaces of Malia and its environs. The resort spreads along the National Highway, which doubles up as a High St. Off this branches a down-leg or beach access road which ends up close by the backshore in a small, pan-shaped turnround point for buses and cars. The area to both sides of this last road is criss-crossed with streets, lanes and tracks and is largely undeveloped, being cultivated. Ploughing, sheep grazing and cane cutting is under way cheek-by-jowl with the random hotel or three, erupting skywards out of a panorama still sheltering the occasional, derelict, skeletal water windmill.

The beach access road is lined with hotels, pensions, *Rooms*, tavernas, beach and cocktail bars, supermarkets, tourist gift shops, discos, Renta-a-Car as well as scooter and bicycle hire firms. Just 'an everyday Greek village'. Well not quite. The foreshore end is blocked off by a small, caique repair yard complete with a crude gantry and double block tackle. Offshore of the very sandy beach to the right is a small chapel interestingly sited on a rocky outcrop.

There can be no doubt that this is an extremely popular resort and with every justification. I must own up to shuddering at the degree of sophistication and have to admit that the more cosmopolitan cafe-bars offend my sensibilities, as do their ever-present television sets belting out an appalling mix of American violence and idiot British situation comedies. The rapid advancement in 'sophistication' of Greek youth is very evident and they have now reached the 1960s and the era evinced by say the film *Grease* and *John Travolta*.

Not all is lost to the backpacker as there is a *Youth Hostel* (Tel. 885075/224160), numerous hotels and pensions including a large clutch of C, D and E Class establishments. It is worth noting that some of the smarter A Class hotels list meals costing more than I would pay for a double room on some islands! The accommodation radiates out from the major 'T' road junction. Travellers trying to keep costs down will have to go for the E Class hotels as even the D Class ones average some 1800 drs for a mid-season double room. Exceptions to these rates are the *Alykon* (Tel. 31394) and *Argo* (Tel. 31636) where en suite single room rates commence at 900 drs and doubles 1150 drs; the *Arcadi* (Tel. 31439) with en suite singles costing 1000 drs and doubles 1500 drs, and the *Golden Bee* (Tel. 31243) with both shared and en suite bathrooms starting off at 650 drs for a single room and

1000 drs for a double, rising to 750 drs and 1200 drs respectively (15th June - 14th Sept). Of the E Class hotels the *Apostolos* (Tel. 31484) comes mentioned in dispatches! It is a pity that the once efficient Malia Camping has surprisingly closed down.

As for the accommodation, eating out is amply catered for (subtle) but I must highly recommend the:

Restaurant Oroscopio, Beach Road
Directions: On the left-hand side, in the corner of the second side street down from the High St.

The patron and his family are all involved and this includes granny and a rather precocious daughter who speaks better English than I (not difficult, do I hear the cry?). Noticeably patronised by locals – yes, there are some in Malia. The staff are most helpful and well-mannered and the food is good. Offerings include moussaka mince (250 drs); stuffed tomatoes (200 drs); swordfish (330 drs); stifado special (450 drs); Greek salad (150 drs) and a large bottle of retsina (110 drs). They might also serve green beans, although it is not on the menu.

A souvlaki snackbar lurks on the right-hand side of the main road going eastwards.

Scooter hire is very expensive averaging 2000 drs per day with three days costing 6000 drs. Machines from **Aries Rent a Vespa** have a spare wheel!

About 2 km out of Malia, going eastwards, a signpost to the left indicates the route to the **Minoan Malia Palace** and the accompanying outlying Minoan remains. The site is perhaps not so striking as those at Phaestos but nevertheless well worth a visit, especially if you are not visiting any of the other excavations.

Back on the main road, a turning off to the left leads to the fishing village of:
SISI (43 km from Iraklion) Tel prefix 0841. When we first arrived on Crete I was being assisted by the ELPA office in Iraklion and naturally asked the manager his choice for the foremost, natural Cretan seaside village. He selected Sisi. After extensive research I am not sure I would totally agree, but this charming, lovely, look-alike for a Cornish fishing village must be very close to the top of the pile. It is worth a visit if only to look over before the development under way swamps both Sisi and its environs. Interestingly enough Anne's notes read "Sisi is waking up...but only a little, don't panic yet". The pleasant approach road gently winds down through the village to, on the left, a hard standing area alongside the small cove and fishing-boat quay. On the right (*Fsw*) there was once a 'good news' taverna but which now trades as a cocktail rock bar – there you go! Halfway down the village, by the *Pension Petsalakis*, there is a sign, pointing along a track to the right, written *Sisi Bay Villas And To Beach*. The road wanders through a number of recently erected villa apartments and three new tasteful package holiday hotels, the *Mikro Xenodoxeio*, the *Porto Sisi* and *Egina*. The route opens out on to a flattened area high above the sea where motor caravans occasionally park up. From here, circumnavigating an old, disused windmill and some apartments, leads down, via a deeply rutted path, to a dry river-bed. Following the bed to the left leads to a bamboo grove beyond which is a deep, narrow bay with a rocky sandy foreshore and large pebbled seabed. It is a beautiful setting, but rubbish and oil-bestrewn. There is a stony cliff path down from the flattened area referred to above.

Back at the 'High St' junction there is another vaguely positioned sign, written *Porto Sisi*, which Anne charmingly advises "favours pointing down to the harbour but actually points vaguely in a diagonal towards nowhere", which is fair enough.

There are a number of pensions and apartments with accommodation including:

Pension Petsalakis
Directions: Half-way down the 'High St', opposite the 'Beach turning'. The pension has expanded in recent years and there are now two buildings, one each side of the road. The accommodation is very nice, spotless and pleasantly furnished. The balconies of the rooms of the right-hand building (*Fsw*) have the better views than those in the left which look out over a backyard. A double room with bathroom en suite and a balcony costs, in the high season, a reasonable 1600 drs. The right-hand building has a pleasant patio area, with tables and chairs, and excellent views over the sea and towards Porto Sisi. The hard-working, very Irish-looking, Greek lady runs the kitchen and serves up a limited menu whilst her 'hubby' does not appear to overdo things.

Another taverna is situated just below the *Petsalakis* on the left. **Rooms** are available on the road in (or out) and a typical example is the very nice looking:

Sophias Apartments (Class A Pension)
A double room with bathroom en suite in high season cost 1700 drs.

Next door to *Sophia's* is the *Pension Eirini* which charges the same rates. There are also **Rooms** on the right almost at the bottom of the High St and across the road from the harbour quay wall. A signpost on the Highway, prior to reaching the Sisi turnoff, points to *Sisi Camping*.

The inner man/woman is well gratified by the light sprinkling of Greek character tavernas throughout the village and the two well situated establishments over-looking the small, almost circular harbour. Of these latter, one, the more expensive, is excellently positioned, accessed by a flight of steps from the quay, and the other, still with a good outlook is the:

To Mouragio Taverna
Directions: Either down the last street to the left off the High St, heading in the direction of the harbour, or around the harbour quay wall to the left (*Fsw*) and along the path from the more expensive, harbour wall taverna.

Excellent food at reasonable prices and less pretentious decor and fixtures than its competitor. That is it manages without table-mounted lookalike gas light lamps! A meal for two of swordfish, a large souvlaki deliciously herb flavoured, cucumber salad, a plate of chips, bread and a large bottle of good wine costs 1175 drs. You'll notice Anne and her Greek husband, a doctor doing his army National Service, are not satisfied with retsina. Oh no they drink 'a large bottle of good wine'. A bottle of the old, tooth gargle would have knocked some 200 drs off the bill. The waitress is English and her father-in-law owns the To Mouragio.

Shops of note include a tourist/gift shop, downhill from *Pension Petsalakis,* and a large supermarket, on the right of the High St (*Fsw*), prior to the 'Beach turning', which sells mainly tourist goods. There is a post box in the wall of a house on the right of the High St and two unobtrusive hire firms, one offering cars and the other scooters.

It is a wrench to leave Sisi but to soften the regret it is only necessary to proceed to:

MILATOS VILLAGE (about 49 km from Iraklion) One of my five-star places but, as with any comments herein, this is a very personal opinion and there are no discos and or cocktail bars. In fact there is not a lot at all, really.

The approach can be made directly via Sisi or from the direction of Neapolis. From Sisi, breasting a ridge opens up a panoramic view of the large Milatos Plain with a rather unusual chapel standing solitarily on a small hillock in the middle distance. The Neapolis road winds steeply up the mountainside past an abandoned, ruined village with a line of derelict, stone windmills.

Both roads lead through the splendid, venerable Greek village of **Upper Milatos** half a mile or so before Milatos Beach. There are a number of old and traditional shops, typical of which is the village store which seems to be part of the family living room. Here we once purchased some feta cheese which had to be dug out of an ancient cylindrical container stored in the fridge. The purchase caused quite a lot of consternation and the whole family became involved.

Close by the village is yet another cave where the villagers, in days of yore, hid only to be routed out by the Turks and massacred.

There is accommodation available at *Rent a Room* (Tel. 32204).

The road falls away from the village down to the seafront and:

Milatos Beach. A number of maps simply use the nomenclature Analipsis which is in fact, the name of the tiny chapel that is set down to the right of the hamlet's small, sea-bordering, irregular square. Only a dozen or so years ago there was just a few houses, a taverna and the chapel but.... Fortunately it is still essentially unspoilt and certainly a pleasant spot.

On the left, where the road spills out on to the square, is the village store which is reasonably well stocked even if the service is rather slow. Technically there are **Rooms** over the shop as indicated by a sign. But the store owner is a reluctant participant in the arrangements and has to be persuaded, okay harangued, to telephone the owner. Best to try elsewhere.

Working around the square in an anticlockwise direction, beyond the chapel, is an indigenous supermarket and, on the far flank, a taverna with a metered phone from which international calls can be made. On the backshore side is the *Restaurant Mary Elen*, less expensive than the *Restaurant Akrogiali* which specialises in fish dishes. My own recommendation is the:

Taverna O Meraklis This now spans the westward shore track off the bottom left-hand corner of the square (*Fsw*) and is a favourite bar of the local fishermen. Here they often while away their spare time, sitting on the taverna's chairs, baiting their fishing baskets. Certainly it is the friendliest of places, and the diminutive lady who runs it is a gentle soul. Her younger brother, Manolis, who is training to be a teacher, helps out when he is at home and speaks some English. Sadly he will finish his course in 1987 and may go away to follow his chosen profession. The prices are on the inexpensive side and after a few nights in the village you may well become one of the inner circle, sharing the family's food at the big table inside. A few regulars speak a little English and are delighted to engage visitors in conversation.

Around the corner from the O Meraklis, a backshore track runs 300m to the left, along the pebbly sea-shore. This leads past a number of tavernas; three lots of **Rooms**, with doubles costing 1500 drs upwards; full scale apartment development underway, the shore being littered with building materials, and to landward a number of skeletal concrete frameworks and 'hopeful' looking pillars. At the far end is the now block booked:

Thalia A condominium of three and four bedroomed cabins, in a pretty setting and with most of the holiday conveniences including a swimming pool. The Thalia was once situated in relative seclusion but apart from the development along the track, there is now, for some very obscure reason, a new harbour being built to the west. The coast is already lined with huge concrete blocks to form the foundations.

Back to the square, there are several notices proclaiming *Yiannis 'Ride on a Storm' Hires motor-scooters, pedaloes and canoes.* Unfortunately the pedaloes are scattered about on the round pebble beach which stretches away to the right (*Fsw*).

A track used to lurch along parallel to the seafront petering out in a flattened patch randomly edged by an old windmill and a number of local houses. Now much of the area has been or is being developed with new houses. Several advertise accommodation, this often being in the only completed room of the particular construction.

Bread is delivered daily to the square by a van at about midday, but it is of the one-hour, brown, round-stone variety. By way of explanation, Greek bread can be quantified by the number of hours in which it must be eaten. One-hour bread is almost beyond redemption before it is purchased. At the other end of the scale is a white, French look-alike which can last 24 hours or more.

If there is a drawback to the village it is the lack of public transport which makes it necessary to use taxis or hire a car or scooter.

NEAPOLIS (some 54 km from Iraklion) Tel. prefix 0841 It is worthwhile turning off the main road to the busy, bustling country town of Neapolis which is certainly not on the tourist track, but nonetheless is friendly and colourful. The many shops are bursting with their various wares. The expansive square is bordered by trees, a large church and a petrol station. The High Street running the length of the town has, on the left, going west, a marvellous yoguteria where creamy yogurt is served up from the vat.

One Petros Philargos, born in 1340 in the village of Kares that existed on the site of present-day Neapolis, was eventually to become Pope Alexander V, but only for about a year, after which he passed away in mysterious circumstances.

Accommodation is not superabundant but there is the:

Hotel Neapolis (Class D) 1 Evangelistrias   Tel. 32268
Single rooms sharing the bathroom cost 800 drs and en suite 900 drs whilst a double room sharing costs 1300 drs and en suite 1500 drs.

From Neapolis, the country route is a pretty, valley road with many old windmills dotted about, passing through the lovely village of **Limnes** and on to **Ag. Nikolaos** (*See* CHAPTER 17). As usual, the presence of any town or village is apparent by the piles of rubbish dumped on the hillsides on the approach to the particular settlement.

ROUTE FOUR

To Knossos and Archanes (5 and 16 km) The road to the amazing
archaeological site of Knossos passes south out of Iraklion through a rather squalid suburb and then dusty and hilly countryside but with flowers and vines in abundance. Naturally enough, considering its prime tourist rating, there are a large number of tour buses to the site. This route leads past the town's hospital on the left and, beyond Knossos, a rather splendid, Venetian, two-tiered water aquaduct at a sharp twist in the road. It was here, I think, that the team of British guerillas and Greek partisans snatched the German General Kreipe in April 1944, during the Second World War.

Just before reaching the entrance to Knossos, a lane leads up to the right to the Villa Ariadne. This was built by Sir Arthur Evans, the prime mover behind the excavation of the magnificent site, and has experienced a history all of its own that would rate tour visits if it were not over-shadowed by the colossus across the road. *Dilys Powell* wrote a very readable and evocative book entitled *The Villa Ariadne*, ostensibly relating to the history of the building and its occupants, but encompassing much Cretan history. Those who have lived in the Villa include Sir Arthur Evans, the famous millionaire archaeologist who spent his fortune and the fortunes of his family in carrying out the excavations; John Pendlebury, a romantic Byronesque archaeologist turned guerrilla fighter in the Battle of Crete; King Paul, monarch of Greece, when fleeing the relentless German advance as well as the German commanders of wartime Crete. One of these, General Kreipe, was dramatically abducted and spirited off the island. This epic act of adventure is well described in the book *Ill Met By Moonlight* by *William Moss*. Readers interested in this period should also obtain a copy of *The Cretan Runner* by *George Psychoundakis* which includes much detail of the events from a partisan's point of view.

I am sure there can be no disagreement with my contention that the Villa is a study subject of its own. Whatever, we must now move on, across the road, to:

KNOSSOS (5 km from Iraklion) The history of the excavations and the archaeology is well documented and makes a fascinating thriller story, from the luck of the draw in identifying the possibilities, the difficulties of acquiring the hillside and the slow realisation that this dig would uncover the jewel in the Minoan crown.

As with most Minoan palace sites, the great palace was built around a central court from which spread a succession of buildings, rooms and cellars connected by staircases, small courtyards, corridors and magazines for pithoi (storage jars and urns).

It is a pity that the imaginative reconstruction that Evans put into train, based on frescoes found on the site and artistic recreations by Piet de Jong, and resulting in a coherent restoration, caused so much academic controversy. There can be no doubt that the other palace remains that have been 'faithfully' excavated are much more enjoyable once Knossos has been visited.

The dig revealed the religious aspect of the complex with sacred double axes, pillars, shrines, purification or lustral baths and the mythological Minotaur bull. This is in addition to the outstanding architectural design, coupled with the complicated installation of roadways, drainage and sanitation systems, water hydraulics as well as what must be the first Greek 'squatty', in the Queen's apartments. It is fascinating to realise that the word labyrinth originates from the lost Minoan language, that is 'labrynthos'.

The site, probably the capital of the Minoan empire, has been continuously excavated from 1900. It has remained a 'British dig', for after Sir Arthur Evans could no longer finance the escalating restoration costs, he bequeathed the site to the British School of Archaeology, based at Athens.

Habitation of the site occurred as early as 6000 BC. The Minoan period commenced circa 2000 BC, continuing after the great earthquake of about 1700 BC and the resultant reconstruction. This was followed by another earthquake circa 1600 BC, after which more rebuilding was necessary until the final apocalypse in 1400 BC. This disastrous conflagration resulting from a 'big bang', possibly occasioned by the cataclysmic eruption of Santorini's volcano, was originally considered to have resulted in immediate evacuation and abandonment of the Minoan sites. More leisurely thought and later excavation suggests that the civilisation did not suffer from a 'here you are, there you go'. There was possibly reoccupation after the disaster followed by a rapid decline and final desertion. Future generations were only too aware of the sacred nature of the remains and kept well clear of the locality.

Recent discoveries include the exciting 'Royal Road' and the accompanying foundations of houses, workshops and possibly viewing platforms. For detailed study and enjoyment it is well worthwhile purchasing a guidebook on the spot. How can one follow that?

It is worth, despite the inevitable anti-climatic feeling, taking the road, now badly potholed in places, to the dusty sprawling town of:

ARCHANES (16 km from Iraklion) Tel, prefix 081. This is a centre for grape production and there is some industry. The rubbish is collected by a municipal dust cart, and the town is the possessor of a sports ground and an electrical goods shop. Despite these 20th century attributes, fortunately Archanes retains a very Greek village feel. Certainly the cafe-bars are dominated by the male population of the village whilst the female gender are noticeable by their absence. As Anne put it, they are probably tending the vines, and why not I say?

Some of the 'great unwashed' make their way here to join in the grape harvest, possibly when richer pickings are no longer available elsewhere. There are the usual kafenions, cafe-bars and tavernas as well as a fairly squalid bar decorated with a stuffed bat and run by a kindhearted proprietor. He 'brews' his own local wine, of a potent nature, and serves up a very good pita bread souvlaki.

Accommodation is available at the *Hotel Dias* (Class B, tel 751810) and there are **Rooms**. The confusing network of roads and streets is 'assisted' by an extremely muddling one-way system.

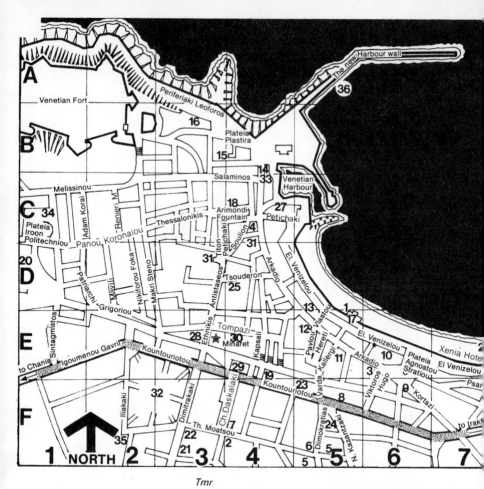

Tmr

RETHYMNON

Illustration 13

144

13 RETHYMNON (Rethymno) ***
Harbour city

FIRST IMPRESSIONS
Seaside tourist town; cultured and industrious; secretive Old Quarter.

VITAL STATISTICS
Tel. prefix 0831. Population about 15,000.

HISTORY
Not so extensively catalogued as the island's two other major cities, Rethymnon has some late Minoan traces. The Venetians, during their occupation, were responsible for much of the town's development. After a Turkish pirate raid the walls and fort were constructed despite which, in common with the rest of the island, Rethymnon was overwhelmed by the Turks in 1645.

GENERAL
It is a cause of some wonderment to note how many guides cover Rethymnon rather *en passant*. Personally I regard it as one of the most all-round, attractive locations for the tourist, and probably the most complete of Crete's major towns. In addition to the 'standard package' of Venetian fortress, City wall, harbour, churches, Turkish Old Quarter, mosques, minaret and fountain, there is a really magnificent sandy beach. I've dreamt of a sandy beach!

As there are no ferry-boats (*See* later notes) or airport, arrival will be by road. The Highway runs to the south of Rethymnon and the main road/'High St', Odhos Kountouriotou, skirts the edge of the City with no clearly marked access. From the main road it is easiest to turn down the streets prior to the *Hotel Valaria* (*Tmr* 8F5) which lead down to Agnostou Stratiou Sq (usually incorrectly (?) named Iroon Sq), beside the Kara Pasha Mosque (*Tmr* 3E6). This is not the most salubrious area from which to start out but is a very convenient point from which to make a sweep to the left along the magnificent seafront Esplanade. The beach backshore, to the right, is planted with embryonic palm trees, and the Esplanade buildings to the left, are fronted by full-grown palms. The avenue ends up at the inner Venetian Harbour (*Tmr* B/C4/5) which it is possible to miss as this miniature, Chania 'look-alike' is tucked away round the corner. It is necessary to jink right and then left to gain entrance to the very small and pretty harbour, the attractions of which are rather spoilt by the massed restaurants that edge the quay wall.

One of the problems in establishing a position in the town is that, to deceive, the layout appears to be a grid but in actual fact is a series of slow curves. The most confusing streets are those of Arkadio and Ethnikis Antistaseos which both start off in the area of the Museum (*Tmr* 4C4) and finish up in completely different quarters, although seeming to run parallel. Know what I mean!

Odhos Ethnikis Antistaseos commences its gently curving, uphill sweep alongside the Venetian Arimondi Fountain (*Tmr* 18C3/4) and marks the eastern edge of the Old Quarter. The street passes the Minaret of Nerantzes (*Tmr* 31D3), climbing on up to the old Town Gate, outside which is another minaret, and a bustling square flanked by the very large, still unfinished, modern Tessaron Martyron Church (*Tmr* 29E4). Diagonally across the main road are the Public Gardens (*Tmr* 32E/F2/3).

Odhos Arkadio also gently curves but parallel to the seafront, and one block back, ending up on Plateia Agnostou Stratiou. Once these two streets are mastered, the rest of the town can be explored.

ARRIVAL BY BUS

More probably arrival will be at the dusty, disorganised, shambling Bus Square set between two bus ticket offices (*Tmr* 5F5) south of the main road, Odhos Kountourioutou.

ARRIVAL BY FERRY

See **Travel Agents, A to Z.**

THE ACCOMMODATION & EATING OUT

Both are plentiful but the cost of accommodation here has risen dramatically over the last 4 or 5 years, even outstripping other Cretan holiday centres. In the case of Rethymnon this is almost entirely due to discovery and expansion by the package holiday tour operators. Generally, accommodation in Rethymnon is more expensive than in towns further west, with the most basic pension rate being around 1200 drs for anything decent, as compared to 1000 drs in Chania.

Wandering around the back streets of the Old Quarter making enquiries of a few householders about their prices results in quotes of 1200 drs and upwards, even in the very back alleys. Those travelling alone in high season, may well find it more advantageous to go to a hotel (C, D, E class) than search out a pension and/or Rooms. In general the hotels reduce their rates more easily for one person, so it is possible to obtain better value for money. For instance a D Class hotel results in a room with en suite bathroom for 1000 drs whereas Rooms will only offer a cheap double at no reduction and the bathroom will be shared.

The Accommodation

Hotel Olympic (*Tmr* 6F5). (Class B) Th. Moatsou/Dimokratias Sts.   Tel. 24761
Directions: It really could not be closer to the Bus offices/terminus unless it was built over them. When arriving other than by bus, turn up Odhos Dimokratias at the square (well romboid) formed by the streets of Dimokratias and N. Kazantzaki (usually listed as Hortatzi St), with the National Bank (*Tmr* 24F5) in the apex. An up-market, mainly tour operator booked, expensive hotel. Added to this it is situated directly diagonally opposite the Bus terminus and as the first bus departs at 0600 hrs it can be noisy, to say the least. There is also a taxi rank across the road.

It goes without saying that rooms are en suite with a single bed costing 2000 drs and a double 2845 drs but breakfast may be mandatory which adds another 520 drs or so to the bill. What's money?

Hotel Brascos (*Tmr* 7F3/4) (Class B) Th. Moatsou/Ch. Daskalaki   Tel. 23721
Directions: In the third block west of the Bus Square.

Comments as for the *Olympic* but less bus and taxi noise. En suite bathrooms with a single room costing 2250 drs and a double 2450 drs rising, respectively, to 2600 drs and 3000 drs (1st June – 30th Sept). The cost of breakfast, which may well be compulsory (you will eat your boiled egg...), rises from 550 drs to 600 drs, depending on the time of year.

Back to (cost) reality, there are **Rooms** turning south from the Bus Sq, along Odhos Kazantzaki and following the narrowing lane to whence it forks. Normal rates for pension accommodation.

Hotel Valari (*Tmr* 8F5) (Class C) 84 Kountouriotou   Tel. 22236
Directions: On the main road, opposite the monument to E. Venizelou which is itself close by the National Bank (*Tmr* 24F5).

On the main road and therefore very noisy. En suite bathrooms with a single room charged at 1400 drs and a double 1825 drs, rising to 1780 drs and 2265 drs (1st June – 18th Oct). Note that the management may require encouragement to reduce the first (overcharging) rate quoted. Nothing like turning as if to leave....

At this juncture I strongly advocate calling into the NTOG office (*Tmr* 1D/E5) presided over by the Anglophile Mr Costas Palierakis. He will not only arrange accommodation but barter on a clients behalf, once he has their exact requirements. More on Mr Costas under **NTOG, A to Z.**

Hotel Acropol (*Tmr* 9F6) (Class D) Plateia Agnostou Stratiou (Plateia Iroon)   Tel. 23477
Directions: From the main road (Odos Kountouriotou) proceed down Ierolohitou St (which becomes Viktoros Hugo) and on to the Square. The spartan hotel is on the right in a not particularly salubrious situation.
   Despite the location and class, the hotel is clean and the bathrooms are cleaned out twice a day – and the staff are very friendly. The supply of hot water can be eratic. A double without bath from 1500 drs and en suite from 1800 drs.

Hotel Achilles (Class E) 151 Arkadio   Tel. 22581
Directions: In the same block as the *Hotel Acropol.*
   A friendly owner with nice double rooms, complete with shower and balcony at the front of the building, costing 1700 drs. However there are less expensive rooms at the back, still en suite, costing 1200 drs.

Pension (*Tmr* 10E6) 11 Arkadio
Directions: To one side of the Esplanade leather shop (of which more later), close to Plateia Agnostou Stratiou, and entered from a flight of steps to one side of the building. Entry can also be effected from Odhos Arkadio exactly opposite the Kara Pasha Mosque (*Tmr* 3E6).
   It is difficult to decide whether the black draped lady owner is as forbidding as the very spartan, almost grim but clean accommodation. A grotty double room costs 800 drs whilst a slightly superior double costs 1000 drs. Naturally the bathrooms are shared.

Hotel Minoa (*Tmr* 11E5) (Class D) 60 Arkadio St.   Tel. 22508
Directions: From Plateia Agnostou Stratiou turn along Odhos Arkadio at the Kara Pasha Mosque (*Tmr* 3E6), and the hotel is on the left.
   Greek provincial in a super part of town in which to reside, with the beach immediately down a short lane and across the Esplanade road. The owner is pleasant and the establishment clean and airy. Officially the en suite rooms cost 1700 drs for a single and 1800 drs for a double room but negotiations can be entered into, especially if prospective guests show an inclination to leave!

This area is a rich vein of accommodation with **Rooms** at No. 68, just along from the *Hotel Minoa,* and the:

Venetia 39 Varda Kallergi St
Directions: In the side street, almost opposite the *Hotel Minoa,* which leads down the Esplanade. Apartments and rooms.

Hotel Zania (Class D) 3 Pavlou Vlastou/Arkadio St.   Tel. 28169
Directions: From the *Hotel Minoa* turn left or north-west along Arkadio St, past Odhos Hereti to Pavlou Vlastou Lane and the hotel is on the left.

Pleasantly Greek provincial but light, airy and clean and, in Anne's opinion, a better choice than either the *Hotels Achillon* or *Minoa*. The landlady is helpful, offering to place single room aspirants with a friend of hers. In high season a double room sharing the bathroom costs 1500 drs and rooftop singles are made available at 600 drs each.

Youth Hostel (Class D) (*Tmr* 12E5) 7 Pavlou Vlastou   Tel. 22848
Directions: A door or two up from the *Hotel Zania* and on the right. The entrance is through a surprising, almost medieval, stone corridor which leads into a pretty, tree shaded courtyard.

Access to the timber-planked upper storey is via a flight of stairs. There is cellar storage for rucksacks, a common room, hot showers in the morning and early evenings, a kitchen and bar. Light snack meals are provided (a Nes costs 65 drs and an omelette 80 drs). The notice board has local tourist information and 'for sale and to buy' cards on display. The per person charge for a night is 300 drs. Valid YHA membership cards are asked for, certainly in the high season, but the management indicate that they would not turn away the desperate.

Hotel Achillion (*Tmr* 13D/E5) (Class E) 151 Arkadio   Tel. 22581
Directions: Slightly further along Odhos Arkadio and stretching through to the Esplanade, with entrances from both front and back.

Dingy but what do you expect from a Class E hotel – the Savoy? It does have an air of long ago, faded elegance. A double room, sharing the bathroom, in high season costs 1200 drs a night.

By proceeding along Odhos Arkadio towards the Venetian harbour, once past the Museum (*Tmr* 4C4) there are **Rooms** on both sides of the road ending with the:

Pension Mikonos (*Tmr* 14B/C4) 303 Arkadio St.   Tel. 29129
Directions: As above

A very large building in an excellent position and one of the best value establishments in town. Mr Kokonas, a friendly young man, quotes singles from 500 drs and a variety of double room options starting off at 1000 drs with possible reductions for more than one day. There is a pleasant balcony overlooking the end of the Venetian Harbour.

Odhos Arkadio opens out on to the Esplanade road. Turn left on to Plateia Plastira to pass the incredibly expensive *Hotel Ideon,* now block booked by various tour operators including SAGA (which does not stand for Sex And Games for the Aged), and look for the sign pointing to N. Plastira lane and:

B. Dokimaka (*Tmr* 15B3/4)
Directions: As above.

Rather Cycladean island 'norm' set around a flower drenched courtyard and run by a very Greek landlady. Rave reviews elsewhere have resulted in double rooms in the high season costing 1500 drs, plus the cost of a shower.

Hotel Kastro (*Tmr* 16B3) (Class D) Periferiaki Leoforos   Tel. 24973
Directions: Just up the road from Plateia Plastira, towards the fortress, in amongst a small row of restaurants, bars and **Rooms**.

The friendly, hunky, very hunky young proprietor (I stress this 'hunky thing' is one of Anne's sexist proclivites surfacing) exudes an atmosphere of congeniality. No singles but he quotes 1500 drs for the double rooms with en suite bathroom. Over a drink or three he, and his friends, assure prospective clients that it is only his inate good nature that precludes him from charging in excess of the official rate of 1850 drs. Oh yes!

Before leaving the subject there are two houses with **Rooms** in Odhos Soulion, close by the Museum (*Tmr* 4C4).

Camping Arkadio. This site (and nearby *Camping Elizabeth*) is some 4 km east of Rethymnon on the Old Road for details of which *See* IRAKLION, ROUTE ONE.

The Eating Out There are three main localities for restaurants and tavernas. One is the stretch of Esplanade between the Beach Pavilion (*Tmr* 17D/E5/6) all the way round to the Venetian Harbour.
Of the Esplanade alternative I can recommend:

The Samaria 37 El Venizelou
The usual offerings but well cooked and good value. A rotisserie supplements the menu options. The owner, in his mid 40s, is attentive and hard working. Initially it is possible to gain the impression that the 'schlepper' is the proprietor. Thank goodness he is not. Costas ('Mr NTOG') sometimes frequents this restaurant and occasionally a delicious suckling pig is put on the menu.

Another 'eatery area' is the Venetian Harbour, the quayside of which is jam-packed with the tables and chairs of restaurant/tavernas that crowd each other cheek by jowl all the way round the harbour's small perimeter. Unfortunately these expensive establishments are prone to advocate fish dishes, thus causing the meals to be even more expensive. Those tavernas with typical Greek offerings are on the far or north end. One at least of the restaurants is comparatively reasonably priced; the:

Taverna Panagos
Directions: Two-thirds of the way round the quay wall from the beach end.
The menu includes tzatziki (65 drs), Greek salad (225 drs), a plate of kalamari (225 drs), the usual fish dishes, pork or lamb chops (350 drs), pork souvlaki (360 drs), a beer (65 drs) or small bottle of retsina (65 drs).

The 'richest' area, and that with the best tavernas in Rethymnon, must be centred around the Arimondi Fountain, on Plateia Diog Moshoviti (*Tmr* 18C3/4).
Perhaps the pick of the bunch is the, once basic, once inexpensive:

Taverna Battela
Directions: Just beyond the Arimondi Fountain on Diog Moshoviti Sq.
Nowadays the food is absolutely excellent but not however desperately cheap. Diners are ushered into the kitchens by Beni the friendly, Israeli waiter. Here the very large, ample but friendly Cretan lady cook is surrounded by 'millions' of pans and steaming trays.
Beni, almost inevitably, is a humourist. Anne observed him, whilst whizzing around with trays of 'on the house' raki, approach a couple of matronly German lady diners. Rather fussed, they refused his offer only to be egged on by Beni with a loud, lightning response "Okay but it's very good for sex you know". The taverna's guests collapsed about his ears. A meal of stifado, bean stew, bread and a full bottle of retsina will set a couple back some 1270 drs, which may well include a free raki or two.

The Fountain Square and surrounds are crammed with tavernas and cafe-bars including the recommended *Rimondi*, all well frequented by locals, expatriates and tourists. Further on from Arimondi Fountain, Thessalonikis St leads past a dancing school for young Cretan girls to a couple of more local offerings, including the typically Cretan restaurant ΠΑΝΟΥ ΚΟΡΟΝΑΙΟΥ on the street of the same name. None are really inexpensive although naturally they are cheaper than the Esplanade establishments.

Back on Odhos Arkadio, on the same side of the road and across a side street from the *Hotel Minoa* (*Tmr* 11E5) are the:

No. 74 'Souvlaki' & No. 70 'Snackbar Souvlaki'
Directions: As above

Separated by a cosmetics shop, these two snackbars are timely reminders on Crete of a disappearing past. Cellar-like in appearance and with the souvlakis cooked over a charcoal fire on long, thin sticks after which, when cooked, the meat is pulled off and jammed into pita bread. (The more modern method is to have a vertical rotating spit on which the meat is packed in the form of an 'upturned ice cream cone' rotating past a semicircular electric element). The two shops certainly offer a very cheap alternative to the rest of the town's eating houses. No. 74, where two souvlaki sticks and a bottle of beer costs some 175 drs, has the 'advantage' of the enactment of a daily pantomime. The patron is 'dis-assisted' by his teenage daughter Marina who sits outside scowling and does no work except when subject to sustained shouting by father! (I'm sure other parents know the feeling!)

Also on Odhos Arkadio, close by the Venetian Harbour, on the sea side of the road, are the:

Sunny Pub & the Pub Why Not
Reputed to serve draught beer and English-style pies. Oh goody! It certainly appears to be a reproduction of the real thing, if you see what I mean. Why leave the home shores?

On the town side of these 'pubs' is the very small, pretty, raised garden of a taverna which seems popular with the locals. Only the early, very early evening bird catches a meal here.

Other 'offerings' take in a good pie shop (including cheese pies) next door to the OTE office (*Tmr* 19E/F4) and one or two small restaurants alongside the football ground (*Tmr* 20D1), just round the corner from Plateia Iroon Politechniou.

THE A TO Z OF USEFUL INFORMATION
AIRLINE OFFICE & TERMINUS (*Tmr* 21F3) The Olympic office is on the corner of Odhos Dimitrakaki, which is a continuation of Ethnikis Antistaseos, just beyond the Bank of Greece (*Tmr* 22F3).

Aircraft timetables *See* **Iraklion and Chania**

BANKS
Bank of Crete (*Tmr* 23E/F4/5). Sited on the High St, Odhos Kountouriotou, to the east of the OTE (*Tmr* 19E/F4). Changes travellers cheques and Eurocheques.
National Bank of Greece There are two; one on Tsouderon St (*Tmr* 24D4) and the other opposite the Town Hall, on Plateia E Venizelos (*Tmr* 24F5).
Bank of Greece (*Tmr* 22F3).

BEACHES Really no need to list this facility which must be one of the best beaches on the island. Generally of excellent sand, the beach stretches from the south side of the Venetian Harbour all the way past the eastern breakwater (which arrows out into the bay from the Restaurant Delfini) and on for a mile or so to where the Esplanade road finally runs out. The *Restaurant Delfini* (*Tmr* 26E7) marks the end of the seaside town, the development from here on becoming scrappier and scrappier.

I suppose there must be a blot on every landscape and I am not sure why the good citizens of Rethymnon allowed the erection of the low, but stark Beach Pavilion (*Tmr* 17D/E5/6) smack in the middle of the vista, nor for that matter the countless 'straw' umbrellas. On the credit side the facilities include fresh water beach showers and toilets which have now been rebuilt and are looked after by attendants who keep them spotless. Perhaps the relocating of the NTOG office in the building resulted in a fundamental rethink. Certainly some years ago the place was a disgrace, but not now.

The beach between the two breakwaters is quite broad and the area adjacent to the palm-tree edged Esplanade is pleasantly covered with sparse, tufted grass. The beach is now cleaned every morning added to which the locals have probably been discouraged from allowing their dogs to roam at will for 'walkies'. The pressures of the traffic have resulted in the necessity for vehicles wishing to park along the Esplanade backshore to purchase a parking ticket from the NTOG office. Needless to say this piece of petty bureaucracy is ignored by everyone.

BICYCLE, SCOOTER, & CAR HIRE The hirers of two-wheeled vehicles are gathered together on Odhos K. Paleologou between the Museum (*Tmr* 4C4) and the Arimondi Fountain (*Tmr* 18C3/4). Cars are rented out by a number of travel agents and there is a **Hertz** office on Kortazi St, up from east of Plateia Stratiou.

Do not forget Mr ('NTOG') Costas as an intermediary. He enjoys obtaining competitive rates for 'his' tourists.

BOOKSELLERS There is a good shop on Ιουλιας Petichaki St, which runs down from the area of the Museum (*Tmr* 4C4) to the seafront, almost opposite the Ladies-Only WC (*Tmr* 27C4). Other book/paper shops of some note, and which sell British newspapers, include one opposite the OTE (*Tmr* 19E/F4) and No 36 Ethnikis Anistaseos, on the left leaving the Town Gate (*Tmr* 28E3) behind one.

BREAD SHOPS One at No. 69 opposite the *Hotel Minoa* (*Tmr* 11E5) in Arkadio St; another behind the OTE (*Tmr* 19E/F4) in Kapsali St, down on the right (followed by a grocer's); one in Hereti St (close by the *Hotel Minoa*) and another in the Old Quarter on Panou Koronaiou (**PANOY KOPONAIOY**) at No. 21, on the right after the branch lane Renieri M.

BUSES The main Bus Square has two offices (*Tmr* 5F5) diagonally opposite each other.

Bus timetables
BUS STATION ONE (*Tmr* 5F5) North or seaside of the Square   Tel. 22212

Rethymnon to Iraklion
Daily   0645, 0730, 0815, 0900, 0945, 1015, 1045, 1115, 1145, 1215, 1245, 1315, 1345,
            1400, 1415, 1445, 1515, 1545, 1615, 1645, 1715, 1745, 1815, 1845, 1945, 2100 hrs.
Return journey
Daily   0530, 0630, 0730, 0815, 0900, 0945, 1015, 1045, 1115, 1145, 1215, 1230, 1245,
            1315, 1345, 1400, 1415, 1445, 1515, 1545, 1615, 1645, 1715, 1745, 1815, 1845, 1930 hrs.
One-way fare 380 drs.

Rethymnon to Chania
Daily 0700, 0730, 0815, 0915, 1000, 1045, 1115, 1145, 1215, 1300, 1330, 1400, 1430,
       1500, 1530, 1615, 1700, 1730, 1800, 1830, 1900, 1930, 2000, 2030, 2100 hrs.
Return journey
Daily 0530, 0645, 0730, 0800, 0830, 0900, 0930, 1000, 1030, 1100, 1130, 1200, 1230,
       1300, 1330, 1400, 1430, 1500, 1530, 1600, 1630, 1700, 1730, 1830, 1945 hrs.
One-way fare 330 drs.

BUS STATION TWO (*Tmr* 5F5) South side of the Square.

Rethymnon to Spili, Ag. Galini.
Daily 0645, 0900, 1030, 1200, 1345, 1745 hrs.
Return journey
Daily 0645, 0845, 1030, 1145, 1445, 1630, 1930 hrs.
One-way fare 280 drs.

Rethymnon to Myrthios, Plakias.
Daily 0600, 0815, 0930, 1130, 1345, 1800 hrs.
Return journey
Daily 0700, 0930, 1100, 1245, 1500, 1930 hrs.
One-way fare 210 drs.

Rethymnon to Chora Sfakion via Plakias.
Daily 0815 hrs.
Return journey
Daily 1630 hrs.
One-way fare 400 drs.

Rethymnon to Arkadi Monastery.
Daily 0600, 1100, 1430 hrs.
Return journey
Daily 0700, 1300, 1600 hrs.
One-way fare 105 drs.

The following is another piece of bus journey information, which as Anne pointed out, says it all!

'How To Cross The Samaria Gorge From Rethymnon
You can leave from Rethymnon early in the morning by the 7.00 a.m. bus from the central bus station (46 Moatsou Street) to Omalos. The bus from Hania to Omalos can leave at 8.30 a.m.
    After two hours driving time you arrive in the longest gorge (18 km) in Europe from 5-7 hours walk. The Samaria gorge, winding its way through awe inspiring grandeur and wild beauty.
    At the exit near the seaside village of Agia Roumeli, there is an attractive beach and communication with the village of Chora Sfakion (Sfakia) by the 1400, 1600 or 1700 hrs motor boat.
    In summer more times.
    At 1830 you can leave from Sfakia by bus back to Rethymnon. You have to stop at Vrisses and from there you get on the bus which comes from Hania.
    Wish you a good trip!'

CINEMAS One in Arkadio St at the Plateia Agnostou Stratiou end and another in the Old Quarter off Salaminos St, close to which is a Pool Hall.

COMMERCIAL SHOPPING AREA Oddly for a town of this size there is no central area, which makes shopping a slow business. The nearest approach to a market area is at the Town Gate (*Tmr* 28E3) end of Ethnikis Antistaseos. Here there are a number of grocers, fish and meat stalls, and ironmongers, in amongst tailors, dry cleaners and hairdressers (men, of course).

The Old Quarter streets of Rethymnon embracing Thessalonikis, and its extension Panou Koronaiou (ΠΑΝΟΥ ΚΟΡΟΝΑΙΟΥ), Melissinou and Salaminos contain a variety of shops including bakers and grocers. Another fruitful area is in the square and side streets dominated by Tessaron Martyron Church (*Tmr* 29E4) and there is an excellent supermarket immediately alongside the Church. Across the High Street/main road, market stalls are set up during the week in the area outlined by the streets of Kountouriotou, Dimitrakaki and Th. Moatsou (*Tmr* E/F3). Tsouderon St (*Tmr* D4) has a preponderance of tailors at the sea end and leather goods at the far end.

With leather shops in mind, I cannot leave the subject without mentioning a father and son duo who dominate this business at the east end of the Town. (I hasten to add, tourist leather goods...) The father will probably first come to one's notice for he performs (sic) from a shop on the seafront, just along from Plateia Agnostou Stratiou. He is bedecked in an evening suit version of the Cretan hillman's uniform complete with lace headshawl, waistcoat, flared trousers and white boots. Watch out if he offers you a raki or two – it can wipe out an afternoon. As Anne points out the hardened traveller will not be amused by his antics, more especially that of handing his girl assistant some of the customers change as a tip! Certainly do not pay the list price – a gesture of absenting oneself from the shop should result in a 20-25% reduction off a 1000 drs pair of sandals. His son, who operates around the corner at No. 52 Odhos Arkadio adjacent to the *Hotel Minoa* (*Tmr* 11E5), commands four or five self-taught languages and is prepared to enter into an argument on political philosophy in English. I must admit that this consists of haranguing on about our Prime Minister and the Government's policies vis a vis the UK and the EEC, but there you go! I mean, do you know the name of the Greek Prime Minister let alone what party he heads up? Son follows in father's footsteps by occasionally 'swamping' customers, to whom he takes a liking, with glasses of ouzo or raki. They both have a repetitive habit of referring to Englishmen as "Capitalista – Ah Thatcher". Should we experience a change in our government I am sure they will, within days, substitute the correct name. Almost opposite, at No. 52, is a local who also runs a leather-goods shop, but one can only feel very sorry for him as he just does not stand a chance against the competition of his voluble, fellow countryman.

DISCOS The *Restaurant Delfini* (*Tmr* 26E7), at the eastern end of the promenade, has a disco-bar and there are a number of 'offerings' sandwiched between the multitudinous restaurants, tavernas and cafe-bars on Leoforos El. Venizelou (The Esplanade road).

FERRY BOAT None despite the odd attempt in the past. *See* **Travel Agents** for details of a trip-boat that makes summer voyages to Santorini island.

HAIRDRESSERS Rethymnon has almost more men's hairdressers than kafenions, if such a thing is possible. There are a number of ladies' hairdressers in Odhos Dion Kastrino Giannaki, off Tsouderon St. (*Tmr* D4)

LAUNDRY In 1986 a brand new coin-op laundrette, 'LAUNDRY MAT' (*Tmr* 30E4), opened its doors at 45 Odhos Tompazi. Open daily 0900 - 1400 and 1700 - 2100 hrs.

MEDICAL CARE
Chemists & Pharmacies A number in the usual streets of Arkadio, Ethnikis Antistaseos and Kountouriotou (the main road/High St). The NTOG can advise which are open all night.
Hospital (*Tmr* 35F2) On Odhos Iliakaki, beyond the Public Gardens.

NTOG (*Tmr* 1D/E5) The office, now located right of centre (*Fsw*) of the backshore Beach Pavilion, used to be dominated by the colourful, but no longer youthful, Mr

Costas Palierakis who has for years gone well beyond the remit of his office. He would assist any tourist but was always especially kind and helpful in his attitude to the English, for whom he has a soft spot, no doubt due to old, wartime memories. Costas is still in evidence but he is now ably abetted by the less demonstrative but also helpful Dimitris and Yiannis. As Costas puts it "Now you see, I am no longer alone, we are all together and no one is captain". The entrance is off the Esplanade and the office is open weekdays 0900 - 1830 hrs, weekends and holidays 0900 - 1300 hrs.

Incidentally in the same building, next door to the NTOG, is a government-run display of Cretan traditional wares, blankets, pottery and leatherwork, which is interesting to look around but neither Anne nor I know why the display is called EOMMEX.

OTE (*Tmr* 19E/F4) Sited on the 'High St' and still, in 1986, open 24 hours a day.

PETROL A number of stations including a fairly central one, opposite Tessaron Martyron Church (*Tmr* 29E4).

PLACES OF INTEREST
Arimondi Fountain (*Tmr* 18C3/4). Only three heads and a part of the back wall of this pretty fountain survive. It stands alongside the vine, grape and gourd festooned Diog Moshoviti Square.

The Fort (*Tmr* A/B1/2). A large Venetian, but interiorless, fortress. The outer walls and one main town gate are now in a good state of restoration but the Turks and Germans, some 300 years apart, ensured that only these and a domed mosque remained standing. The fort is open Tuesday - Thursday between 0800 - 2000 hrs; weekends and Monday between 0930 - 1800 hrs.

The Museum (*Tmr* 4C4). Located in the original 16th century Venetian Loggia. It is worth a visit, but the exhibits are rather disjointed. The entrance fee is 100 drs and the museum is open daily between 0830 - 1500 hrs; Sundays and holidays between 0900 - 1430 hrs.

The Old Quarter One of the most interesting sights. The overhanging, wooden first storeys of the Turkish buildings almost blot out the sky from the narrow lanes, with the occasional Venetian stone facade to a building. Start out from Arimondi Fountain Sq (*Tmr* 18C3/4) and wander along the almost parallel streets of Salaminos and Thessalonikis and their interconnecting side lanes.

Odhos Titon Petichaki, which connects Fountain Sq with Ethnikis Antistaseos, forms the eastern end of the Old Quarter. Keep an eye open for the shop in this street with a massive vine growing all over the ceiling of the interior.

Public Gardens (*Tmr* 32E/F2/3). The formally arranged gardens were originally a Turkish cemetery. They now contain an aviary with the exhibits cooped up in undersized cages. Every year, at the end of July, a wine festival is held in the grounds. It may have been a serious affair originally, but has now turned out to be a rather fairground, 'razamataz' event, with funny hats and false noses not entirely out of place.

Religious Buildings These include the Mosque of Kara Pasha (*Tmr* 3E6), and, if only for curiosity's sake, the newly constructed and as yet externally unfinished Church of Tessaron Martyron (Four Martyrs) (*Tmr* 29E4) which possesses splendid, vast interior murals.

Venetian Harbour Small, very attractive and full of caiques, with its quay walk crowded out by restaurant/taverna chairs and tables.

POLICE
Port (*Tmr* 33B/C4/5). Adjacent to the Venetian Harbour, at the northern end of Arkadio St.

Tourist (*Tmr* 34C1). The office was once closer to the action, adjacent to the Museum, but ostensibly due to the old building collapsing, they have moved up to Plateia Iroon Politechiniou. They have an extensive list of **Rooms** and hotels as well as a simple but reasonably effective town plan.

Town Also at the other end of Odhos Thessalonikis, on Plateia Iroon Politechniou, alongside the football ground (*Tmr* 20D1).

POST OFFICE (*Tmr* 2F3/4). Moved in 1986 to Odhos Th. Moatsou, opposite the *Hotel Brascos*.

TAXIS There are ranks on the Tessaron Martyron Church Sq (*Tmr* E4) as well as the Bus Square area, alongside the *Hotel Olympic* (*Tmr* 6F5).

TELEPHONE NUMBERS & ADDRESSES

Hospital: (*Tmr* 35F2) Iliakaki St.	Tel. 22550/27491
NTOG: (*Tmr* 1D/E5) Beach Pavilion, El. Venizelou	Tel. 29148/14143
Olympic Airways: (*Tmr* 21F3) Dimitrakaki St.	Tel. 22257
Taxis: 24 hr service	Tel. 24000/25000
Tourist Police: (*Tmr* 34C1) Plateia Iroon Politechniou	Tel. 28156

TOILETS

Ladies' Facilities (*Tmr* 27C4) On the left of Odhos Ιουλίας Petichaki leading down from the Museum to the Esplanade. A splendidly clean WC presided over by a lady attendant. Clean they may be, but despite this they are rather smelly. The overseer has her other senior-citizen, lady friends round for a Sunday afternoon tean in the ante-room. Well, why not?

General. In the Beach Pavilion (*Tmr* 17D/E5/6).*See* **Beaches** for fuller details of this, now, excellent facility. There are also toilets in the Public Gardens (*Tmr* 32E/F2/3).

TRAVEL AGENTS

Nearchos Travel This office is located at the Venetian Harbour end of Arkadio St, opposite the *Sunny Pub* (*Tmr* C4). The young lady speaks good English and they carry details of a catamaran service to Santorini island. I am fairly certain this is the same craft with which the agency tried to establish a daily connection to Piraeus. If so, it is quite likely that if the Santorini idea does not prove financially satisfactory then they will rethink. Should the service continue, a one-way fare costs 2300 drs, a 'cruise excursion' 6150 drs and the journey time is 2½ hrs. The catamaran departs from the New Harbour (*Tmr* 36A5) at 0745 hrs, returning from Santorini at 1800 hrs. The service probably only runs on a daily basis at the height of the season, out of which months it might run only two or three times a week. One-way tickets are only available when they are not fully booked on the excursions, which is a lot of the time!

Creta Travel Bureau Situated to the east of Rethymnon, beyond Plateia Agnostou Stratiou, on the Esplanade road, halfway between the Square and the *Xenia Hotel*. They offer a comprehensive and enterprising list of excursions throughout Crete.

ROUTE FIVE

To Chania via Petras, Georgioupolis, Vamos, Kalyves & Souda

(72 km) To understand the benefit that the New Highway has been to the island transport it is only necessary to compare the new and old route on this journey. The Old Road winds its way inland via **Atsipopoulo** and Georgioupolis, where the roads cross. There is little point in using the Old Road unless especially wishing to make a particular trip on this very pleasant but winding road and/or to see Episkopi, which is a large, pretty rural village. None the less the excursion is described in CHAPTER 14, ROUTE TWELVE.

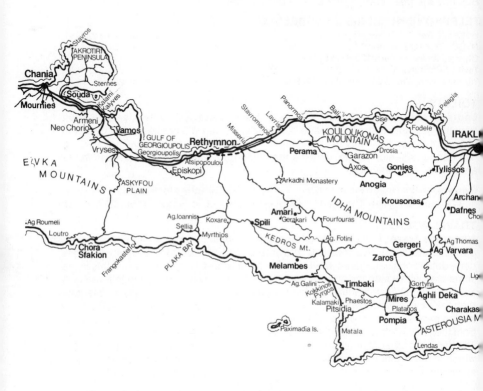

Illustration 14   Crete centred on Rethymnon

The Highway speeds past the **Gerani** turning to the left, opposite which, is a nice bay and chapel set at sea-level. From here on, the splendidly rugged coastline with good beach is the subject of extensive civil engineering works. A newly scraped, unsurfaced, coast-hugging track runs parallel to the Highway seeming to serve little purpose. The occasional connecting tracks are signposted 'Beach Exit'. The actual entrance eventually crops up at the small hamlet of:

PETRAS (literally 'stones', about 12 km from Rethymnon) Set down to one side, on a headland complete with a rocky beach, a number of dwellings including a taverna and a cultivated, bamboo-enclosed field edged by ground vines,.

.The Taverna's proprietor is Yiannis, who is aided by his wife Agapi, and they serve interesting but not inexpensive meals. Roast rabbit, Greek salad, chips, a beer and a bottle of wine costs some 1300 drs. Yiannis' wife has a friend Tasse (short for Anastasea) who occasionally helps out in the taverna. She is a rather interesting young woman who lived in Australia with her Greek husband for 15 years and not only speaks 'perfect Australian', but is also a very liberated lady. I am sure her more conservative, Cretan neighbours in Episkopi find her more radiacal theories rather unsettling.

The Gulf of Georgioupolis is edged by a long, empty beach which goes on for several miles and on the shores of which white breakers leisurely roll and crash. The only disturbance to the untouched scenery is the installation of a big drainage system. There is a beach taverna at the far, west end and the Highway here is oleander lined. At the end of the gulf is:

GEORGIOUPOLIS (32 km from Rethymnon). Tel. prefix 0825. Once one of the finds of Crete but now very popular at the height of season, so much so that accommodation can be a problem. The approach roads are lined with sizeable eucalyptus trees as is the very large Main Square. From the Square a lane runs down to the side of the River Almyros, which flows into the sea (that is the river, not the lane, runs into the sea...) Caiques, benzinas and the occasional yacht line both banks of the river.

The concrete-banked, nearside of the river is flanked by a wide, open, flat, sheep-cropped area, part of which is used by the village lads as a football ground. The far bank is grassed with a path that leads up to a taverna near the lovely river mouth. The near or village side of the river is bordered by a narrow rocky causeway, which sallies forth into the sea and at the extremity of which is a solitary chapel built on a rocky plinth. As one correspondent pointed out, where else on the islands, if not in Greece, would be found in the height of Summer, not one but three full flowing rivers – and icy cold water at that?

Around to the right is the delightfully sandy village beach. Sensibly the locals have set down vented 40 gallon drums to be used as incinerators for visitors' rubbish. The result is a very clean appearance to the village and its environs.

Around the tree, flower and rose-planted Main Square, and on the road to the quay, are a few tavernas, food shops, stores, hotels, pensions and **Rooms**. The quay lane has a cavernous taverna with a souvlaki and chips snackbar stuck in a corner of the patio.

Accommodation includes the *Hotels Amfimalla* (Tel. 22470) and (opposite) the ΠΗΝΕΛΟΠΗ (*Penelope*) (Tel. 22477), both Class E with doubles at about 1100 drs. The *Gorgona Hotel* (Class C, tel. 22378) is beautifully sited at the far end of the beach, with en suite rooms costing 1750 drs. (1st June and 31st Oct). Unfortunately this hotel is now block booked by a British tour company, leaving only the balconyless ground floor available for 'independents'.

Towards the end of the Second World War Georgioupolis was the eastern extent of the beleagured German garrison, which had retreated into an enclave based on Chania. The old roadway out towards Rethymnon marked the boundary and was gated and barricaded. As the inevitability of their eventual defeat sank in, the Germans held out, refusing to surrender to the Cretan guerrilla bands. They preferred to give themselves up to the British, fearing the probable settlement of old scores that the Cretans would indulge in if they could get their hands on their erstwhile conquerors. In an attempt to smooth the path of events to come, the Germans, prior to surrendering, were persuaded to exchange prisoners at this gate.

On a more mundane note, beside the Rthymnon road out of Georgioupolis is the small but very neat looking (possibly package booked) E Class *Hotel Nickolas* (Tel. 22482). En suite rooms with singles cost 1100 drs and doubles 1500 drs.

The Old Road out to Chania crosses the Highway and leads to **Vryses**, which is a most attractive tree lined, working village. It is here that the Chora Sfakion bus for Chania draws up and must be disembarked from by passengers wishing to proceed to Rethymnon and/or Iraklion.

It is probably preferable to take the resurfaced country road to:

VAMOS (46 km from Rethymnon) The atmosphere engendered on the Vamos headland is unique and decidedly very pleasant but..., the roads hereabouts are not only rough, but also badly potholed.

Vamos village is very Greek, not at all touristy. There is a Post Office, the usual tavernas and lovely views from Vamos to:

KALYVES (60 km from Rethymnon) This is a well-cultivated area with some new apartments. Petrol is available in Kalyves and the shops, including a butcher, baker and supermarket, are open on Sunday. The charm of the village is increased by the small river and old buildings.

There is a dimunitive, sandy bay at the east end of the town, alongside the fishing quay. The rest of the foreshore is very rocky and an unmade dirt track runs parallel to the High Street.

There are a few, if any, tourists, and only the *Hotel Koralli* (Class E, tel. 31356) to accommodate them. The small, neat hotel, peacefully set in a screen of bamboo and olive groves, is built on the backshore of the lovely, sandy bay and green peninsula beyond Kalyves. A double room with bathroom for the period from 1st July to 30th September costs 2500 drs.

A kilometre prior to the village of Kalami is a pleasant taverna on the edge of a sandy beach serving basic fare and there are beach showers. **Kalami**, site of the old Turkish fort of Izzedine, is only a few metres long and from here on the road, set halfway up the hillside, skirts the edge of the very lovely, large and azure Souda Bay. From the road much of the view is obscured by the trees lining the road's edge. It is a pity that much of the bay is taken up by the Greek and NATO Navy forces, which organisations restrict access. At the far side of the bay, on the water's edge of the Akrotiri peninsula, is the very neatly laid-out British and Commonwealth cemetery. (*See* EXCURSIONS TO CHANIA CITY SURROUNDS, CHAPTER 14).

SOUDA (some 64 km from Rethymnon, 9 km from Chania) Tel. prefix 0821. Apart from the Naval base, the Chania ferryboats use this port as the terminal. In common with many seagoing ports throughout the world, Souda has its attractions and detractions, in this case not a lot of attractions!

Most visitors sally forth to more attractive pastures as soon as possible. A bus departs every 15 minutes during the day and there is a taxi rank on the square, at the junction of the main road and the ferryboat quay road. If stuck in Souda, there are some **Rooms** and two grotty hotels, the:

Knossos (Class D) 31 Plateia Pringhipos Georgiou   Tel. 89282
Directions: On the Main Square.
Doubles from 1000 drs with shared bathroom,

and the:
Parthenon (Class D) Plateia Pringihipos Georgiou/29 El Venizelou   Tel. 89245
Directions: As for the Knossos

Souda has a bank, a Post Office, tavernas, bars, a laundry, baker, grocery shops and a petrol station.

After 8 km the outskirts of Chania are reached (*See* CHAPTER 14)

ROUTE SIX
To Plakias & Ag. Galini via Spili (62 km) The winding road from the City
gives a fine view of Rethymnon (if one's attention can be diverted long enough to glance backwards). The journey passes through a very Cretan landscape, being dry, rocky, brown and grey, up and down, with sheep and chapels everywhere.

To Plakias
At 21 km a turning off to the right leads up to **Ag. Ioannis** (29 km from Rethymnon). The now wide, newly surfaced road winds breathtakingly, via hairpin bends, down the Kotsifou Gorge, complete with sea views, towards Sellia. The twisting road to Plakias turns off before Sellia is reached, towards the village of:

MYRTHIOS (36 km from Rethymnon) A large village with a Post Office, colourful *Youth Hostel* (Tel. 31202) above *Georgious*, and the usual 'services' i.e. tavernas.
  The road corkscrews another 4 km down through olive groves, **Rooms** and camping to:

PLAKIAS (40 km from Rethymnon) Tel. prefix 0832. At the entrance to the village there is a sign that decrees *No Wild Camping Is Allowed*, which dictat is extensively ignored! This rather disjointed community lies to the right whilst the seashore spreads out along the very long frontage edging the large Plaka Bay. At the far, west end of the village are remains (nearly archaeological) of fishing activity as well as tavernas, the tables of which crowd out on to the tree lined, large pebbled, backshore. There is a baker. Plakias' hotels include the reasonably priced:

Livykon (Class C)   Tel. 31216
Directions: The western end of the village.
  All rooms have en suite bathrooms with singles costing 930 drs and doubles 1400 drs.

and the much costlier:

Alianthos (Class C) Plateia Ag Nicolaou   Tel. 31227
Rooms are en suite with a single room charged at 1900 drs and a double room 2200 drs rising to 2100 drs and 2600 (1st June - 30th Sept).

  At the more reasonable end of the scale is a *Youth Hostel* – private and youthful (!) – on the right-hand side of the road into Plakias, charging 300 drs a night per head. The village is full of **Rooms** with a going rate of 1100 drs for a double. Keen villagers 'arrest' arrivals as they decant from their transport. There is, I'm afraid, also a *Pub-Time Out* and *Dancing Pub Sunshine*!

The best sand is at the far eastern end of the bay, reached along a track running parallel to the shore. The track is edged by small, spindly trees and scrub amongst which, despite the signs forbidding the same, are tents and motor caravans. It is a pity that the rubbish bins, so thoughtfully installed, are not emptied (so what's new) which helps contribute to the rather messy, dirty appearance. On the other hand the swimming here is really excellent.

At the far end of the bay is:
Beach Bar/Rest
A bar/restaurant block, the expensive rooms of which cost 1620 drs with en suite bathrooms.

A further 3 km to the east is another 'camping' beach favoured by Germans, with shower heads on the backshore.

To Ag Galini

Back on the Rethymnon to Ag. Galini thoroughfare a branch road off to the right, 1 km on from the Plakias turning, heads through **Koxare** and the impressive Kourtaliotiko Gorge to Preveli Monastery. It is necessary to turn left in **Asomati**, as the other road forges on to Plakias, and left again at the next turning. The impressively sited monastery, overlooking the sea, achieved fame as a clearing house for British and Commonwealth troops trapped on the island after the Battle of Crete.

Once again on the Rethymnon to Ag. Galini route the road passes through straggling **Mixorrouma**, where there is petrol. The setting is very impressive and the road, lined by oleanders with lovely flowers all around, has now been totally rebuilt all the way to:

SPILI (30 km from Rethymnon) This is a lovely, even beautiful, clean, bustling, 'alpine' village almost smothered in flowers and set in a green, fertile, cultivated plain snuggling at the foot of the mountain. It is a base for mountain walkers and organised ramblers. There is a hotel, restaurants, shops, two banks, a Post Office, OTE and four petrol stations. The bus station is north of the town's big statue, to the west, and a taxi rank is to the east of the road through the village. Incidentally taxi drivers often 'siesta' for long periods of the day, thus being unavailable for hire. Spili sports a car rental firm, an ANEK ticket office, a bakery and many **Rooms**. The tree shaded settlement, as if to emphasise its mountain-stream feel, possesses an attractive row of lion's-head fountains endlessly spewing forth cold springwater into a long, rectangular, stone trough, all set in an arboured square. It may well be that it will prove as much a wrench for readers to leave Spili as it was for the authors.

The road on from Spili to the mountainside village of **Akoumia** is still (in 1986) badly potholed. The next section on to **Nea Krya Vrisi** and the **Melambes** turn off, set in very dramatic scenery, is newly surfaced. In fact all the way from Nea Krya Vrisi to Ag. Galini is in very good condition except for.... There would be a but, wouldn't there! Travellers should note that, as if to keep drivers on their toes, there is a nasty, unsigned, unheralded 1% of the road which has been inexplicably allowed to deteriorate – no disappear.

The final approach to Ag. Galini spirals down to the quayside (*See* CHAPTER 16).

ROUTE SEVEN
To Ag. Galini via Amari (about 69 km) This is an alternative to the Spili route skirting the other side of the Kedros mountain. The thoroughfare passes through groves of large olive trees, climbing out of Rethymnon on to **Prasses** village on the right, with **Rooms** and a big quarry (there is no connection!). The road tops a rise revealing a very green, fertile valley on which herds of sheep graze. A deep gorge borders the road, fortunately edged with an old stone wall and, unusually,

there are a number of visible water points. This winding route does not endure much traffic, but what there is appears to thunder down the middle or wrong side of the road. The continually climbing road is set for something 'big' if the hug piles of gravel and numerous road construction plants represent clues! The surface is of 'good character' as the road approaches mountainside straddling **Apostoli**, an attractive tree lined village, with a deteriorating road surface, followed by a road junction at muddy **Ag. Fotini**, where petrol is available and which serves as a bus change-over point.

The left-hand fork leads to **Fourfouras** and the right to **Gerakari**. The Fourfouras turning crosses a wide plain to the south, and on a lovely country stretch, leaves the Asomati religious school on the left. The route passes through pretty **Vizari** and **Fourfouras**, a not so pretty village, but where petrol is available.

The road surface in the region of **Kouroutes** is very poor and many of the old houses in this valley, from a distance, resemble beehives. The next village of **Nithavris** is narrow and scrappy but possesses a brand new petrol station. The very nice lady who runs it is most helpful and might well offer lone travellers a coffee and help in securing accommodation by telephoning ahead. How's that for service? The route passes on through **Apodoulou**, after which the right-hand (unsignposted) turning must be taken at the road junction for Ag. Galini *(See* CHAPTER 16). The islets of **Paximadia** can be seen from hereabouts prettily set in the 'oh so blue' shimmering Mediterranean.

The olive groves in this area are neatly laid out and the moth-eaten road surface is imprinted with white lines! Off to the left, a track leads down to *Camping Ag. Galini. (See* **The Accommodation, Ag. Galini,** CHAPTER 16).

ROUTE EIGHT
To Iraklion via the Old Road (about 80 km) The coast road (or Highway) can be used as far as the seaside settlement of **Stavromenos** where the Perama turning crosses the Highway. The old, narrow road winds through olive groves and the villages of **Nea Magnisia**, **Viranepiskopi** and **Alexandrou** lying in the low, scrubby foothills strong with the smell of wild thyme, but sporadically littered with plastic. The giant cacti on the left of the road are eye-catching. Alexandrou has a petrol station as has the small working town of:

PERAMA (22 km from Rethymnon) Tel. prefix 0831. Complete with a 'proper' supermarket and market square but no concessions to tourists.

Perama can be used as the jumping off point for a trip to **Melidoni Cave**, the route casting off to the left to **Melidoni Village**, left again for 3 km and then a short walk to the cave's entrance. It has mythological connections, but achieved comparatively recent historical fame, or more correctly infamy, when, in 1824, a marauding band of Turks fired the entrance, killing a couple of hundred villagers who had taken refuge inside. The Turks seemed to have a predilection for this sort of 'unchappish' behaviour.

From Perama the road runs down a small gorge, lined with white rhododendrons, and through **Ag. Silas**. Here the road narrows down, with a wall to one side, and proceeds to **Dafnedes** whose taverna, lemon grove and charcoal burner inhabited green valley is towered over by Kouloukonas Mountain to the left.

Mourtzana is a pretty tree lined village from whence the road bridges a river-bed amongst the vines and winds round the bottom of the mountain to the very attractive village of **Drosia**. From the intensely cultivated, open countryside, heavy with grape vines growing in the red earth, the valley road rises dramatically via a narrow, winding route to a mountain ridge at **Marathos**. This small village is set in a boulder-strewn plateau, at the edge of which, over the next ridge, is a splendid view out over the sea and Iraklion (*See* CHAPTER 12). From here the road tumbles and winds its way down to the outskirts of Iraklion City. Halfway down, a turning off to the right leads, after 4 km, to the village of **Tylissos**, where there are fairly extensive remains of a Minoan villa.

ROUTE NINE

To Arkadhi Monastery (About 24 km) The old coast road must be taken, proceeding eastwards out of Rethymnon. The prettier route involves using the direct and winding lane to **Pigi** village but the signpost for Pigi faces east, so is rather difficult to see coming from the Rethymnon direction. Note that the first available road leads via the villages of **Adele** but does not pass through as attractive countryside. The narrow streets of Pigi are set between high walls and whitewashed houses.

The road on this route has been under reconstruction for the past four years and the section under assault, in 1986, was that between the villages of Pigi and Loutra. The constructions workers have a fairly casual attitude towards dynamiting the mountain rock. None of the red tape we would experience in England, oh no. But the chaps do try and save the travelling public from injury, even if it is by means of last minute, or even last seconds, warnings!

At the very next small settlement of **Loutra**, petrol is available as is accommodation at *The Panorama*. The road to Arkadhi climbs up rolling hillsides covered with olive trees and passes through or by a number of villages, including **Kyrianna**, (large tree lined, with a big square) and **Amnatos**, and across a deep ravine edging the roadside for this stretch. Years of massive reconstruction have now resulted in an up to six car width road of motorway proportions and super flat tarmacadam. The old road used to be so dangerous it induced caution – this new highway is so fast that it encourages terminally dangerous speed.

Close by the Monastery the road leads over a very narrow bridge built by the monks as long ago as 1685 and the final approach is on cobbled surfaces.

Of all Cretan historical and religious monuments, if only one could be visited then it should be:

Arkadhi Monastery
To read the account of this highly revered site is to understand Cretan history and attitudes, more especially the Greek disposition towards the Turkish nation. Apart from the symbolic importance, the buildings are extremely attractive and still house a working religious community, which is an added bonus. Anne adds that another perk is the cheap, powerful raki on offer. She reckons that at 200 drs for a bottle of pure alcohol it must be good value!

The cloistered Monastery, to which entrance is free, is set out in the form of a rectangle which encloses a very pretty church. The site may well date back to the 5th century AD but most of the existing buildings were built in the 16th and 17th centuries.

As with many of the religious establishments of Crete, Arkadhi has, over the millenium, been the centre of resistance for the oppressed natives, which tradition included guerrilla fighters' actions against the German occupation trops during the Second World War.

The fame of the Monastery is soundly and dramatically based on the events of 1866 when Cretan patriots and villagers were beseiged by an overwhelming force of Turks. The story goes that after a number of days' heroic resistance, rather than be taken alive by the marauding, bloodthirsty assailants, the Abbot gave instructions for the powder magazine to be blown up, resulting in the death of up to 1000 Cretans and some 2000 Turks. It would be inappropriate, even blasphemous, to suggest that it was a fluke Turkish canon shot that hit the magazine resulting in the big bang, wouldn't it?

A small museum (entrance 100 drs) displays various artifacts and the story of the Monastery is amply and colourfully set out in an English language guide book. There is a cafe and toilets close by but bring your own paper!

Arkadhi Monastery

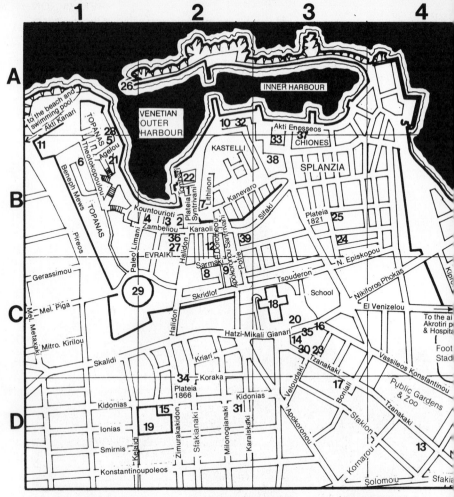

Tmr

1 Hotel Plaza B2
2 Hotel Piraeus B2
3 Hotel Manos B2
4 Pension Mouragio
  & Hotel Lucia B2
5 Pension Meltemi A/B1
6 Pension El Greco B1
7 Domenico Travel B2
8 Orthodox Cathedral C2
9 Hotel Fidias B/C2
10 Hotel Ariadne A2
11 Hotel Xenia A/B1
12 Taverna B2
13 Airline office D4

14 National Bank C3
15 Change office D2
16 Bank of Greece C3
17 Sunny Tours C/D3
18 Market C3
19 Main Bus station D1/2
20 Souda Bus stop C3
21 Atlantis Pension
   & disco B1
22 N.T.O.G. B2
23 O.T.E. C3
24 Ag Anargyri Church B3
25 St. Nicholas Church B3
26 Lighthouse A1/2
27 Archaeological
   Museum B/C2

28 Naval Museum A/B
29 Shiavo Bastion C1/
30 Post Office C3
31 Tourist police D2
32 Port & Town police
33 Customs A/B3
34 Plateia 1866 C/D2
35 ANEK Ferry-boat
   office C3
36 Minoan Ferry-boat
   office B2
37 Venetian Arsenals A
38 St. Marks Arcade B
39 Cheese pie shop B

CHANIA

Illustration 15

Tmr = Town map refere
Fsw = Facing seawards
Sbo = Sea behind one

14 CHANIA (Hania, Xania, Khania) ★★★★
Second city, port & airport

FIRST IMPRESSIONS
Venetian quarter and harbour; old world enterprise; sophisticated, cosmopolitan activity; elegance; lovely, friendly people.

VITAL STATISTICS
Tel. prefix 0821. Population about 55,000.

HISTORY
Chania stands on the site of ancient Kydonia. Neolithic and Minoan remains have been found in the Kastelli Quarter of the city. Chania remained important in the post-Minoan period, even up to the Arabian seizure in AD824. The Venetians, after their initial purchase of the island circa 1204, named the city *La Canea* but lost it to the Genoese for a few years between 1267 and 1290. The Venetians then retook it, not to let go until 1645, when the Turks overwhelmed the whole island. The Venetians built many fine buildings and had to fortify the city after pirate raids in the 1530s, but the walls were not to prove as impregnable as those of Iraklion. The Turks converted some of the Venetian buildings as was their habit and made Kastelli (as they named Chania) the island's capital in the 19th century. The Turks were expelled in 1898 and Prince George became the High Commissioner responsible to The Great Powers (Britain, France and Russia).

GENERAL
As Iraklion can disappoint, from the first acquaintance Chania will surely enchant and continue to do so with every day that passes. It is not that Chania has anything that Iraklion does not. Perhaps it is the spacing and harmonisation of the elements. On the other hand the commercial ferry facility is inconveniently situated 6½ km to the east, at Port Souda, and the airport, used only for internal Greek flights, is at Sternes some 18 km to the east, on the Akrotiri peninsula. Admittedly the harbour is magnificent, as are the Castle walls; the Venetian Arsenals are perhaps more noteworthy as they are in a comparatively unrestored state; the harbour quayside activity is fascinating; the Topanas, Kastelli and Chiones Old Quarters are aesthetically pleasing and the Market is incomparable. Surely these factors have all contributed to the indefinable difference, or have they?

Whatever the reason or reasons may be, Chania is a city that richly rewards exploration. The Quarters encompassed by the old walls are particularly interesting with their many winding back streets and lanes yielding up fascinating glimpses into the past at each twist and turn. Outside the walls, the streets around Plateia 1866 (*Tmr* 34C/D2) are quaintly commercial, many acts of engineering being carried out on the pavement and in the gutter. In strict contrast, the area to the south-east is rather palatial, with fashionable 19th century houses and apartments of some grandeur. This latter ambience is probably because Prince George (who became the island's High Commissioner in 1898) set up home in this district. Naturally, it became the smart thing to reside here if a person wished to move up the ladder of social success. Eleftherios Venizelos, a Republican Prime Minister and statesman of international repute, after whom seemingly nearly avenue, street and square has been named in Greece, was born on Crete and also took up residence in this area.

The hub of the city is Syntrivani Square (*Tmr* B2), situated at the bottom of Odhos

Halidon up against the Outer Harbour. The quayside Esplanade is an explosion of bars, restaurants, hotels and tavernas. In the evening the wide harbour thoroughfare is awash with the citizens of Chania, Greek armed service personnel and tourists. They perpetuate a constant *ramblas* or *volta*, the cacophony of their voices accompanied by an ill-assorted and discordant musical background. Entertainers freelance along the waterfront and may include an 'American amateur hooker', a French accordionist and a fire eater. Added to all this activity the tavernas employ a *schlepping* technique to influence passers-by, potential customers constantly being regaled to see this kitchen or that display of food on offer. It can prove quite exhausting!

From the south, left-hand corner of Syntrivani Sq a panoramic view encompasses the square, the rather lovely, domed roofs of the old Turkish mosque (which now houses the NTOG office), the lighthouse and the sweep of the harbour quay.

Moving westwards, or to the left, leads round to the turn of the old walls at the harbour entrance, just beyond Odhos Agelou (Angelou), and the Naval Museum (*Tmr* 28A/B1). Parallel to the quayside road, Zambeliou Lane twists its way up to the headland and Theotokopoulou St. On the way along Zambeliou the Venetian Loggia is passed on the left and steps scurry off hither and thither. For a glimpse into the past take a look down Beneph Mews that branch off Theotokopoulou St.

South from Syntrivani Sq and Halidon St rises past the Museum (*Tmr* 27B/C2). This is housed in the once grand Venetian Church of St. Francis, built in the 16th century, and converted into a mosque by the Turks - what was not? A few strides further up the slightly rising street and almost opposite each other are the Catholic Church to the right and the Square and Orthodox Cathedral of the Three Martyrs (*Tmr* 8C2) to the left. The Cathedral was built in the 1860s on the instructions of a thankful Turk whose son had been the subject of a miraculous cure. This was supposedly brought about by the healing powers attributable to an icon belonging to an earlier church that stood on the site. At the top of Halidon St, and across Leoforos Hatzi-Mikali Gianari, is Plateia 1866 (*Tmr* 34C/D2), notable for its splendid underground toilets.

Left along Leoforos Hatzi-Mikali Gianari, (which is fine if you are on foot as this is part of a one-way traffic system going the other way), and the City Market hoves into sight. This is housed in a very large building (*Tmr* 18C3), beyond the traffic lights and on the left, which, under one roof, meets the day-to-day needs of Chania and the surrounding districts. Across the avenue to the right are a number of streets that radiate out and contain the majority of the city's commercial undertakings.

Left again, down the far side of the Market, leads, with a wiggle, past a solitary minaret towards the tree-dominated Plateia 1821. I say 'tree dominated', but that would be to ignore San Rocco Church on the north side of the square and St Nicholas Church (*Tmr* 25B3) on the eastern flank. St Nicholas has experienced, over the years, the usual changes of 'official' God. Originally built as a Dominican place of worship, it was then used by the Turks as a mosque, eventually to become an Orthodox church. This convuluted religious background is evident by the building possessing both a campanile and a minaret.

From St Nicholas Church down to the inner Venetian Harbour leads through a grid layout of side streets towards the Venetian Arsenals (*Tmr* 37A/B3) on the waterfront. The Arsenals were arched buildings for shipbuilding and repairs, elegant Venetian stonework equivalents of wartime Nissen huts - well perhaps not! Turning back towards Plateia Syntrivani from the Arsenals, the quayside streets are paved ways cluttered with the paraphernalia of the fishing-boat industry. Immediately behind them, raised up on the hillside of the Splanzia Old Quarter, are the remains of St Mark's Arcade (*Tmr* 38B3). Behind this, in the region of Kanevaro St, are the areas of Minoan excavations.

The city is well fitted out with litter bins but the locals around the harbour still appear to use the sea for disposal of their rubbish, more is the pity.

ARRIVAL BY AIR
It is improbable that a tourist will arrive by plane at Sternes airport. If so there is an Olympic Airways bus which meets the flights and shuttles passengers back and forth to the Chania Olympic office (*Tmr* 13D4) at a cost of 100 drs one-way.

ARRIVAL BY FERRY
The port of Chania is across the neck of the Akrotiri peninsula at Souda. An excellent bus service makes the connection, departing every 15 minutes from the Bus stop (*Tmr* 20C3), in front of the Market.

THE ACCOMMODATION & EATING OUT
All that could be desired within an olive stone's throw of the Outer and Inner Harbour and its encircling Esplanade road, Akti Kountourioti.

The Accommodation Radiating out from Syntrivani Sq (*Tmr* B2) are the:
Hotel Plaza (*Tmr* 1B2) (Class C) 1 Tombazi   Tel. 22540
Directions: As above.
Not the quietest location in town for, apart from the fact that the area is throbbing with activity, there is a restaurant immediately beneath the hotel. If this were not enough, in the alley way behind the hotel are two of the noisiest, liveliest cocktail bars in town, pulsating with juke-box music and a clientele who seem to be under the impression that their nearest neighbours are some miles away. Single rooms, sharing the bathroom, start off at 800 drs and double rooms 1500 drs rising to 900 drs for the single and 1700 drs for a double (1st April - 31st Oct). Double rooms with en suite bathroom are only 50 drs more a night. But note that the hotel fills up early, even in mid season.

Most of the accommodation that overlooks Akti Kountourioti and the harbour have their entrances in Zambeliou St, one back and parallel to the quay. The comments appertaining to the *Hotel Plaza* must be taken into account for any accommodation situated in this quarter. Admittedly Zambeliou St itself is fairly quiet but, despite being very narrow, motorbikes do occasionally roar down the alley.

Hotel Piraeus (*Tmr* 2B2) (Class E) 14 Zambeliou   Tel. 54154
Directions: In the first block, to the west of Syntrivani Sq.
All rooms share bathrooms with single rooms costing 610 drs and doubles 910 drs. These rates rise to 870 drs and 1450 drs (1st July - 30th Sept). Well it is E Class.

Off Odhos Zambeliou, to the left on Odhos ΚΟΝΔΥΛΑΚΗ, there are **Rooms** at No. 13. Much of area south of Odhos Zambeliou is undergoing extensive rennovation or at least rebuilding of collapsed buildings and many of the old pensions are being modernised.

Hotel Manos *(Tmr 3B2) (Class C) 17 Akti Kountourioti*   *Tel. 29493*
Directions: Further along the Esplanade from the *Hotel Piraeus*. It can prove difficult to raise the management but identification of the premises is made easy by the 'interesting' drinking fountain in the entrance which resembles a small boy spewing water into a toilet. Very salubrious..!
In actual fact this well-regarded accommodation is classified as a pension. A single room sharing the bathroom costs 1200 drs and a double room 1500 drs. An en suite double costs 1700 drs. The rates rise to 1600 drs for a single, 1800 drs for a double sharing the bathroom and 2000 drs en suite (1st July - 31st Dec).

Pension Mouragio (*Tmr* 4B2)
Directions: Next door to the *Hotel Lucia* on Akti Kountourioti, the building has a rather careworn appearance but is good value.

A mid season double room costs 1200 drs. There is a restaurant on the ground floor (*See* **The Eating Out**).

Hotel Lucia (*Tmr* 4B2) (Class C) Akti Kountourioti/Paleo Limani St   Tel. 21821
Directions:Naturally, next door to the *Pension Mouragio!*

Rather more expensive than neighbouring establishments but all rooms have en suite bathrooms. A single room costs a princely 2120 drs and a double room 2650 drs, rising respectively to 2280 drs and 2850 drs (1st July - 30th Sept).

Pension Meltemi (*Tmr* 5A/B1) Odhos Agelou
Directions: On round the Harbour Esplanade all the way to where the rampart walls appear and then left up Agelou Lane. The first building on the right is the Navy Museum (*Tmr* 28A/B1) and the next is the pension.

This is a narrow fronted, tall building with a bar and table outside. Drab double rooms cost 1200 drs in mid season.

Next door is the:-

Pension Theresa (Thereza) 8 Agelou   Tel. 26122
Directions: As above.

The pension, occupying a lovely, seven hundred year-old house, is run by an English girl (would you believe Teresa) and her Greek husband. Anne has asked me to point out he is very, very pleasant and hunky 'to boot'. This insistence on Anne's part is based on the foundless supposition that I am sexist and only mention, in detail, the ladies. In my defence I must point out that when I call or stay at a pension, or taverna, husbands are usually absent at some 'watering hole' or other so I do not always meet them. We first came across Theresa some years ago, writing home to her parents and nostalgically recalling the delights of English roast beef and Yorkshire pudding. She has lived in Chania for six years. The house is simply but tastefully decorated and the winding, somewhat rickety staircase ascends to the various floors. Do not miss the plain, circular murals on the first floor. The rooms have glorious views of the harbour. They are simply furnished but with much care.This is evident in the small inset dressers complete with a few books and brochures, flowers and individual bedside lamps with shades. (I used to dream of bedside lamps with shades in Greece). These rooms are available for 1300 drs with shared bathroom and shower, and there is a self-contained apartment for two costing 1500 drs. A small but excellently positioned roof terrace is available for all, but not everybody should turn up at once. Oh, I nearly forgot, the hooks for hanging clothes are positively workmanlike and will actually do the job without collapsing under the strain. (*See* ISLAND ACCOMMODATION, CHAPTER 4).

Agelou Lane climbs up to Theotokopoulou St and at the junction is:

El Greco Pension (*Tmr* 6B1) (Class B) 47-49 Theotokopoulou St.   Tel. 22411
Directions: As above.

Smart with pine walled reception and clean-cut female receptionist added to which there is a roof garden.These embellishments are reflected in the charges. Single rooms sharing the bathrooms start off at 1550 drs and en suite 1700 drs. Double rooms sharing are charged at 2150 drs and en suite 2300 drs. These rates rise to 1750/2000 drs for a single room and 2350/2600 drs for double rooms (1st June - 31st Oct).

Hotel Argyro (Class B) 13 Theotokopoulou St.   Tel. 55019
Directions: Halfway down on the right-hand side.

There are a few double rooms sharing a bathroom which cost 1300 drs and rise to 1800 drs (1st April - 30th Sept). But the hotel is part package tour booked and the hotel's forte is furnished apartments complete with fully fitted kitchen, shower, bathroom and maid service. They cost between 3600 and 4200 drs, rising to 5000 drs (1st April - 30th Sept). There is a roof garden.

Enquiries about this accommodation, and the *Domenico Pension* on Odhos Zambeliou, should be made to the **Domenico Travel Agency**, (*Tmr* 7B2) – *See* **Travel Agents.**

There are less expensive, very, very pleasant apartments next door (to the *Hotel Argyro*) at No.9 Theotokopoulou St (Tel. 56935). These are run by Kiria Irene, who can be found on the premises, or contacted via the General Store across the street. The rooms are well equipped, very clean and only two years old. The kitchens include a fridge, cooker and plenty of space. The building also has a roof garden. Charges are 1800 drs a night.

Back to the hub of things, as it were, possibly the most prolific area for **Rooms** is in the locality of the Greek Orthodox Cathedral (*Tmr* 8C2). Odhos Halidon has **Rooms** on both sides of the street from Skridlof St down to the harbour.

Behind the Cathedral is:-

Pension Fidias (Phedias) (*Tmr* 9B/C2) (Class E) 6 Apokoronou Santrivani
Tel. 52494/53975

Directions: As above along Odhos ΣΑΡΜΑΚΗ (Sarmaki) and right on to Odhos Apocoronou Santrivani.

Fidias has a very friendly atmosphere, and the walls are covered with posters of Greece and tourist information. Prices are 1000 drs for a double room sharing the clean bathroom, but singles are also let at the rate of 500 drs per bed in shared rooms. The main drawback is the awful clamour due to the pension being sited next to the Cathedral Square, used as a racetrack all night long by the local youth and their horrificaly noisy motorbikes. Added to this the Cathedral bells sound like out of tune fire engines clanging loud and long on Sundays and, for that matter, on all or any other relevant religious occasion, often at irreligiously early hours! The sound of loud speaker aided chanting and prayer drifts pleasantly down the surrounding streets on Sundays which is certainly more pleasing and civilised than the bells.

There are a number of other pensions and **Rooms** on the same street. In the three side lanes between the streets of Sarmaki and Karaoli (*Tmr* B/C2) are, respectively, the:-

Pension Lito Odhos Dorotheou   Tel. 53150
Directions: As above.

Nikos is the proud owner of the establishment and as a retired plumber, naturally fitted the bathrooms himself resulting in very hot water all day long! He sits downstairs in an incredibly old, vaulted, cave-like room which occupies all of the ground floor. He bought the place four years ago, "It was all falling down", and to believe him just look at next door... or don't! The rooms, whitewashed and very clean, are quite small but beautifully furnished with a wardrobe, desk, two chairs, bedside table, wall mirror, hooks and suitcase stand, all new and in solid pine. The front bedrooms have balconies with a washing line and peg (sic) – and Anne's room had a rubber plant. Towels are provided. Doubles cost 1000 drs, sharing the clean, aromatic, and very well plumbed bathroom. Showers are listed at 170 drs each extra but Nikos often refuses payment, which at that price he should! Nikos has every right to be proud added to which he is also very friendly, constantly offering coffee, cake, company and a game of backgammon!

Pension Lito must be considered as a contender for the 'Number One' spot in Chania – although the exhaust bellow of motorbikes and scooters still results in some noise down here. A room at the back is the answer to that.
The:-

Pension Afroditi 18 Ag Deka   Tel. 57602
Directions: As above.

All rooms share the bathrooms with a single charged at 600 drs and a double room 1110 drs. These rates rise to 610 drs and 1290 drs in the height of summer (1st July - 30th Sept).

and the:-

Pension Kydonia Odhos ΕΙΣΟΔΙΩΝ
Directions: As above.

Looks wonderful from outside, but is no longer well recommended! The rooms are sparse, bare and purely functional. Better accommodation for two is available in Chania at 1000 drs per night...

Hotel Ariadne (*Tmr* 10A2) Akti Enosseos
Directions: From the Outer Harbour proceed round the quayside to the right (*Fsw*) and the hotel is alongside the Police station.

Splendid position but there was a disco in the basement (closed in 1986) and this harbour situation can get very busy in the summer, at almost any hour. En suite double rooms only, start off at 2000 drs and rise to 2200 drs (1st June - 31st Oct).

The hotels in the area of Plateia 1866 (*Tmr* 34C/D2), which include the *Canea* (Class C, tel. 24673) at 16 Plateia 1866, the *Samaria* (Class B, tel. 291265) on the corner of Kidonias and Zimurakakidon St and the *Omalos* (Class C, tel. 57171) at 71 Kidonias St, are rather expensive. The *Omalos* starts off at 2720 drs for an en suite double room and breakfast. There are **Rooms** opposite the Bus station (*Tmr* 19D1/2) on Kidonias St but do not forget that any accommodation in this area can prove to be very noisy.

In the elbow of the north part of the old wall, at the end of Theotokopoulou St are the:-
Xenia (*Tmr* 11A/B1) (Class B) Theotokopoulou St   Tel. 24561
Directions: As above.

Superb position, but it would have to be as a double room with en suite bathroom costs 2750 drs, breakfast 225 drs and dinner 780 drs. It is possible to watch TV and have a drink in comfort but why leave the U.K.?.

Pension Europa
Directions: Signposted up to the left from Akti Kanari, just beyond the city's swimming pool.

A sign on the roof advertises *Rooms and Luxury Apartments*.

Despite the inconvenience, well recommended is the:-

Youth Hostel 33 Drakonianou St   Tel. 53565
Directions: It is necessary to catch a bus from the stop opposite the Market (*Tmr* 20C3), or just round the corner on Odhos Apokoronou, for about a 5 minute bus ride in a southerly direction. Get off at Dexameni Sq or the 5th stop.

Rather off the beaten track but certainly quiet. A bed costs 300 drs, there is hot water and membership cards are not usually demanded.

Camping Hania   Tel.51090
Directions: Take the Main Road out of Chania westwards along the coast. Buses depart from the Bus terminal (*Tmr* 19D1/2). After about 3 kilometres a sign to the right leads to a complex of newly laid roads complete with street lighting but no buildings (Spanish style?) This area sports a number of not so clean beaches divided by small tree clad hillocks which show evidence of illegal camping.

The neat, newly 'renovated' site is really very, very nice. The pleasant owners, who also run the taverna, a bar and supermarket, are hard working and rightly proud of the place. Tents are pitched between rows of shady olives and bougainvillea. Other facilities include a washroom and a clothes washing room. It's very close to the beach, but even in high season doesn't entirely fill up. Unlike many bossy Greek campsite owners, the only rules they make are "quiet and respect of others". Prices work out at 220 drs per person and 150 drs per tent.

The Eating Out There are a number of souvlaki snackbars. These include one at the Syntrivani Sq end of Halidon St, with a good offering for 80 drs and a small bottle of beer from 50 drs, and another stall near the junction of Halidon St with Leoforos Hatzi-Mikali Gianari. Both are on the left side of the street *(Fsw)*.

Cheese Pie Shop *(Tmr* 39B2/3) Odhos Ποτιε.
Directions: At the bottom of the lane *(Fsw)* on the right.
Anne couldn't find it but Iain Morris (who is acknowledged) could, but it was always sold out. Excellent value, scrumptious shop-made pie sold by weight. Open Sunday mornings but customers have to be quick as the locals have 'heard about it' and a queue usually forms.
N.B. Please note Anne maintains this establishment is in the next street along, Odhos Apokoronou Santrivani!

An abundance of restaurants with outside tables and chairs almost encircle the Outer Harbour and there are a few, more local tavernas on the edge of the Inner Harbour. These include two local restaurants about 20m up the wide streets, just beyond the Arsenal *(Tmr* 37A/B3), and another, good fish taverna, at the far east end of the Inner Harbour. But arrive early as they fill up with knowedgeable Greeks.
Incongruously set in the row of traditionally Greek eating places, to the left of Syntrivani Sq *(Fsw)*, is a 'Kentucky Fried Chicken'. Most of the establishments have an illuminated glass cabinet displaying their various offerings. Compare prices because, despite the fact that it would make sense for the closely packed rivals to be competitive with each other, prices can vary by several hundred drachmae for the same dish. In amongst this 'wash of offerings' the following proffer good value:-

Restaurant Mouragio Akti Kountourioti
Directions: As above.
Cane lampshades and good, hot food. Moussaka, stuffed tomatoes, fried potatoes, beans, Greek salad, bread, a beer and retsina cost about 1200 drs for two.

and further along the Esplanade, the *Restaurant Zepos*.

If the usual run of the mill eventually palls try the:-

Coucher Du Soleil
Directions: Beyond the NTOG office *(Tmr* 22B2).
Admittedly a rather posy if apt name as the sunset views are lovely but the prices are reasonable and the situation is quiet and calm. The pleasant owner migrates from Athens for the summer months. A meal for two of stuffed tomatoes, salad, beer, bread and an indulgence of fabulous strawberries and cream (250 drs per head), costs some 1134 drs.

Taverna ΑΠΟΒΑΘΡΑ *(Tmr* 12B2) ΕΙΣΟΔΙΩΝ St
Directions: Opposite the *Kydonia Pension* off Karaoli St or Odhos Samaki.
Super find with one of the widest choice of offerings to be found on Crete at reasonable prices although a correspondent advises that the range is now perhaps not so varied. The menu can include snails, lamb stew (not fricasse), octopus, rabbit with onions, pork with celery, squids, sausages (Mykonos or Chania), meat balls, taramasalata, tzatziki, spinach (cold), salads, saute potatoes, baked (Cretan) beans and (good) wine from the barrel. A specimen bill for two of several small jugs of retsina, lamb, pork, spinach, saute potatoes and bread works out at about 1000 drs. A quiet young man with good English and his redheaded wife (there are quite a number of redheads on Crete) run the taverna and their two children help, with dignity. A lot of locals eat here, although they are now outnumbered by tourists. As

the taverna is open for much of the year, the owners sometimes holiday at the height of the season, which is most unreasonable of them.

An expensive but very good English breakfast is served at:-

The Cafe Remetzio
Directions: On Syntrivani Sq, beneath the *Hotel Plaza* (*Tmr* 1B2)
A pint of fresh orange juice, coffee, two eggs, some bacon, a slice of tomato, large toasted bun, butter, jam and cake for two costs about 840 drs.

The Cafe Bonatsa
Directions: Immediately to the left (*Fsw*) on entering Syntrivani Sq.
A splendid cafe-bar to while away an idle morning writing cards or musing about life. The service is slow but very reasonably priced, when the order eventually arrives. A large 'Nes meh ghala' costs 67 drs and the coffee is hot. Clients are not hustled and there is a pleasant swell of background music.

One slight but startling intrusion into any holiday reverie can be the habit of the Greek Air Force to unexpectedly overfly Chania.

THE A TO Z OF USEFUL INFORMATION
AIRLINE OFFICE & TERMINUS (*Tmr* 13D4) Some official maps still detail the office at the junction of Tzanakaki and Veloudaki Sts, but it is much further up Odhos Tzanakaki, opposite the far end of the Public Gardens.

Aircraft timetable
Chania to Athens
Three flights daily   0720, 1955, 2155 hrs.
From 15th June additionally
Daily except Thursday   1155 hrs.
Return
Daily   0555, 1810, 2010 hrs.
From 15th July additionally
Daily except Thursday   1030 hrs.
One-way fare 3030 drs, duration 45 mins.

BANKS The major bank for changing travellers and personal cheques is the **National Bank** (*Tmr* 14C3), opposite the Market. The **Credit Bank** (on the east side of Syntrivani Sq and Kanevaro St) and the **Change Office** (*Tmr* 15D2), alongside the *Omalos Hotel*, exchange travellers cheques. Foreign paper money, acquired whilst on the way to Greece, say in Yugoslavia or Italy, can only be changed at the **Bank of Greece** (*Tmr* 16C3).

BEACHES There is a small beach in downtown, unfashionable east Chania on the coast road out to the Akrotiri peninsula, but it is set amongst a backcloth of low-rise factories.
The main beach is a few kilometres to the west round the fortress wall (passing on the tree lined route, the city's swimming pool, which is often drained). Prior to the swimming pool, a breach in the fortifications allows a road to climb up into the Old Quarter just before the *Xenia Hotel* (*Tmr* 11A/B1). Sharply outlined against the background is an outstandingly attractive, old three-storey building, the upper two storeys of which are overhanging, clapper board. Immediately beyond the swimming pool is a small, squalid beach, with a stony seabed covered in various seaweeds. Pass by and proceed beyond the Bank Sports Club, an olive factory and a small fishing boat harbour on to a road running the length of a very sandy beach. There are two tavernas across from the backshore and **Rooms** at the far end of the promenade road. The inshore is protected from the worst seas by an incomplete reef and joy, oh joy, there is a beach shower. At the far, west end of the flat bay, alongside a

beach bar, is a large pile of rusting missiles gravely marked *Greek Air Force 1969*. Oh yes!

Further on are two more half-mile stretches of beach, each separated from the other by a small headland, as discussed under *Camping Hania*. (*See* **The Accommodation**).

BICYCLE, SCOOTER & CAR HIRE Scooter and car hire outfits, including **Zeus**, mingle with the cafe-bars to the right, on entering Syntrivani Sq. Should these prove a bit expensive, wander along Odhos Karaoli, off Odhos Halidon. This becomes Sifaki St where there are some 'Rent-A-Scooter' outfits. A number of car hire firms are located in Tzanakaki St, including **Sunny Tours** (*Tmr* 17C/D3) at No.38 (*See* **Travel Agents**).

BOOKSELLERS An excellent bookshop is on the left or west of Syntrivani Sq, but what is not? There is another vendor operating out of a 'periptero-like' kiosk in the central part of the Market (*Tmr* 18C3).

BREAD SHOPS One in Zambeliou St, behind the *Hotel Manos* (*Tmr* 3B2) and another on Odhos Theotokopoulou, south of the *El Greco Hotel* (*Tmr* 6B1). Alongside this latter baker is a small grocer and next door a fruit and vegetable shop, both clean and offering good value. Bread is also available on various stalls in the Market (*Tmr* 18C3).

BUSES The main Bus terminal is on Kidonias St (*Tmr* 19D1/2), alongside the *Hotel Samaria*, and is an all-action, bustling, chaos. There are a number of small shops selling most requirements, including a garage tool accessory shop. Perhaps this is for the bus drivers?

Other local buses depart from Plateia 1866, (*Tmr* 34C/D2) and a stop (*Tmr* 20C3) adjacent to the Market. There is another on Nikiforos Phokas, beyond the School where Leoforos Hatzi-Makali Gianari splits into Nikiforos Phokas and El Venizelou.

Some of the desk clerks at the main Bus station speak excellent English and can be very helpful. Note, I say 'can'. It is vital to make enquiries at this main depot about the various departure points and at the same time establish whether tickets must be pre-purchased or if it will be a free-for-all on the bus. It must be understood that buying a ticket from the desk does not do away with the joy of fighting for a place, it simply means there is a better chance of getting on the conveyance.

Bus timetables
Note a certain amount of vigilance is required to ensure at what time and from where a particular bus departs!
Main Bus Depot (*Tmr* 19D1/2)   Tel. 23052
Chania to Rethymnon, Iraklion
Daily   0530, 0645, 0730, 0800*, 0830, 0900, 0930, 1000, 1030, 1100, 1130, 1200, 1200*, 1230,
        1300, 1330, 1400, 1430, 1500, 1530, 1600, 1630, 1700, 1730, 1800, 1830, 1930 hrs.
Return journey
Daily   0530, 0630, 0700*, 0730, 0815, 0900, 0930, 1000, 1000*, 1115, 1145, 1215, 1230*, 1245,
        1315, 1345, 1430, 1515, 1545, 1615, 1630*, 1645, 1715, 1745, 1845, 1930 hrs.
* Officially indicates non-express, Old Road bus route – 5 hrs journey duration.
One-way fare 710 drs; distance 140 km; duration 3 hrs.
Chania to Stalos, Ag. Marina, Maleme, Chandris
Daily   0600, 0715, 0800, 0830, 0900, 0930, 1000, 1030, 1100, 1130, 1200, 1230, 1300, 1330,
        1430, 1530, 1600, 1630, 1700, 1715, 1730, 1800, 1830, 1900, 1930, 2000, 2030, 2130 hrs.
Return journey
Daily   0830, 0900, 0915, 0930, 1000, 1015, 1030, 1100, 1115, 1130, 1200, 1215, (then a gap
        according to the official printed timetable...!) 1630, 1700, 1730, 1800, 1815, 1830, 1900,

1930, 1945, 2030, 2230 hrs.
One-way fare 90 drs

Chania to Kolimbari, Platanios, Kastelli
Daily   0600, 0715, 0830, 1000, 1100, 1200, 1300, 1430, 1530, 1630, 1730, 1830, 2000 hrs.
Return journey
Daily   0500, 0600, 0700, 0730, 0800, 0830, 0930, 1030, 1130, 1230, 1400, 1530, 1615, 1730,
        1900 hrs.
One-way fare 210 drs; distance 42 km; duration 1½ hrs.

Chania to Paleochora
Daily   0900, 1030, 1200, 1430, 1700 hrs.
Return journey
Daily   0700, 1200, 1330, 1530, 1700 hrs.
One-way fare 360 drs; distance 77 km; duration 2 hrs.

Chania to Omalos (for the Samaria Gorge)
Daily   0615, 0830, 0930, 1630 hrs.
Return journey
Daily   0730, 1000, 1100, 1800 hrs.
One-way fare 210 drs; distance 42 km; duration 1½ hrs.

Chania to Souyia
Daily   0900, 1330 hrs.
Return journey
Daily   0700, 1430 hrs.
One-way fare 330 drs; distance 70 km; duration 2½ hrs.

Chania to Platanos
Daily* 1100, 1630 hrs.
Return journey
Daily* 0700 hrs (next day).
* Sunday bus schedules, if any, must be carefully checked.
NB *To be honest folks, I am a little perplexed, no, more perplexed about this schedule.*
One-way fare 305 drs; distance 63 km; duration 2 hrs.

Chania to Chora Sfakion
Daily   0830, 1100, 1400, 1530 hrs.
Return journey
Daily   0700, 1100, 1630, 1830 hrs.
One-way fare 350 drs; distance 72 km; duration 2 hrs.

Chania to Ag. Galini
Daily   0530, 0730, 0900, 1030, 1230, 1530 hrs.
Return journey
Daily   (Yes – well some six a day. Um!)
One-way fare 330 drs.

Chania to Vathi (via Elos).
Daily   1300 hrs.
Sunday/holidays   0930 hrs.
Return journey
Daily   0615 hrs
Sunday/holidays   1400 hrs.
One-way fare 315 drs; distance 63 km; duration 2½ hrs.

Chania to Spilia (Kissamou)
Daily*   0800, 0900, 1030, 1300 hrs.
Sunday/holidays*   0730, 0930, 1100, 1300, 1500 hrs.
Return journey
Daily*   0900, 1100, 1200, 1500, 1730 hrs.
Sunday/holidays*   1400, 1630, 1845 hrs.
* *These times require careful checking at the time of travel.*
One-way fare 135 drs; distance 25km; duration ½ hr.

Chania to Fournes
Daily   0645, 0800, 0900, 1100, 1200, 1330, 1630, 1930 hrs.
Sunday/holidays*   0730, 1700 hrs.

Return journey
Daily   0730, 0830, 0930, 1230, 1430, 1800 hrs.
Sunday/holidays*   0815, 1745 hrs.
* *Double-double check*
One-way fare 110 drs; distance 20 km; duration ½ hr.

Chania to Frangokastello, Skaloti
Daily*   1400 hrs.
Return journey
Daily*   0700 hrs.
* *Sundays/holidays schedules will require further enquiries.*
One-way fare 370 drs; distance 82 km; duration 2½ hrs.

Chania to Kalyves, Vryses
Daily   0845, 1145, 1445, 1935 hrs.
Sunday/holidays*   0800, 1000, 1200, 1300, 1800 hrs.
Return journey
Daily   0700, 1000, 1300, 1700 hrs.
Sunday/holidays*   0700, 1000, 1200, 1630, 1800 hrs.
* *Again please double check.*
One-way fare 165 drs; distance 33 km; duration 1 hr.

Chania to Vamos
Daily   0700, 0845, 1145, 1415, 1930 hrs.
Sunday/holidays*   0800, 1200, 1600, 2000 hrs.
Return journey
Daily   0700, 0900, 1100, 1300, 1500, 1700 hrs.
Sunday/holidays*   0715, 0930, 1330, 1630, 1815 hrs.
* *Sundays/holidays will require enquiries at the time.*
One-way fare 135 drs; distance 26 km; duration ½ hr.

Chania to Almyros, Gavalochori
Daily*   1430 hrs.
Return journey
Daily*   ? (yes, a query).
* *There may not be Sundays/holidays schedules!*
One-way fare 135 drs; distance 27 km; duration ¾ hr.

Chania to Chordaki (Akrotiri Peninsula)
Daily   0630, 1300 hrs.
Sunday/holidays*   0730 hrs.
Return journey
Daily   0700, 1400 hrs.
Sundays/holidays*   1700 hrs.
One-way fare 85 drs; distance 16 km; duration ½ hr.
* *Must be checked out at the time.*

Chania to Chorafakia, Stavros (Akrotiri Peninsula)
Daily*   0700, 1000, 1200, 1800 hrs.
Return journey
Daily*   0730, 1030, 1230, 1830 hrs.
* *Sundays/holidays will require checking with the office.*
One-way fare 86 drs; distance 16 km; duration ½ hr.

Please NOTE that these are high season timetables, outside of which few months, schedules are severely curtailed, even in mid season.

The bus journeys from Chania are the most beautiful, stunning, breathtaking and frightening on Crete. If of a nervous disposition, take some tranquillisers before commencing the journey!

CINEMAS One in the far corner of the Public Gardens, between Vassileos Konstantinou and Tzanakaki St.

COMMERCIAL SHOPPING AREA (*Tmr* 18C3) Under one roof in a unique market building in the form of a cross and reminiscent of, say, Leadenhall market in London and supposedly based on the Marseilles market. The whole interior is jam-packed with stalls selling almost everything and interspaced by the occasional cafe-bar with a few chairs. Simple food is cooked on tin stoves and in smoking charcoal ovens, the smoke piped through the roof or side walls by rickety pipes.

The west wing is occupied predominantly by fish vendors and around the periphery of the building are various wholesalers. The whole arena is swarming with people and in amongst the hubbub, the stall owners shout their wares. The Market is closed on Sundays but the odd 'market barrow' is open in the vicinity for the sale of vegetables and fruit.

Tsouderon St, in the vicinity of the Market, has a preponderance of shoe shops. Skridlof St is an 'Athens Plaka look-alike', overflowing with leather shops down both sides. Also *See* **Bread Shops.**

DISCO BARS One drawback to listing discos is that they tend to be rather 'fragile', transitory businesses. When in operation they seem to me to very rarely need attention drawn to them, but here we go. There is at least one 'circling' the Outer Harbour, that is beneath the *Hotel Ariadne* (*Tmr* 10A2). The two jukebox-throbbing cocktail bars behind the *Hotel Plaza* (*Tmr* 1B2) hardly need any advertisement and there is a jazz bar on the right of Agelou Lane, beyond *Pension Meltemi* (*Tmr* 5A/B1).

ELPA Signposted to the right of Tzanakaki St or to the left of Apokoronou St, leaving Chania in a south-east direction.

FERRY-BOATS The boats dock at Souda port, the main function of which is as a Navy base and NATO operations centre. Despite the beauty of Souda Bay, the port is a dump and it is best to make for Chania as soon as possible.

Ferry-boat timetables
Chania (Souda) to Piraeus (M).
Daily: FB Kydon or Kriti. Departs 1900 hrs.
Tuesday, Thursday and Saturday: FB Ariadne. Departs 1830 hrs.
Note that in the high season the FB Ariadne schedule becomes:
Tuesday, Thursday, Sunday: 1830 hrs.
Saturday: 0800 hrs.
Much the same general comments apply to Chania ferry-boat as detailed under Iraklion.

FERRY-BOAT TICKET OFFICES The ANEK ticket office is on Leoforos Hatzi Mikali Gianari/Sofokli Venizelos Sq (*Tmr* 35C3) (opposite the Market) and Minoan Lines is at No. 8 Halidon St (*Tmr* 36B2), close by Syntrivani Sq.

HORSE-DRAWN CARRIAGES (Monipos). There are a couple ranked alongside the Outer Harbour on the edge of Plateia Syntrivani. The rather decrepit owners are in stark contrast to their horses and colourfully painted carriages. I always worry if the horse is suffering from having to stand hour on hour in the extreme heat of the day. Anne notes that as they wear hats and she did observe an owner wash down and cool his nags legs, I should rest assured as to their welfare. Establish the cost before hiring one of these archaic methods of travel.

LAUNDRY One very large dry cleaner and laundry service at No.40 Sifaki St (*Tmr* B3), and another on Tzanakaki St, opposite the **National Bank** (*Tmr* 14C3).

MEDICAL CARE
Chemists & Pharmacies Numerous, with the majority concentrated in Odhos Tzanakaki with others in the streets of Vassileos Konstantinou and Apokoronou, all of which radiate out from Plateia Sofokli Venizelos (*Tmr* C3).

Hospital: East on El Venizelou, right on Victor Hugo, immediately left on Odhos Dragoumi and the Hospital is on the junction of Dragoumi St with Kapodistriou St. There is a daily outpatients' clinic.

NTOG (*Tmr* 22B2) In my awards table for NTOG offices throughout Greece, let alone Crete, the Chania office must be one of the country's best. The competition is fierce and includes the Corfu Town (Ionian Islands) and excellent Rethymnon offices. It may well be that the attractive ladies of Chania tip the balance and they certainly could not be more helpful. Additionally the information available is first class, including leaflets in respect of bus and ferry timetables, the Samaria Gorge, Cretan festivals, holidays and high days. Added to this the situation of the office is rather pleasant, located as it is in an old, domed mosque alongside and to the right of the Outer Harbour (*Fsw*). It seems a pity that the elegant lines of the building have been rather spoilt by a very large, flat-roofed extension to the side which accommodates an extensive cafe-bar. Another part of the structure contains a display of Cretan artistic works. The NTOG office is open weekdays 0730 - 1800 hrs and weekends between 0800 - 1400 hrs.

OTE (*Tmr* 23C3) From the Market proceed up Tzanakaki St and the OTE is on the left, beyond the Post Office. Open daily 0600 - 2400 hrs.

PETROL STATIONS Plentiful.

PLACES OF INTEREST

Churches
The Church of Ag Anargyri (*Tmr* 24B3). Possesses some venerable icons.
The Church of St Nicholas (*Tmr* 25B3). Situated on the edge of Plateia 1821 and remarkable for its coupling of a minaret and a campanile.
In the area of the Market is an elegant minaret.
Harbour Area Interesting *tout ensemble*. Viewing the Outer Harbour from the area of the NTOG office (*Tmr* 22B2) brings Venice powerfully to mind. On the edge of the harbour wall there is a distinctive Venetian lighthouse (*Tmr* 26A1/2), the subject of extensive rebuilding. Moving eastwards around the harbour waterfront there are yachts, motor boats, commercial fishing boats, of about 50 ft to 60 ft in length, and some Greek Navy vessels. Beyond the Venetian Arsenals (*Tmr* 37A/B3) the craft become much smaller, finally grading down to rowing boats.

Museums
Archaeological Museum (*Tmr* 27B/C2). The interesting exhibits are located in a building that was the old St Francis Church. There is a garden to one side containing a Turkish fountain, a leftover from the Church's days as a mosque. Closed Tuesdays, open daily 0800 - 1700 hrs.

Historical Museum Proceed up Odhos Tzanakaki to the junction with Sfakianaki St, which is named Solomou St to the west. The exhibits are considered to be outstanding, covering the period from the Byzantine Empire up to and including the German occupation of Crete, between 1941 and 1945.

Naval Museum (*Tmr* 28A/B1) Naturally, a maritime exhibition.

Venetian Arsenals & Walls The original Venetian Arsenals despite rapidly crumbling are still inspiring. The remains of the old walls are best viewed from the west end where there are distinctive outlines of the original large moats, which lead down to the reasonably well preserved Shiavo Bastion (*Tmr* 29C1/2).

POLICE
Tourist (*Tmr* 31D2) The office is at No.44 Karaiskaki St, a hop, skip and walk round from the Bus terminal. Helpful but deskbound with a board bearing names and addresses of various accommodation.

Port & Town (*Tmr* 32A/B2) Alongside the *Hotel Ariadne*. (The Customs authorities are tucked away at *Tmr* 33A/B3).

POST OFFICE (*Tmr* 30C3) On Tzanakaki St.
The various vans and lorries have a habit of pulling right up on to the main steps to unload, obscuring the entrance, which can thus be missed. The usual hours are extended by the provision of a stamp machine outside the office. By the way, the listed times in English, French and Greek used to differ slightly, but as only the English details are now decipherable this is no longer a problem.

Tourist requirements, especially banking facilities, are aided by the provision of a 'Portacabin' Post office, a very large kiosk cum-cabin located on the Square in front of the Cathedral (*Tmr* 8C2). Open daily 0800 - 2000 hrs, with Sunday/holiday hours of 0900 - 1800 hrs. The 'cabin' carries out exchange transactions, obviously filling a very necessary requirement as testified to by the long Bank holiday queues!

TAXIS In and around the Market; on Plateia 1866 (*Tmr* 34C/D2) and alongside the Cathedral (*Tmr* 8C2), off Halidon St.

TELEPHONE NUMBERS & ADDRESSES

Hospital. Dragoumi St.	Tel. 27231
NTOG (*Tmr* 22B2). 6 Akti Tombazi	Tel. 26426
Olympic Airways office (*Tmr* 13D4). 88 Tzanakaki St.	Tel. 27701
Shipping Offices:	
ANEK (*Tmr* 35C3) Leoforos Hatzi-Mikali Gianari/Plateia Sofokli Venizelou	Tel. 23636
Minoan (*Tmr* 36B2) 8 Halidon St.	Tel. 24352
Tourist police (*Tmr* 31D2) 44 Karaiskaki St.	Tel. 24477

TOILETS Almost an abundance including a clean, underground one on Plateia 1866 (*Tmr* 34C/D2); an ethnic, underground one on the Market Square (*Tmr* 18C3), alongside Leoforos Hatzi-Mikali Gianari, and a clean one on the far side of the harbour, behind the *Hotel Ariadne* (*Tmr* 10A2).

TRAVEL AGENTS
Domenico Tourist & Travel (*Tmr* 7B2) 10 Kanevaro/Syntrivani Sq.   Tel. 53262
This is an up-market but helpful office, situated just off Plateia Syntrivani on Kanevaro St, and run by a Greek ably assisted by a couple of English people. Probably 'master of all trades', they offer various accommodation possibilities mainly at the upper price end of the market. (You know, 'hot and cold running maids'). Fully equipped double rooms with towels 'et al', all for about 2800 drs, and more. They can arrange baby-sitters and do have less expensive options on their books if clients can tolerate a hard world with fewer comforts! They also exchange money, hire boats and cars and no doubt do all sorts of other things.....
Sunny Tours (*Tmr* 17C/D3) 38 Tzanakaki St.   Tel. 54502
Yannis, the owner, operates one of the most helpful travel agents in Crete, let alone Chania. The office is situated almost opposite the *Hotel Kypros*, his English is very good, and if you want it, he can get it!
Krit Plimakis
Another tour operator located in a side street, not marked on the maps, alongside the OTE office (*Tmr* 23C3).

At the 'Tragic Bus', cheap, student ticket end of the scale is a tourist agency at No. 46 Skridlof St, on the right, going westwards.

EXCURSION TO CHANIA CITY SURROUNDS
Excursion to Akrotiri Peninsula Before embarking on the route descriptions, a few words will not come amiss regarding Akrotiri promontory. I must admit I do not find it a very attractive area of Crete but apart from the airport at Sternes there are the outstanding historical sites of the Hill of Profitis Ilias; the Monastery of Ag Triada; the Gouverneto Monastery and Katholiko Cave.

The beautifully laid out English and Commonwealth cemetery, at shore level on the neck of Akrotiri, is a moving site. The graves date, in the main, from the Second World War but visitors of an emotional nature should not make too close an inspection. Numerous families have, over the years, visited the burial plots and left very moving, written tributes and testimonials to their fallen relatives. These are still readable and many are heartbreaking, almost harrowing testaments to their loved ones.

The dusty, unmade roads and the signposting on Akrotiri are very bad and finding the way round can be quite a trial.

Profitis Ilias (4 km from Chania). The hill is indicated by a signpost to the left to the Venizelou grave on the hilltop. There are great views across and over the sea and Chania. Profitis Ilias was also the site of a Cretan uprising against the Turks in 1897 signalled by running up a flag of Independence. Rumour and legend has it that this was shot away and a resistance fighter took the standard in his own hands whence the land and naval guns battering the Cretan forces stopped firing.

Following the signs to and through the hamlet of Kounoupidiana, beyond which the airport indications, not Chorafakia, and then the signs to Agia Triada leads to the: **Monastery of Ag. Triada(Tsanagardou) (17 km from Chania)** The last stretch is on a track, edged by an avenue of trees, over the surrounding fields. This celebrated working monastery, Venetian in style and founded in the 1630s, has been restored. Notable features are the entrance way and a campanile.

Further north from Ag Triada Monastery, some 3 km along the main, unsurfaced but driveable track is the: **Gouverneto Monastery.** Sixteenth century, fortified in appearance and renowned for its domed roof and icons.

Beyond the Monastery, about half an hour's walk, are the: **Monastery of Katholiko.** Ruined but close to early Christian rock face caves, a bridged ravine and the: **Katholiko Cave.** A stalactitie hung chamber, the one-time residence and death place of John the Hermit.

John the Hermits saint's day is October 7th when the area is rather busy with the comings and goings of pilgrims.

At the extreme north-western end of Akrotiri is **Stavros**, a scattered settlement, inset in a sandy, scrubland peninsula which is topped off by a small, Greek armed forces base. There are apartments, a taverna complex and signs of an infrastructure for future development.

ROUTE TEN
To Chora Sfakion via Vryses (73 km) The route is east on the Rethymnon road until signposts for Vryses, to which there is a turning from the Highway through **Neo Chorio**, and also a minor, ill-indicated turning off, almost adjacent to: **VRYSES (33 km from Chania)** The village, situated in a fertile lowland, is pretty and the main street tree lined. Petrol is available, there are a few tourist shops, plenty of tavernas, some statues and a river. It is a major bus swop-over point for switching

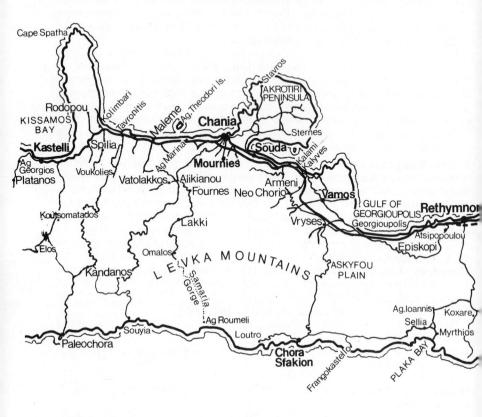

Illustration 16   Crete centred on Chania

from the Chora Sfakion/Chania bus to pick up a Rethymnon or Iraklion bus. There are supposedly two pensions and a hotel with 30 beds.

Beyond Vryses the road slowly climbs through the pretty countryside planted with olive groves and vineyards. Between Vryses and **Alikampos** the Turks suffered two massacres at the hands of Cretans, who were probably Sfakiots.

At about 50 km the flat **Askyfou Plain**, hedged in by encircling mountain peaks, startingly opens up below and in front of the road, which skirts the plain on its western perimeter. Where the route swings over the crest, a Venetian fort, built on a large but isolated hill, dominates the lovely, cultivated valley. The encircling road passes through very rural hamlets and villages which include **Kares, Ammoudari** and **Petres**. Each village is well endowed with tavernas, there are a few *Rooms*, churches are scattered about and there is the occasional petrol station.

At the tiny halt of **Imbros** the road finally tops the rise out of the plain. It then takes a turn, as it were, to the terrifyingly dramatic beginning of the hairpin descent, through in excess of one hundred bends, to Chora Sfakion. The small port is hidden from sight way, way, down below and the south Mediterranean Sea appears to stretch out forever with the rugged coastline extending to either side. Those of a nervous disposition, who should have already taken some pills, if not driving could close their eyes. Bus passengers might consider praying, remembering that the driver has covered the ground many, many times (you hope!).

With 2 km to go to Chora Sfakion (to which we will return in a few paragraphs), a surfaced turning off to the left runs parallel to the coast leading through **Komitades** and **Vraskas** to **Patsianos**. Only the last 3 km of the route is unsurfaced, whatever the maps indicate to the contrary. A footpath prior to reaching **Patsianos**, or a rough (well rougher) car track beyond, leads down to:

Frangokastello Castle (approx. 9 km from the Chora Sfakion road junction, despite the sign detailing 11 km). The beach is sandy, the swimming good, there are two inexpensive hotels, a number of *Rooms* and some tavernas. There is the *'DISGUOTEC AND ROC BAR BLUE SKY* (sic) – well actually more a road side hut – *OPEN EVERY NIGHT*. I bet it's not open every night out of season!

The Venetian fortress dominates the scene and was built in the 14th century in a vain attempt to dominate the eternally troublesome locals. All that survives are the castellated walls and corner towers laid out on a square ground plan. In 1828 the Turks slaughtered the locals defending the fort and it is alleged that, every year in May, their ghosts appear and dance around the fort.

To save returning via the Askyfou Plain, it is feasible to turn right (not left towards Chora Sfakion) and continue, well bump, along the unmetalled road through **Skaloti**.

Beyond Skaloti it is possible to descend some 2 km off the road, down to the peaceful, sandy grey beach of **Kalogeros,** set on a small bay. The gently shelving sand is spattered with pebbles and stone. At the large rock-bordered eastern end, on the edge of the beach, there is a dilapidated hovel and behind this is a flattened area with a few long-stay tents, motor caravans and 'the great unwashed' in evidence. To the right (*Fsw*) at the western side, there is a sign *Stop* indicating a taverna located around the bluff. Sure enough, following the wide unmade donkey track to the right, leads past a series of pretty, small, sand and rock coves to a couple of tavernas battling it out in this comparatively deserted spot. I can never understand the Greek predilection to spoil each other's trade by immediately throwing up competition wherever one business seems to be pulling in a few drachmae. I normally choose the startlingly simple taverna nearest the sea and soak in the enjoyment of, on average, being the only visitor in this isolated spot, that is apart from a couple of distant scuba divers.

Back on the 'main' road (sic), the mountain track winds through **Ano Rodakino** and **Kato Rodakino** (both with *Rooms* and hanging on the mountain side overlooking the sea) to **Sellia**, it's very large church sitting on a mountain top. Here connection is made with the Rethymnon to Plakias road (*See* CHAPTER 13, ROUTE SIX).

Back on the main Chania route, and the road descends to:

CHORA SFAKION (Chora Sphakion, Khora Sfakion, Hora Sfakion, Sfakia) ***

Harbour village

FIRST IMPRESSIONS
Dogs; inhabitants' disinterest.

VITAL STATISTICS
Tel. prefix 0825.

GENERAL
Most people visit Chora Sfakion as a part of the Samaria Gorge tourist undertaking. There are few reasons to pass through or stop over, if not participating in the Gorge junket or catching a local ferry to one of the other small, south-west coast port villages of Loutro or Souyia.

This harbour has developed solely because there is only one way out from Ag. Roumeli, the village at the bottom of the Samaria Gorge (apart from retracing one's steps), and that is by boat. From Ag Roumeli the small ferries ply, to the west, to Paleochora (*See* ROUTE FOURTEEN) and, to the east, to Chora Sfakion. The tourist organisations prefer the shorter Chora Sfakion route so the ferry-boats are forced to plough their watery course to a timetable that fits in with the tour operators' and their clients' descent of the Gorge. Most visitors to Chora Sfakion trudge their weary way up from the Ferry-boat quay (*Tmr* 13), along the harbour wall path and through the 100m spread of the awning-covered 'Main Street', lined by taverna tables and chairs to the Main Square (*Tmr* 11). This Plateia is at the far east end of the village, where the buses, tour coaches and cars pile up in terraced banks awaiting the serried ranks of walkers who have streamed round in endless hordes from the Gorge.

One or two of the tavernas entertain particular tour excursion participants to a 'typical evening out' in a 'typical Cretan fishing village'. Probably because of the constant and regular stream of tourists, numbering a minimum of a thousand per day during the season, the villagers are fairly disinterested and none go out of their way to tout for trade from the bus or ferry-boat arrivals.

Smaller than Ag. Galini, Chora Sfakion has a certain fascination despite the beleaguered air of the residents. Not that the 'Sfakiots' are downtrodden. They represent a rugged breed of Cretans who live on the southern coastline of the foothills of the Levka Mountain range stretching from Paleochora to Chora Sfakion. Over the centuries the Sfakiots fought and evaded submitting even to the all-powerful, all-conquering Venetians and Turks and in so doing they established a deserved reputation for being extremely tough, individualistic characters.

It is perhaps a conundrum that on the one hand the majority of visitors to Crete, and Chora Sfakion, are Germans. On the other hand this is the site of a plaque recording that Chora Sfakion was the port where the majority of the British, Australian and New Zealand troops were evacuated to North Africa. This was in 1941 when the Germans finally overran the island, after the Battle of Crete. Perhaps they have returned to complete the unfinished job!

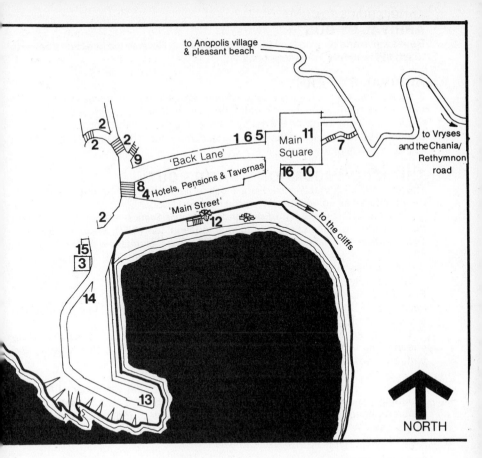

Tmr

1 Pension Sofia
2 Rooms
3 Hotel Xenia
4 Sofia Souvenirs
5 Bakery
6 Supermarket
7 Hospital
8 O.T.E.
9 Post Office
10 Police
11 Main Sq/Bus park
12 Beach
13 Ferry-boat quay
14 Ferry-boat ticket office
15 Taverna
16 Disco Zorba

Tmr = Town map reference
Fsw = Facing seawards
Sbo = Sea behind one

CHORA SFAKION

Illustration 17

CANDID GUIDE TO CRETE

ARRIVAL BY BUS

Buses arrive and park on the Main Square (*Tmr* 11). Reverse the directions below to reach the ferry-boat departure point.

ARRIVAL BY FERRY

From Ag. Roumeli the local passenger ferries motor round, sometimes via Loutro, to moor up at the quay on the end of the breakwater (*Tmr* 13). It is necessary to walk round to the right, following the gently curving quay wall, which leads past the block of hotels/restaurants above the narrow beach (*Tmr* 12) and on to the Main square, set to the east side of the village.

THE ACCOMMODATION & EATING OUT

The two are inextricably mixed up, most of the hotels on the main pedestrian thoroughfare having restaurants on their ground floors.

From the Square to the right (*Fsw*) range the *Hotels Samaria* (now only a restaurant but considering reinstating the accommodation for 1987), *Bradoukis Brothers, Rooms Livikon* and *Sfakia*. They are all of about Class C standard with a double room en suite from 1500 drs. Meals for two average out at around 800 drs and generally prices are reasonable.

Other lodgings include:

Pension Sofia (*Tmr* 1)

Directions: Situated in the narrow, 'Back Lane' that parallels the 'Main Street' and a few buildings beyond the bakery (*Tmr* 5).

Run by a very helpful English girl married to a Greek. Clean and a few drachmae cheaper than the hotels on the front with high season doubles, sharing the bathroom, costing 1200 drs and en suite 1700 drs.

At the other end of the village, keeping to the 'Lane', are a number of **Rooms** including: *Stavris* (rooms with bath), next door to which is the *Taverna Perikles* with a metered phone and where exchange can be transacted, and the *Lefka Ori* (rooms with a bath). At the turn of the quay, where it bends round to the left to form the seawall, is the Class B *Hotel Xenia* (*Tmr* 3).

Generally it is true to say that the hoteliers, restauranteurs and their staff are rather blase and operate on a 'take it or leave it' basis, but this is probably as much to do with the 'Sfakiots' character as disinterest or boredom.

THE A TO Z OF USEFUL INFORMATION

BANKS None. **Sofia Souvenirs** (*Tmr* 4), in the main block of buildings on the 'Main St', offers a reasonable change facility as does *Perikles Taverna* and the Post Office (*Tmr* 9).

BEACHES Beneath the high seawall is a narrow, shingly, grey sand, rather dirty beach (*Tmr* 12) edging the pleasant, small bay.

There is a sign at the far end of the village to *Nice Beaches*. The path leads out on to the Anopolis road. This initially skirts the coastline, and some way along which is a steep path down to a narrow cove. Incidentally it is from this road that the cliff walk to Loutro takes off across the mountain rock face but this scramble is not for the fainthearted. At the height of the summer it is a long, hot walk to this beach and back so do not forget to pack a picnic bag. There are no supplies or services on the way or at the beach.

184

CHANIA

BREAD SHOP *(Tmr 5)* On a corner of the Main Square, diagonally opposite the Police Station *(Tmr 10)*.

BUSES The buses tend to wait for the trip boats to arrive from Ag. Roumeli. As most of the buses start on the steep climb out of Sfakia at about 1600 hrs, it would seem unwise to drive down to the port between 1600 - 1700 hrs.

Bus timetables
These are not listed but the very helpful policeman will tender the information.

Chora Sfakion to Chania*
Daily 0730, 1100, 1600, 1700 hrs.
     & "about 1900 hrs if there are enough people" says the policeman.
* To reach Rethymnon or Iraklion get off the Chania bus at Vryses and catch a connecting bus, BUT do ensure baggage is placed on the correst side of the bus storage compartment, prior to departure.
Chora to Plakias
Daily 1600 hrs.
Chora to Ag Galini
Daily 1600 hrs.
Chora to Anopolis
Daily 1600 hrs.
Return journey
Daily 0700 hrs (next morning as it were).
Chora to Frangokastello
Daily 1600 hrs.
Return journey
Daily 'between 0650/0730 hrs'!
Note these are high season schedules.

COMMERCIAL SHOPPING AREA Naturally there is none, but a number of shops ensure most goods and supplies can be purchased. In narrow 'Back Lane', one back from the 'Main Street', are grocers, a butcher, a dairy and a 'supermarket' *(Tmr 6)*, which is reasonably well stocked and also exchanges foreign currency.

    Opening hours are the usual but the souvenir shops open seven days a week during the season.

DISCOS There is **Disco Zorba** *(Tmr 16)* on the edge of the Main Sq and **Disco Scorpio** 200 m up the winding main road to Chania.

FERRY BOATS The information regarding the timetables of these local, excursion sized ferry-boats differs from port to port. This route connects the south-western coastal village ports of Chora Sfakion, Loutro, Ag. Roumeli, Souyia and Paleochora. I have argued, over a bottle or two, the unreliability of the ferries with one of the skippers, but he was not prepared to own up. The confusion is not helped by the NTOG offices issuing official printed timetables that substantially differ in detail from the various ports information. Oh dear me! Certainly either side of the height of season the schedules are foreshortened.

    All of us have our tale of woe on this particular journey and Anne proved to be no exception as her own cautionary tale explains.

    "I took an early boat to Loutro, and asked the ticket office in Sfakia if it would be possible to get the last ferry from Loutro on to Ag. Roumeli. Yes, I was assured, I could get the 1650 hrs boat, buying my ticket in Loutro. I checked with the boat, when I got off, that the relevant craft would call later and was assured it would. The good people of Loutro told me the same. As it was, I stood on the quayside at 1700 hrs only to watch the boat sail merrily by in the direction of Ag. Roumeli, without stopping! Of course there is no point in getting angry with anyone, ever in Greece, and Loutro is as pleasant a place as anywhere else (if not more so) to be stranded, if you have to be. But I was CROSS all the same!"

Ferry-boat timetables
Chora Sfakion to Loutro, Ag. Roumeli
Daily   1015, 1100, 1530, 1650 hrs.
Return journey
Daily   0945, 1430, 1700 hrs.
One-way fares: Chora to Loutro 125 drs; Chora to Ag. Roumeli 525 drs.
   Also listed are the following:
Chora Sfakion to Ag. Roumeli
Daily   1015, 1100, 1530, 1700 hrs.
Return journey
Daily   1545, 1745 hrs.

Although I detail a number of ports, if planning to proceed westwards beyond Ag. Roumeli, it is necessary to change boats, but beware, because there is little effort to synchonise the services. If wishing to travel on to say Paleochora it may well be necessary to stop-over at Ag. Roumeli.
Travellers MUST CHECK the schedules at the time.

Chora Sfakion is now also a departure port for **Gavdos island** as listed below. For fuller details *See* PALEOCHORA (this chapter), ROUTE FOURTEEN.

Chora Sfakion to Gavdos island
Mid June to end of September
Every Saturday   0900 hrs.
Return journey
Every Saturday   1530 hrs.
Duration 4 hrs.

FERRY-BOAT TICKET OFFICE (*Tmr* 14) To the west side of the harbour, on the way round to the Ferry-boat quay.

HOSPITAL (*Tmr* 7) A small building adjacent to the Main Square.

OTE (*Tmr* 8) At the far end of 'Back Lane', opposite the Post Office.

PETROL No sign of pumps but a building on the left, after leaving the Main Sq, advertises, on large signs, petrol – so they must have some tucked away.

PLACES OF INTEREST
Cave of Daskaloyiannis Just to the west of Chora and one of several caves in the area. Daskaloyiannis was a Cretan revolutionary who led an uprising against the Turks in 1770. Unfortunately he agreed to attend a peace conference, was snatched by the Turks, tortured and skinned whilst alive. His heroic, if possibly involuntary death was celebrated in *The Song of Daskaloyiannis'*.
Churches These include the Church of the Apostles.

POST OFFICE (*Tmr* 9) Opposite the OTE, at the west end of 'Back Lane'.

POLICE (*Tmr* 10) There is a Police station on the edge of the Main Square.

TAXIS Rank on the Main Square.

LOUTRO (Lutron, Loutron)

Harbour hamlet

Loutro cannot be reached by road and the closest contact tourists normally have is to sail by, or make a ferry-boat stop, whilst travelling between Ag. Roumeli and Chora Sfakion. Some fit and fearless walkers make their way along the cliff path from Chora Sfakion or Paleochora via Souyia. It is possible to walk down the mountain-face, goat track from Anopolis village to Loutro. Mind you, the last chap I met who completed the journey, admittedly in unsuitable shoes, was suffering badly ulcerated feet.

Loutro lies inset at the far end of a mountain-enclosed bay and the small hamlet spreads thinly around the sea-shore.

The Cretan people of the south-west coast, usually typified by the Chora Sfakiots, exhibit many characteristics in common with the more infamous Sicilians. They were once a warring people, unconquerable and prone to blood feuds, marriage by abduction (with the subsequent vendettas) and sheep stealing. Modern-day folk of this area reveal some of the traits of their ancestors, especially a dislike of all or any authority. There are many manifestations of this individualism, probably mainly rumours, of course, but a few examples might not go amiss and may help to highlight the rebellious nature of the people of this region.

The local ferry-boat operators' modus operandi best exemplifies their competitive nature. When they first commenced operations the various craft raced each other from departure to destination. This only ceased when they realised the futility and self-defeating nature of the exercise and got together to pool their efforts. In so doing they 'forgot' to include the Paleochora operators, who have been pressing for new licences, a move strongly resisted by the Loutro men.

Litigation has in many respects replaced killing as a method of obtaining revenge, as is proved by some of the more recent, humorous events. The village, as a whole, is being sued for stealing stones from a distant beach to use them for building purposes. Meanwhile, the self-same inhabitants of the village are, via the Port police, suing one of their own. He is a wealthy expatriate who, returning home from America, built a restaurant on the waters edge with a new quay protruding into the sea. The villagers maintain that this quay is ugly and spoils the appearance of Loutro, conveniently ignoring the existing, but not particularly pretty, quays of the extant tavernas. So the Port police are fining him for 'stealing' part of the sea-shore. The problem is exacerbated by the fact that the only way that the entrepreneur can do away with the quay, in order to comply with the law, is to use dynamite. As the possession of dynamite is illegal, he maintains he is unable to carry out these instructions. This would seem very reasonable if one ignored the number of one-armed fishermen or the occasional, out of sight but clearly audible explosion close to shore. Any suggestion that fisherman would have, or are using dynamite to catch fish, is strongly denied. Incidentally, the quay story assumes a new slant and a further insight into the locals' character. A couple of years ago the quay in question was washed away by a great storm but the owner defiantly rebuilt it all over again, where it still stands....

ARRIVAL BY FERRY BOAT

The boats dock at the small quay to the extreme left of the village (*Sbo*).

GENERAL

The first, left-hand (*Sbo*) half of the bay encircled by Loutro consists of, in the main, lodging houses and tavernas connected by a series of concrete paths and quays. A small, stony beach takes over halfway round, adjacent to a large garden wall and, alongside a periptero. This is situated on the edge of the backshore, close by the cliff path to Chora Sfakion which winds off from the seafront.

At the bottom of the ferry-boat finger pier a footpath loops up the hillside to the headland top whereon is sited a very small, ruined Venetian fort whose walls are almost intact. Nearby is an interesting, sunken Arsenal inside which is a well. Continuing down the other side of the headland, in a westerly direction, is the small, pleasant Bay of **Finix** dominated by a taverna with **Rooms** and a large verandah. There is solid evidence of other unfinished buildings to one side.

The Venetians used Loutro as a medieval spa or watering hole and alongside the small church, in the centre of the village, are two small Arsenals.

All paradises have a drawback and Loutro's is in its slightly brackish water. This is strange considering that, on the Chora Sfakion cliff walk, the largest bay, to which the path descends, is called 'Sweet Water Bay' for good reasons. In addition to the fresh water springs, there are a few small caves at the foot of the steepling rock faces, that hem the edge of the beach. These help to make a long stay occupation that much more comfortable and the 'great unwashed' appear to summer on this long, narrow, sandy beach. (Monte Carlo in the winter I suppose?).

VILLAGE DETAIL

Back at the Ferry-boat quay (*Sbo*), the splendidly situated house to the left is *Katerina's*. The family lived much of their life in America and Katerina's daughter Christina speaks excellent, if very fast, American. Mother and daughter are both very pleasant and helpful. Once only **Rooms**, they have 'bolted on' a tasteful, patio cafe-bar. The tables and chairs are scattered around, close by the water's edge with a display cabinet tucked up to the wall of the house. Ice-cream and a variety of tasty 'tosts' are served. The accommodation has now been supplemented by three new, wholesome bathrooms and double rooms sharing these start off at 1200 drs. When we first stayed here it was Christina, a keen sub-aqua swimmer, who explained that the trapped octopus knew to go for a diver's face mask and that only recently hers had been wrenched off by an octopus in its death throes.

On that same visit we were privileged to hear the 'ghostly' dynamite blasts of non-existent fishermen!

Next door and moving to the right, is the 'stick man' who is reported to be rather irascible and the cause of some local trouble. Every village has one, doesn't it? The next building is a taverna with rotisserie which has **Rooms**. Alongside that is one-handed and likeable Yannis's light blue painted taverna. He was once in partnership with his less agreeable brother, who has started up a taverna restaurant in the last building circling in a clockwise direction (*Sbo*), beyond the expatriate American's Restaurant. Consuela does the cooking for Yannis and her daughter looks after mother's periptero to which reference has previously been made.

Next one along from Yannis's is a building with **Rooms**. This is followed by a dark blue painted taverna, the outside tables of which are shielded from the heat of the midday sun by large, gracefully spreading tamarisk trees. This taverna houses the village phone. There is also a wall mounted post box, but I am not sure if and when it is emptied.

Following round the sea-shore, the next *Pension* reputedly has the best accommodation in the village with en suite bathrooms, but naturally the price reflects this excellence. The pension is closely followed by a small office where currency can be changed, a shop with a limited amount of goods, books and postcards.

Next along is the beach on which lie a few disconsolate pedaloes and behind them, the periptero.

The once slightly ramshackle taverna, three buildings beyond the beach, has now been replaced by a new structure but is still run by Stella and Stavros. The eighty year old grandmother, who used to do most of the simple but excellent cooking, has retired to the 'bright lights' of Chora Sfakion. Still a good haunt for morning coffee or the meal of the day, seated at the chairs and tables outside on the sea-lapped patio, shaded by a few trees.

Just beyond Stella's is the American Cretan's quay and restaurant, rising phoenix-like from the sea, and referred to in the introductory paragraphs. Beyond is the Restaurant/Taverna belonging to Yannis's brother.

If you are lucky you will bump into Alison whose husband Stavros heads up the Loutro syndicate of ferry-boat owners. On the other hand, if you have no sense of humour perhaps it would be best to avoid a meeting, for she will surely have you in stitches.

To conclude, Anne reports that the beach has large signboards, warning *NO TOPLESS*, which are only ignored at a lady's peril. I assume bottomless men would also invite some warranted community displeasure! One young, topless lady who surfaced from the sea and stretched out at the far end of the ferry-boat quay, attracted the attention and extreme ire of Katerina's clients. After a few moments of doubtless lynch talk, Katerina's husband stalked down the quay armed with a large stick. The luckless object of mass fury initially had her back to the approaching 'horseman (of the apocalyse)' but, prompted by some sixth sense, turned to see her field of vision filled by a stick-brandishing Greek, making furious gestures. Village gossip has it that the unfortunate woman broke the world record for dressing, whilst in the seated position!

ROUTE ELEVEN
To Ag. Roumeli via Omalos and The Samaria Gorge (60 km)

Follow the Kastelli road for a few kilometres and take the turning to the left, signposted for Omalos. The road ascends through verdant orange groves to the turning off to **Alikianou** at 12 km, where there is a memorial to Cretan partisans killed by the Germans.

The road to **Fournes** (15 km), still in 'orange grove' countryside, starts to climb at the village in a series of loops, passing through **Lakki**. This picturesque mountain village served as the military headquarters of the Cretan guerillas during their intercine struggles with the Turks. The orange groves recede as the altitude rises, giving way to olives, which themselves give way to mountainous hillsides and a vista of granite rocks speckled with conifers. Finally the road tops a rise and opens out on to the fairly fertile **Omalos Plain** and its straggling hamlet (37 km), where there are **Rooms** and a taverna. The large open plain, on which crops grow and goats and sheep graze, is enclosed by gaunt, granite mountains, bringing to mind 'The Hidden Valley'. At the far end of the plain, the road again climbs, now to the head of the Gorge (42 km from Chania).

There is a car and coach park and a dramatic view through the mountains. A wooden fence surrounds the rim of the almost vertical face of the Gorge and the xyloskalo (or wooden steps) which descend to the floor of the Gorge. To the right, up a sharp, short steep drive is the:

Xenia Pavilion (Class B)   Tel. 93237
Only three rooms with seven beds sharing bathrooms. The single bed rate is quoted at 1300 drs.

SAMARIA GORGE

Bearing in mind the bus timetable it is possible, by catching the 0615 or 0830 hrs bus, to make the round trip in a day from Chania to the top of the Gorge, descend and walk the 18 km to Ag. Roumeli, catch a passenger ferry to Chora Sfakion and a bus back to Chania that evening. But why burst a blood vessel? Why not stop over at Ag. Roumeli or Chora Sfakion?

The Gorge opens from 1st April to 31st October, with due allowance for exceptionally inclement weather, at either end of the season, if it causes the river to rise to dangerous levels. Before discussing the walk itself it might well be germane to enlighten the waverers and the doubters as to why they should disturb the happy holiday rhythm of late rising, flesh-toasting during the day with breaks for 'drinkies' and joyous rioting all night. I can appeal to two emotions: curiosity and self-satisfaction. The Gorge is possibly the longest and largest in Europe. It is undoubtedly extremely beautiful, engendering various reactions from awe at the sheer majesty of the scenery, curiosity at the various buildings, interest in the flora, fauna and wild life, and possibly amazement, if not thankfulness, when the jaunt is finished. Well, now readers should be persuaded.

It is easy to imagine the inaccessibility of the location without the modern day advantages of the wooden staircase. This was exploited through the ages by both bandits and guerrilla fighters, especially during the Turkish occupation and up to and including the Second World War. It is reported that even the partisans fighting the Germans were at risk to small bands of Gorge brigands.

It is worth taking a small holdall containing a snack and something to drink despite the fact that there are the occasional water points and the river water can be drunk. Private enterprise has reared its ugly head at Old Ag. Roumeli, close to the end of the walk. Here is an untidy bar and an elderly lady twiddling cans of soft drinks (my copy typist interposed 'drunks' and why not?) in a bucket of water by the pathside. These offerings are expensive. Wear sensible shoes, not flip-flops.

The walk commences by descending the wooden staircase for some 2 km after which, on the right, is a small chapel set in a copse of firs. At about half distance is the now uninhabited village of **Samaria** and another church. The journey is mainly a matter of picking a way over, round and through the boulderous river bed. As in excess of a 1000 people a day pass down the length of the Gorge, there are unlikely to be any unexpected hazards. Another church on the left precedes the narrowest part of the Gorge, where the towering walls slim down to a mere 2 m in width. This section is known as the 'Iron Gates', after which the path picks its way through the stone walled pathways of the village of **Old Ag. Roumeli**. Here a few houses are being restored, there is a kafenion, bar and a donkey service runs (or rather clip clops) down to Ag. Roumeli. After the hamlet, the mountain walls are pushed back and the Gorge widens out into a narrow river valley. The last kilometre or two does drag a little, more especially as walkers are now in the full glare of the sun's rays. The walk should have taken some four or six hours, depending on the participant's state of health, his or her partner's condition and whether or not children were included in the expedition. Members of guided tours tend to be regulated by the pace of the weakest member of the party.

The path wends its way seawards down the unmade, dusty and dirty surface, that doubles for a road, to where it joins with another, rough surfaced thoroughfare that runs parallel to the seashore of:

AG. ROUMELI (60 km from Chania). Tel. prefix 0825. There was an ancient settlement here in the 5th century BC evidenced by excavations to the left of the Gorge (*Fsw*) and the Turks built a fort (surprise, surprise!).

Ag. Roumeli resembles a hot, Alaskan shanty town. The only institutions missing are John Wayne and a bordello. The inhabitants ('Sfakiots') have had a pretty hard life for the last 1000 years or so, what with tending and skinning goats and sheep in order to earn a crust. But now they are engaged in tending and skinning the tourists so as to be able to afford holiday apartments in Chania, Rethymnon or Iraklion.

At the main junction, and to the right (*Fsw*), are a profusion (is there a collective adjective*?) of bars, restaurants and pensions. The native feel of the place is accentuated by the wandering, foraging chickens, goats and sheep but a note of (* *A rubbish, slurp, wash of....*)

caution would not go amiss. Ag. Roumeli has the dubiously unique distinction of being the only gathering of Greeks where I have been, have observed and heard of tourists being 'ripped off' by Greeks, not you will note, fellow tourists.

At the far, right end of the path, parallel to the waterside, is a 'supermarket', well more a shop located in a garage. Everywhere check the prices charged against the labelled price – a nod is as good as a wink. On the path from the Gorge is a little shop in a windowed hut, grandly named 'Mini Market', where bread is available (nod, nod again). All goods and supplies arrive by boat and are trucked about the place. Very little attempt is made to finish off any of the buildings, either externally or internally.

The Restaurant & Pension Tara   Tel. 29391
Directions: The last building from the Gorge and straight ahead, or alternatively, the first to the right from the Ferry-boat quay, with a large patio edging the seafront.

The brothers Stavrondakis run the show and both speak English. I can recommend the accommodation. A double room en suite with a nicely tiled bathroom (well a few are missing, but there you go), costs 1000 drs, or 1400 drs at the height of the season. Be careful climbing the precast concrete steps on the way up to the first storey. There is an irregularity in the rise which causes the unwary to trip, and that is without taking into account any intake of retsina. A meal at the Tara, on the superbly positioned, covered terrace, is good value. Moussaka for two, one green beans (hot), a Greek salad, bread, three beers, a Metaxa and lemonade and one bottle of retsina all for about 1100 drs (so now you know why I fell upstairs).

All the accommodation in the village is advertised 'with hot shower' but mosquitoes are present and the dawn chorus of the village's stray dogs will probably wake the heaviest sleeper.

The surprisingly large beach, to the right (*Fsw*), is made up of fine pebbles and the sea is beautifully clear and blue. To Gorge walkers the beach may well look like paradise and it tends to fill up and empty contemporaneously with the arrival and departure of the ferry-boats. There is quite a lot of unofficial, overnight beach camping going on. Edging the beach are some cliffs, over and around which goats perform a miraculous cliff-walking act.

Ferry-boats The ferry-boat ticket office hut is to the quay side of the *Restaurant/ Pension Tara* and an oft altered timetable is pinned to one of the outside walls.
Ferry-boat timetable For details of both ferry-boat and connecting bus schedules *See* **Chora Sfakion** and **Paleochora** (this chapter), but note the timetables appear to alter at the whim of the operators. Both fares and schedules must be double checked, bearing in mind that very little information ties up, from whatever source it emanates.

Incidentally a beer is very expensive on the ferries at 110 drs a bottle and neither coffee nor food are served.

ROUTE TWELVE
To Rethymnon, via the Old Road From Chania, initially the main road is used. After some 18 km the branch road to **Armeni** is signposted which should be taken. This village lies in a fertile valley full of olive groves with a lovely avenue out of the village. The road bypasses a dying, be-flowered village and proceeds to **Neo Chorio** which has a long irregular square, a disco (yes a disco), and little else. The route winds up and out of Neo Chorio, past a chapel built into the rock on the left, whilst across the valley another settlement sprawls over a lump of rock. The landscape is strewn with cypresses, in amongst which is a steep gorge and very many trees followed by massed grape vines.

Ag. Pantes is a small, pretty, tree lined settlement set in farming country with sheep and chickens everywhere, and charcoal burners in evidence. This section of the route·is particularly attractive, being heavily wooded and with many chapels.

From Vryses (*See* ROUTE TEN) sorties can be made to Georgioupolis (*See* ROUTE FIVE, CHAPTER 13) and the overrated, small freshwater lake at **Kournas**. Back on course, **Episkopi** (tel. prefix 0831) is a large, long, winding settlement with some industry, a Post Office, tavernas, a petrol station, as well as one hotel, *The Minos* (Class D, tel. 61208).

The road traverses a lovely, green ravine very nearly devoid of mechanical traffic but there are plenty of donkeys clip clopping along, usually laden down with a heavy load plus the owner.

Ag. Andreas squats in a landscape of olives but there are signs of development at the roadside, despite which the local charcoal burner is in evidence. From here the road loops via the large, compact village of **Atsipopoulo** to Rethymnon (*See* CHAPTER 13).

ROUTE THIRTEEN
To Kastelli via Ag. Marina, Platanias, Maleme, Tavronitis & Kolimbari (42 km) The main road out of Chania, westwards, passes along or
near the coast through a stretch of haphazard, urban, seaside development. After some 2km, on the left-hand side, is the rather bellicose statue of a mounted, stooping eagle. This is to commemorate, or more truly mourn, the heavy losses of the crack 7th German Parachute Regiment that spearheaded the German invasion during the Battle of Crete, in May 1941. The main assault took place on this stretch of coast but the attrition was so heavy that Hitler is supposed to have ordered that no more attacks of this type were to be undertaken.

AG. MARINA (about 5 km from Chania) Tel. prefix 0821. The lovely beach is surrounded by surfboards, cafe-bars, tourist shops and hotels. These include the expensive, tour operator booked *Santa Marina* (Class B, tel. 68570) with double rooms from 2900 drs and a nice garden down to the beach. There are usually vacancies in the out-of-the-height-of-the-season months. Other accommodation includes the Class C *Ta Thodorou* (Tel. 68510) as well as a number of pensions and *Rooms*, both in Ag. Marina and either side of the sprawling road to the west.

Some 6 km out of Chania, a lovely, sandy stretch of beach runs along the roadside. Just offshore is the bold looking island of **Agii Theodori** which is reputedly a refuge for the legendary Agrimi or Kri-Kri, (the Cretan wild goat or chamois), an object of veneration in Minoan times.

At the far end of the beach is:
Camping Ag. Marina   Tel. 48555
Not as desirable a site as *Camping Hania* (*See* **The Accommodation, Chania**) but reasonable facilities including a taverna, supermarket and shower/toilets block. Daily charges are 240 drs per person and 150 drs for tent hire. Bus travellers should catch the Chania/Ag. Marina/Maleme/Chandris conveyance.

PLATANIAS (some 8 km from Chania) Tel. prefix 0821. The original village has spread down off its small, flat-topped hill into a sprawl of 'Costa-like' development, with the reinforced concrete skeletons of buildings randomly sprouting out of cultivated fields and bamboo groves. There are two Class B hotels, the *Filoxenia* and *Villa Platanias*. The beach here is low, flat and sandy.

The road now narrows down and corridors through tall bamboo-fencing wind breaks, pierced by poorly made doors of tin and plastic. A river is crossed prior to reaching the village of **Pyrgos**, where there are **Rooms**, and the larger, industrial but flower-bedecked village of:
MALEME (16 km from Chania) Tel. prefix 0821. In the centre of the village is a wine factory. At harvest time the main road has vehicles of every shape and description lined up along the kerb, loaded down with grapes, the drivers patiently waiting to deliver their towering loads.

Beyond Maleme, sited between the road and sea-shore, is the very smart *Crete Chandris Hotel* complex (Class A) and the E Class *Karnezi* (Tel. 91291). To the left is the German Second World War cemetery. By a strange quirk of fate this was, and probably still is, tended by George Psychoundakis, the author, with the guidance of his mentor Patrick Leigh Fermor, of *The Cretan Runner*. This book is the moving story of Crete's involvement in the Second World War struggle with the Germans, written from a partisan's point of view – a must for anyone interested in the period.

Another kilometre further on is a small military airfield which was the centre of the German airborne assault in 1941. A large, wide, dry river-bed is quickly followed by the village of:

TAVRONITIS (19 km from Chania) *Rooms*, vegetable shops, a petrol station and the junction with the turning off to Voukolies, Kandanos and Paleochora (*See* ROUTE FOURTEEN). The main road passes through vine filled fields, the very small village of **Kamissiana** and a lovely chapel on the left, whilst to the right, is a dirty seashore of grey sand and dunes.

The churches in this area are constructed in the Cycladean style with a minaret tacked on the end. At the limit of the flat plain, is the turning off to:

KOLIMBARI (23 km from Chania) Tel. prefix 0824. The site of a large wine factory with shining, stainless steel tanks lying around on the ground. There are *Rooms* and two hotels, the:

Hotel Rose Marie (Class D)   Tel. 22220
En suite rooms with singles from 900 drs and doubles 1100 drs. These rates increase to 1000 drs and 1300 drs (1st June - 30th Sept).
and the:
Hotel Dimitra (Class E)   Tel. 22244
Double rooms only sharing starting off at 1500 drs rising to 1800 drs (1st June - 31st Oct).

Back on the main crossroads, a narrow road leads to the interior and the village of **Spilia.** Here is a church with some magnificent frescoes above which is a large cave. Some kilometres beyond the village of **Episkopi** (not the large, Rethymnon Episkopi, its cousin....), is a very old church.

The deteriorating main road swings past a large, scale, charcoal burner's 'HQ' to the left and on to **Kalydonia**, set in large olive groves. From this village the winding route passes by narrow ravines and through scrubbly hills, emerging suddenly on the lip of the mountainside. This vantage point overlooks the Gulf of Kissamos, edged by the elongated, mountainous headland of Gramvousa, the plain far below and Kastelli Town in the far distance. Up here a local entrepreneur has erected a bamboo-thatched cafe-bar.

It is a long, winding descent to the highly cultivated, green, undeveloped plain and the small village edging the foot of the mountain with many churches dotted about. A signpost indicates *Camping Mithimna* to the right, whilst the main road advances to **Drapanias** village, the working community of **Kaloudiana**, (whence the Elos turning, *See* CHAPTER 15, ROUTE SIXTEEN), after which appear the outskirts of Kastelli (*See* CHAPTER 15).

ROUTE FOURTEEN
To Paleochora via Kandanos (77 km) Proceed along ROUTE THIRTEEN
as far as Tavronitis. Here take the branch route off to the left along a road which is under reconstruction, with the resultant indeterminate ride. The route ascends slowly, weaving through fields of olives, oranges, lemons and vines whilst to the left is a large, dry, river-bed being quarried for shingle. The small village of **Neriana** is

across the river and, from this area to Voukolies, the road passes through a very green valley with bamboos, a petrol station and several war memorials.

Voukolies is a large village which has a square, whereon is an extensive Saturday market, and a number of shops including a baker. There is also a petrol station and tyre shop, yes a tyre shop which, due to the generally bad state of the roads in the area, is a very adroit piece of opportunism. On the public square, well more beneath it, are the dirtiest and smelliest public lavatories Anne reckons she has ever seen. The roads in this area are (in 1986) in an absolutely dreadful condition.

En route to the tiny village of Dromonero, the road narrows again, winding steeply upwards and the vegetation becomes less dense. At **Dromonero** the bus drivers often pop out, drop down a few steps and refresh themselves from the village fountain.

The pretty, tree lined village of **Kakopetros** clings to the side of the towering mountain whose surfaces are bare granite, fissured with deep valleys. Between Kakopetros and **Mesavlia** the road, still in bad shape, slowly descends through more cultivated surrounds which alternate with sandy gorse, heather and wild thyme. Clusters of coloured beehives are seemingly haphazardly dotted about.

The long descent leads to modern **Kandanos** which has a large wine factory. The modernity of the settlement is due to the Germans' destroying the town during the Second World War, having found the citizens difficult to control and reluctant to give up their 'unsporting', resistance activities.

Towns and villages on this route are famed for the various Byzantine churches, frescoes and paintings. The road now makes a craggy, ravined descent towards:

PALEOCHORA (Palaiokhora)
Seaside village.

FIRST IMPRESSIONS
A town-like village port; the 'great unwashed'; self-service, a large, sweeping, magnificent beach.

VITAL STATISTICS
Tel. prefix 0823.

GENERAL
I am not sure what initially triggers the feeling of uneasiness, a suspicion that something is not quite normal, but the feeling persists and grows. Depending upon one's susceptibilities, this sensation explodes into the realisation that under the weight of the 'great unwashed' the locals have mutated, developing a parochial strain to cope with a problem which they appear unwilling to deal with. This manifests itself in several noticeable ways and, I am sure, in numerous others I was unable to detect. The usual Greek service, excruciatingly slow but normally polite and interested, is displaced by a sullen, even slower pace. Many bars have instituted 'self-service', that is, clients have to go to the counter, order and immediately pay for their requirements. I would not go so far as to say that drinks and food are indolently served, with scarcely veiled disinterest and distaste, but it is a very fine distinction. The *Neon Cafe* is a particular example, advertising fresh orange juice but serving up orange squash and even if challenged in Greek – by a native (got the idea), refusing to change the same. True to say that once a proprietor realises that a client has bathed that week, that he (or she) does not intend to sit at a table all night nursing one shared drink, is not bringing convenience food from other sources to his tables, doesn't have a stray dog in tow nor several dirty, unwashed children, is not begging,

or stealing or both, then service may well return to normal. But it will be necessary to persevere.

Paleochora was a fishing village as evidenced by the disproportionately large harbour installation at the lighthouse end of the peninsula. Here the small fleet weathers out the worst weather. Many fishermen now content themselves as proprietors of apartments and pensions in order to cater for the spin-off from the Samaria Gorge traffic.

The differing faces of the village are evidenced by the two seashores. The left-hand or eastern, initially rocky shoreline is reasonably 'polite' with a small quay where the ferry-boats pull up. It is edged by a neat Esplanade with bench seats. The right-hand or western beach is probably one of the finest on Crete with a huge, gently curving, large, tree fringed, sandy shore set in an impressive, distantly cliff edged bay. Where is the snag? Ah well, this is where the 'great unwashed' camp out in their hundreds, strewing the backshore trees' thick foliage with tents and plastic-covered shelters of every size and description.

Keep an eye out for the handless and sightless villager, probably an ex fisherman, who walks his pelican around the village. (*See* LOUTRO for further explanation and edification of the limblessness.)

ARRIVAL BY BUS

The bus thunders down the middle of the village, through the cement faced buildings. These whitewashed rectangles, arranged on a grid layout, are gently squeezed in between the two sea-shores. The peninsula narrows down to the bulbous, lighthouse-mounted, headland that encompasses the harbour proper, some way beyond the main town. The buses pull up on the High St, towards the headland end of Paleochora, in amongst a welter of bars, restaurants, tavernas and souvenir shops.

Sharp left is the eastern shore and Ferry-boat quay, sharp right the western beach and, back the way the bus has travelled, the centre (if it can be called that) of the village.

ARRIVAL BY FERRY

Ferries dock on the very small, eastern shore quay across the Esplanade from the *Pelican Bar/Restaurant*, a convenient and good watering hole.

It is perhaps unfortunate for the natives that Paleochora seems to have lost out, to some extent, in the ferry flow of tourists disgorged (disgorged, oh yes) from Ag. Roumeli. Although there is a service from Ag. Roumeli via Souyia it does not run so often, nor is it as popular as the admittedly shorter Chora Sfakion route. Rumour, only a vile rumour, has it that this rather shameful state of affairs is a result of skullduggery, avarice and collusion by the skippers that ply the other route – but it could be true. Hush my mouth!

THE ACCOMMODATION & EATING OUT
The Accommodation There is a plethora of **Rooms** but not a lot of official hotels. The local populace do not hesitate to offer their accommodation as soon as travellers disembark from bus or ferry. The convenient and good goes quickly, the further out and not so modern may stay available for some time.

Officially listed hotels include the:

Pension Eliros (Class B)   Tel. 41348
En suite rooms with singles costing 1100 drs and doubles 1400 drs which charges rise to 1200 drs and 1900 drs (1st April - 30th Sept).

Pension Lissos (Class C)   Tel. 41266
No singles, with doubles sharing bathrooms costing 1100 drs and en suite 1410 drs.

Hotel Oasis (Class E)   Tel. 41328
Double rooms only, sharing a bathroom cost 1200 drs and with an en suite bathroom, 1550 drs.
Hotel Paleochora (Class E)   Tel. 41225
Only double rooms, sharing the bathroom for 1100 drs.

My favourite is the excellent:
Hotel & Taverna Dionisos (Class D)   Tel. 41243
Directions: Sited in the High Street and offering good clean accommodation. Nearby are *Rooms Lafonissi.*

The Taverna Dionisos offers extremely friendly service and inexpensive meals but get there early as the place fills up very quickly. An example for two, includes one small and one large chicken portion, aubergines, Greek salad and a bottle of retsina for about 700 drs. All on offer is laid out in the unusually large kitchens for clients to view.

Pension Maria's
Directions: On the eastern seafront, 100m down the Esplanade.

Only two rooms but the pension offers simple, clean, if slightly disjointed accommodation with a shared bathroom.

The taverna part of the building serves a very limited, inexpensive menu.

Generally prices for **Rooms** in Paleochora start at 1000 drs for a double room with shared bathroom and about 1300 drs for a double with en suite bathroom.
Koulieros Rooms & Tavernas
Directions: Next door to *Pension Maria's.*

Room prices with shared bathroom start at 1500 drs, a little expensive but agreeable.

The taverna is pleasant and reasonably priced. A meal for two of stuffed tomatoes, stuffed aubergines, bread, two bottles of beer, two cokes, and two plates of chips all for 660 drs. Christos Koulieros is a very nice fellow, certainly not one of the 'indifferent' Paleochorians.

There are also the **Hotels Livykon** (Class D, tel. 41250) and **Grigorakis** (Class E).

The Eating Out Numerous but apart from the tavernas detailed above, good value is offered at the:
Pelican Bar Taverna
The locals breakfast here, the position is very convenient, being adjacent to the Ferry-boat quay, and there is a large outside patio. Unfortunately a lot of reconstruction and rebuilding work is taking place to the right of the Ferry-boat quay and sitting in or outside the Pelican is a noisy, dusty experience (in 1986 and may well be so in 1987).

THE A TO Z OF USEFUL INFORMATION
BANKS The **National Bank of Greece** is situated next door to the *Pension and Taverna Dionisos* and opens the usual hours.

The Travel Agent, close by the bus stop, changes money and the office hours are: daily 0830 - 1330 & 1700 - 2130 hrs, Sundays 0900 - 1330 hrs.

BEACHES Referred to in the Introduction to Paleochora. The eastern, Ferry-boat quay shore is boulderous for the first 100m or so and then breaks into a long, large pebble and shingle foreshore which curves off into the distance but is littered with plastic sheeting. There is a beach shower.

The extensive, sandy, western beach has showers, which must be a great joy to the tent dwellers, and is edged by a thick, elongated grove of trees. The foreshore is

sufficiently large to be able to ignore the 'undressed' element.
Evenhandedly there are olive-oil factories adjacent to each beach.

BICYCLE, SCOOTER & CAR HIRE 'Rent-a-Bike' run by Giorgos.

BOOKSELLER Yes

BREAD SHOPS Two bakers clustered one or two streets back from the eastern seafront.

BUSES There is a ticket office in the side lane off the High St, alongside the Bus stop. This lane leads down to the Ferry-boat quay and the office is on the right, prior to the *Pelican Taverna.*

Bus timetable
The bus timetable is screwed to the wall of a convenient taverna on the same side as the ticket office.
Paleochora to Chania
Daily   0700, 1200, 1330, 1530, 1730 hrs.
Fare 360 drs.

CINEMA There is a daily, open-air performance in the summer months. No need to give directions as signboards are displayed on the pavements and most of the village expatriates appear to troop off to watch.

COMMERCIAL SHOPPING AREA None, as would be expected in a village of this size, but the wide diversity of tourists has ensured that there are sufficient shops and general stores. Shops keep the usual hours.

DISCO Yes. On the western beach backshore, past the Post Office, is the **Studio Music Club.**

FERRY-BOATS The Paleochora, Souyia, and Ag. Roumeli passenger boat connection is less reliably scheduled, but as we divined it, the following is a guide. Our suspicious attitude is due to the fact that on various occasions we have been thwarted in our plans by the non-appearance of the boat, but there you go. The timetable is posted up on the 'Bus ticket office Taverna' BUT differs from the official NTOG handout. So what's new!
Gavdos (Gavdhos) island
The passenger boats also connect with the island of Gavdos some 50 km south of the 'mainland' and a four hour journey. Gavdos has some simple rooms and shelters as well as about twenty or so inhabitants, but it is back to the 'roots' as it were. For further information in respect of this route *See* **Travel Agents**. Those wishing to get away from it all certainly should consider this as a most attractive option.

Ferry-boat timetable
Paleochora to Souyia & Ag. Roumeli
Daily: 0900* hrs.
Return journey
Daily: 1600* hrs.
One-way fare 265 drs.
* *Note the NTOG leaflet stipulates outward 0830 hrs and return journey 1700 hrs.*
Paleochora to Gavdos island
Monday, Thursday   0800 hrs.
Return journey
Monday, Thursday   1600 hrs.

OTE Perhaps surprisingly, there is one.

PETROL Yes.

POST OFFICE Across from the backshore of the western beach.

POLICE Both Town and Port.

TRAVEL AGENTS *See* **Banks. Brown's** (sic) is an enterprising outfit running organised trips to **Gavdos island** *–See Greece as it was 100 years ago*. Details of these four day jaunts, which include accommodation in simple homes, are posted on a board on the eastern (Ferry-boat quay) seafront. Potential clients are urged to make advance bookings as the number of rooms is strictly limited.

TOILETS A recently constructed, flat-roofed building on the eastern shore Esplanade, a few blocks down from the *Pelican Taverna*, but for use only in dire emergencies as it is usually left in an 'eye-watering' state.

SOUYIA (Sougia, Soughia) Seaside village. Tel. prefix 0823.
Not so isolated as, say, Loutro with a twice daily bus service to and from Chania at the height of the summer. Souyia is also linked with the Ag. Roumeli to Paleochora ferry-boat connection and the energetic can cliff scramble from either location. The modernish seaside hamlet, with a pebbly but clean beach has sufficient, inexpensive accommodation and cafe-bar/tavernas to ensure its growing popularity.
   The only classified accommodation is the *Pension Pikilassos* (Class B, tel. 51242). For details of the ferry-boats *See* **Ag. Roumeli** and **Paleochora**.

Loutra, from the cliff path walk

Knossos Royal Way

Paleochora ferry-boat – rarely seen when wanted!

FIRST IMPRESSIONS
An English market town.

VITAL STATISTICS
Tel. prefix 0822

GENERAL
This small, thriving town radiates out from a busy little square which is above, and some 200m from the seafront. The wide dirt track, connecting the two, is routed around the Castle walls, through cultivated fields, past the occasional house before spilling on to a small fishing boat quay square. To the right (*fsw*) is a road edging the long, seafront which faces up the very large Bay (or Gulf) of Kissamos.

Some years ago it was true to say that "there is very little backshore development...", but now there must be reservations and as Anne points out, changes and developments have and are happening. It might be true to say that if each case is inspected individually it would not give cause for alarm or despondency but when looked at as a whole it is our opinion that Kastelli is poised for 'one giant step...', or more correctly is on the brink of a rapid tourist build up. Certainly whereas the beach backshore was simply and only edged by cultivated small holdings, there are now some six places with **Rooms** as well as a couple of restaurants.

If tourism does take off much of the credit (!) will be due to the locals' enthusiasm, and efforts. Naturally the Germans are in the vanguard and many of the accommodation and taverna signs are in that language.

ARRIVAL BY BUS
These pull up on the west side of the Main Square.

ARRIVAL BY FERRY
The ambitious quay, at which ferry-boats dock from the Peloponnese, is about 2½ km westwards out of town. The pier has a Customs office and a bar. The curving walk round to Kastelli can prove to be uncomfortably hot at the height of a summer's day. On the ambit from the pier, after about 1 km, there is a little chapel set into a cave followed by a picturesque, caique fishing boat anchorage, a huddle of houses, a couple of tavernas and a small cove with pleasant swimming. Keep left where the road forks.

THE ACCOMMODATION & EATING OUT
The Accommodation There has been a marked increase in the availability of beds with a number of new **Rooms**, pensions and hotels and while there are less tourists than rooms, owners will 'negotiate'!

Castelli (Castle, Kastron) Hotel (Class C) Plateia Kastelliou   Tel. 22140
Directions: On the right (east) of the Main Square(*Fsw*). Incorporated with the hotel is a large restaurant (*See* **The Eating Out**).

The hotel is clean, very convenient and reasonably priced. A single room en suite costs 1400 drs, a double with shared bathroom 1600 drs, whilst an en suite double costs 1900 drs. Outside the height of season the owner offers a double room for about 1500 drs. Breakfast may be mandatory in the months of July – September and costs 180 drs per person.

The Galini Beach Hotel
Directions: Signposted to the right, from the main Chania approach road, and situated on the seafront at the eastern end of the beach.

The Hotel Morpheus
The hotel, just off the Chania road, close by the centre of the town, is closed down for the foreeable future. The owner, Mr. Papadakis, has, in the meantime, opened up the *Hotel Kissamos* but he is still toying with the idea of reopening the *Morpheus*. On the other hand the local tourist officer is of the opinion that there is too much work required to bring the place up to any standard!

Restaurant/Pension
Directions: From the seaward, or north end of the Main Square, Plateia Kastelliou, the road to the fishing boat quay jinks left, then right and straightens out past the remains of the Castle. Halfway down to the waterfront, on the left, is the restaurant and rooms.

Hotel Kissamos (Class C)   Tel. 22086
Directions: 100m beyond Plateia Kastelliou, on the principal road west out of town, in the direction of Falasarna.

This hotel has, apparently, been built gradually, one floor at a time, over the past few years and the good news is that the top floor is now complete. The hotel is very modern, comfortable, spotlessly clean and quieter than the usual square-side hotels, despite the building procedure. The proprietor is pleasant, helpful, friendly and serves good wine from the barrel. All rooms are en suite and most have balconies, with singles from 1600 drs and doubles 2000 drs rising, respectively, to 2000 drs and 2500 drs (16th June – 15th Oct). Anne reports that the price quoted for a double in high season was 2812 drs, despite the official rate of 2500 drs (!), but she managed to rent a double room as a single for only 1000 drs, which included a phone, towel and hot water.

One of the six places with accommodation on the seafront is the very smart, new:
Manty   Tel. 22830
Directions: As above.
Double bed furnished apartments cost about 3000 drs per day.

Another is the:
Elena Beach Hotel (Class B)   Tel. 23300
Directions: On the backshore of the beach.
New with en suite double rooms and breakfast costing 2800 drs.

A further waterfront location is the restaurant at the bottom of the 'Town-to-Beach' track, immediately on the right(*Fsw*). Double rooms sharing the bathroom cost 1400 drs. There is a similar establishment on the left.

The best 'bargain basement' accommodation must be:
Rooms Antonia   Tel. 22073
Directions: At the very west/left-hand end (*Fsw*)of the fishing-boat quay square, in fact the last house and in a splendid location.

Owned and run by the delightful Mrs. Antonia Douganatsi who offers very pleasing, clean double rooms for 1000 drs sharing the bathroom but with a washbasin fitted in each room. Admittedly Antonia confides that when her daughter marries she might want all the house for private use, in which case the rooms would no longer be available. But nuptials, as mother puts it, may be one, three or seven years away, who knows? Well exactly!

Apartments Chryssani   Tel. 23390
Directions: Situated about 2 km out of Kastelli, overlooking a fishing boat anchorage.

   This is a new apartment complex run by Dimitris Chryssani, who is also involved in the Ferry-boat ticket office (**E. Xyrouhakis**). The suites are 'equipped' with a full bathroom, sitting room, kitchen complete with fridge, sea-view balconies and telephone. There are also entertainment rooms and a children's playground all of which has to be paid for with a cost of 3000/4000 drs per night rising to 4000/5000 drs (1st July – 30th Sept). Golly gosh!

The Eating Out Not a lot. Endaxi (OK), there are some but the pace of their expansion is not as fast as the abundance of accommodation – yet!
The Castelli Restaurant
Located in the ground floor of the *Hotel Castelli* but closed for 1986, as was the *Morpheus*.
Souvlaki/Grill Snackbar
Directions: New and across the High St from the Tourist office, which is off the western end of the Main Sq. Due to Anne once again being 'treated', this time by 'Mr. Tourist Office', we are unable to report the prices.

There are several breakfast cafes around the Main Sq and the:
Cafeteria
Directions: Across the High St from the Church, at the eastern end of town.
   Coffee here cost 70 drs (but once Anne again enjoyed a 'freebie', paid for this time by the owner).
   On the way down to the waterfront and on the left, after the Castle, is the *Restaurant/Pension* and two once sleepy tavernas on the fishing boat quay, which have now been spruced up.
   The *Galini Beach Hotel*, at the eastern end of the beach, serves meals.
   The tavernas at the caique harbour, to the west of Kastelli, are a bit distant from the town for a quick snack but will suffice very well for diners who wish to work up an appetite and then walk off the meal on the way back.

THE A TO Z OF USEFUL INFORMATION
AIRLINE OFFICE On the Chania road into town.

BANKS
Commercial Bank of Greece The Chania side of the High Street, on the right. They cash Eurocheques, backed by a card, as well as travellers cheques.
National Bank Further down, on the left-hand side of the road. They accept major credit cards and change travellers' cheques.

BEACH As described in the Introduction to Kastelli.

BICYCLE & SCOOTER HIRE
Rent from Anthony   Tel. 22909
Anthony, a smiling, bearded 35 year old Greek, speaking adequate English, and an old aquaintance, hires out a variety of two-wheeled velopeds. His shop is on the left up the little side street opposite the National Bank. A Vespa costs 4500 drs for three days and a larger engined one works out at 6000 drs for the same period.

BREAD SHOPS Rather unusually there is almost a surfeit of bread shops, as well as a baker with ovens in the shop front, at the western end of the High St.

BUSES The buses park upon the Main Square, on the west side of which is the ticket office into which is incorporated a small snackbar.

Bus timetables

Anne's notes in respect of the bus schedules reveal an initial raw fury followed by a refined, coded plea for the Greeks to get their act together. "Aargh – why bother?" Okay....logically, these should match the times for the same buses as handed out in Chania. Most are similarly listed but some are not! There you go.

Kastelli to Chania

Daily	0600, 0700, 0730, 0800, 0830, 0930, 1030, 1130, 1230, 1400, 1530, 1615, 1800, 1900 hrs.
Sunday/holidays	0730, 0930, 1015, 1100, 1230, 1400, 1530, 1700, 1800, 1900 hrs.

Return journey

Daily	0545, 0715, 0830, 1000, 1100, 1200, 1300, 1430, 1530, 1630, 1730, 1830, 2000 hrs.
Sunday/holidays	0730, 0830, 0930, 1100, 1200, 1400, 1530, 1700, 1830, 2000 hrs.

Kastelli to Falasarna

Return journey

Daily	1100 hrs.

Kastelli to Sfinari

Daily	1400 hrs.

Return journey

Daily	0700 hrs. (next day).

Kastelli 'round trip' to Samaria Gorge & back

Summer months only

Daily	0500 hrs.

The return bus departs from **Chania Sfakion** at 1630 hrs.
Incidentally, this information was validated by the bus driver whose indicator board simply says Kastelli (sic). Perhaps he drives round the houses.

Note that Athens to Githion buses run as follows:

Athens to Githion (M), 100 Kifissou St   Tel. 5124913

Daily	0730, 1030, 1345, 1700 hrs.

Return journey

Daily	0800, 1145, 1230, 1530, 1730 hrs.

One-way fare 1200 drs; duration 6½ hrs.

COMMERCIAL SHOPPING AREA None, but the High St contains most requirements including a bridal dress shop! The usual opening hours.

FERRY-BOATS They dock at the Ferry-boat quay as described in the Introduction. Schedules are even regarded by the Greeks as highly unreliable, so they must be! Locals talk of at least two hours leeway either side of the listed/quoted arrival and departure times. The major problem is that one of the ferry-boats motors all the way round from Piraeus via various Peloponnese mainland ports of call as well as the islands of Kithira (Kythira) and Antikithira.

Ferry-boat timetables

Arrivals (from Githion (M))	Day	Arrival time
	Tuesday	0530 hrs*
	Friday	0530 hrs*
Departures		
	Tuesday	0800 hrs*
	Friday	0800 hrs*

* One-way fare from Githion 1420 drs; duration 6 hrs.

In addition I have a notion that the **CF Ionian** departs from Piraeus on Monday and Thursday at 0900 hrs calling at:
Kiparissi* (M), Gerakos* (M), Monemvasia (M), Neapolis (M), Elafonisos Island*, Ag Pelagia (Kithira island), Githion (M), Kapsali (Kithira Island) and Antikithira island – but....?
* Mondays only.

FERRY-BOAT TICKET OFFICES
E. Xyrouhakis, Plateia Kastelliou   Tel. 22655
Situated on the west side of the Main Sq, in the same block as the Bus office. The Githion (Peloponnese) agents are Th. Rozakis, Peloponnese. Tel. 0733 22207.

LAUNDRY At the western end of the High St.

MEDICAL CARE
Chemists & Pharmacies One sandwiched in between the Bus and Ferry-boat offices as well as several others scattered about.

OTE On the right of the main Chania road, east of the Main Sq.

PETROL Two stations on the Chania road.

PLACES OF INTEREST These include the Castle, which was built in the 16th century, and a Museum, sited in the Church and clock-tower block on the Main Square (that neither Anne nor I have visited). There is also a 'static exhibit' in the shape of a stranded tanker in the bay, between the town and Ferry-boat quay.

POST OFFICE on the left-hand side of the main Chania road, east out of the town.

POLICE Well more a Customs house sited, rather dispiritedly, on the left-hand side of the fishing boat quay.

SPORTS FACILITIES Not a lot, but why not try your hand at the Greek equivalent of snooker in the two-table hall, just beyond the Commercial Bank? Thinking about it, the game is probably 'pool' – another American corruption of a worthy, 'why not leave it alone', British game. Incidentally, what was wrong with rounders?

TAXIS Rank up on the High Street side of the Plateia Kastelliou Church.

TRAVEL AGENTS
General Toyrist (sic) Agency/Dictynna Travel   Tel. 22434
Directions: The office is on the High St, just off the western end of the Main Square.
    This business opened its doors in 1986 and is symptomatic of the increasing ground swell of tourism that is rippling towards the west of the island. The very helpful proprietor, Stefanos Rimantonakis, who speaks good English, is assisted by his 'American speaking' daughter, "when I can afford to pay her". They have connections with **Sunny Tours** of Chania. (*See* **Travel Agents, A to Z, Chania,** CHAPTER 14). Although a travel agency, they also act as an unofficial information office and gladly supply details of accommodation, local events and timetables. In fact they are so helpful and enthusiastic that you would think they had shares in their various recommendations. Perhaps they have...? Incidentally, they handle '*Airville*' and....*Tickets*' (sic).

ROUTE FIFTEEN
To Falasarna (13 km) The road proceeds west from Kastelli through flat scrubbly countryside planted with olive groves, to **Ag. Georgios**, then commences to climb in a southerly direction. At **Platanos** village, which has two petrol stations, fork left entering the village and then turn right for Falasarna. There are extensive

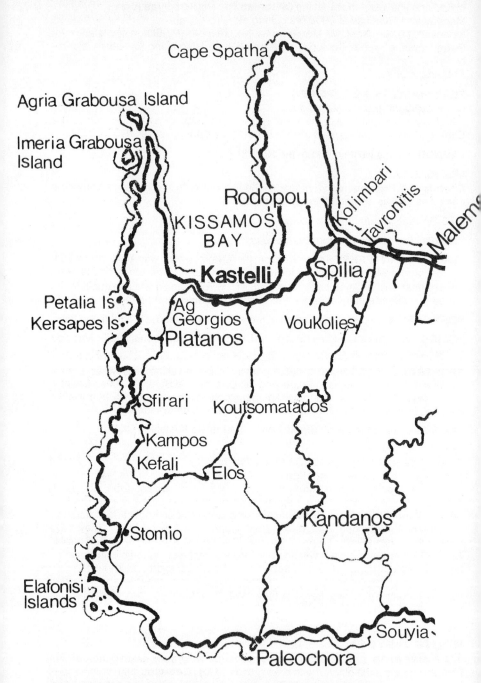

Illustration 18 Crete centred on Kastelli

roadworks underway and the road becomes a dirt track followed by an asphalted stretch again when passing a taverna in **Kavousi**, after which the route leads through vines to a rise. From here is a most impressive view of the long narrow plain way down below, edged by a very yellow beach and the sea, in which are dropped the small, low islands or rocky outcrops of Petalia, to the north, and Koursapes, to the south.

The sounds of sheep and goat bells drift across the countryside as do the familiar smells of Greece – wild thyme, broom and oleander. Access to the beach is gained from a flattened area to the side of the main dirt track which continues to work it's way to the north of the plain and the Minoan ruins of Falasarna, some 3 km further on. From the narrow plateau, about 30m directly above the wide expanse of sand and blue, blue sea, a steep goat track weaves down through the huge, litter-covered, fallen rocks, to the backshore. The plain, now above, was probably once the sea bottom which explains the 'aggregate' look to the rocks.

Incidentally, the Falasarna tomato festival is a movable feast, usually held in July, but of course only celebrated when the tomatoes are ripe and harvested.

Unfortunately on closer inspection it becomes apparent that the beach is littered with blobs of tar, so great care is needed when laying down clothes or a beach towel.

To the north and to the west or left of the top of the peninsula, beneath the island of Agria Grabousa, is the island of Imeri Grabousa. This was once an almost impregnable pirates' lair, the raiders using an abandoned Venetian fort as their base.

On the way back to Kastelli, a TV aerial clamped to the side of a small chapel, on the edge of Kavousi village, seems rather out of place. It may well be the village community 'TV mast'.

ROUTE SIXTEEN
To Stomio Bay & Elafonisi islets and return via Elos (98 km).

Take ROUTE FIFTEEN to Platanos village where fork left for Sfinari along a flower-bush lined, surfaced road, despite most maps still detailing it as unpaved. The route is built on the mountain side with breathtaking views down to the sea, overlooking deserted beaches and rocky outcrops before dropping down to:

SFINARI (about 22 km from Kastelli). The village has several tavernas and **Rooms** which competition has prompted to develop a rather interesting form of 'product discounting'. One establishment offers 'Free Camping', another free boat trips and yet another 'Free coffee'!

A narrow dirt track leads down to the seafront from the main village where is a taverna and a sign to (yet another) 'Free Camping'. The lovely lady who runs the place is most informative and will describe the route on to Stomio as well as narrate the scenes in Sfinari when the first motor car arrived, in 1964, on the then new road. "Great excitement, we were all in the streets waving", she exclaimed whilst taking off her apron and flapping it about as a demonstration. This taverna used to be a fish weighing station for boats from North Africa... but at that point Anne advises her Greek began to overheat a little!

Unfortunately Sfinari lacks a beach but does possess shallow blue, blue water and flat rocks with fishing boats bobbing about in the inlets. However....the taverna-lady explained that the villagers realise (that the lack of a beach) "....is a bad thing for tourism", so they are setting about building their own beach, and the digger is now in situ. Oh dear me! Sfinari is most definitely a find, a place with a 'miles from anywhere' ambience and Anne's notes reveal that if it was not for this '------ guide' she would have stayed there for weeks and weeks and ....

From Sfinari the road continues to be asphalted for about a further 2 km, passing down a beautiful, green and flowering valley then over a bridge, where the surface ceases to be asphalted, continuing on to climb the other side of the valley.

KAMPOS (about 43 km from Kastelli). Many *Rooms*.

Despite the state of the road between **Amygdalokefali** and Kefali being the worst on this route, the views along the whole of this stretch are dangerously stunning and attractive, especially when one should be concentrating on driving. The coastline is generally similar to that at Falasarna (*See* ROUTE FIFTEEN).

At Kefali a left-hand turning leads down to **Vathi**, then to **Stomio** and on to the coast and the:

Chrysoskalitissa Nunnery (53 km from Kastelli). The priory is supposed to have a golden stair-tread on one of its ninety odd steps which can only be seen by those who have not committed a sin. I don't suppose it has been found by many. There is a rather inaccessible beach with beach bars down below the Nunnery. But as it is possible to carry on to a 'find' why not proceed to:

ELAFONISI BEACH (57 km from Kastelli). There are *Rooms* about a kilometre prior to reaching Elafonisi.

Offshore is the stunning:

ELAFONISI ISLET. A paradise of beach on beach on beach reached by wading across the shallow blue-lagoon waters. Definitely one for the 'off the beaten track' travellers.

To save making the return journey back along the outward road, it is feasible to turn right at Kefali along the unmade dusty road to:

ELOS (19 km from Kastelli) A very pretty village which is the centre of the local chestnut industry and where a chestnut festival is held every year, on the third Sunday of October. There is a petrol station, bakery, shop, and, would you believe, a taverna or two?

The road descends through massed chestnuts and deciduous trees set in the heather-clad hills and olive trees with black nets draped around them on the ground.

Halfway to Koutsomatades, a poorly surfaced track advances off to the right passing through **Strovles**, where keep straight on, to the main Kandanos – Paleochora road (*See* ROUTE FOURTEEN).

Back on the Elos road beyond a large number of domed piles of smoking timber set down by the local charcoal burner, the road passes through:

KOUTSOMATADES (about 14 km from Kastelli) In this village a taverna proclaims its presence with a sign written in English – such a change from the more ubiquitous German.

Beyond Koutsomatades the poorly surfaced road plunges through a tunnel in the gaunt mountains to emerge and run along the side of a deep gorge, sensibly edged with a crash barrier. There are several *Rooms* along this part of the route.

About ½ km prior to Topolia, on the left, is a chapel built into the mouth of a cave, the Ag. Sophia cave, which has been inhabited since the Neolithic period.

TOPOLIA (9 km from Kastelli) A very beautiful mountain village with a narrow, tight turn in the thoroughfare.

The road, now country lane in nature, becomes narrow and descends through **Voulgarou**, with a petrol station and large church, to dusty **Potamida**, where there is a post box and the remains of the old road. The valley road becomes bumpy and runs alongside a river-bed through groves of oranges and lemons to the village of **Kaloudiana** after which is the junction with the main Chania-Kastelli road.

ROUTE SEVENTEEN
To Polyrrinia (8 km) More a good walk (if you must) than a drive, from the petrol station on the Chania side of Kastelli, up into the lower mountain slopes on which is laid the very attractive village of:

POLYRRINIA Although archaeologists will be interested in the few visible remains of the ancient site of Polyrrinia, some twenty minutes' climb on from the village, the narrow, steep lanes that clamber through the dwellings of the village are probably of more interest to the average traveller. Added to which, there is a superbly situated, vine trellised taverna from which to enjoy the excellent views out over Kastelli and the Gulf of Kissamos.

Cleaning the beach or walking the donkey?

Romeo, Romeo, where art thou.....?

16 AGIA GALINI (Ayia Galini) *
Once a fishing harbour village – now...

FIRST IMPRESSIONS
Look alike for a Cornish fishing village; masses of villa tourists.

VITAL STATISTICS
Tel. prefix 0832

GENERAL
I was once able to write:
> A smaller, prettier 'look-alike' to Ag. Nikolaos. It is often bemoaned by travel writers that the simple, innocent, fishing villages have all but disappeared, in the 1980s, under a welter of package tourists, and their attendant hotels, pensions, restaurants, tavernas and bars. This may be undeniable, but the manner of the metamorphosis here has been such that Ag. Galini has uniquely retained much of its charm and beauty.....Ag. Galini has managed to evoke an intimate and somewhat refined air in contrast to many other resorts where 'chips with everything' and funny hats are prevelant.

Well, yes. The years of constant development and exploitation have not been kind to Ag. Galini. The elitism that I referred to in the previous edition has squeezed out any residual Cretan characteristics, thoroughly desanitising the place of the unique, uncapturable 'essence of Greece' - just as one writes of a Hilton Hotel, that a guest could be anywhere in the world, well almost. And all this without even a presentable beach!

The village is sandwiched in a narrow defile. This has resulted in most development having to be either alteration of existing buildings or their replacement by new structures which are now stacked up along the one and only road in (or out). Very little of the original, old-world, fishing village charm of Ag. Galini has been retained. There are no 'Places of Interest' to view, not even a Venetian or Turkish fountain, anywhere. No, I forgot, on the path round to the beach there are some caves, now sealed off, which were used by the Germans during the Second World War as machine gun nests. Incidentally I'm not sure how anyone would find it possible to declare war anywhere on Crete during the summer months. Would anyone take it seriously and how could a tank carrier make its way through the droves of tour buses?

The main road winds steeply, descending the hillside and the defile around which the village is layered, spilling out on to the very large, Main Harbour Square. In the middle of this concrete plateia are railings surrounding a small fountain, which fountain is not a Venetian, or even a Turkish relic, more a modern and rather pathetic dribble.

The village rises up from the north side of the Square with three side-by-side streets leading off in a north-south direction. The left-hand street (*Sbo*) is Odhos El Venizelou, the High St, to the right and next to which is 'Petrol Pump' Street and next along, the steps to Odhos Vas. Ionnis. The left and right flank of the Main Square are edged by trees, the only blot on the visual effect being a fuel tank, to the right (*Sbo*), raised on stilts for fuelling fishing boats. Facing seawards the west side of the harbour is protected by a massive, curving seawall/breakwater cum quay that angles off from the edge of the Square.

ARRIVAL BY BUS
The buses used to informally park up on the Harbour edging Square, but no longer. The Bus Square is now set down on the outskirts of the 'core of the village', alongside

THE ACCOMMODATION & EATING OUT

The Accommodation The apartments, hotels, pensions and houses line the road down to the Harbour-Quay Square. I do not think I have seen as much accommodation in any one village, but most of the beds are block-booked by tourist firms. The charges made by hotels in Ag. Galini are very sensitive to tourist fluctuations and a shortage of visitors, results in prices plummeting, even in the height of season. *Rooms* are not much cheaper than the less expensive hotels.

Hotel Kydon (Class E) El Venizelou   Tel. 91228
Directions: On the north, far side of the Bus station Square, on the left of the High St, Odhos El Venizelou, *(Sbo)*.
   Mid season double rooms sharing the bathroom can fall as low as 800 drs, rising to 1150 drs in the high season.

Hotel Ikaros (Class D) 23, 4 Martyron   Tel. 91270
Directions: Directly behind the Bus station.
   The small number of buses that arrive and depart do not cause an unsociable amount of noise. In any case the first bus start-up and off is as late as 0645 hrs! This is a nice, clean hotel with a pleasant owner and, possibly, a resident priest! In the high season, double rooms, with en suite bathrooms, cost 1200 drs.

Other reasonably priced hotels on the three parallel streets, (including the High St, Odhos Venizelou), and the road that connects them laterally, include:

The Pantheon (Class E) Kountouriotou   Tel. 91293
Directions: As above.
   Very clean double rooms with bathrooms en suite costing 1200 drs but package holiday booked. (*Sun-Med* in 1986).

Aktaeon Hotel (Class E) 4 Kountouriotou   Tel. 91208
Directions: As above.
   Run by a very pleasant landlady but she does adjust the official rates in an upwards direction by some 100/200 drs per night! Double rooms sharing a bathroom cost 1100 drs and en suite 1200 drs.

In Bizaniou St are located the *Hotel Cristoe* (Class C – tel 91229), *Hotel Chariklia* (Class D – tel 91257) and the *Hotel Miramare* (Class C – tel 91221).
   On Odhos Vas. Ionnis is the:

Hotel Livyi   Tel. 91216
Directions: As above.
   Double rooms en suite start off at 1000 drs.

On the edge of the village, at the top of the hill, beside the main road in (or out depending on which way one is going) and with magnificent views over the sea, are the:

Hotel Areti (Class D)   Tel. 91250
Directions: As above.
   All rooms have en suite bathrooms. Single rooms start off at 850 drs and doubles 1150 drs rising to 950 drs and 1450 drs (1st June - 31st Oct).
and the:
Hotel Minos (Class D)   Tel. 91292
Directions: As above.
   A single room en suite costs 1000 drs and a double room with bathroom from 1200 drs.

212

Hotel Soulia (Class C) El Venizelou   Tel. 91272
Directions: Overlooks the Harbour Square.
A double room en suite costs 1500 drs.

Camping Ag. Galini.
Directions: The site is some 2 km east along the coast and is signed with a decrepit board from the beach. (*See* **Beaches, A to Z**).
Charges per person are 200 drs and 200 drs for a tent.

The Eating Out

The majority of restaurants squat on the town side of the Harbour-side Square or line both sides of the pedestrian way - Vas Ionnis. This is the third street from the left (including the High St) off the north of the Main Sq. (*Sbo*), approached up a flight of steps. One or two eateries are scattered down the top, right-hand side of the second street from the left (*Sea still behind one*), which I have nicknamed 'Petrol Pump' St as there are few if any, road name signs and (surprise, surprise) there is a petrol pump at the top end. Alongside the petrol pump are two cheese pie/pita bread/souvlaki bars.

THE A TO Z OF USEFUL INFORMATION

BANKS There is only a **National Bank** change office, which is supplemented by many other unofficial facilities, the most enterprising of which must be the:
Everything Shop
Directions: At the top of Odhos Vas Ionnis.
   The owner will change anything including cash, cheques and Eurocheques. This enterprising gentleman also appears under Commercial Shopping Area and the OTE. The doors are open 0800 - 2300, apart from a siesta, including weekends.

BEACHES It is necessary to walk round the eastern or bottom edge of the Harbour Square, past the caique slipway and a sign proclaiming that *It Is Forbidden The Nudism And The Camping*.
   The concrete and rock path clings to a cliff-edge, composed of 'replica aggregate', which appears, every so often, to fall off in great chunks. The first, very small bay is boulderous (see what I mean?) with a large pebble shore usually edged during the day by naked sunbathers lying in lines like smoking kippers. ('And how did he pass away my dear?' 'Oh, quickly thank you..... beneath tons of Cretan rock, but died happy, sunbathing, face-up reading the Mail on Sunday'.) Sea urchins show up menacingly on some of the underwater rocks.
   Swinging round to the next, long, rambling and ramshackle bay, the path edges past some old wartime machine-gun nests (which Anne, quite unnecessarily, noted she felt was the most interesting and attractive thing in Ag. Galini! Well, she was reading *The Cretan Runner* at the time). The narrow beach is made up of slate-grey shingle mixed with large, rounded stones and is infested with flies, whilst the sea edge is fine pebbles and sand. Close by the cliff are two beach discos, three beach bars (one of which serves hamburgers), three tavernas and the skeletal outline of an unfinished, prestressed concrete building (that is, still unfinished in 1986). Sunbathers tend to pile up the pebbles in semicircular walls to form sun-traps/wind breaks. The 'beach' possesses the delights of sunbeds, pedaloes, windsurfers and, possibly, gigolos for hire!
   To the east, towards the far end of the bay, a sign indicates the 200m or so track up to *Camping Ag. Galini*. It does not entice one to enquire!
   To make up for the lack of any self respecting beach, 'sea-taxis' ply for hire, ferrying clients to more far-flung alternatives. Certainly there are a series of long bays curving all the way round to Kokkinos Pyrgos. Scenically the distant view is magnificent with the Gulf of Messara edged by the eastern landmass.

BICYCLE, SCOOTER & CAR HIRE Naturally.

BOOKSELLERS There is a book shop on Odhos Vas. Ionnis selling popular English books and newspapers as well as guides and maps.

BREAD SHOPS One on the High St, on the way out of the village, in the area of the Post Office, set in a modern block.

BUSES As discussed in the introductory paragraphs, the Bus office and terminus is on the Square to the side of the High St.

Bus timetables
The times are listed on a signboard outside the office.
Ag. Galini to Rethymnon (& Plakias)
Daily	0645, 0845, 1030, 1200, 1400, 1430, 1600, 1930 hrs.
Saturday, Sunday & holidays	1200, 1500, 1930 hrs.
Return journey	
Daily	0530, 0645, 0900, 1030, 1330, 1445 hrs.
Saturday, Sunday & holidays	0645, 0900, 1030, 1330, 1645 hrs.

Ag. Galini to Iraklion
Daily	0800, 0930, 1030, 1215, 1315, 1500, 1630, 1830, 2000 hrs.
Sunday/holidays	0800, 1030, 1230, 1500, 1730, 1930 hrs.

Note: To get to Matala it is necessary to take the Iraklion bus and change at Phaestos.

Ag. Galini to Chora Sfakion
Daily	0830 hrs.
Return journey	
Daily	1600 hrs.

COMMERCIAL SHOPPING AREA None, which is not surprising in a village of this size, but a number of scattered shops serve most needs and requirements. The most zealous must be the:

Everything Shop
Directions: Situated at the top of Odhos Vas. Ionnis.
Open daily including Sundays, 0800 - 2300 hrs, except for the afternoon siesta.

Apart from this gentleman, the village's opening hours are the usual.

DISCO/COCKTAIL BARS Yes. 'Petrol Pump' St boasts a cocktail bar and the beach sports two discos, which at least keeps the thumping, earsplitting sounds to a muffled and distant echo of sound. The cliff walk round to the beach is illuminated at night, possibly to save losing, with any sort of regularity, the odd client here and there!

OTE From the Bus Square bear left at the top left-hand corner (*Sbo*), keep left past the first turning off to the right, along and to the top of Odhos 4 Martyron. Open weekdays 0730 - 1510 hrs.
The 'Everything Shop' on Odhos Vas. Ionnis (mentioned before) has a metered telephone which is in constant use.

PETROL In the street parallel to the High St, Odhos El Venizelou, at the top end and on the left (*Sbo*).

POST OFFICE On the High St.

POLICE An office on the west of the Harbour Square, up a small flight of steps.

TAXIS When available they rank beneath the spreading trees on the left of the Harbour Square (*Sbo*).

TRAVEL AGENTS Two at the top of Odhos Vas. Ionnis, offering any number of 'goodies'.

TOILETS A modern block, up a flight of steps that also leads to the curving, rather massive seawall, just down from the Police station.

Modern they may be but the facilities are very primitive and smelly. The gentlemens is open air with the urinals fixed at a toe stretching height whilst the ladies', only just separated from the men's, are 'squatties'.

ROUTE EIGHTEEN
To Lendas via Phaestos, Matala and Gortyna (a minimum of 59 km) After rounding the mountains to the east of Ag. Galini, the very large Messara Plain unfolds below. The nearside of the landscape looks to all intents as if it is a flood plain, an illusion created by the massed, shiny plastic greenhouses glinting in the sunlight. Close inspection reveals an appallingly squalid situation with the greenhouses and their surrounds resembling a plastic shanty town. The pity is that the authorities do not insist that the farmers clear up the old, windblown, shredded, dirty brown sheets of plastic that flap in the breeze and lay scattered over the countryside.

KOKKINOS PYRGOS (approx. 9 km from Ag. Galini) Tel. prefix 0892. This sprawling village epitomises the worst of the Messara Plain, being simply awful. The dirty, plastic sheeting waves about in the slightest wind, from one end of the road that fringes the waterfront to the other. A small caique mole divides the seafront into shingly sand to the right (*Fsw*), with a couple of anchorages, and rocks to the left.

There are Pensions, ***Rooms*** and at least three hotels including the *Brothers*, *Libyian Sea* and *El Greco* as well as a few tavernas.

Yes, well. My notes simply keep repeating plastic, plastic, plastic... Wherever the glance falls, modern, prestressed concrete buildings are interspaced with plastic greenhouses, a few threadbare trees, some bamboos and the odd donkey (also threadbare).

At the junction of Kokkinos Pyrgos and the main road, there is a Greek Air Force base, and beyond, mountain-to-mountain olive groves leading to:

TIMBAKI (approx. 12 km from Ag. Galini) Tel. prefix 0892. An industrial town with no concessions whatsoever to tourism (and why not?) apart from a few hotels, including the *Ag. Georgios* (Class C – tel. 51678) and *Kriti* (Class E), as well as a pension. There is, as befits a place of this size, a bank and petrol station. The dusty sprawl is complemented by an Army camp and a concrete works.

From Timbaki the road plunges back into a countryside of plastic greenhouses and olives. Most of the peasants are donkey-borne (this phrase is acceptable as long as the typesetter gets it right!).

A turn off leads through a much prettier landscape with no plastic, to:

PHAESTOS (approx. 20 km from Ag. Galini) This well placed Minoan site, situated on a hillside overlooking part of the Messara Plain, was largely excavated by the Italians. Serious digging commenced in 1900 and has continued on and off to the present time. To the layman the ruins are confusing, there being little imaginative above ground reconstruction, as at Knossos, but this is a personal viewpoint. Archaeological purists regard Phaestos as classical restoration and Knossos as having experienced restorational rape. The excavations are open daily, 0800 - 1700 hrs and between 0800 - 1700 hrs on Sunday. It is possible to purchase detailed

Illustration 19   Crete centred on Agia Galini

guides from the staff attending the admission ticket booth, and entrance costs 150 drs.
The car and coach park 'sports' a few natives, dressed in Cretan costume, selling various goodies and begging. One of these touts offered Anne a job at his hotel, located in Kokkinos Pyrgos, which presumably explains why he was selling plums at the Phaestos excavations!
For a small treat and to get away from the stream of Phaestos excursion coaches, from the parking space outside Phaestos take the Matala road and then after some 200m, the first right-hand fork for the 3 km drive to:

Agia Triada A small Minoan site, now named after an adjacent Byzantine church, is believed to have been closely linked with Phaestos.

Before proceeding to Matala, a diversion can be made on the dusty, unmade roads to the agricultural village of:

KAMILARI (approx. 24 km from Ag. Galini) Apart from **Rooms** there is the unlikely:
Hotel Oasis (Class E)   Tel. 42217
All rooms share the bathrooms with singles starting off at 590 drs and a double room 900 drs. These charges rise to 620 drs and 960 drs (16th May – 30th June) and on to 645 drs and 1020 drs (1st July - 10th Oct).
There is also **Rent-A-Scooter**. Oh dear.

From the village a track makes off to the small settlement, by the sea, of:

KALAMAKI (approx. 27 km from Ag. Galini) Travellers should note that the signposting in this area is poor, so be warned and ask as often as possible, as even some of the locals are not sure!
It is surprising to find, in this almost deserted and out of the way location, a number of regularly spaced, unlovely concrete-box homes set in the surrounding sand dunes. The long, gently curving bay possesses a grey, sandy beach in which are embedded slightly angled slabs of sandstone.
There are a number of **Rooms** and self-contained apartments, including those at the:

Pension Phillarhomenie
Surprisingly chic and constructed in a facsimile Spanish-villa style. A double bedroom with en suite bathroom costs 1700 drs.

Overlooking the beach is the:

Cafe-bar Vangellis
Enquiries can be made here from the proprietor Vangellis about other accommodation but as he owns the *Pension Phillarhomenie* ...! He does supply details of other **Rooms** which he says start off at 900 drs a double sharing the bathroom.
The service at this bar makes most Greek establishments seem unseemingly hasty, but it is 50/50 self-service. The first '50' being if you do not get served, take the second '50' and go and get it yourself.
I have no doubt the style of service and charges are influenced by the proximity of:

MATALA (approx. 28 km from Ag. Galini) Tel. prefix 0892. The approach via Pitsidia village, which has many **Rooms**, passes, to one side of the road, an *Olympic Holidays campsite* and the *Hotel Matala Bay*, both at the edge of the village. The road spills out on to a large square with a building plonked down in the middle around which traffic must circulate. Parking is not allowed on this square and a large sign ensures visitors are aware of this 'local parish council' dictate. But there is a well signed, large, bumpy surfaced car park behind the beach which is free.

217

Matala's fame is based on a departed culture – the hippies and flower-power children of the 1960s – some whom lived in the old cliff-face caves overlooking the neat little bay. Now a 'tourist trap' for holiday-makers intent on experiencing this Mecca of the once present, vacationing, international set, which the Greeks exploit to the full. Only 'film extras' need apply for job vacancies. A present day, stereotype male holiday-maker (Matala man?) is a middle-aged 'youngster', his paunch ill-disguised by a necklace supported, rectangular bar dangling over a greying, hirsute chest, with long sideburns and a thinning head of hair frizzed and frantically combed to cover the balding patches. The older hedonists mix with the very young who still make the pilgrimage to this erstwhile 'hot spot'.

The comparatively small beach, set at the bottom of the indented bay, consists of fine, grey shingle and a smooth, rock foreshore. The high cliffs, forming the right or north horn of the bay, contain the serried caves which were certainly used by Christians in the fifth century. The northern cliffs are matched by a lower hillside to the left, into which the rest of the village is built. A Greek official now patrols the caves and insists that 'bottomless' sunbathers dress. Oh yes, unless I forget, it is possible to hire pedaloes and sunbeds on the beach.

The Accommodation
Matala Sun
Directions: On the entrance to the village.
A double room en suite costs 2400 drs in the high season.

Pension Romantika (Class E)   Tel. 43257
Directions: Next on the right to the *Matala Sun*.
The clean and pleasant single and double rooms have en suite bathrooms. Singles start off at 900 drs and doubles 1200 drs rising to, respectively, 1000 drs and 1400 drs (1st July – 30th Sept). The owners have the high season charges for a double room listed at 1575 drs, despite which they may cut the price to 1350 drs!

Matala Bay (Class C)   Tel. 22100
Offers both single and double en suite rooms with charges starting off at 1300 drs and 1800 drs rising to 1500 drs and 2000 drs (16th June – 30th Sept). Maybe the swimming pool pushes the listed double room price up to 2600 drs, including breakfast?

In the town centre itself are the:

Hotel Zafira (Class D)   Tel. 42366
Directions: As above.
All rooms have en suite bathrooms. A single room costs 1100 drs and a double room 1350 drs rising to 1350 drs and 1676 drs (16th May – 30th Sept). But rates quoted tend to be 200 drs in excess of those printed in the official handbook.

and the:

Hotel Bambou Sands (Class C)   Tel. 42370
Exactly the same prices as the *Zafira*.
There are numerous **Rooms**, all more expensive than most other Cretan holiday locations.

Matala Camping
Directions: Signposted from the end of the car park.
Perversely the campsite charges of 100 drs per head and 100 drs for a tent are inexpensive but the showers are cold.

Those tempted to camp out either in the main bay caves or on the beach should reconsider as the police are both vigilant and the fines very expensive. But bear in mind that **Rooms** in Pitsidia village, some 4 km back along the main road, are up to 400 drs less expensive per head.

BEACHES A number of desirable beaches exist within fairly easy reach either side of Matala. To the north, about 50 minutes walk, is 'Komos' Beach. The easiest route is to travel back along the main Pitsidia road and take a track off to the left, the second I think, from the outskirts of Matala. The beach is about 2 km in length and has its own 'summer months' community of squatters.

To the south of Matala is another beach. This 2 km hill walk leads past more caves in which reside the old-hand, long-stay squatters who the authorities appear to leave in peace.

BUSES The buses pull up on the Main Square and there is a timetable notice board on the square.

Bus timetables
Matala to Iraklion via Phaestos*
Daily   0700, 0930, 1215, 1430, 1700, 1830 hrs.
Sundays/holidays   1000, 1200, 1430, 1600 hrs.
*Travellers wishing to get to Ag. Galini should take the bus to Phaestos (except for the 0700 hrs bus) and change there to catch a connecting bus.

The building in the centre of the Main Square contains **Sports Rent-a-Car** (scooters, etc) and there is a notice on the wall announcing that *the doctor come to Matala every Friday 5-8pm.*

Alongside the Main Square is a covered market, but most supplies are that little bit more expensive than elsewhere on the island, and there is a baker, money exchange and book shop. All this and Zorba's Disco – *Every Night Under Open Air.* How can one resist the lure of this resort?

Personally, I think Matala has the discernable sound of money grabbing and the odour of 'rip off', but that is only my opinion.

To reach Lendas and Ag. Deka (for Gortyna), the choice revolves around returning to the main Timbaki to Ag. Deka road or taking the poorly signposted, rough, cross country route via Petrokefali and Platanos. It just depends on your sensibilities. Anne is of the opinion that the word sensibility should be replaced by common sense. Her notes may help waverers make up their minds. "Only an IDIOT would take the road via Petrokefali, Peri and Platanos by choice. I did it through duty but got totally lost and then accidentally went through Alithini as well as Pompia. The road between Platanos and Pompia is appallingly bad and Peri has many bumpy bi-ways which I would have preferred not to see. Much better to go back to the main road". You see the girl has no sense of adventure!

Whatever, **Petrokefali** is a pretty Greek village with a white chapel, beflowered gardens, central square, pleasant road, and charcoal burners in the area. A traveller may divert through **Pompia** which is a dusty, untidy, sprawling town with unmade roads.

At **Choustouliana** village there is petrol. Beyond **Plora**, the road climbs, after the badly signed right-hand turning to Lendas, in a series of hairpin curves with, behind one, magnificent views across the lovely Messara Plain. The road passes a spectacular, sheer rock face, disused ruins and, before going through the pass to Miamou, a massive building under current construction which is simply miles from anywhere. Goodness only knows what's being built and for whom. Once through the mountain hanging village of **Miamou**, the road surface (surface?) is awful for a mile or so, as it passes through brown, moorland hills, but eventually reaches the top of the steep, very long, cliff edge descent to Lendas where the road surface, thankfully, becomes acceptable. Eagles may well be seen soaring back and forth – that is a long as the locals haven't shot them all!

LENDAS (59 km from Ag. Galini) It is questionable if the journey is worth the effor The place really is a flyblown, messy huddle of tavernas with little or no roa structure, resulting in the odd unintentional foray through a native's backyard (ofte to his or her anger). The irregular, earth-surfaced bus and car park is connected by series of downward tracks to the four tavernas that edge the little cove. The hous and taverna surrounds are litter bestrewn and 'campers' are to be found in mos nooks and crannies. There is a public toilet, and a local who 'fills-in' as a mone exchange.

Although all four backshore tavernas used to offer accommodation, only one c them now regularly proffers **Rooms** (1000 drs for double with bathroom). Two other have ceased renting rooms and the last is reluctant. Generally the toilet facilities ar Cycladean in style, sited at ground floor level on the edge of the patio.

There is one other house in the village offering basic **Rooms** with a share bathroom at 1000 drs. Whatever, accommodation in Lendas is not that easy to com by, nor are the locals that helpful.

Regarding the bus schedules, perhaps the sign says it all –

'BUSES CO-OPERATIVE   Tel. 283073
Daily Passing Hours from Lendas
To Iraklion 0630 - 1445 hrs
Same on Sundays
To Iraklion 1600 hrs.'

As the spirit of the natives seems hardened against tourists, added to which the appear to be bent on making as much as they can from the xenos or visitors, it is mystery why one of the package holiday companies includes Lendas on the schedules as an excursion. Certainly if moved to visit the place, it seems prudent t avoid the days on which the tour buses drop in.

Journeying back to Ag. Deka involves a traveller in all the glorious uncertainties c Greek cartography as most road maps are inacurrate when detailing this area.

AGHII DEKA. The large village is centred around a not very lovely, long High Stree with roads off to either side. There are **Rooms**, petrol, a Post Office and chemist i addition to the usual cafe-bars. But the fame of the village, named after ten loca martyrs who refused to worship Roman gods, is its proximity to the site of:

The Gortyna (Gortys) Excavations Gortyna came into its own, as a City Stat controlling the Messara Plain, from about 800 BC, after the decline of the Minoa society. Fame was based on its code of laws, the Gortyna Code, set down in the fift century BC. The Romans invaded some time in 67 BC, when mopping up the island and made it their island capital. Plans were formulated to build a grand city, but thes ideas were never fully implemented. Gortyna's importance continued through th Byzantine period, finally being laid low by the Saracens in AD 820/30.

Excavations commenced in the late 1800s and have continued spasmodically u to recent times. The remains are not visually very impressive and it is easy t accidentally drive past them.

The main road back to Ag. Galini leads via **Mires** which is another busy, dust industrial, Messara Plain town. Accommodation is available at the *Olympic Hote* (Class D – tel. 22777) where the rooms share the bathroom, with a single costing 85 drs and a double room 1260 drs.

Tmr		
	16 Hotel Cronos E3	33 Commercial Bank D/E4
1 Ferry-boat quay B/C5/6	17 Hotel du Lac E4	34 General Hellenic
2 Bus park G2	18 Hotel Akratos E4	Bank D4
3 Bus office &	19 Hotel Levandis E/F5/6	35 National Bank of
terminus G3	20 Hotel Sgouros F5/6	Greece E/F3/4
4 Rooms	21 Hotel El Greco E/F7	36 Babis scooter hire G2
5 Pension Atlantis G3	22 Hotel Kriti E6/7	37 Bread shops
6 Pension Elpida F/G2/3	23 Pension Pergola D6/7	38 O.T.E. E/F4
7 Hotel Magda E/F1	24 Pension Marigo D4	39 Chapel E4
8 Hotel Apollon F/G1/2	25 Youth Hostel D4	40 Cathedral F3
9 Hotel Iris F1	26 Hotel Alcestis C/D4/5	41 Museum B2
10 Hotel Elena F1	27 Pension Perla A3	42 Post Office E3/4
11 Pension New York G1/2	28 Restaurant Nefaro F/G6	43 Tourist Police B/C2/3
12 Hotel Kera G1	29 Papas Kafenion E3	44 Port Police/Municipal
13 Hotel Zefiros G1/2	30 Snackbar F2/3	Tourist Office D4/5
14 Hotel Sunrise G1/2	31 Souvlaki	45 Hospital A1
15 Hotel Dias G1	Snackbar C/D3/4	
	32 Airline office E3	

AGIOS NIKOLAOS Illustration 20

Tmr = Town map reference
Fsw = Facing seawards
Sbo = Sea behind one

222

17 AGIOS NIKOLAOS (Aghios, Ayios Nikolaos)

Harbour town and package holiday resort

Purists ✶✶
Disco Swingers ✶✶✶✶

FIRST IMPRESSIONS

Tourists; discos; pop music; cocktail bars; souvenir shops; very attractive; hilly harbour town; mosquitoes.

VITAL STATISTICS

Tel. prefix 0841. Population 6500.

HISTORY

Not a lot, the modern day town being a comparatively recent development of the 19th century. There are a few Hellenistic, Roman and Venetian bits and pieces but Ag. Nikolaos lacks the usual Cretan breadth and depth of Minoan remains, churches, and Venetian and Turkish buildings. Mind you the site was the harbour for the relatively adjacent, ancient Lato City (*See* EXCURSION TO AG. NIKOLAOS SURROUNDS). That is not to say that the clean, lovely, tree lined avenues, pretty lake and harbour do not adequately compensate for the lack of the usual historical prerequisites.

Most of the growth of this once backwater harbour town, has occurred since the 1960s. Mark you, Ag. Nikolaos has certainly made up for lost time and is probably the most touristic of all Cretan holiday resorts – I can only presume the Minoans are now rotating in their graves.

GENERAL

Ag. Nikolaos is a conundrum, perhaps more correctly it could be described as a schizophrenic town. Undeniably it is a tourist trap, with some of the shortcomings that intense exposure to the package holiday industry brings about. Despite this, in the strata beneath the annual invasion , and not totally submerged, is a delightful, interesting seaport settlement.

There are several indicators that point to a possibly unacceptable level of tourism which include a high incidence of tourist shops, including 'ethnic' products and jewellery shops; convenient, 'fast-food' snackbars; parking restrictions; Greek voices in a minority; waiters who will not hear out customers' halting efforts in Greek; an inability to purchase a cup of Greek coffee and that 'Costa Brava' ambience. There is hope yet, for as I have previously postulated (sounds pompous I know), the Greek character is not one that is easily submerged or prostituted to suborning influences. Considering that historically the Cretans did not allow the Venetians or Turks to gain the upper hand, I am sure a plethora of sunburnt, obese, swinging, fun-loving tourists are not going to sublimate their natural characteristics completely. Let us hope I am right.

Ag. Nikolaos is the subject of an all-embracing one-way road system. The usual approach to the town is via the south-western corner to the Bus park (*Tmr* 2G2) and up to Plateia Eleftherios Venizelos, crowning the hill which dominates the town. From the far side of the Main Square, the High St (Odhos Roussou Koundourou) plunges down to the harbour front, over the Lake Voulismeni sea inlet bridge and climbs up Odhos K. Paleologou, out of town on the Iraklion road. Incidentally the lake is supposedly bottomless but research has established a depth of some 60m.

Ag. Nikolaos is larger than at first appears to be the case, the concentration of tourist activity being centred in an area stretching from the Bus park, in the south, to the harbour and its surrounds. But this would be to ignore N. Pangalou Kitroplatia

Bay (*Tmr* F6) to the east, the coastal stretch south of the Bus park and developments to the south-west.

Arrival at Ag. Nikolaos will be by road or, possibly, by ferry-boat.

ARRIVAL BY BUS

Buses park up on a dusty 'bomb-site lot' (*Tmr* 2G2) and turn round/terminus on Plateia Atlandithos (*Tmr* 3G3) to the south of the Main Square centre of town.

ARRIVAL BY FERRY

The layout and size of the port is similar to that of an Aegean island. Inter-island ferries dock on the right-hand side (*Fsw*) of the harbour (*Tmr* 1B/C5/6). A short walk around the quay road of Akti Koundourou leads past a row of restaurants and shops including 'traditional' Cretan art, music and gift shops (one aptly named 'Schmuck') and a Rent-A-Car office, to the centre of the waterfront.

THE ACCOMMODATION & EATING OUT

The Accommodation Ag. Nikolaos is 'package holiday country' with many hotels block booked by the tour operators. This, plus the many demands on the *Rooms* and pensions that are available, results in the town quickly filling up in the height of summer. Mosquitoes are a problem, so the strictures in CHAPTER 1 should be followed. But the biggest drawback is that most hotel and pension owners request a substantial amount more for height of season accommodation than the 'official' rates. *C'est la vie.*

The noisy areas around the Bus park (*Tmr* 2G2) and Bus terminus office (*Tmr* 3G3) are particularly rewarding when searching out accommodation. Radiating out from Plateia Atlandithos, with beautiful views over the bay, there are:

Rooms (*Tmr* 4G3)
Directions: Just across the side street of Tavla from the Bus office.

Pension Atlantis (*Tmr* 5G3) (Class C)   Tel. 28964
Directions: Up Tavla St and first right and on the right.

Only double rooms available with shared bathroom from 850 drs and en suite from 1100 drs rising to 1000 drs and 1300 drs (16th June - 30th Sept).

There are also **Rooms** almost opposite *Pension Atlantis.*

Pension Elpida (*Tmr* 6F/G2/3)
Directions: On the street that edges the north side of the Bus park, and connects up with Kontogiani St., halfway along on the right. Remember the general limitations in respect of lodgings adjacent to Bus termini.

Turning north up Kontogiani St and taking the first left at the bottom of V. Merarchias St, leads into a side road whereon are two houses with **Rooms** (*Tmr* 4F2), on the left-hand side of the road. Continuing to the end of this street, turning left down the steps and taking the first right, leads to the:

Pension Magda (*Tmr* 7E/F1) (Class B) 13 Gournion St   Tel. 23925
Directions: As above and on the left.

Although pronouncing itself a hotel, Magda is actually licensed as a pension but room prices are rather, no are very expensive. Single rooms sharing the bathroom start off at 1540 drs and en suite 1806 drs whilst double rooms en suite cost 2350 drs rising to, respectively, 1890 drs, 2350 drs and 3260 drs (1st June - 30th Sept).

Back at the main road of Kontogiani St, turn in the Sitia direction (south-west). The next left is the far, south boundary of the Bus park. Adjacent to this is the *Hotel*

Aphrodite which contains furnished apartments for package tourists. The siting of this accommodation brings to mind the general pitfalls of booking locations from holiday brochures that display 'well positioned' photographs. I am quite sure tour operators do not indicate that this or that hotel overlooks the railway/airport/bus terminal as may be appropriate, nor, in the case of the Aphrodite, that the street is subject to the constant coming and goings of buses, the earliest of which bursts into life as early as 0630 hrs. Here endeth the lesson!

Almost immediately on the right, across the main road from the *Hotel Aphrodite,* is Plateia Minoos, an elongated square with central aisle gardens and bars, shops, hotels, scooter hire and travel agents round the periphery.

Hotel Apollon *(Tmr* 8F/G1/2) (Class C) 9 Minoos   Tel. 23023
Directions: As above.

Very smart with all rooms en suite. Singles cost 1431 drs and doubles 1707 drs rising to 1564 drs and 1973 drs (1st June - 14th Sept). Despite these official rates Anne reports that 2700 drs was the requested rate for a high season double.

Hotel Iris *(Tmr* 9F1) (Class B) Minoos Sq.   Tel. 22407
Directions: Across the side street of K. Loukareos from the *Hotel Apollon.*

Actually categorised as a pension. All rooms are en suite with singles costing 1250 drs and doubles 1530/1800 drs increasing to 1500 drs and 1785/2100 drs (1st June - 30th Sept). Here again Anne advises 2500 drs was the quoted rate for a double room.

Hotel Elena *(Tmr* 10F1) (Class C) 15 Minoos   Tel. 28189
Directions: A few buildings down again from the above accommodation.

Modern, and rates as for *Hotels Apollon* and *Iris,* but block booked for seven months of the year.

Back on Kontogiani St, leaving Plateia Minoos (on the right), and on the left, at the next junction, is the:
New York *(Tmr* 11G1/2) (Class C) 21a Kontogiani   Tel. 28577
Directions: As above.

Classified as a pension and likely to have rooms available as it is not used by the package tour operators. This is not surprising as the pension fronts on to the Main Road into Ag. Nikolaos, the Bus park is just around the corner and this area is 'downtown'. Single rooms sharing the bathroom start at 600 drs, en suite 800 drs with double rooms sharing costing 900 drs and en suite 1050 drs. Between 31st May and 30th September the rates increase to 700, 900, 1100 and 1300 drs respectively. Anne found that, in July, the management demands 1800 drs for an en suite double room including breakfast, which is a bit of a price hike.

Hotel Kera (*Tmr* 12G1) (Class C) 34 Kontogiani   Tel. 28711
Directions: Across the road from the *New York.*

Only en suite double rooms which start off at 1600 drs and rise to 2000 drs (1st June - 30th Sept) but note that 2250 drs was required in the high season.

Turning down the side street alongside the *Pension New York* leads to the:
Hotel Zefiros (Zephyros) *(Tmr* 13G1/2) (Class C) Odhos Idomeneos   Tel. 23631
Directions: As above and on the right.

Only en suite rooms with singles charged at 1300 drs and doubles 1600 drs rising to 1500 and 1900 drs (1st July - 30th Sept). A high season request was made for 2100 drs here.

Hotel Sunrise *(Tmr* 14G1/2) (Class B) Odhos Idomeneos   Tel. 23564
Directions: A few buildings down from the *Hotel Zefiros* and classified as a pension.

All rooms are en suite with singles costing 1050 drs and doubles 1350 drs. These rates rise to 1100 drs and 1450 drs (16th May - 30th June), increasing to 1200 drs and 1800 drs (1st July - 30th Sept). High season doubles were quoted at 2000 drs and 300 drs for breakfast, compared to a listed 180 drs!

Hotel Dias (*Tmr* 15G1) (Class C) 2 Latous   Tel. 28263
Directions: Back on the Main Rd, Kontogiani St, and continuing out of town in a south-westerly direction leads to a fork in the road. Take the main, Sitia right-hand turning and the hotel is on the right. A noisy area.

En suite rooms with singles charged at 1340 drs and double rooms 1607 drs which increases to 1660 drs and 2188 drs (1st July - 30th Sept).

Rooms (*Tmr* 4G1)
Directions: To the left side of the *Hotel Dias* but facing on to the Sitia road.

From Odhos Kontogiani, proceeding up V. Merarchias, or the parallel street of S. Venizelos, leads to the top of hill and the Plateia El. Venizelos. Across the square to the left and up the side street is the *Hotel Cronos* (*Tmr* 16E3) but it is tour operator block booked.

From El. Venizelos Sq, the two parallel streets of 28th October (Octovriou) and Roussou Koundourou plunge down to the harbour front.

Hotel du Lac (*Tmr* 17E4) (Class C) 17, 28th October.   Tel. 22711
Directions: A third of the way down from the Main Sq., in a superb position over-looking the small, sea-connected lake in the centre of the town.

Very expensive and all rooms have en suite bathrooms (as they should do at these prices). Single rooms cost 1847/2067 and double rooms 2300/2753 drs. These rates rise to 2023/2300 drs for single rooms and 2507/3034 drs for double rooms. Breakfast is charged at 250 drs. Despite the official listed charges the management requests 3450 drs in the high season for a double room.

Down and across a side street is the totally block booked *Hotel Akratos* (*Tmr* 18E4)

Towards the bottom of Odhos Roussou Koundourou, turning right up Odhos M. Sfakianaki leads along a street with a surfeit of fast food, 'Costas Toast' and *ad nauseam et al* all the way to Plateia N. Pangalou Kitroplatia. (Beware, there is a K. or N. Sfakianaki St halfway down Odhos Roussou Koundourou.) On the left of M. Sfakianaki St is the:
Hotel Levendis (Leventis) (*Tmr* 19E/F5/6) (Class B) 15, M. Sfakianaki   Tel. 22423
Directions: As described above, three blocks down.

The cocktail bar has a juke box that belts out the old favourites – oh goody! Probably much of the accommodation is booked by smaller tour operators. Rooms have en suite bathrooms with singles charged at 1575 drs and doubles 1890 drs. These charges rise to 2000 drs and 2400 drs (1st June - 30th Sept).

Unfortunately the hotels on Plateia N. Pangalou Kitroplatia (*Hotel Sgouros, Tmr* 20F5/6) and Akti Kitroplatias Milos (*El Greco, Tmr* 21E/F7; *Hotel Kriti, Tmr* 22E6/7) and *Pension Pergola, Tmr* 23D6/7) are now taken over by tour operators for most of the summer months.

The harbour quay road, Akti Koundourou, encircles the harbour, crossing over the towns bridge alongside which is the *Cafe Asteria*. They advertise *Information here for rooms at the Sgouros, Dias and Pergola Hotels*. However, any enquiries within are met by an unhelpful lack of information and the terse instruction to go and enquire at the hotels in question. Oh well!

The bridge spans the small inlet connecting the harbour to Lake Voulismeni and allows easy access from the east to west of the town at sea-level. On the west side of the bridge is Odhos K. Paleologou (up which makes off towards Iraklion) and the continuation of Akti Koundourou, which leads out along the coast to Minos and Elounda beaches, and Spinalonga island.

Pension Marigo (*Tmr* 24D4) (Class B) K. Paleologou   Tel. 28439

Directions: From the bridge a few metres up Odhos K. Paleologou and the pension is opposite the town car park, on the corner of a row of tavernas and a souvlaki shop. The town car park tends to obscure the view of the lake.

This establishment is part and parcel of another pension, the *Amalthia* (Class B, tel. 28914) which is just around the corner, at Odhos 13 Pringipos Georgiou. The charges for both are the same but only the *Amalthia* has single beds. All rooms have en suite bathrooms with a single room costing 1250 drs and a double room 1650 drs. These rates rise (officially) to 1540 drs and 1860 drs. On the other hand, in late July, a double room and breakfast was quoted at 2800 drs despite breakfast being officially listed at a cost of 260 drs!

Youth Hostel (*Tmr* 25D4) Koraka St.

Directions: The first turning up to the right from the north side of the bridge, between the taxi rank and the General Hellenic Bank.

This is a very pleasant Youth Hostel with a bunk costing 300 drs per night. It has the dubious, added attraction of 'open air' beds, well not quite. The room at the top of the building was not finished in 1986 and the bunks up there are in a half-built/concrete pillar area. Certainly cool, but what about the mosquitoes? The place also has a bar.

Hotel Alcestis (Alkistis) (*Tmr* 26C/D4/5) (Class C) 30 Akti Koundourou   Tel. 22454

Directions: From the bridge, turn right past the office of the Port police (*Tmr* 44D4/5), following the quay wall round to the left out along the Spinalonga coast road.

Well situated, but at the start of a very busy, disco-bar, taverna bestrewn road. All rooms have en suite bathrooms with singles starting off at 1200 drs and double rooms 1500 drs which charges rise to 1560 drs and 1800 drs. (1st July - 30th Sept). Breakfast is listed at 220 drs. Despite the official rates, 2025 drs is asked for a double room in late July.

The Hotels Rea (Class B), *Hermes* (Class A) and *Coral* (Class B) follow on the footsteps of each other on, or adjacent to, the coast road of Akti Koundourou. Naturally charges reflect their delightful siting and classification. Additionally the ambience is heavily weighted to the Mediterranean, fun-loving, swinging disco, jet set, package tourist holiday-makers, rather than Greek traditional.

Not all is lost though for situated in this area is the:

Pension Perla (*Tmr* 27A3) (Class C)   Tel. 23379

Directions: On the corner of Akti Koundourou and Odhos Salaminos.

Pleasant owners run this clean and well furnished pension which must rate as a find if only because of the reasonable rates charged. Additionally the Perla is in a fashionable, well placed position. High season doubles, with en suite bathroom, cost about 1500 drs, yes 1500 drs and that includes breakfast. The front facing rooms have a balcony overlooking the sea but the downstairs rooms, at the rear of the building, can be a bit smelly due to their proximity to the toilets.

The Eating Out There is no shortage of eating places. They range from 'tost', 'fast food', hamburger and souvlaki snackbars to tavernas and restaurants. In this 'plethora of cooking oil' I mention just a few offerings out of the numerous establishments that range around the edge of Lake Voulismeni, the quay and coastal road of Akti Koundourou, Plateia N. Pangalou Kitroplatia and on Odhos M Sfakianaki. Prices are generally higher than elsewhere on Crete. A number of the tavernas on Odhos K. Paleologou, which overlook the lake, claim to be that used by the cast of one or two British television thriller series filmed in Ag. Nikolaos a few years ago.

Limni Restaurant Odhos K. Paleologou

Directions: Opposite the lake, to the side of the Hellenic Bank (*Tmr* 34D4), just beyond the Taxi Rank.

Proclaims itself to have been the culinary headquarters for the cast of the *Lotus Eaters* and more a taverna than a restaurant. Naturally, the usual offerings of stuffed tomatoes, meat balls, green beans and chipped potatoes. A meal for two of 'special' salad, chicken curry and rice, swordfish, chips, 2 beers and bread costs 1272 drs. This represents very good value for Ag. Nikolaos, especially when one considers that the establishments the other side of the lake charge about double for a similar meal!

Restaurant Nefaro (*Tmr* 28F/G6) Plateia N. Pangalou Kitroplatia.
Directions: At the far, right-hand side of the small bay (*Fsw*).

Smart, with an outside paved patio edged by railings, lanterns and potted palms. Table cloths and well-dressed waiters all add up to an above-average meal cost of some 700 drs per head, but the fare is excellent (albeit small portions).

Papa's Kafenion (more correctly **Terpsis**) (*Tmr* 29E3) Plateia El. Venizelos
Directions: On the north side of this hilltop Main Sq.

Two old boys run this splendid establishment. The tables and chairs are shaded by several spreading trees. In direct contrast to much else in Ag. Nikolaos, this establishment could not be more Greek, restoring one's faith that there are some locals left in town. Reasonably priced drinks, and mezethes are served with the brandy. A coke costs 45 drs and a bottled beer 80 drs.

Toulipa's Snackbar (*Tmr* 30F2/3) V. Merarchias St.
Directions: Two-thirds of the way down from Plateia El. Venizelos, on the right-hand side.

A good range of reasonably priced Greek snacks and meals.

Souvlaki (Convenience Food) Bar (*Tmr* 31C/D3/4)
Directions: Sited on the right of Odhos K. Paleologou, just beyond the car park.

Of smart appearance, with awning-covered tables and chairs across the road, on the edge of the car park. I would like to recommend the place but the offerings are quite often sub-standard in my experience.

There is a 'greasy' snackbar alongside the Bus office (*Tmr* 3G3) which serves up good looking souvlakis.

THE A TO Z OF USEFUL INFORMATION
AIRLINE OFFICE & TERMINUS (*Tmr* 32E3) As is often the case on Crete (and elsewhere on the Greek islands for that matter), the Olympic Airways office is not sited where indicated on many of the town plans. It is actually situated on Odhos Plastira, which skirts the cliff-edge, overlooking the south end of Lake Voulismeni. The usual quiet, calm, slow, polite service. Office hours are daily 0730 - 2030 hrs & Saturday 0730 - 1500 hrs.

BANKS
Commercial Bank (*Tmr* 33D/E4) On Odhos 28 Octovriou, close by the harbour. Normal bank hours.
General Hellenic Bank (*Tmr* 34D4) Located at the outset of Odhos Paleologou, across the road from Lake Voulismeni. Changes travellers and Eurocheques, but do not forget to take a passport and the Eurobank card when changing a personal cheque.
National Bank of Greece (*Tmr* 35E/F3/4). Odhos Roussou Koundourou, just down from Plateia El. Venizelos.

BEACHES Not a lot for a town with this density of tourists. Plateia N. Pangalou Kitroplatia (*Tmr* F6) gives access to the fairly small, grey sand, stony beach which fringes a bay to the east of the town. The foreshore is mainly large pebbles and the very small rubbish bins provided are emptied every morning but overflow during the day.

The other beach is a narrow strip of sand bordered by Akti Atlandithos, which runs south of Plateia Atlandithos, the Bus Square (*Tmr* G3). The only other bathing area is off large, flat, slightly shelving rocks that edge and protrude into the sea beside the Spinalonga road.

BICYCLE, SCOOTER & CAR HIRE
Rent a New Bike. Scooters for hire and located across the side street from the *Hotel Levendis* (*Tmr* 19E/F5/6), on M. Sfakianaki St.
Babis (*Tmr* 36G2). Scooter hire and located on Kontogiani St, just down from the Bus park. A Vespa costs 1200 drs per day.
Car rental outfits, including **Hertz** and **Avis**, are located on the streets of K. Paleologou, Roussou Koundourou and M. Sfakianaki.

BOOKSELLER A very good shop, halfway down 28th October or Roussou Koundourou from Plateia El. Venizelos, the shop stretching laterally between the two streets.

BREAD SHOPS On the streets of M. Sfakianaki (*Tmr* 37E5), Kontogiani (*Tmr* 37F3) (close by the Bus park), Pringipos Georgiou (*Tmr* 37C/D4) (just up from the *Hotel Marigo Tmr* 24D4) and the west side of Plateia El. Venizelos (*Tmr* 37E/F3).

BUSES The Bus park (*Tmr* 2G2) is on the north-west of Plateia Atlandithos and the buses pull up, 'for the off', on Plateia Atlandithos, on the edge of which is the Bus office (*Tmr* 3G3).

Bus timetable
Ag. Nikolaos to Malia, Iraklion.
Daily	0630, 0730, 0810, 0900, 0930, 1030, 1100, 1130, 1230, 1300, 1330, 1400, 1430, 1600, 1630, 1700, 1730, 1800, 1830, 1900, 2000, 2100 hrs.

One-way fare 330 drs; duration 1½ hrs; distance 69 km.
Ag. Nikolaos to Schisma, Elounda.
Daily	0715, 0900, 0930, 1000, 1030, 1100, 1200, 1300, 1400, 1500, 1600, 1700, 1800, 2000, 2100 hrs.
Saturday/Sunday holidays	0800, 1030, 1230, 1430, 1630, 1800, 1930 hrs.

One-way fare 60 drs; duration ½ hr; distance 12 km.
Ag. Nikolaos to Ierapetra via Gournia.
Daily	0630, 0900, 1000, 1100, 1200, 1300, 1500, 1600, 1700, 1800, 2000 hrs.

One-way fare 75 drs; duration 1 hr; distance 36 km.
Ag. Nikolaos to Sitia via Gournia.
Daily	0630, 0900, 1000, 1100, 1200, 1430, 1630, 1900 hrs.

One-way fare 360 drs; duration 2 hrs; distance 74 km.
Ag. Nikolaos to Kritsa.
Daily	0615, 0700, 0810, 0900, 0930, 1000, 1030, 1100, 1200, 1300, 1400, 1500, 1600, 1700, 1800, 1930 hrs.
Saturday/Sunday holidays	0700, 1000, 1200, 1400, 1600, 1730, 1900 hrs.

One-way fare 55 drs; duration ½ hr; distance 11 km.
Ag. Nikolaos to Lasithi Plain.
Daily	0830, 1400 hrs.
Sundays/holidays	0830 hrs.

One-way fare 270 drs; duration 2 hrs; distance 55 km.

There is an Elounda bus stop on the harbour quay, by the bridge opposite the Port police office (*Tmr* 44 D4/5).

COMMERCIAL SHOPPING AREA No specific district. Most grocery, fish, meat, general stores and shops are centred on the parallel streets of V. Mararchias and S. Venizelos (which are attractively lined with mature trees down both sides) and the top of Roussou Koundourou St, on the right-hand side, from Plateia El. Venizelos.

Odhos S. Venizelos has greengrocers most of the way up and down its length and there is an Ironmonger's on the left, close by Plateia El. Venizelos. Descending down V. Merarchias St, from the Main Square, on the right-hand side is a Fish shop and a General Store (which sells salami) and on the left a Dairy shop, 'Greek' general food store and a Butcher. Going down Roussou Koundourou St towards the harbour, on the right is a Fish shop, a store named 'Super Way', a 'Mini Market', and a Supermarket.

As mentioned in the Introduction to this Chapter, Ag. Nikolaos has a plethora of gift, traditional wear and jewellery shops, in fact, probably more than any other town in Crete.

Lastly, to gasps of incredulity and general whoops of amazement, there is a 'Freezer Centre' on Odhos V. Merarchias. Fortunately this is simply a line of small freezer cabinets down the centre of a shop packed with frozen goods, but it cannot auger well for Hellenic civilisation!

Opening hours are the usual, with some allowances for the tourist nature of the town.

DISCOS No problem!

FERRY BOATS Quite a busy port with well-worthwhile connections to various other Greek islands.

Ferry-boat timetable

Day	Departure Time	Ferry-boat	Ports/Islands of Call
Wednesday	0800 hrs	G. Vergina	Kasos, Karpathos, Rhodes
Thursday	1215 hrs	Nireus	Sitia (Crete), Kasos, Karpathos, Diafni (Karpathos), Chalki, Rhodes, Simi, Tilos, Nisiros, Kos, Kalimnos, Astipalaia, Amorgos, Paros, Piraeus (M).
	2300 hrs	Kyklades	Anafi, Santorini, Folegandros, Milos, Piraeus (M).
Saturday	0800 hrs	G. Vergina	Kasos, Karpathos, Rhodes.
Sunday	1030 hrs	Kyklades	Sitia (Crete), Kasos, Karpathos, Diafni (Karpathos), Chalki, Rhodes, Kos, Kalimnos, Leros, Ikaria, Samos, Chios, Mitilini (Lesbos), Limnos, Kavala (M).

FERRY-BOAT TICKET OFFICES

Massaros Travel. 29 Roussou Koundourou   Tel. 22267
Directions: On the left, on the way down from Plateia El. Venizelos to the harbour. Mr Massaros must be one of the most helpful vendors of ferry-boat tickets in all of the Greek islands. Almost unbelievably he produces typed schedules of ferry-boats that arrive and depart not only from Ag. Nikolaos but Iraklion, Souda (Chania), Kastelli as well as Santorini and Rhodes. These details include detailed ticket prices. Well, well.
Knossos Travel. Akti Koundourou   Tel. 28114
Directions: On the quay road, north of the bridge between the Port police (*Tmr* 44D4/5) and some steps.

MEDICAL CARE

Chemists & Pharmacies Quite a number on the major streets.
Hospital (*Tmr* 45A1) On the top left of Odhos K. Paleologou.

NTOG (*Tmr* 44D4/5) More a Municipal Tourist office really, which only opened in September 1985 and is situated in the same building as the Port police, but facing directly on to the bridge. One of the regular staff is a very pleasant, friendly girl who tries very hard and is keen, even if she is not always accurate. The office is open daily 0730 - 1900 hrs.

OTE (*Tmr* 38E/F4) Halfway down Odhos Roussou Koundourou from Plateia El. Venizelos and one street to the east. The turning is to the right along Odhos K. Sfakianaki. Open daily 0600 - 2400 hrs.

PETROL On Odhos V. Merarchias as well as outside Ag. Nikolaos on the National Highway to Iraklion.

PLACES OF INTEREST
Cathedrals & Churches
The lovely little chapel sandwiched in between the tourist dross, towards the bottom of Odhos Roussou Koundourou, is rather unexpected and comes as a complete surprise (*Tmr* 39E4).
The Cathedral is situated on Odhos S. Venizelos (*Tmr* 40F3).

Museums
The Archaeological Museum (*Tmr* 41B2) A small collection of exhibits housed in a new building towards the top of Odhos K. Paleologou. Open daily 0845 - 1500 drs; Sundays/holidays 0930 - 1430 hrs and closed Tuesdays. Admission 100 drs.
Folk Museum Located in the same building as the Tourist office/Port police (*Tmr* 44D4/5). Opened in June 1986, their blurb says it all –

> We announce that in our town Agios Nikolaos the Folk Museum is at work.
> It is at the ground floor below the post Authority (sic).
> In the museum several things of popular art are exhibited.
> The museum is open daily from 10am to 1pm and from 5pm to 8.30pm.
> Except Monday.
> The entrance costs 50 drs.
> We ask you to recommend to your customers to visit us.
> We believe that the acquaintance with our genuine Folklore art is in indispensable (sic).
> Foreign Friends.

There are some pathetic bird cages alongside the steps that descend from Odhos Plastira to Lake Voulismeni.

POLICE
Port (*Tmr* 44D4/5) Situated in the corner of the building opposite the town bridge.
Tourist (& Town) (*Tmr* 43B/C2/3) In common with most Greek Tourist police offices, they are taking a back seat as it were and the old prime site, on the side of the lake, has been abandoned. (It is fair to say that there is now an extremely conveniently positioned Municipal Tourist office (*See* **NTOG**). The Tourist and Town police are now merged in a combined office on the left of Odhos K. Paleologou, which climbs north-west from the town bridge. They, that is up to four of the officers, are still friendly and helpful and, despite the official hours, may well be found *in situ* well into the early hours of the evening. Maybe because of their lower profile, the information sheets are kept in the electricity meter cupboards! Open daily in the Summer season from 0730 - 1430 hrs.

POST OFFICE (*Tmr* 42E3/4) Down 28th October St from Plateia El. Venizelos, and on the left. Usual hours.

TAXIS The main rank is outside the Port police office (*Tmr* 44D4/5), in the corner of the quay formed by the buildings. There used to be a board displaying the charges to various destinations but this has disappeared. If possible ascertain the 'going' rate and negotiate with taxis at other points in the town, including the Squares of El. Venizelos, Atlandithos and Minoos, which may well result in a lower quote.

TELEPHONE NUMBERS & ADDRESSES

Hospital (*Tmr* 45A1) Odhos K. Paleologou,	Tel. 22011/22369
NTOG – (more a Municipal Tourist office) (*Tmr* 44D4/5)	Tel. 22357
Olympic Airways (*Tmr* 32E3) Odhos Plastira	Tel. 22033
Taxis 24 hr. rank,	Tel. 24000/24100
Tourist police, (*Tmr* 43B/C2/3) 17 Odhos K. Paleologou,	Tel. 22321/22251

TOILETS Sometimes marked on town plans as situated on Plateia El. Venizelos but these facilities are now no longer there. I am afraid it is left to the bushes, friendly hotels, tavernas or perhaps the sea!

TRAVEL AGENTS

Creta Travel. As remarked elsewhere in the book, this firm offers an unequalled and extensive range of tours. They have an office on Odhos K. Paleologou, across the road from Lake Voulismeni.

Massaros Travel. Their offices are at 29 Roussou Koundourou on the left-hand side of the road (*Fsw*). Eulogised about under **Ferry-boat Ticket Offices.**

EXCURSION TO AG. NIKOLAOS SURROUNDS

Excursion to Kritsa, Lato & Kroustas (about 16 km). Proceed along the Sitia road from Ag. Nikolaos and, instead of turning on to the Main Highway, take the hill road to:

KRITSA (11 km from Ag. Nikolaos) An attractive mountain village, famed for local handicrafts. But Kritsa is now on the coach excursion schedules, as well as being served by a busy, local bus route, and is billed as an 'authentic', rural village untouched by the (destroying) hand of tourism. Oh yes! Visitors should note that buses to this 'quiet, Cretan Eden' get very crowded in the height of season months.

The main road narrows down into the High Steet which winds up through the balconied, vine trellised houses to the Main Square. There are spectacular views out over the rooftops of the serried houses to the Gulf of Merambellou.

Despite the despoiling waves of tourists that 'assault' the village daily to plunder the now not always genuine wares, exhibited by the locals, sanity returns as nightfall approaches. For those prepared to sit it out, there are several pensions and some **Rooms**, the rates for which are up to half those demanded in Ag. Nikolaos. Most of the taverna/restaurants are located on the High St and their prices reflect the situation.

The village was the setting used for filming one of Nikos Kazantzakis's novels but there is some confusion as to which one.

It is not for any of the preceding that Kritsa is famed but due to:

Panagia Kera Church. The whitewashed building, surrounded by a whitewashed wall, is situated some 600m prior to the village, on the right-hand side of the main road set in olive groves. Reputedly one of the island's most remarkable Byzantine churches built between the 13th and 15th centuries and with magnificent, richly executed interior murals. The many frescoes, depicting various religious themes, almost entirely cover the walls of the three naves/aisles. Check on the daily opening

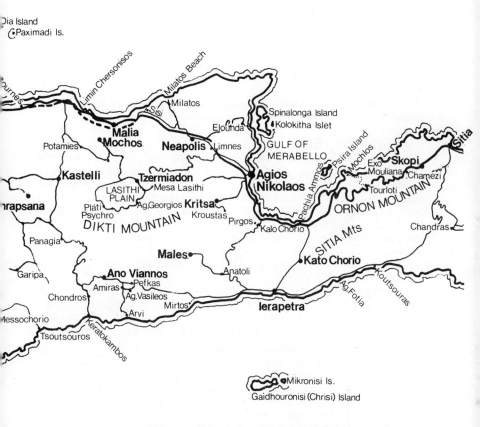

Illustration 21   Crete centred on Agios Nikolaos

hours as the church is administered by an attendant and admission costs 100 drs.
Lato Excavations (13 km from Ag. Nikolaos). The right-hand turning off the main road at Kritsa for the excavations is immediately prior to the village, signposted along a rough track and takes about an hour to walk.

There are substantial remains of the ancient city which some authorities consider to have been one of the finest in Crete. It started to take shape in the 18th/17th century BC with building proceeding until about the 3rd century BC. Lato was constructed between two hills with extensive views out over the Gulf and the City's harbour, now the site of modern day Ag. Nikolaos. Well worth a visit.

Five kilometres can make quite a difference and nowhere more so than the 5 km separating Krista from:
KROUSTAS (16 km from Ag. Nikolaos). This village is as yet relatively unsullied by the hordes that descend on Kritsa and Lato.

ROUTE NINETEEN
To Sitia via Pachia Ammos (73 km) The stretch of coast from Ag.
Nikolaos, round the Gulf of Merambellou, as far as and beyond Istron, is 'Villa Country'. The coast is gently rugged, with little sandy coves here and there. The views are magnificent, with the distant headlands to east and west curving round like the horns of a bull. The problem with holidaying in a villa on this stretch is the comparative isolation and holiday cost calculations must include an allowance for taxi fares or vehicle hire. There are buses, but the timetables are limited, so be warned.

Almiros has few hotels, after which the coast road climbs, winds and descends in and around the various bays.

At **Ammounda** there is a small bay, the rocky coast is beset by olive groves and the villas start in earnest. The turning off to the right, where the bridge is being widened, is for Pirgos. The junction is marked by some tavernas and flowers. In this area there are a number of fashionable villas in amongst the occasional, old house.

KALO CHORIO (11 km from Ag. Nikolaos) Tel. prefix 0841. The hill above the village, which is to the right, is shaped like a pyramid. Hereabouts a backwards angled, unmade track, from behind the taverna on the left, sheers off through well watered, cultivated fields, past a sandy football pitch, edged by bamboo groves, to a stony, gently curving beach. Away to the right is a small chapel and two boat houses. The sea-shore stretches away to the left, with goats and donkeys in fields that reach down to the very edge of the backshore. A pleasant spot.

Back at the development on the main road there is a 'Mini Market' and two large tavernas.

Hotels in Kalo Chorio include the:
Elpida (Class C)   Tel. 61403
All rooms have en suite bathrooms. Single rooms are charged at 1556 drs and a double room 2044 drs, rising to 1911 drs and 2578 drs. Breakfast which is mandatory is listed at 250 drs. Even if the Elpida does have a swimming pool, it seems unreasonable of the management to demand 3400 drs for a double in high season.

Around the next corner in the road is another pretty bay followed, at Istron, by the remarkable:
Istron Bay Hotel   Tel. 61303
This de luxe emporium is built on the side of the vertical cliff face. The hotel's swimming pool and tennis court are spread around the small, sandy beach set in the lovely little cove which it totally occupies. Not that I would like readers to be under the misapprehension that the facilities only include a swimming pool and (floodlit)

tennis court. Oh no, there are a night club, pool bar, boutique, jewellery shop, games rooms with table-tennis and billiards, childrens' pool, water skiing, sailing, pedaloes, canoes, a hotel caique, wind-surfing and skin diving, to name but a few! Mark you, the charges reflect these small trifles, to which must be added air conditioning. Single room rates vary between 5000 - 8000 drs whilst double rooms cost 7500 drs - 11000 drs, and this is not per week. No, these are the daily rates.

The coast road on this stretch is very dramatic but alters quite suddenly on the approach to Gournia where the scenery changes to moorland terrain. Prior to arriving at the archaeological site, a large signboard to the left declares the existence of:
Gournia Moon Camping. This would appear to be an all-action, all-swinging facility. An additional fringe benefit is the provision of 'built in' tarpaulin shades over the tents.

Gournia. The contrast between the campsite and the archaeological remains could not be more extreme if it was not such a ridiculous concept. The first time I viewed the ancient Minoan town of Gournia was when driving over from Ierapetra. The coastal plain, edged by the sea to the north and surrounded by hills on every other side, spreads out down below and the site is laid over a small hillside. From a distance and height it requires several long looks to establish that it is not a comparatively recently abandoned village, but a place of great antiquity. This helps prove what I have always suspected, namely that not a lot has changed in Greek architectural development from Minoan times to the present day. The approximate area was initially pinpointed by Sir Arthur Evans and taken up by a young American lady in 1901, who almost completed the task of excavation by 1904. It appears to have existed as a working, self-supporting community, with harbour installations in the bay, now submerged and lost.

PACHIA AMMOS (21 km from Ag. Nikolaos). Tel. prefix 0842. The dusty, dirty, seaside village and small port is spread around a long, flat bay with, in the background, the towering Sitia and Ornon Mountains. Depsite the setting, Pachia Ammos has managed to make a real mess of things. The grey, stony beach and mossy foreshore is absolutely littered with rubbish, added to which there is no heart or centre to the place. Clumps of bamboos appear here and there and a few fishing boats are dejectedly moored up alongside a small harbour mole. Petrol is available.

Accommodation includes:
Hotel Xenios Zeus (Class D)   Tel. 93289
Directions: On the main road.
    Despite its grand sounding name and size, it is only a D class hotel, although all rooms are en suite. Single rooms cost 1000 drs and double rooms 1400 drs rising to 1300 drs and 1800 drs (1st July - 31st Dec). Anne pointed out that she would expect to be paid to stay in this particular hotel!

Hotel Golden Beach (Class C)   Tel. 93278
Directions: Down a side road from the Main Road towards the waterfront.
    The Golden Beach is ineptly, if not ludicrously, named as it is located across the road from the backshore of the greyest, filthiest beach I have ever seen. The litter is piled thickly along the whole stretch. The rates are much the same as for the *Hotel Xenios*.

The villas fade away to the east of Gournia. At the very pretty village of **Kouvousi**, which lies snuggled at the foot of the mountains set in olive groves, the road commences on a long climb initially edging a dramatic, oleander filled canyon. Trees and flowers line the road all the way up the steep incline which dramatically ends at the viewpoint platform of **Platonos**. This looks out over the sea, which way down below washes the base of the towering cliffs. A few kilometres off shore is **Psira island,** set in the bright blue, shimmering sea.

The village of **Lastros** stretches out to the left on a spiny projection from the mountain, edged by a gorge. Similarly at the Mochlos turning, the village of **Sfaka** clings to a mountain ridge.

MOCHLOS (50 km from Ag. Nikolaos). Tel. prefix 0843. The hamlet lies at the end of an unmade track on the pebbly sea's edge. Two hundred metres from the foreshore is a small islet named after the settlement. There are tavernas as well as a couple of hotels which include the:

Sophia (Class D)   Tel. 94240
Double rooms en suite only, cost 1700 drs.
and the:
Mochlos (Class E)   Tel. 94205
Rooms share bathrooms with a single costing 750 drs and a double room 1200 drs.

Back on this Cretan corniche, the road winds past the village of **Tourloti**, again set to one side of the highway, as is **Myrsini**. From here, there is a magnificent view of the bays below, with soaring eagles, seemingly suspended over the junction of cliff-edge and sea. The road descends past **Mesa Mouliana**, where petrol is available, and **Exo Mouliana**, which straddles the road and is a mix of dusty, old and new buildings. From hereabouts the white blob of Sitia comes into view and the slow, even descent passes **Chamezi** above the plain, then through terraced olives to the large, rambling flat roofed town of **Skopi** below the road. Beyond Skopi is one more frightening (no, dramatic) piece of road and ravine to Sitia (*See* CHAPTER 18).

ROUTE TWENTY
To Tsoutsouros via Kalo Chorio, Anatoli, Mirtos, Arvi, Keratokambos (103 km). Take ROUTE NINETEEN to the Kalo Chorio junction and turn right on to the narrow, winding road which passes through the large village of Kalo Chorio. Once past the side turning to Meseleri, the road improves, enabling a traveller to concentrate on the scenic delights of the mountain vistas, trees, scrub, olives and bends.

Prina is small and clings to the side of the hill with fruit and vegetables growing and three cows grazing (well maybe more or less when the reader visits). Between Prina and the village of **Kalamafka**, which nestles in the mountains, it is possible to observe the sea to the north and south of Crete. Unusually there is plenty of water available at the roadside but from hereabouts the beautiful views are marred by the now familiar plastic. The road descends by a vast quarry works where the surface of the thoroughfare is very bad, probably due to the weight of haulage traffic, and litter and dust are everywhere. The route rolls down to the coastal plain which is inflicted with rubbish, and plastic greenhouses.

The road west of Ierapetra, messy and planted with bamboos, leads to **Gra Lygia**. This village is subject to much new development, petrol is available, and the beach is small, squalid, rocky, grey and litter strewn. From here the road arrows over the flat plain bordering the sea, with *Rooms* and villas in amongst the sprawling ribbon development and acres of plastic. Beyond **Nea Anatoli**, with it's large church, is **Nea Mirtos** situated above the sea and its pebbly beach. After the road passes a wide river-bed to the right, the turning down to Mirtos is opposite the:
Hotel Esperideis (Class C)   Tel. 51207/51298
A nice looking hotel on the road's edge.
All rooms have en suite bathrooms. A single room cost 1519 drs and a double

room 1856 drs which charges rise to 1823 drs and 2228 drs (16th June - 30th Sept). Opposite, on the junction, is a lovely bougainvillea.

MIRTOS (52 km from Ag. Nikolaos). Tel. prefix 0842. The village stretches along the sea's edge. The long, grey shingle, pebble beach is edged with tavernas, a Post Office, baker and general store. There are **Rooms** from about 900 drs upwards for a double bedroom and the *Myrtos Hotel* (Class C, tel. 51226).

A few local fishing boats moor up on a small amount of litter but the really noticeable thing is that the atmosphere is decidedly uncordial. The pretty and pleasant village is still engaged in a long struggle to repel an unsavoury invasion by the 'great unwashed', who are attempting to move in. Perhaps the fact that the Germans destroyed the village and disposed of all the males may have soured the residents against any blitzkrieg, including the present-day, tourist inspired invasion.

Close to both Mirtos and Nea Mirtos are two archaeological sites, that is, one close to each.

The road climbs west out of Mirtos, turning inland and gently winding up through fire wracked countryside. The brown foothills of Mount Dikti lie to the right and, in the area of **Kalami** village, are a number of beehives set in amongst the lemon groves and on the hillsides.

At **Pefkos** there is petrol, some tavernas and a turning off to Ag. Vasilios high above a green ravine. Apart from a bus stop in **Ag. Vasilios** there are kafenions and **Rooms**, with caves above the road and pomegranates in the trees. The side road curves back to the Main Road and a little further on there is the turning for Arvi, via the narrow, old Greek village of **Amiras**. The tightly twisting, downward plunging, reconstructed road runs on to a track edging the backshore of a pebbly beach. Turn left for the still unspoilt, seaside village of:

ARVI (81 km from Ag. Nikolaos). Tel. prefix 0895. A pleasant halfway house between the isolation of Keratokambos and busy Tsoutsouros. Arvi is simply a narrow street parallel to the beach. A store, baker's, souvlaki stall, grill-bar, kafenion and four tavernas line the 'High St' and the beach as do many **Rooms** and the:
Hotel Ariadne (Class C)   Tel. 31200
Single rooms en suite cost 1200 drs per day and doubles 1540 drs. In the high season (16th June - 15th Oct) a single room is 1500 drs, a double sharing the bathroom 1600 drs and en suite 1925 drs.

It was at Arvi some years ago that I witnessed the quintessence of indolence. A local is in the habit of frequenting one of the beach tavernas and, whilst sitting idly drinking at a patio table, casts his line across the beach and then settles down to a comfortable chat with his mates, occasionally twitching the twine that extends across the terrace and beach into the breaking seas. The really noticeable part of the performance is that he stretches his leg out on a convenient seat and threads the fishing line between his toes.

From Arvi more sober minded citizens will retrace their 'wheel marks' to the main road beyond Amiras and turn left for the large, appealing, very, very spectacular, mountain clinging village of **Ano Viannos**. Here turn left down and along the pretty route to **Chondros** (which is attractive but not so spectacular as Ano Viannos), from whence the road is asphalted to within a couple of hundred metres of Keratokambos. On the other hand.....instead of rejoining the main road, it is possible to journey from Arvi along the coast, on an unmade, rocky, dusty, donkey track. This roughshod route passes a good looking, sandy beach and continues on edged by plastic greenhouses, which contain banana palm trees, all the way to:

KERATOKAMBOS (90 km from Ag. Nikolaos). Since I first wrote about Keratokambos, despite detailed changes, this seaside hamlet has remained largely undeveloped and I still regard it as an unspoilt, if tawdry Shangri-la. I have to admit that one person's idea of beauty, desirability or heaven on earth is not necessarily that of another observer.

Apart from evaluating whether or not Keratokambos is a 5 star location, another conundrum a guide book writer has to weigh in the balance is whether or not to inform readers of the delights of this or that location. Certainly most travellers enjoy finding an untouched place on their holiday travels but, having found one, to tell or not to tell, that is the question? To do so can lead to an ever increasing number of visitors, which then despoils the very isolation and, ultimately, its charm. Whatever, it would be presumptuous to think that others have not already stumbled across Keratokambos, so here goes.

After that introduction of course, anything I write might well be an anticlimax and that is not too difficult as very little goes on in this dusty, straggling little place. The tiny hamlet faces a long, tree lined seafront beach of pebbly sand that stretches away to the left and right. A chapel sits on a small square in the centre of the development and, to one side, there are two tavernas which offer simple meals. Opposite the chapel, on the backshore, is a beach shower and there is now a good general store, but accommodation is sparse. On the Ano Viannos-Chondros road down to Keratokambos, immediately prior to the junction with the High St/Esplanade – no, more correctly the coastal track, there is:

Rooms Ve (sic)

A nice digs. The en suite double room includes the use of full kitchen facilities – fridge, cooker and full sets of crockery and cutlery – all for a high season rate of 1300 drs. Particularly welcome are the provision of a washing line, pegs and a few, well four, English paperbacks ranging from Neville Shute to Alistair McLean.

Along the track to the west, or right *(Fsw)* of the village, in the direction of Tsoutsouros, is a fairly new seafront taverna with a few **Rooms** which are often full during the height of the season months. Meals and accommodation are available at the *Pension Kastro*, next door to which are a fish taverna and a cafe.

My preference is *Nickos's Taverna*, which is second left *(Fsw)* from the 'Main Square', but this is purely a personal choice. Meals are simple and the locals' English is almost nonexistent. Nickos has a weak heart, so do not expect a rowdy party every night, and it is advisable to reserve dinner, but do not be surprised if the food proffered is not quite that expected. On our first visit, some years ago, the patron hauled a steak out of the fridge and then showed us some Cretan beans. Goody, steak and beans. Ah no! We actually received meat flavoured bean soup. Rosemary was of the opinion that the steak was simply dragged through the murky liquid, but there you go.

The wasteland opposite the sea to the east is still showing signs of some development, one day, so visit Keratokambos before it is too late. Reluctantly we leave the quiet charm of this peaceful hamlet to go west (young man).

The stony track to Tsoutsouros passes out through the rural end of Keratokambos, all chickens, goats, donkeys and dust, and winds and switchbacks round a rocky headland with a beautiful bay down below. From here the route drops down to a sandy plain alongside the sea where the direction to take becomes distinctly problematical. If it's any help, after 5 km turn left. Hereabouts a shanty settlement of three or more houses is centred around a dried-up river-bed. The road (why use that word – the surface is nearly too bad for tanks) crosses over a rudimentary bridge, swings left and passes through the occasional olive grove. After climbing a steep incline, crossing a small plateau littered with plastic, through another olive grove and rounding a small bay, the traveller approaches:

TSOUTSOUROS (103 km from Ag. Nikolaos). This seaside development is set on a narrow area edging a small, flat bay and surrounded by steep mountain sides to the west.

Frankly Tsoutsouros is a disappointment (as Keratokambos was a delight). It can get very busy in the height of the season, being very popular with the Greeks (what do they know that I don't?). Apart from this there is much recent development along the sea's edge. This now includes some ten tavernas overlooking the long, grey shingle beach, (which is cleanest at the right end (*Fsw*)), a new house or three and two hotels, the:
Hotel Ag. Georgios (Class C)   Tel. 51678
Double rooms cost 1600 drs in the high season.

and the *Hotel El Greco* (Class E, tel. 51182).
Apart from the aforementioned tavernas there are **Rooms**, a restaurant or two and a post box (I often wonder when and by whom these widely scattered receptacles are emptied). To the right are the remnants of the original fishing hamlet.

Some years ago at the west end of Tsoutsouros 'High St', I made one of those errors in direction which, in the safety of the local pub, allows one to give the 'chaps' a good laugh but that at the time was extremely worrying. The main track out of Tsoutsouros, in the direction of Kasteliano, was not immediately evident but I found what I thought was the way and headed for it. It was on the fourth hairpin of the large, rocky, boulderous and very, very steep sward that my companion baled out – just like a sky diver. The problem was that I could not stop as the vehicle (a heavy, unwieldy, old, converted ambulance) was lifting off the front wheels due to the weight transferring to the back. Nothing for it but to go on and on and on.....Finally I was able to pull up on a piece of the track that was still climbing and switchbacking up the seemingly enormous mountain face, with a precipitous drop to one side. To cut the story short, it took 2½ hours to travel the 15 km of this hair-raising journey, with not a soul in sight and, near the summit, eagles beneath us, yes soaring about the gorge to the right below our vehicle. The ever-present, nagging worry was that the engine, gearbox or back axle, or all three, would fail! "Hello, is that the Basingstoke office of the AA? Well, I'm stuck on this mountainside...." "Where, Sir?" You can picture it.

When we finally reached the first village, **Messochorio**, I checked the map and sure enough there was no road, not even one of those imaginative lines that Greek cartographers are prone to lightly sketch on to the odd, open looking places. I knew it had been rough, but that was ridiculous!

ROUTE TWENTY ONE
To Elounda, Spinalonga & beyond (12 km) The road from Ag.
Nikolaos chicanes out along the coast coves at Minos beach, skirting slab-like rocks that almost seem to float on the sea's surface. Sunbathers, from the surrounding hotels, lie in their hundreds on towels and beach mats spread out over these platforms.

The road rises to **Hera** village, sited halfway up the mountainside. From this vantage point there is an amazing view of the peninsula of Spinalonga and the causeway connecting the offshore land to the 'mainland'. In the way of this causeway, there were originally salt flats but these have lain derelict for many years.

The approach road from Ag. Nikolaos passes through clean countryside dotted with isolated hotels, cafes and bars, olive groves, some old houses, classy apartments and a number of **Rooms**. It then falls to sea-level towards the village of:

ELOUNDA (12 km from Ag. Nikolaos). Tel. prefix 0841. A signpost to the right indicates the route to the ancient site of Olous and the causeway. Olous was a port and important city, but little now remains although there is an early mosaic and basilica in the area.

Elounda village is really very, very smart with a Riviera feel to what was originally a simple fishing port, but is now an international holiday resort. The number of luxury and Class A hotels gives adequate testament to the exclusivity of this tourist haven.

Cheaper accommodation is located at **Schisma** immediately prior to Elounda and includes the:

Hotel Olous (Class E)   Tel. 41357
Only double rooms are available sharing the bathroom, charged at 800 drs per night rising to 900 drs (1st June - 15th Sept).

Back at Elounda, additionally, and presumably necessary to preserve the widespread acclaim and acceptability of the location, there are a few discos and night clubs including, for instance, the 'Playboy Bar'.

The small main square houses the Post Office, one block north of which is the Police station, the National Bank of Greece and an international telephone in a store opposite the Church. The square is situated close by the rocky seafront where are moored up some fishing boats and from which caique excursion trips can be enjoyed. Elounda's fine, gravelly, small beach is some way beyond the village. A few of the old buildings have survived, which is a pleasant surprise.

Elounda was the location for the BBC TV series *Who Pays the Ferryman*, a fact that is used to advertise the various hostelries favoured with the crew and cast's patronage.

A branch road off to the left, through the 'old quarter' of Elounda, winds up to the pretty village of **Fourni**, surrounded by stone-walled vineyards and with no concessions to tourists. From Fourni the road, lined with a lovely avenue of white trunked eucalyptus trees, advances to the pretty little village of **Kastelli** (not that western Crete Kastelli) where there is petrol and a post box.

Half-way along the coast road to the north from Elounda, brings into sight magnificent views out over the fortress isle of Spinalonga with Spinalonga peninsula to the south and, to the north, the headland of Cape Ag. Ioannis rearing up in the background.

PLAKA (16 km from Ag. Nikolaos). A lovely, quiet hamlet and tiny fishing-boat port at the end of the sea-level road that edges the coastline from Elounda. The beach is acceptable, if pebbly, with marvellous views of Spinalonga. There are a number of **Rooms** and several tavernas even if the fare is rather limited. Probably the pick of the eateries is the:

Kalimera Taverna
They offer excellent dishes, carefully prepared at reasonable prices. A very good meal for two of loukanika, thousand island salad (tuna, meat *et al*), a bottle of good wine and bread cost 1000 drs.

Local fishermen have made a business of ferrying people (400 drs each) to and from:

SPINALONGA ISLAND Known as 'the island of the living dead' whilst used as a leper colony. The island's fortress was built by the Venetians in 1579 and the structure proved so impregnable that they managed to hold out against the all-conquering Turks until 1715 (the rest of Crete having fallen by 1669). Interestingly enough the Turks in their turn stayed in occupation of this remarkable outpost for some years after they had departed 'mainland' Crete. Some time in 1904 it became a leper colony, which only finally closed in 1957.

Chania arsenals

Tmr

1 Ferry-boat quay B/C5
2 Bus Square H6
3 Bus Office H6
4 Alice Hotel I.2/3
5 Rooms – No 53 I./J2
6 Pension Apolonia H/I.2/3
7 Hotel Mariana G2
8 Hotel Krystal G2/3
9 Hotel Mysson G3
10 Rooms – No 29 G/H3
11 Hotel Via H6
12 Hotel Elena G6
13 Hotel Flisvos G6
14 Hotel Itanos G4
15 Hotel Denis F4
16 Rooms – No 35 F2/3
17 Rooms – No 54 F2
18 Rooms – No 19 D/E2/3
19 Hotel Archontikon C2
20 Pension Creta D2/3
21 Rooms A/B3
22 Souvlaki Snackbar F4
23 Zorbas Restaurant F4
24 Yuras Restaurant H4
25 Cafe-Taverna G/H3
26 Commercial Bank G3/4
27 National Bank G3/4
28 Bank of Crete H/I.3/4
29 Car Hire G5/6
30 Petrol Station G5
31 Bread shop F/G3
32 Bread & pie shop D2
33 Cinema I.2/3
34 Supermarket/Store H/I.3
35 Zorbas Disco D3
36 O.T.E. F/G2/3
37 Venetian Fort A1
38 Folklore Museum E1/2
39 Post Office I.3
40 Town police I.2/3
41 Port police B/C3/4
42 Ferry-boat ticket
   office C/D3/4
43 Public lavatories G6
44 Olympic office G3/4

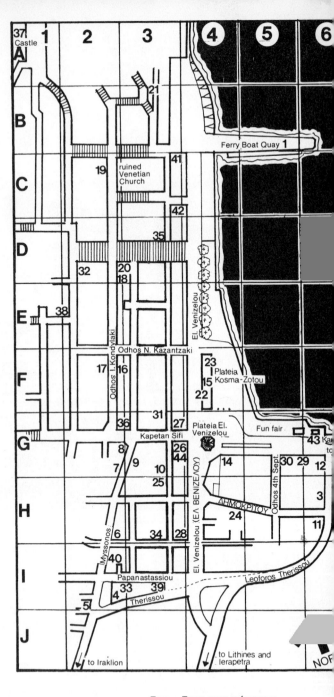

SITIA Illustration 22

242

Tmr = Town map reference
Fsw = Facing seawards
Sbo = Sea behind one

18 SITIA (Siteia) ***
Harbour town

FIRST IMPRESSIONS
A Cycladean-island 'look-alike' Chora and port; steps; white cubic houses; taverna quay; sea-town sprawl; lack of Venetian or Turkish remains.

VITAL STATISTICS
Tel. prefix 0843. Population about 6500.

HISTORY
There are possible connections with the Byzantium Eteia. Previously named La Sitia, the Venetians built a fortified wall and castle but history appears to have side-stepped this area, apart from the occasional earthquake and pirate raid.

GENERAL
First impressions may well be mixed. The town to the north of the main road is pure island harbour charm. The terraces of square white houses are interspaced with steep, broad steps, both of which climb upwards, seemingly ever upwards. The hillside is topped by, to one side, a fort and chapel cemetery which overlook the harbour scene of boat quay, long triangulated waterfront Square and Esplanade.

The areas to the west and south, are generally messy, urban sprawl, possibly one of the factors that has kept the tidal flow of holiday-makers to a mild swell. Other reasons contributing to Sitia not (yet) losing its innocence in the tourist rape, that has defiled so many other resorts, must include the lack of an overall picture-book appearance and the distance from Iraklion airport. This latter is a most important factor. The comparative remoteness is accentuated by the fact that much of the road, although fairly well surfaced, is of a sinuous, 'island quality' after the National Highway runs out just beyond Ag. Nikolaos.

The usual approach is on the main road from the direction of Iraklion, which drops down from the low, gentle hills west of the town. Once on the outskirts, the descending road curves fairly sharply past the Ierapetra turning, to the Esplanade. At the waterfront, to the right (or south-east) leads out of Sitia, alongside a very long, gently curving beach of several miles length, towards Vai, Palaikastro and Zakros. To the left leads immediately into the town proper which is in the form of an 'L' with the broad quayside Esplanade edged by house, shop, taverna and restaurant fronts.

Unusually little Venetian or Turkish influence is visible apart from the fort and one particular building several blocks up and back from the quay front. The houses are much more biased and in the style of the Cycladean islands, being coloured cubic shapes.

Sitia might well be considered an ideal seaside resort. There is a splendid beach, complete with a sunken ship and wind-surfing school (of which more later); an interesting old town; a fishing and cargo boat harbour and Ferry-boat port; lively quayside tavernas with busy industrial activity surrounding the whole. Sitia is famed for its sultanas and there is a rave-up, no, no a festival held in the month of August to celebrate the fruit. A 450 drs ticket allows visitors to drink as much of the local wine as can be consumed whilst watching Cretan folk dances. The town is well endowed with five sided litter bins.

ARRIVAL BY AIR
The flights only connect with the Dodecanese islands of Rhodes, Kasos and Karpathos. The airport is about 1 km south of Sitia Town but unusually there is no Olympic Airways bus, it being necessary to walk or catch a taxi.

ARRIVAL BY BUS
The Bus Square (*Tmr* 2H6) is now in a much more convenient location for both driver and passengers, being sited on the right of the road into Sitia, close to the waterfront. This Main Road, Leoforos Therissou, is rather featureless and drab, although the central island has been landscaped and planted out.

ARRIVAL BY FERRY
The Ferry-boat quay (*Tmr* 1B/C5) is almost at the far north end of the town in the shadow of the Venetian fort, well not quite, but with some poetic licence....After disembarking, straight on from the broad finger pier leads past the Port police office (*Tmr* 41B/C3/4) and up steps that climb the hillside. Sharp left leads along the waterfront Esplanade to the centre of the town.

THE ACCOMMODATION & EATING OUT
The Accommodation. There is a surprisingly wide variety, quite sufficient unto the day thereof.

Hotel Vai (*Tmr* 11H6) (Class C) Leoforos Therissou   Tel. 22528
Directions: On the left of the main road into town (*Fsw*), at the junction with Odhos ΔHMOKPITOY and a step or ten diagonally across from the Bus terminus.
  Smart and expensive despite its Class C rating and all rooms have en suite bathrooms. Singles start off at 2134 drs and double rooms 2456 drs which charges rise to 2330 drs and 2720 drs (1st July - 30th Sept). In the high season the management may demand as much as 3400 drs for a double room (They may, but I wouldn't pay it!)

Hotel Elena (*Tmr* 12G6) (Class C) Leoforos Therissou   Tel. 22681
Directions: Further on down the road from the *Hotel Vai*, almost on the 'T' junction with the Esplanade.
  The rooms have en suite bathrooms with singles charged at 1560 drs per day and doubles 2080 drs. Rates rise to 1820 drs and 2340 drs (16th June - 31st Oct) but height of season enquiries may well be met with a request for as much as 3100 drs, admittedly including a 260 drs breakfast.

Hotel Flisvos (*Tmr* 13G6) (Class D) 4 C. Karamanli   Tel. 22422
Directions: On the Esplanade, just around the corner from the Bus terminus and on the right.
  Good seafront view, but this is a busy, noisy road. Single rooms, sharing the bathroom, cost 670 drs and doubles, sharing, 966 drs whilst en suite double rooms cost 1170 drs. These charges rise, respectively, to 760 drs, 1090 drs and 1320 drs. Despite these 'official' rates the management quote 1200 drs and 1500 drs for double rooms.

Pension Asteria
Directions: Next door but one to the *Flisvos*.

Hotel Itanos (*Tmr* 14G4) (Class C) Plateia El. Venizelou.   Tel. 22900
Directions: At the west end of the Esplanade, alongside the small Public Garden in front of the Tax office, close to the Main Square.
  Smart but booked up by rambling groups and coach parties. Naturally (at these

prices) all rooms have en suite bathrooms with a single costing 1740 drs and a double 1980 drs per night. These rates rise to 2100 drs and 2375 drs (1st July - 30th Sept). Breakfast costs a 'mere' 250 drs and lunch/dinner 700 drs.

Hotel Denis (*Tmr* 15F4) (Class B) 60 Plateia El. Venizelou   Tel. 28356
Directions: At the end of the palm tree lined Esplanade is a raised, small roundabout hosting a stone memorial, in the shape of a recumbent soldier, and four large palm trees. To the right, where the road divides, is a fairly large block of buildings. The hotel is behind the *Cafe Tsirilakes*.

Actually licensed as a pension so Class C rates apply to this well-situated accommodation. Depending on your viewpoint (or age), it is either in the thick of things or very noisy – take your choice. Only shared bathrooms with a single room costing 1250 drs and a double room 1550 drs. These daily charges rise to 1500 drs and 1920 drs. 'Quotes' can rise as high as 2170 drs for a double room in the height of the season months.

The Hotel Krystal (*Tmr* 8G2/3) (Class C) 17 Kapetan Sifi/Myssonos Sts.   Tel. 22284
Directions: In the third block up from Plateia El. Venizelou, along Odhos Kapetan Sifi, and on the left, on the corner.

A modern, stylish hotel with en suite bathrooms. A single room costs 1560 drs and a double room 2080 drs, which rates rise to 1820 drs and 2340 drs (1st June - 31st Oct). They may well request 3000 drs for a double room, including breakfast, in the high season.

The Hotel Mysson (Minos, Mison) (*Tmr* 9G3) (Class D) 82 Myssonos.   Tel. 22304
Directions: Almost opposite the *Hotel Krystal* in, naturally enough, Odhos Myssonos.

Clean, sparse and very Greek provincial ('indigenous') as might well be expected for a Class D hotel. Doubles cost 1000 drs, sharing the bathroom, in mid-season.

Hotel Mariana (*Tmr* 7G2) (Class C) 67 Myssonos   Tel. 22088
Directions: On the other side of the road from the *Hotel Mysson.*

The average C Class hotel rates, but the place is taken up by package holiday-makers.

Further along Odhos Myssonos (that is in a south-westerly direction), a store on the other side of the road from the *Hotel Mariana* advertises **Rooms** on a piece of cardboard stuck in the window.

There is accommodation at:
'NO 29' (*Tmr* 10G/H3)
Directions: In the narrow lane that branches off Kapetan Sifi, one down from Odhos Myssonos, and which runs parallel to Odhos El. Venizelou.

Pension Apollonia No. 22 (*Tmr* 6H/I.2/3) off Odhos Myssonos.
Directions: On the left, a block before the Police station (*Tmr* 40I.2/3). The building is on the corner of Odhos Myssonos and the side street.

Picturesque, literally, with the odd mural here and there. Steps from the side street lead to the rooms and a pleasant balcony off which are a washroom and toilets. Singles cost about 600 drs and double 900 drs in the high season.

Alice Hotel (*Tmr* 4 I.2/3) (Class C) 34 Papanastassiou   Tel. 28450
Directions: Odhos Papanastassiou branches off the top (south) end of Myssonos St, very close to the Iraklion road. Papanastassiou St is where the buses used to 'terminus'.

A modern hotel beyond which is the Cinema. Rooms have en suite bathrooms, a single room costing from 1560 drs and a double from 2080 drs which rates rise to 1820 drs and 2340 drs (16th June - 31st Oct).

Also at this end of town are:

'Rooms' (*Tmr* 5 I/J2) 53 Myssonos St.

Directions: A few buildings down and on the same side as the BP Petrol Station, on the corner of a side street off Myssonos St.

Simple, island lodgings not-withstanding-which rates are about the average for a Class C pension.

Youth Hostel 4 Therissou St   Tel. 22693

Directions: 400m up the Iraklion road, on the left going out of town.

Well spoken of with a very friendly, 'camp-fire' atmosphere (as are many Cretan Youth Hostels). A single bed costs about 300 drs per night.

Odhos I. Kondylaki, most easily reached from Plateia El. Venizelou and climbing Odhos Kapetan Sifi, branches off to the right beyond the OTE office (*Tmr* 36 F/G2/3) and is rich in accommodation including:

Rooms (*Tmr* 17F2) No. 54 I. Kondylaki St.

Directions: On the left of the street

Typically disorganised, 'Greek family ethnic' accommodation. The rooms are jumbled up with the owners living quarters and the washing machine is in the guests' bathroom. Despite the above remarks, accommodation is rather overpriced with high season doubles, sharing the bathrom (and the family's 'personabilia'), charged at 1200 drs.

Rooms (*Tmr* 16F2/3) No. 35 I. Kondylaki St.

Directions: Across the road from the above establishment.

Similar comments to the above.

Continuing along Odhos I. Kondylaki, over the branch street of N. Kazantzaki, leads to **Rooms** (*Tmr* 18 D/E2/3) at No. 19. Further along the street, a large flight of steps sedately but steeply makes a right angle junction with Odhos I. Kondylaki.

Descending and then first right (*Fsw*) turns off on to a lower but parallel street and *Pension/Rooms Creta* (*Tmr* 20D2/3) at No. 37, on the right-hand side.

Back on Odhos I. Kondylaki and across another widely spaced flight of steps, climbing the hillside from the waterfront, leads to:

Hotel Archontikon (*Tmr* 19C2) (Class D) 16 I. Kondylaki   Tel. 28172

Directions: As above, on the left-hand side.

Neat appearance with double rooms only, sharing bathrooms. Rates start off at 1000 drs rising to 1100 drs, but enquirers might be asked up to 1400 drs at the height of the season.

Directly across from the Ferry-boat quay (*Tmr* 1 B/C5) is a flight of steps that ascends the hillside. The lane branching off to the right, at the bottom of this flight of steps gives access to the outer-harbour quay. Sandwiched in between the lane and another flight of steps, climbing drunkenly away up to the left, are **Rooms** (*Tmr* 21 A/B3).

Further on, halfway to the outer harbour quay and on the left, is the:

Hotel Stars (Astra) (Class D) 37 M. Kolyvaki   Tel. 22917

Directions: As above.

Not only nicely positioned but probably the best value in town. Additionally it is convenient to the Ferry-boat quay and away from the general hurly-burly. Double rooms, sharing the bathrooms, are charged at 950 drs in high season. Anne plaintively wished she had found it earlier!

The Eating Out A plethora of waterside taverna tables and chairs under bright awnings stretch along from the Plateia El. Venizelou towards the Ferry-boat quay. Their fare is extremely well presented and the standard of fish dishes excellent. Naturally clients must have very deep pockets to order fish, but this is maybe one of the occasions to be tempted to shell out (whoops!) the extra drachmae.

Possibly it is unfair to select one particular establishment from the pack but at the Plateia El. Venizelou end of this attractive row of restaurants and tavernas is:
Zorba's (*Tmr* 23F4) Plateia Kosma-Zotou
Directions: In the same block as the *Cafe Tsirilakes/Hotel Denis.*
A 'wide range of menu' to fit most pockets and sensibilities.

At the other end of the spectrum, or possibly from the sublime to the ridiculous, is the:
Souvlaki Snackbar (*Tmr* 22F4)
Directions: Sandwiched (must one!) between the *Cafe Tsirilakes* and the *Hotel Denis* on El. Venizelou, under the 'Lowenbrau' sign.
A good offering by a 'bird-trilling' (sic) owner. The locals who crowd in are a noisy testament to the quality.
Yura's (*Tmr* 24H4) Odhos ΔΗΜΟΚΡΙΤΟΥ.
Directions: From Plateia El. Venizelou proceed in a southerly direction along Odhos El. Venizelou, past the Public Garden, and the first street on the left slants down past Yura's, which is on the right, beyond the *Peacock Pub.*
Average fare at a reasonable price in a nicely laid out, high-ceilinged room. The colourful waiter has a tendency to break into a spot of self-indulgent 'Greek country and western music'. Perhaps he is hoping to be spotted by a talent scout. Ladies inspecting the menu must expect their 'tiny' hands to be clasped to his bosom. Moussaka, Greek salad, beans, bread and retsina for two cost about 900 drs.

I must admit that the last eating place to receive a mention has not received my patronage, but is included for the owner's 'point of sale' offer. With Plateia El. Venizelou as a starting point, head up Kapetan Sifi St and turn along the first left after the National Bank. Halfway along on the right, is a:
Cafe-Taverna (*Tmr* 25G/H3)
Directions: As above.
A low ceilinged, old fashioned, not inexpensive establishment with a signboard pronouncing *If You Don't Like The Food You Don't Pay.* I presume diners who make a habit of 'not liking' are discouraged from future patronage.

THE A TO Z OF USEFUL INFORMATION

AIRLINE OFFICE & TERMINUS (*Tmr* 44 G3/4). There is an Olympic ticket office at No. 56 Plateia El. Venizelou but there are no airport buses to the 'small island' airport. It is thus necessary to take 'Shanks pony' or a taxi (at a cost of about 120-150 drs). Flights do not connect to Athens but very conveniently make a link with three of the Dodecanese islands. The office is open Monday-Saturday, 0830 - 1300 hrs & 1700 - 2030 hrs.

Aircraft timetables

Day	Departures Departure time	Islands	Arrivals Departure time
Tuesday & Thursday	1125 hrs	Kasos	1045 hrs.
		Karpathos	1030 hrs.
		Rhodes	0925 hrs.
Saturday	0800 hrs.	Rhodes	0645 hrs.
Saturday & Sunday	1155 hrs.	Karpathos	1030 hrs.
		Rhodes	0925 hrs.

One-way fares to Kasos   1880 drs, duration 30 mins.
             Karpathos   2450 drs, duration 35 mins (via Kasos 1 hr 5 mins).
             Rhodes   4760 drs, duration 55 mins.

BANKS The Commercial Bank of Greece (*Tmr* 26G3/4), which accepts Euro-cheques, and the **National Bank** (*Tmr* 27 G3/4) span the entrance to Odhos Kapetan Sifi, just off Plateia El. Venizelou. The **Bank of Crete** (*Tmr* 2H/I.3/4) bridges two streets. Close by, to the left (*Fsw*), and also on El. Venizelou, is the **Ionian & Popular Bank.**

BEACH The town's sandy beach describes a gentle curve for a mile or so, in an easterly direction and is edged by the Vai road.

BICYCLE, SCOOTER & CAR HIRE A number of establishments ranged along the waterfront at the Vai end of town, which include **Apollon** and **Vai Rent-a-Car**. There is a car hire office (*Tmr* 29G5/6), diagonally across the road from the town's Toilet block, as well as scooter hire outfits on Leoforos Therissou, a few metres up from the seafront.There are two more opposite each other on Odhos 4th September (ΣΕΠΤΕΜΒΡΙΟΥ) which leads off the Esplanade alongside the petrol station (*Tmr* 30G5). Rates as for other Cretan towns.

BREAD SHOPS From Plateia El. Venizelou climb Odhos Kapetan Sifi towards the OTE office, and take the first turning to the right for:
No. 85 (*Tmr* 31F/G3) A tiny bread shop on the left with a post box on the wall, alongside the shop.
   Back on Odhos Kapetan Sifi, the fourth lane that branches off to the right (that is the fourth lane from El. Venizelou but third from the side street in which is the baker above), leads to:
Picadilly Bread & Pie Shop (*Tmr* 32D2) The shop opens seven days a week and is sited on the right, alongside a lovely but dilapidated Turkish timber building with an overhanging first storey.

BUSES The Bus Square (*Tmr* 2H6) is located on the right of Leoforos Therissou (*Fsw*) at the Esplanade end of the road. The Bus office (*Tmr* 3H6) is across the Avenue.

Bus timetables
A number are listed on the 'super-duper' timetable issued at the Iraklion bus office (*See* **Chapter 12, Iraklion, Buses, A to Z)** so let's hope they tie in with the listings that follow!

Sitia to Ag. Nikolaos, Malia, Iraklion
Daily: 0630, 0915, 1115, 1215, 1415, 1430, 1615, 1715, 1915 hrs.
Return journey
Daily: 0730, 0830, 0930, 1030, 1300, 1500, 1715 hrs.
One-way fare 690 drs; duration 3½ hrs; distance 143 km.

Sitia to Vai
Daily: 0900, 1100, 1200, 1400, 1600, 1730 hrs.
Sunday/holidays: 0900, 1100, 1200, 1400, 1600, 1730 hrs.
Return journey
Daily: 0900, 1000, 1200, 1300, 1500, 1730, 1830 hrs.
Sunday/holidays: 1000, 1200, 1300, 1500, 1700, 1830 hrs.
One-way fare 140 drs; duration 1 hr; distance 29 km.

Sitia to Zakros
Daily: 0615, 1400 hrs.
Return journey
Daily: 0700, 1500 hrs.
There are no buses on Sundays/holidays

Sitia to Ierapetra
Daily: 0615, 0900, 1215, 1400, 1800, 1930 hrs.
Sunday/holidays: 0900, 1200, 1400, 1800, 2030 hrs.
Return journey
Daily: 0630, 0830, 1000, 1200, 1400, 1630 hrs.
Sunday/holidays: 0800, 1000, 1200, 1400, 1630 hrs.
One-way fare 300 drs; duration 2 hrs; distance 61 km.

CINEMA (*Tmr* 33I.2/3) Located in the triangulated block below the *Hotel Alice*. Although it may well be closed at the height of season, it is not a 'dead' cinema.

COMMERCIAL SHOPPING AREA No real centre. Sitia is, in the original plan of things, a difficult town in which to shop, with much 'to and fro'ing'. There is a small, pavement-based market on the first street to the right off Odhos Kapetan Sifi (*Sbo*), and another, one street up at the far end of the first block. In amongst the first mentioned street market is a Dairy shop.

Not all is lost if you require one-stop shopping as parallel to Odhos Papanastassiou is a street in which is located a busy Supermarket – well more a General Store (*Tmr* 34H/I 3). Odhos Myssonos contains a number of stores and a Butcher's shop along it's length. Shops generally do not open on Sunday.

Useless information includes the fact that Sitia must have more Barbers than bars.

DISCOS
The **Disco La Nuit** is on Karamanli St, the 'Ocean Side Drive' from Sitia towards Vai, opposite the *Beach Bar*. At the other end of town is **Zorba's Disco** (*Tmr* 35D3) accessed up the wide terrace of steps leading to the Church from the Esplanade, El. Venizelou.

FERRY-BOATS These arrive and depart from the Ferry-boat quay (well, well). I call it that, although small merchant ships and local boats moor up here. If a cargo ship is alongside the quay, and the ferry is due, they simply slip the after line and let the ferry nose in between ship and quay.

Ferry-boat timetables
For full details *See* **Chapter 17, Ag. Nikolaos, Ferry-boat timetables, A to Z.**

FERRY BOAT TICKET OFFICES
K. Tzortzakis (*Tmr* 42C/D3/4)   Tel. 22631
Directions: On the way to the Ferry-boat quay.

MEDICAL CARE
Clinics & Pharmacies. Plentiful and a rota system operates.

NTOG None, nor are there any Tourist police. Help!

OTE (*Tmr* 36F/G2/3) At 22 Kapetan Sifi and only open Monday to Friday between 0730 hrs and 2200 hrs.

PETROL A Shell petrol station is situated on the junction of the Esplanade and Leoforos Therissou but it closes for siesta early every day as well as Sundays, holidays and highdays. The 'in place' is on the corner of the Esplanade and Odhos 4th September (*Tmr* 30G5), but it is inconveniently sited and causes many a traffic jam in the area.

PLACES OF INTEREST There is a shortage of the usual offerings but all is not lost.

To one side of the bay, opposite the Class A *Kappa Club* (not detailed as the very expensive suites are block booked by a French holiday company), is the interesting, half-submerged shipwreck of a merchant ship that lies just off the beach. It has proved to be quite a focal point but was not the only wreck to grace these shores. During most of the 1983 summer season, there was another, but the town authorities decided that two was one too many. Such decision making!

Folklore Museum (*Tmr* 38E1/2) Rustic but interesting exhibits in a house the same side of the road as the high wall surrounded, hilltop church. Open daily 1000 - 1400 hrs and 1600 - 1900 hrs.

Venetian Fort (*Tmr* 37A1) Built in 1204, it is small and plain with extensively restored walls and a pleasant keep. The elderly attendant has a piece of paper with, written on it, the following dates: *Spanish pirates 1538; Turks 1651; Greek 1870*. Were that all history lessons proved that easy!

POLICE
Town (*Tmr* 40.I.2/3) On the way out of town, just off Odhos Therissou on the right of Myssonos St.
Port (*Tmr* 41B/C3/4) On the corner of the block facing the Ferry-boat quay.

POST OFFICE (*Tmr* 39.I.3) In the same block as the Cinema and *Hotel Alice.* Open the usual hours. There is also a postal services 'porta-cabin' kiosk opposite *Yura's Restaurant* (*Tmr* 24H4), on Odhos ΔHMOKPITOY.

SPORTS FACILITIES On Karamanli St (the 'Ocean Side Drive' road to Vai) and alongside the (last) *Beach Bar*, on the left, is a **Windsurfing School**. This is set down in the corner of the beach formed by the bar, the road and the sea's edge. Valerie and John, a Rhodesian, run the school. Let us hope they continue to do so in future years, for you will have to travel a long way to meet such a pleasant, helpful and knowledge-able couple. But I must admit to bias. Some summers ago we (well Rose actually) lost a pair of reading glasses in the sea, whilst jibing one of the school's sailboats (which we had been warned against). Both Val and John diligently searched the sea bottom for hours, and next morning located, dived and recovered them. All beyond the call of duty but very much appreciated.

Hire rates per hour include:
Windsurfers 600 drs per hour; pedaloes 400 drs p.h; canoes 200 drs p.h; sailboats 800 drs p.h and parascending* 2000 drs p.h.
Anne's notes cryptically state 'a boat sails (fast!) round the bay – you "fly" above!'

TAXIS There are taxis ranked in front of the Post Office (*Tmr* 39.I.3) and alongside the Public Garden, on Plateia El. Venizelou.

TELEPHONE NUMBERS & ADDRESSES
Olympic office (*Tmr* 44G3/4) 56 El. Venizelou   Tel. 22270
Town police (*Tmr* 40.I.2/3) 24 Myssonos St   Tel. 22266

TRAVEL AGENTS *See* **Ferry-boat Ticket Offices**

TOILETS There is a Public Toilet block (*Tmr* 43G6) on the knuckle of the quay, almost opposite the junction of Leoforos Therissou and the Esplanade.

ROUTE TWENTY TWO
To Vai and Erimoupolis (27 km) The very poorly surfaced road leaves Sitia over an almost makeshift bridge via pretty countryside on one side and, on the other, a long, grey, shelving, sandstone beach edged by groves of trees. At the village of **Ag. Fotia** there are *Rooms*, small apartment developments and Villas to let. In this area, in 1971, a Minoan cemetery was discovered. The road, subject to diversions and roadworks, is clearly in the process of constructive destruction!

The route wanders along the coastline and the countryside changes from the mountainous ravines west of Sitia to gentle, sloping, scrub covered mountain and sandy hillsides reminiscent of the west coast of Ireland. Here and there a development hoves into sight, often surrounded by plastic littered land. The major parting of the ways, that is to Toplou/Vai and Palaikastro, is a particularly good example of confusing Greek signposting. Two signs, which should point down the same road, indicate totally opposite directions. A worthy citizen has made some free-hand amendments but remember at the fork, left is for Toplou Monastery, Vai and Erimoupolis and right is for Palaikastro, Zakros and Kato Zakros. The junction is notable for the presence of a large number of coloured beehives.

As detailed, the left turning leads to:
Toplou Monastery (21 km from Sitia) Not at all as I had imagined. The strange looking building, a fortified Venetian monastery, is built on a sparse, bare and isolated location. The site of a much earlier religious building, earthquake and predators caused the rebuilding in the 16th century. The nomenclature Toplou is derived from the Turkish, and means 'canon ball'. On display are some interesting relics, historical documents and icons.

From here, a hop, skip and a jump leads to:
VAI (some 29 km from Sitia) More correctly named Finikodasos, the renowned seaside spot is a sandy beach whereon groves of palm trees grow, giving the appearance of a tropical location. That is, a much visited, tour excursion crowded, beach bar, car park encircled and thus highly overrated tropical location.

An interesting diversion, in order to escape the overpowering tourism and 'beach sleeping unwashed', is to slip northwards to the comparatively isolated, rocky bay and small beach of **Erimoupolis.** This was the site of Itanos, originally a Minoan settlement that, unusually, retained its importance and expanded during the Roman and Byzantine eras. The setting is magnificent with **Elasa island** to the east and the Cape of Sideros curving away in the distance. No further exploration to the north can be undertaken as the Greek Navy have occupied the rest of the peninsula.

ROUTE TWENTY THREE
To Kato Zakros via Palaikastro & Zakros (35 km) Take ROUTE TWENTY TWO as far as the Vai turn off but keep to the right, following the main road as it curves round to:

PALAIKASTRO (24 km from Sitia) Tel. prefix 0843. A large village with petrol, an OTE, a baker, a few shops, a 'pub', tavernas, hotels, pensions, *Rooms* and a rather confusing road system. Despite signs indicating a taxi rank on the town square, this has been erected by a 'false prophet', and enquiries evince the information that it is necessary to telephone Sitia.

Accommodation available includes the B Class *Pension Hellas*, the:

Illustration 23 Crete centred on Sitia

Hotel Itanos (Class E)   Tel. 22508
Rooms share the bathroom, single rooms costing 500 drs and doubles 710 drs.
and the:
Hotel Paleokastron (Class E)   Tel. 61235
Double rooms sharing the bathroom cost 900 drs.

A lovely diversion is at hand by taking the signposts for the *Hotel Marina Village.* The unmade, dusty track makes a straight run through the highly cultivated olive groves, beneath the shady branches of which sheep peacefully graze. The small village of **Agathia** is to the right, and the track becomes very flinty. *The Marina Village* (Class C, tel. 61284) complex, signed off to the left, is set in the olive trees.

There are treats to come by keeping to the right, which leads to a succession of lovely, deserted, sandy bays alongside the Palaikastro Minoan remains overlooked by Kastri Hill. This is another of the 'guide finds' of Crete.

In the lee of the hill, and to the left (*Fsw*) of the first and largest sandy bay, is a collection of buildings including a kafenion and the Mitsakakis family's *Maistrati Taverna*. This seaside hamlet is known as Hiona of Palaikastro.. A meal at the far taverna is first class. Another, nearside, taverna sits astride the junction of the foreshore and the various rocky tracks that criss-cross the area. The family running this establishment keep home made feta. If milk is requested they are just as likely to send a son across the field with a glass and fulfil the order there and then by milking one of the goats. No question of its freshness!

Interestingly the locals clean up the beaches and put the rubbish in plastic sacks but..... they are propped up on the side of the beach, only to be left *in situ* until the bags split and the rubbish spills out again when the locals collect up the resultant mess and... The area is heavily shepherded and it is best not to camp out in the line of one of the regular sheep runs.

To seawards, lying in the large curve of the land, are the **Grandes islands.** Occasionally a laid up tanker idly swings at anchor between the islands and the bay. By keeping along the right-hand track, on the north side of the Petsofas headland, further bays come into view as well as the wreck of a small tramp steamer which can be seen run up on the far side of the offshore islands.

Back at and from Palaikastro the moorland appearance of the countryside persists and the winding road weaves on through neat groves of olives, slow foothills, and a long valley. This is one of the prettiest roads on Crete and the villages, which are very interesting, include: **Langada** (small, spread out, new development); **Chochlakies** (as for Langada plus cubes); a ruined village; several spectacular chapels (two stark white and another pink based and multicoloured); **Azokeramos** (very Greek, a kafenion, a few new houses); a dome covered well by the roadside and **Kellaria** (clinging narrowly to the hillside).

The soil in this region is startlingly pinky-purple. A number of cows are to be seen grazing which appear to be treated like household pets, often wearing a twisted rope noseband and usually looking in excellent condition.

Adravasti, a lovely, quaint old village with a large number of donkeys, is set in heavily cultivated surrounds.

ZAKROS (Ano) (37 km from Sitia) Tel. prefix 0843. Zakros does not come as a disappointment after the beauty of the preceding journey. On the approach to the village is a sign to the right indicating spring water which I think is that found flowing into a large concrete system.

The Main Street curves sharply through the village and contains a few tavernas, a cafe, bars, stores, baker and the:

Hotel Zakros (Class C) 1 Eleftherias. Tel. 28479
Not inexpensive considering the rather 'far flung' position of the village. Rooms have en suite bathrooms with a single room costing 1150 drs and a double room 1500 drs. These rates rise to 1300 drs and 1750 drs (1st July - 30th Sept).

A splendid meal of the day is to be enjoyed by 'troughing' at:

Taverna ΜΑΕΣΤΡΟ
Directions: On the left of the 'High St' approximately where it describes a sharp curve.
The old lady presiding over this Greek, very indigenous taverna advertises her establishment's presence with a large sign bearing the words *Finest Greco Cookery*. That homely phrase and the simple meal does not let down her boast. No frills but excellent home cooking.

The main purpose of (Ano) Zakros is to give access to Kato Zakros, or so it would seem. Personally I am of the opinion that Zakros can stand on its own.

On the way out of the village the ruins of a small Minoan house are indicated on the trackside, but once again they look very like any other average, derelict Greek dwelling. The asphalted road arrows on southwards, whilst the left-hand branch turning to Kato Zakros is now surfaced for half its length, skirting a very, very steep gorge famed as a Minoan burial ground. I suppose they tipped them over the edge. You know – there goes granny in her sarcophagus. Beyond the gorge, the route becomes a third-rate donkey path which hairpins down the mountain, flattening out to wander through banana groves and past the impressive remains of the Palace of Zakros to the flat, curved bay of Kato Zakros. Incidentally the presence of at least three steam rollers parked along the last stretch of unsurfaced track must indicate that 'once upon a time', in the future, the road will be completed.

KATO ZAKROS (45 km from Sitia) Cultivated fields edge the rim of the clean, pebbly beach, the approach track to which is dominated by two tavernas set on the backshore. The track meanders through the gap between the two tavernas, only to turn sharp right along the edge of the tree lined beach whereon it peters out.
To the left, (*Fsw*), the sea's edge is broken up into small stony beaches. The half dozen or so fishing boats that work out of the bay are moored up in this area, overlooked by a string of buildings, fronted by a large patio. There are some **Rooms** in these little houses, a bar alongside a small hut-like construction that sports a telephone, and was once magnificently signed *OTE*. Behind, on the other side of the track, are the Port police.
There are, including the two aforementioned establishments, a total of four tavernas spread along the front offering sustenance, accommodation, and the use of their toilet/shower facilities.
It is impossible to leave Kato without eulogising about the informal and simple remains of the:

Palace of Zakros Excavations were started at the turn of the century by one Hogarth, a British archaeologist but it was not until the Second World War that the Greeks realised the true potential of the site. Entrance costs 100 drs.

It is possible, just possible, to avoid returning to Sitia via Palaikastro. To achieve this 'short cut' from Zakros, (possibly inadmissable as an accurate description if measured in time), take the road to the village of Adravasti, Karidi and Mitato in order to rejoin the Sitia road below Roussa Eklissia. The route is rough (very rough) but awe inspiring and worth it if only to see the village of Karidi.
The track of pink, purple earth and gravel, winds up and up and up above Adravasti, affording panoramic views down to Zakros and across the plains. The

turn-off to the right to Vrisidi is invisible and when the 'road' is viewed from the other end, in Mitato, this can only be regarded as a good thing! Apart from which the diversion along two sides of a triangle requires a traveller to observe Karidi's beauty. At the end of the climb, the road wanders between beehives across the mountain top and approaches **Karidi** down a shallow, fertile valley. The valley is filled with vines, there are a few beautifully cared-for, tethered donkeys and the road passes a circular stone threshing floor. Ahead is the lovely, lovely white village set in a peaceful, lush countryside scene.

The village of **Mitato** is rather an anticlimax. Furthermore the maps should be ignored. The road only becomes surfaced on the downward slope, beyond the village of **Krioneri**, where it joins a military road (not marked on maps) from the summit of Mt. Prinias. What a drive!

ROUTE TWENTY FOUR
To Ierapetra via Piskokefalo (57 km) The first leg of the road across the
island follows the normal pattern and mix of good and bad road, pretty and ugly villages, cultivated and barren countryside, valleys and mountains, chapels and chapels, villages that straddle the road, villages that tower over the road, villages that snug away beneath the road, and above all, magnificent, dramatic and squalid views.

The first seaside village is **Pilalimata** which is not a particularly pretty sight, enduring the double blow of being enveloped in plastic and seemingly under constant construction. Beyond, there is a lovely looking bay but with no sign of access, followed by a wide, sweeping crescent of another bay beset with flowers, **Rooms**, a clean, pebbly beach and the *Tavernas Havai* and *Ammesis*.

From here to (and beyond) **Makryalos,** there are as many **Rooms** and Villas to let, in amongst the vines and the backshore, as there are old houses. Unfortunately there is also a lot of plastic and the surrounds have a ripe odour.

Koutsouras is the subject of both messy civil engineering and agricultural development. This is to distinguish between house and hotel buildings and the race to cover large regions of Crete with plastic greenhouses! There is a bank, bus stop and petrol. The foreshore is very rocky and accompanied by urban ribbon development.

West of Koutsouras is prettier and greener, with fruit and flowers growing, and the road is lined with oleanders. A rather unusual blue and white double chapel is perched above the road to the right, across from which is a pleasant bay. They are followed by more plastic, a pebbly beach and yet another bay complete with a taverna, a sandy pebbly beach, **Rooms** and a pension.

Ag. Fotia lies in a wide ravine edging a grey shingle seashore bay surrounded by olives and vines. Apartments and the *Villa Fillipos*.

The road winds down to the village of **Ferma** set in olive groves with tavernas and **Rooms** as well as Flat and Villa development in hand. The *Taverna Emilios* is grouped with a supermarket, some agricultural plastic, hotels rimming the beach, a huge church and disco/taverna, all widely spaced out. Petrol is available. The fine grey shingle of the seashore gives way to a strip of beach. Beyond Ferma there is a splay of Corfu-type villas, hotels and bungalows, followed by a camping site and a petrol station, set in a low, scrub covered, sandy plateau edged by a rocky beach all the way to unlovely:

KOUTSOUNARI (47 km from Sitia) This village now has a campsite with a restaurant and bar, charging 150 drs per person and 100 drs for a tent. The smart *Hotel Blue Sky,* on the right of the road, is plonked down in a lunar landscape followed by rough, uneven, 'firing-range' terrain all the way to:

IERAPETRA
Seaside town

FIRST IMPRESSIONS
Scattered, messy, industrious town; lack of charm and a centre; very small old quarter and fort.

VITAL STATISTICS
Tel. prefix 0842

HISTORY
The modern town is sited on the ancient seaport of Ierapytna which had substantial trade links with North Africa. The Romans established a large development of which there are a few remnants. Naturally enough the Venetians and Turks occupied the site as evidenced by the Venetian fort and the Turkish minaret.

GENERAL
The immediate surrounds to Ierapetra are squalid and the initial impressions tend to linger. It is difficult to pick one particular reason for the town's lack of charm and inability to captivate. The lack of a substantial Old Quarter does not help, nor does the absence of a coherent street layout or town centre. Whatever the reasons, Ierapetra, despite being the only settlement of any size on the south coast, remained a backwater until it experienced rapid growth in the 1960s due to the wealth generated by the plastic greenhouses. This was followed by the discovery of Ierapetra as a potential holiday resort, although I have been unable to discover the charms that resulted in this turn of events, apart from the generally available abundance of sun and sea. Why spoil the industrial squalor with an overlay of tourist requisites?

Most of the hotel development has taken place along the eastern end of the town. At the western end is the very small Old Quarter, a Venetian fort, Turkish minaret; Clock Tower and a small cargo harbour.

ARRIVAL BY BUS
The Bus station and terminus is in the wide, one-way street of Giannakou. The pandemonium has to be seen to be believed, especially when the school children are arriving and departing.

THE ACCOMMODATION & EATING OUT
The Accommodation *Rooms* are advertised on the wall at the entry to the Bus office.

Hotel Atlantis (Class C) Agios Andreas.   Tel. 28555
Directions: To the east of town.
Rooms have en suite bathrooms. A single costs 1422 drs and a double 2311 drs, which charges rise to 1778 drs and 2844 drs (16th June - 30th Sept).

The Youth Hostel
Directions: Within a couple of hundred metres of the *Hotel Atlantis*, to the east.
Usual rates.

Hotel Creta (Class C) Plateia El. Venizelou   Tel. 22316
Note the times the buses start up as the hotel is on the route.
A single en suite costs 1690 drs and a double with bathroom 2225 drs. In the busy summer months breakfast is obligatory at a further cost of 200 drs.

Hotel El Greco (Class C) 40 M. Kothri   Tel. 28471
Directions: Close to the Bus office and adjacent to the seafront.
A double with bathroom costs 3000 drs at the height of the season.

Guest House Venizelos (Class E) 17 Koraka   Tel. 28675
Directions: Across the road from the Bank of Crete but displays no name.
Very, very ethnic with double rooms only, sharing the bathroom. Rates start off at 800 drs and rise to 1000 drs.

Guest House
Directions: Next door to the *Venizelos* above, to which refer for comments.

Hotel Alkyon (Class D) Dom. Theotokopoulou Paralia   Tel. 22211
Directions: On the quay front.
Single rooms sharing the bathroom cost 700 drs and en suite 800 drs whilst double rooms sharing cost 1000 drs and en suite 1200 drs.

Kritiki Villa (Cretan) (Class D) 16 Lakerda   Tel. 28522
Directions: To the north-east of Plateia El. Venizelou.
Recommended, with a vine covered trellis shading the patio, a communal kitchen and a roof-top area for basking.
Single dormitory beds are charged at 600 drs, single rooms sharing the bathroom cost 800 drs, doubles sharing and/or with en suite bathrooms are charged at 1650 drs.

Hotel Lygia (Class C) Parados Kyrba   Tel. 28881
Recommended by a knowledgeable reader as a friendly and comfortable little hotel.
All rooms are complete with en suite bathrooms, singles starting off at 1200 drs and doubles 1400 drs rising to 1400 drs and 1600 drs (1st July - 30th Sept).

The Eating Out Most of the bars, restaurants, tavernas and their chairs and tables are grouped along the concrete Esplanade which runs from the small, rocky mole to the east of the harbour breakwater through to the main town beach. The menus are similar to each other and prices are comparable. A reader recommends that diners look out for the restaurant run by an extrovert but very hen-pecked chef. Ah, well yes.
Opposite the Bus office is a 'Ierapetra-style' souvlaki snackbar, that is, the meat is served up on a stick with a bag of chips and a hunk of bread.

THE A TO Z OF USEFUL INFORMATION

BANKS The Bank of Crete is on Koraka St, and the **Ionian & Popular Bank** on Plateia El. Venizelou.

BEACH The grey, sandy, main town beach spreads eastwards, but beyond the harbour, to the west, is another long stretch of beach.

BICYCLE, SCOOTER & CAR HIRE Generally charges from the two or three outfits are at the top end of the Cretan pricing scales. Is this because most of the visitors are desperate to get away?

BUSES The buses park up on Odhos Giannakou and the office is here as well.

Bus timetables
Ierapetra to Ag. Nikolaos, Malia, Iraklion
Daily   0615, 0730, 0830, 1030, 1230, 1430, 1500, 1600, 1800, 1900 hrs.

Return journey
Daily: 0730, 0830, 0930, 1030, 1130, 1330, 1430, 1530, 1630, 1830 hrs.
Ierapetra to Mirtos
Daily: 0615, 1000, 1200, 1345, 1630, 1930 hrs.
Ierapetra to Mirtos, Vianos, Iraklion
Daily: 1000, 1630 hrs.
Sunday/holidays: 1630 hrs.
Return journey
Daily: 0630 hrs.
Ierapetra to Koutsounari, Koutsouras, Makryalos
Daily: 0630, 0830, 1000, 1200, 1400, 1630, 1930 hrs.
Sunday/holidays: 0800, 1000, 1200, 1400, 1630 hrs.
Return journey
Daily: 0615, 0900, 1215, 1400, 1800, 1930 hrs.
Sunday/holidays: 0900, 1200, 1400, 1800, 2030 hrs.
Ierapetra to Sitia via Lithines
Daily: 0630, 0800, 1000, 1130, 1400, 1730, 1930 hrs.

COMMERCIAL SHOPPING AREA There is no central market. The majority of the shops are gathered together on Odhos Kountourioti, one back from the waterfront as well as in the adjacent, parallel streets. The usual opening and closing hours.

DISCOS Yes.

MEDICAL CARE
Chemists & Pharmacies. Plentiful.

OTE 25 c,Koraka St. Open daily 0730 - 2200 hrs but closed weekends.

PETROL A number of stations, mainly on the outskirts of town.

PLACES OF INTEREST These include the aforementioned Fort and Minaret, the Museum, a Turkish fountain and a house close by the Fort, where it is rumoured that Napoleon stopped on his way to campaign in Egypt, in June 1798.

Archaeological Museum A one room exhibition in the Public Library. The Museum houses a remarkable Minoan sarcophagus with painted hunting scenes.

POLICE
Town To the west of the Bus office on the seafront Esplanade.

POST OFFICE Situated on Odhos Houta reached via Kothri St.

It is with some regret that I have to close this guide dwelling on Ierapetra, which must not be considered in any way a typical example of the majority of Cretan seaside towns.

I was with Hercules and Cadmus once,
When in a wood of Crete they bay'd the bear
With hounds of Sparta: never did I hear...
So musical a discord, such sweet thunder.

Chora Sfakion

INDEX

A
AA, the, 19, 20
A to Z,
Agia Galini, 213-215
Agios Nikolaos, 228-232
Athens, 83-98
Chania, 172-179
Chora Sfakion, 184-186
Ierapetra, 257-258
Iraklion, 121-131
Kastell , 203-205
Paleochora, 196-198
Piraeus, 105-108
Rethymnon, 150-155
Sitia, 247-251
Accommodation, 31-35
Agia Galini, 212-213
Agios Nikolaos, 224-227
Athens, 69-77, 93-95
Chania, 167-170
Chora Sfakion, 184
Ierapetra, 256-257
Iraklion, 116-120
Kastelli, 201-203
Matala, 218-219
Paleochora, 195-196
Piraeus (M), 103-104
Rethymnon, 146-149
Sitia, 244-246
Acropolis, The, 68
(Athens)
Addresses, See Useful...
Adele, 162
Adravasti, 253, 254
After-sun, 3
Agathia, 253
Aghii Deka, 220
Aghios Nikolaos, See Agios
Nikolaos
Agia Galini, 211-215
Agia Triada, 217
Agii Theodori island, 192
Ag (Agios)
Andreas, 192
Fotia (north coast), 251
Fotia (south coast), 255
Fotini, 161
Georgios (Iraklion), 136
Georgios (Kastelli), 205
Ioannis, 159
Konstantinos, 135
Marina, 192
Pantes, 191
Pelagia, 131-133
Roumeli, 190-191
Silas, 161
Triada Monastery, 179
Vasilios, 237
Agios Nikolaos, 223-232
Agora, The Greek, 68
(Athens)
Agora, The Roman,68
(Athens)
Agria Grabousa, See Grabousa
Airline flights
Athens, 63, 83
domestic, 25
international, 9-12
fares, 9-12
Airports
Athens, 12-13, See Athens
Chania, (Sternes), 167, 172
Iraklion, 116, 121
Sitia, 244, 247-248

UK, 12
Air temperatures,
See Weather
Akoumia, 160
Akrotiri peninsula, 179
Alarm clock, See Clocks
Alcohol, See Drink
Alexandrou, 161
Alikampos, 181
Alikianou, 189
Alithini, 219
Allowances, 5, 21
Almiros, 234
Alphabet, Greek, See Language
Amiras, 237
Ammoudari, 181
Ammounda, 234
Amnatos, 162
Amnisos, 136
Amygdalokefali, 208
Ancona, 19
(Italy)
Ano Rodakino, See Rodakino
Ano Viannos, 237
Apodoulou, 161
Apostoli, 161
Archanes, 142-143
Ariadne, Villa, See Villa Ariadne
Arkadhi Monastery, 162-163
Armeni, 191
Arrival by Air, See Airline flights
& Airports
Arrivals by Ferry-boat, See
Ferry-boats
Arvi, 237
Askyfou Plain, 181
Asomati, 160
Aspirin, 4
Athens, 63-98
airport, 12, 63
camping, See Camping

Atsipopoulo, 155, 192
Australia, 11
Avdou, 135
Avrakontes, 136
Ayia Galini, See Agia Galini
Ayios Nikolaos, See
Agios Nikolaos
Azokeramos, 253

B
Backpacks, 3
Bad buys, 53
Bakers, 54
Bali, 133-134
Banks, 5, 55-56
Bank cards, 5
Bari, 19
(Italy)
Bathrooms, 32-33
Battle of Crete, 141
Beaches, 33, 37
Bedroll, 3
Bedrooms, See Accommodation
Beer, See Drink
Best buys, 53
Beverages, non alcoholic, 45
Bicycles, 39-40
Bin liners, 4
Books, 4
Bottle-opener, 3
Brandy, See Drinks
Bread shops, See Bakers

Brindisi, 15, 19, 21
(Italy)
Buses
Athens, 63, 84-86, 96, 97
domestic, 25, 38
international, 17-18, 63
Piraeus, 101, 105
Butchers, 54

C
Cafes, 46, 47
Calamine lotion, 3
Cameras, 5
See Photography
Camping, 33, 77-78 (Athens)
Canada, 11, 16
Car
hire, 39-40
travel by, 19-21
Cards, playing, 4
Chamezi, 236
Chania, 165-179
Charter flights, 9-12
Chemists, 4
Chochiakies, 253
Chondros, 237
Chorafakia, 179
Chora Sfakion, 182-186
Choustouliana, 219
Chrysoskalitissa Nunnery, 208
Cigarettes, 5, 21
Cigars, 5, 21
Climate, 5
Clocks, 4
Clothes pegs, 3
Clothing, 3
Coaches, See Buses
Coffee, See Beverages
Compass, 4
Condiments, 3
Containers, 3
Conversion tables, 5-6
Cooking equipment, 3
Creams, 3
Credit cards, 5
Crete, 109-258
General, 110-111
Introduction, 109-111
Religious holidays &
festivals, 109
Specialities, 109
Vital statistics, 109
Cruise ships, 27
Currency, 5, 21

D
Dafnedes, 161
Denmark, 12, 17
Department of Health,
See National Health Cover
Dia island, 136
Dialling Codes, See OTE
Disinfectant, 4
Donkeys, 38
Drapanias, 193
Drink, 5, 21, 45-46, 53
Drinking Places, 46
Drivers & driving
requirements, 20-21
Dromonero, 194
Drosia, 161
Duty free, 5, 21

Artwork by: Type Setting & Ted Spittles
Plans & maps by: Graham Bishop
Typeset by: Type Setting, Portsmouth

GROC's Candid Guides
introduce to readers

Suretravel '89

A comprehensive holiday insurance plan that 'gives cover that many other policies do not reach', to travellers anywhere in the world. In addition to the more usual cover offered, the **SURETRAVEL HOLIDAY PLAN** includes (where medically necessary): 24 hour World Wide Medical Emergency Service including, where appropriate, repatriation by air ambulance.

Additionally, personal accident, medical and emergency expenses EVEN while hiring a bicycle, scooter or car.

An example premium, in 1989, for a 10-17 day holiday in Greece is £13.50 per person.

Note: All offers & terms are subject to the Insurance Certificate Cover

For an application form please complete the cut out below and send to:
Willowbridge Publishing, Bridge House, Southwick Village, Nr Fareham, Hants. PO17 6DZ

Mr/Mrs/Miss...Age.............................

of...

....

request a **SURETRAVEL** application form.

Date of commencement of holiday...............................Duration ....

Signature...Date.....................